Frommer's®
EASYGUIDE
TO
LAS VEGAS
2017

Quick to Read • Easy to Carry • For Expert Advice
In All Price Ranges

By Grace Bas

FROMMER'S STAR RATINGS SYSTEM

Every hotel, restaurant, and attraction listed in this guide has been ranked for quality and value. Here's what the stars mean:

★ Recommended
★★ Highly Recommended
★★★ A must! Don't miss!

AN IMPORTANT NOTE

The world is a dynamic place. Hotels change ownership, restaurants hike their prices, museums alter their opening hours, and busses and trains change their routings. And all of this can occur in the several months after our authors have visited, inspected, and written about, these hotels, restaurants, museums and transportation services. Though we have made valiant efforts to keep all our information fresh and up-to-date, some few changes can inevitably occur in the periods before a revised edition of this guidebook is published. So please bear with us if a tiny number of the details in this book have changed. Please also note that we have no responsibility or liability for any inaccuracy or errors or omissions, or for inconvenience, loss, damage, or expenses suffered by anyone as a result of assertions in this guide.

Artist Dale Chihuly covered the ceiling of the Bellagio (p. 57) with a garden's worth of exquisite, hand-blown glass flowers.

CONTENTS

The famed fountains outside the Bellagio (p. 158).

A LOOK AT LAS VEGAS

G litzy, gritty, gaudy, glamorous, and sometimes goofy, Las Vegas may well be the most colorful city in America. That goes for the people who call it their home (or make it their home for the weekend), the lights and playful structures, the multi-hued desert and mountain scenery that surrounds it, and the ever-changing cityscape. Las Vegas is constantly in flux: new attractions and restaurants constantly appearing, new efforts to challenge the normal standards of morality that some cities cherish. That's why we revise this guidebook yearly. Our author has captured the very latest and most outrageous Las Vegas efforts to shock, amuse or intrigue you. What follows now are some of the sights you'll see, the adventures you'll have, and everything else that "Vegas" provides in such awesome amounts.

Arthur Frommer

The myth about the pyramid-shaped Luxor (p. 53), with its sphinx out front, is that the beam of light shooting from its peak can be seen from outer space. That isn't true, but it makes quite an impact on the Las Vegas Strip.

THE LAS VEGAS STRIP

Hand-painted frescoes, 25-foot high Bottocino marble columns, and a floor that's an exact replica of the one in Venice's Church of Santa Maria Rosario greet guests checking into the Venetian (p. 60).

Singing gondoliers serenade visitors both inside and outside the Venetian.

Glam chandeliers are draped throughout the lobby of The Cosmopolitan (p. 194).

The facade of New York–New York (p. 54) features a 150-foot replica of the Statue of Liberty, a 300-foot-long "Brooklyn Bridge," and a taxi-themed rollercoaster—just for fun.

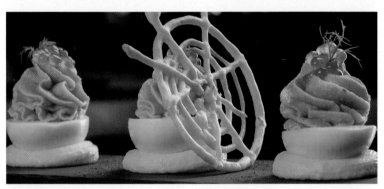

The food (smoked salmon- and caviar- deviled eggs in this case) is as swank as the setting at the Venetian's db Brasserie (see p. 109).

It's not unusual to see Elvis on the Las Vegas Strip. And sometimes Elvi roam in packs. You'll be expected to tip if you ask for a photo with one of them.

Britney Spears is just one of the many stars who play Vegas in lieu of touring.

Cirque du Soleil's *KÀ* (p. 206) combines spectacular feats of daring with exquisite sets and costumes.

Though *Absinthe* (p. 205) is *not* a Cirque du Soleil show, like them it features jaw-dropping acrobatics.

Broadway shows, like *Rock of Ages* (pictured), are now a fixture of the performing arts scene here.

A DJ gets the crowd going at Light (p. 231), one of Sin City's most popular nightspots.

Just off the Strip, the Hard Rock's Pool Party (p. 79) is considered as sizzling a scene as anything that happens after dark.

For some, watching the dancing waters in front of the Bellagio (p. 57) is all you need to do to have a great night on the town.

The jam-packed floor of the Planet Hollywood casino (p. 66).

Musician Mayer Hawthorne at the craps table of the Cosmopolitan.

Getting hitched can be a thrill ride: a bride and groom on the Stratosphere's Big Shot (p. 159).

The High Roller (p. 155) is the world's tallest ferris wheel.

Luxury brands are the focus of the Crystals mall at City Center (p. 192). Nearby are stunning works of contemporary public art.

ABOVE: **The Conservatory Gardens of the Bellagio (p. 158).**

RIGHT: **Elegant and extravagant: the Forum Shops at Caesar's Palace.**

DOWNTOWN LAS VEGAS & OFF THE STRIP

Outdoor bars, with photogenic bartenders, are part of the scene at the Fremont Experience in the heart of downtown.

The LED above the Fremont Street Experience plays high-tech sound and image shows of all sorts.

Guests "swim with the sharks"—literally—at the Golden Nugget pool (p. 73).

Culinary Dropout (p. 135) is just one of the hip new restaurants taking root away from the Strip.

The thought-provoking Mob Museum (p. 161) explores the role of organized crime in history and popular culture.

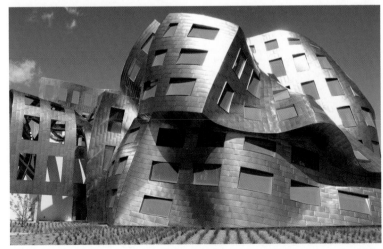

Frank Gehry is the architect of this cutting-edge hospital. It's not a tourist venue, so you won't be invited inside, but the exterior is an awe-inspiring sight.

Audience participation is encouraged at the Chippendales' show (p. 210). Bring your earplugs: the screaming of bachelorette parties can get intense.

Visitors can play out NASCAR fantasies at SpeedVegas (p. 165). Here anyone with a driver's license—and the cash—can take an exotic muscle car or supercar out for a zoom around the 1.5 mile Formula One–inspired race track.

At the Heart Attack Grill (p. 131) waitresses dress as cardiac nurses and the grub contains an artery-busting number of calories.

The big cats that used to entertain guests at the MGM Grand (p. 50) can now be visited at the more humane Lion Habitat (p. 167).

More than just a driving range, Topgolf features an entertainment stage, plus multiple kitchens and bars.

At The Neon Museum, you'll see many of the spectacular vintage signs that once adorned the city.

Though the Grand Canyon can be seen on a day trip from Las Vegas (p. 254), we recommend a several day stay, allowing you to climb below the rim, and to see its turrets, buttes, and striations in different lights throughout the day.

Completed in 1936, the Hoover Dam (p. 241) transformed the landscape and lives of Westerners, and is still considered one of the nation's marvels of engineering.

Handsome Red Rock Canyon (p. 250) is only a 25-minute drive from the Strip.

Ancient petroglyphs dot the striated rocks of the Valley of Fire (p. 246).

A Vegas ski vacation?!? It's doable if you add a visit to nearby Mount Charleston (p. 252).

THE BEST OF LAS VEGAS

The flamboyant showman Liberace once said, "Too much of a good thing is wonderful!" He may very well have been talking about Las Vegas, a city in which he was a frequent headliner and one that has built its reputation on the concept of excess.

There's too much to look at, too much to do, too much to eat, too much to drink, and certainly too many ways to lose your money. Indulgence is the level at which most people start their visit, and why not? You can run out of room on your memory card trying to snap pictures of all the postcard-worthy sights, from dancing fountains to blasting volcanoes; the hotels are so big that getting from your room to the front door requires rest periods; the dining scene has turned this town into a culinary destination; and the nightclubs have elevated Sin City to the biggest, most successful party spot in the world. And all of that is before you get to the shows, the shopping, and the sheer madness of glittering casinos. Look at the faces of those waiting for their flights out of town: tired, maybe a little hung over still, but then there's that little smile when they think about one of those "what happens in Vegas . . ." moments they just had. When it comes to Las Vegas, Liberace may have had a point.

THE best AUTHENTIC LAS VEGAS EXPERIENCES

- **Strolling on the Strip After Dark:** You haven't really seen Las Vegas until you've seen it at night. This neon wonderland is the world's greatest sound-and-light show. Begin at Luxor and work your way past the incredible hotels and their attractions. You'll probably be exhausted both physically and mentally by the time you get to the halfway mark around Caesars Palace, but forge ahead and you could go all the way to the Stratosphere Tower for a bird's-eye view of the city from more than 1,000 feet up. Make plenty of stops en route to see the Mirage Volcano erupt, take a photo of the full moon over the Eiffel Tower, and marvel at the choreographed water-fountain ballet at Bellagio.

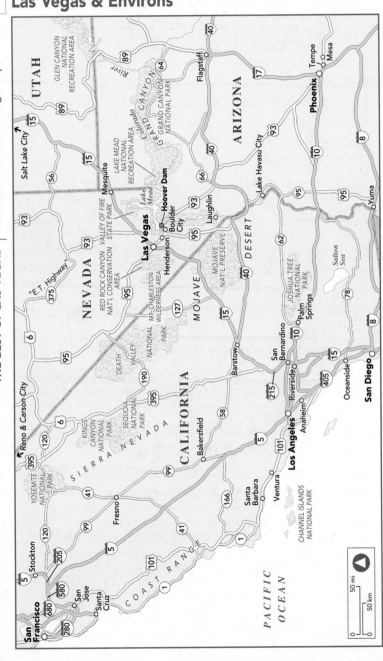

- **Casino-Hopping on the Strip:** The interior of each lavish hotel-casino is more outrageous and giggle-inducing than the last. Just when you think they can't possibly top themselves, they do. From Venice to Paris, from New York City to the Manhattan-style chic of CityCenter, it is all, completely and uniquely, Las Vegas. See "The Best Las Vegas Casinos" later in this chapter.

- **Sleeping In:** Come on! You're on vacation! Yes, there are lots of things to see and do in Las Vegas, but with tens of thousands of the most luxurious hotel rooms in the world, don't you just want to stay in one of those big fluffy beds and maybe order room service? We know we do. See "The Best Las Vegas Hotels" below.

- **Visiting an Only-in-Vegas Museum:** Take a breather from the casino floor and learn something new about Sin City: Go nuclear at the **National Atomic Testing Museum** (p. 164), get "made" at **The Mob Museum** (p. 161), or get lit up at **The Neon Museum** (p. 161).

- **Spending a Day (and Night) in Downtown:** Glitter Gulch is undergoing a renaissance with fun, modern hotels and casinos like **The Downtown Grand** (p. 73); terrific new and affordable dining options such as **Eat** (p. 131) and **La Comida** (p. 128); fun and funky bars like **The Commonwealth** (p. 222) and **Atomic Liquors** (p. 219); and must-see attractions like the **Fremont Street Experience** (p. 160). Oh, and there's a giant, fire-breathing praying mantis at the **Downtown Container Park** (p. 198). If that doesn't make you want to go, nothing will!

- **Shopping Until You're Dropping:** Take what Napoleon called "the greatest drawing room in Europe," replicate it, add shops, and you've got **The Grand Canal Shoppes** at the Venetian (p. 196)—it's St. Mark's Square, complete with canals and working gondolas. See chapter 7 for the lowdown on the shopping scene.

- **Dressing Up for a Show:** Despite the fact that you'll see plenty of cats in Bermuda shorts, hoodies, and Hawaiian shirts, there's something about putting on your best suit or fanciest dress for an evening at the "thea-tuh" that can't be beat. See chapter 8 for reviews of the major shows and check out "The Best Las Vegas Shows" later in this chapter.

- **Breaking Some Records:** You can find thrills in many parts of the United States, but a few of the adrenaline-pumping attractions here are worthy of spots in *The Guinness Book of World Records*. **High Roller** (p. 155) is the world's tallest observation wheel; the **Stratosphere Tower & Thrill Rides** (p. 157) are the highest in the United States; and **SlotZilla** (p. 162) is the world's tallest "slot machine," which is the launching platform for zip lines down Fremont Street.

- **Getting Away from It All:** Las Vegas can be overwhelming, so be sure to create some time in your itinerary to find your Zen at such scenic spots as the **Valley of Fire State Park** or **Red Rock Canyon.** See chapter 9 for more ideas for day trips from Vegas.

THE best LAS VEGAS RESTAURANTS

- **Best Strip Restaurants:** **Restaurant Guy Savoy** (p. 111) is a legend in Paris and this offshoot is just as stellar. A second choice? **Estiatorio Milos** (p. 110) which serves impossibly fresh Mediterranean seafood.

- **Best Downtown Restaurants:** The gourmet-yet-cool specialties at **Carson Kitchen** (p. 130) and the authentic, homemade-style Thai dishes at **Le Thai** prove that the dining scene in Downtown has arrived.

- **Best Off-Strip Restaurant:** **Raku Grill** (p. 142) is a 10- to 20-minute drive from the Strip, but the flavorful Japanese grill specialties here make it totally worth the trip.

- **Best Comfort Food:** The heaping portions of classic American comfort food at **Tom's Urban** (In New York–New York; p. 54) will satisfy even the most ravenous of eaters, while the funky twists on the genre served at **Culinary Dropout** (p. 135) will charm the most jaded.

- **Best Theme Restaurant:** Generally speaking, we think theme restaurants are overpriced tourist traps, but **Gilley's** (p. 116) has such great down-home cooking that we're willing to overlook the mechanical bull.

- **Best Steakhouse:** The Vegas staple restaurant is alive and well in the hands of modern chefs like Gordon Ramsay, whose **Gordon Ramsay Steak** (p. 110) celebrates the one thing that matters in a steakhouse: the meat. One of the stars of the show (in addition to Ramsay, when he's in the open kitchen) is the multi-tiered, mirrored steak cart that lets you check out all the luscious prime cuts from every angle. The only better look you'd get of that beef is if you were face to face with the cow itself.

- **Best Cheap Eats:** **Fat Choy** in the Eureka Casino, 595 E. Sahara Ave. (www.fatchoylv.com; ✆ **702/794-0829**) serves both Asian and American comfort foods—think pork belly bao and short rib grilled cheese sandwiches—at a slots-only locals' casino just off the Strip.

- **Best Splurge:** Food should not cost as much as it does at **Joël Robuchon at the Mansion** (p. 97) and its slightly less expensive sibling **L'Atelier de Joël Robuchon** (p. 98), but a few bites of the exquisite cuisine will make you understand why it does.

- **Best Buffets:** It's expensive, but the **Bacchanal Buffet** (p. 145) serves high-quality food worthy of tablecloths and candlelight. Bargain hunters, however, won't need to sacrifice quality at the **Main Street Garden Court Buffet** (p. 147).

- **Best Hamburgers:** **Holstein's** (p. 117) grinds it out at the Cosmopolitan, putting out really inventive burgers such as the Gold Standard, topped with bacon, goat cheddar cheese and tomato confit. Not into beef? Not to worry, they've got pork, turkey, and veggie burgers to suit everyone. Plus some killer milkshakes.

- **Best Desserts:** An off-shoot of the NYC original, **Serendipity 3** (p. 119) is known for enormous plates of food, but we think the Frrrozen Hot Chocolate is the best treat on a hot Vegas day.

- **Best Views:** You can see the entire city and big chunks of southern Nevada from the revolving **Top of the World** (p. 125), situated more than 800 feet up the Stratosphere Tower, while at **Alizé** (p. 132), at the top of the Palms, you get a virtually unobstructed view of the Strip and delightfully crafted French cuisine that may make you forget the vista entirely.
- **Best Breakfasts:** The home-style fare at **The Pantry** (In The Mirage; p. 63) features daily pancake specials adorned with expensive chocolate (and sometimes gold leaf, depending on the season), while **Eat** (p. 131) offers dizzyingly fresh and flavorful choices that have won legions of fans.

THE best LAS VEGAS HOTELS

- **Best Classic Vegas Hotel:** Most of historic Las Vegas has been imploded (often spectacularly), but at **Caesars Palace** (p. 57) you can still get a taste of it as themed Roman decadence meets classic Sin City opulence.
- **Best Modern Vegas Hotel: The Cosmopolitan of Las Vegas** (p. 58) offers a blueprint for what the next generation of Las Vegas hotels will be like: as over-the-top visually as any theme hotel, but with a sexy, contemporary edge.
- **Best for a Romantic Getaway:** No, it's not the real Eiffel Tower, but the one at **Paris Las Vegas** (p. 65) is almost as charming as the rest of this ooo-la-la themed resort, providing you ample opportunity to re-create a romantic French retreat.
- **Best for Families:** Las Vegas is not a family destination, but if you can't leave the little ones with Grandma, your choice for a major Vegas hotel is **Circus Circus** (p. 71), where there are almost as many things for the wee ones to do as there are for adults.
- **Best for Business Travelers: Westgate Las Vegas'** (p. 82) location next to the Convention Center makes this a no-brainer from a geographical perspective, but the large rooms, classic casino, and raft of restaurants give it a decidedly Vegas spin.
- **Best Rooms on the Strip:** There are less than 200 rooms at **The Cromwell** (p. 60), and compared to more modern hotels, they can run on the smaller side. But cool design touches (art! real books!) and a prime location center Strip make up what you lack in space.
- **Best Rooms Downtown: The Downtown Grand** (p. 73) took the bones of the old Lady Luck hotel and turned it into a modern yet comfortable resort that ups the ante considerably for this neighborhood.
- **Best Rooms Off the Strip: Red Rock Resort** (p. 90) lives up to the resort part of its name as a true desert retreat, complete with gorgeous, modern rooms that you'll never want to leave.
- **Best Bathrooms:** This one is a toss-up for us, with the bigger-than-many-apartments-size retreats at **The Venetian** (p. 60) and the sumptuous luxury fixtures at **Wynn Las Vegas** (p. 68) both winning our, er, hearts.
- **Best Bang for Your Buck:** Almost everything you can find at a Strip hotel (nice rooms, full casino, multiple restaurants, former Las Vegas mayor/

martini aficionado Oscar Goodman!) can be gotten at the **Plaza** (p. 78) in Downtown Las Vegas for a fraction of the cost.

o **Best Non-Casino Hotel:** They can't get your money gambling, so they get it through high room rates, but to stay at the **Mandarin Oriental** (p. 49) is to immerse yourself in luxury.

o **Best Splurge:** Rooms at **Wynn/Encore Las Vegas** (p. 68) will almost always be among the most expensive in town, but you'll totally feel like you are getting your money's worth, especially with the gorgeous spas, pools, casinos, and other amenities at your disposal.

o **Best Hotels for Spas:** The **Spa at Encore** (p. 191) is a 70,000-square-foot oasis for the mind, body, and spirit, with gorgeous Moroccan-infused design and a full menu of pampering delights. Meanwhile, we only wish our own gym were as handsomely equipped as the one at the **Canyon Ranch SpaClub** (p. 189) in the Venetian, which also has a number of other high-priced treatments on which you can blow your blackjack winnings. For more great spa options, see p. 189.

THE best FREE THINGS TO DO IN LAS VEGAS

o **Watching the Waters Dance:** The intricately choreographed water ballet that is the **Fountains at Bellagio** (p. 158) would be worth repeated viewings even if they charged to see it. The fact that they don't makes it an almost perfect Vegas experience.

o **Enjoying the Changing of the Seasons:** There are five seasons in the elaborately designed botanical gardens of the **Bellagio Conservatory** (p. 158): Winter (holiday), Chinese New Year, Spring, Summer, and Fall. No matter which is on display during your visit, make sure your digital camera has a full battery charge. You'll want lots of pictures.

o **Seeing a Volcano Erupt:** When the free **Mirage Volcano** (p. 158) first "erupted" in 1989, shooting flames and faux lava into the sky, it literally stopped traffic on the Strip. That it doesn't today only means that it has more competition for your attention, not that it is any less fun.

o **Watching the Sky Light Up:** Many people considered it almost sacrilegious to convert the famed Glitter Gulch in Downtown Vegas into a pedestrian mall with a free light-and-sound show broadcast on a massive LED canopy overhead. Now the **Fremont Street Experience** (p. 160) is considered a must-visit.

o **Playing a Penny Slot:** Yes, in order to win the big bucks—sometimes millions of them—on a modern penny slot you have to bet much more than just one penny. But if you're okay with smaller rewards and losses, you could stretch a dollar into 100 spins.

o **Beating the High Score:** It's free to just look at the restored classic machines at the **Pinball Hall of Fame** (p. 167), and if you want to do more than just look, it'll only cost you a couple of quarters. What other museum lets you play with its works of art?

○ **Making Your Own Postcard:** Just down the road from the southern-most edge of the Strip is one of the most photographed and imitated signs in the world. Get a picture of you at the **Welcome to Fabulous Las Vegas Sign** (p. 158), and you'll have a postcard-worthy souvenir.

THE best WAYS TO SEE LAS VEGAS LIKE A LOCAL

○ **Gambling on a Budget:** Finding a local at a Strip casino is rare. Why? Because Vegas residents know the limits are lower and the payback is often higher at neighborhood casinos like **Red Rock Resort** (p. 90) and **Green Valley Ranch Resort** (p. 86).

○ **Eating off the Strip:** Those same locals who don't gamble on the Strip usually don't eat on the Strip either, unless they are trying to impress visitors. Instead they dine at the less expensive but still fantastic local eateries such as **Carson Kitchen** (p. 130) or **Made L.V.**

○ **Becoming an Arts Lover:** Leave the tacky Las Vegas snow globes for the souvenir-hunting tourists and get yourself some unique Vegas keepsakes at one of the arts collectives instead. **Emergency Arts** (p. 160) and **The Arts Factory** (p. 159) are leading the charge for the burgeoning arts scene in the city.

○ **Hunting for Treasure:** It may be surprising to find out that in a city like Las Vegas, where history is often disposed of with carefully timed implosions, antique shopping is a favored pastime of locals and visitors alike. Check out the fun finds at **Retro Vegas** (p. 199).

○ **Catching a Broadway Show:** The 2012 opening of the stunning (both visually and aurally) **Smith Center for the Performing Arts** (p. 162) has been a boon to the cultural life of Las Vegas, giving a proper home to everything from the philharmonic and dance troupes to their popular Broadway Series featuring titles like *Book of Mormon* and *Hamilton.*

○ **Walking the Streets:** No, not that way. Instead, check out the fun **First Friday Las Vegas** street fair (p. 164), which brings the local (and tourist) community together with live entertainment, art vendors, and lots of state fair–type food. Did we mention deep-fried cookie dough? We thought that would get your attention.

THE best LAS VEGAS CASINOS

○ **Best Classic Casinos:** On the Strip there is no place that honors its history quite like **Caesars Palace** (p. 57), where you can still enjoy the classic Roman splendor that has been wowing gamblers since 1966. And though they no longer have the World Series of Poker, serious players still head directly to **Binion's** for its swingers vibe and lively table game action.

○ **Best Modern Casinos:** When we first saw the contemporary, cutting-edge decor at **Aria Las Vegas** (p. 45), we thought that nothing could top it in terms of modern casino luxury. But then along came the bold, artistic statement of **The Cosmopolitan of Las Vegas** (p. 58), and we realized we just might have a competition on our hands.

o **Best Glitter Gulch Casinos:** Downtown Las Vegas casinos often have lower limits and friendlier dealers, two things that can make losing money less painful. The best of the breed in the area are the **Golden Nugget** (p. 73), all warm hues and laid-back fun, and **The Downtown Grand** (p. 73), which manages to be both modern and charmingly retro at the same time.

o **Best Local Casinos:** Most neighborhood casinos are low-limit, no-frills joints, but the casinos at **Red Rock Resort** (p. 90), **Green Valley Ranch** (p. 86), and **M Resort** (p. 88) are as stylish as many on the Strip. That they can be that visually appealing, and still maintain most of the thrifty attitude that the locals' casinos are known for, is almost a miracle.

o **Best Budget Casinos:** You won't find any ostentatious opulence at **The Orleans** (p. 83), but you will find thousands of low-limit slot and video poker machines and dozens of gaming tables that won't cost you an arm and a leg to join. Meanwhile the **Four Queens** (p. 75) in Downtown Las Vegas offers similarly low-priced gambling options in comfortable and friendly surroundings.

o **Best Splurge Casino:** Yes, you can find high-limit slots and table games pretty much anywhere, but why not surround yourself with the opulent decor and high-class furnishings of **Wynn/Encore** (p. 68)?

o **Best Blast from the Past Casinos:** Both the **D Las Vegas** (p. 72) and the **Eastside Cannery** (p. 86) have a selection of "classic" machines that still take and dispense actual coins!

THE best LAS VEGAS SHOWS

o **Best Overall Show:** A perfect intersection of music and artistry can be found at *Michael Jackson ONE* (p. 206), featuring the music and choreography of the King of Pop and the stunning visual theater of Cirque du Soleil.

o **Best Big Shows:** The wow-factor winner is a toss-up between **Cirque du Soleil's** *KÀ* (p. 206) and *Mystère* (p. 208). The latter is more traditional—if you can call a human circus that mixes dazzling acrobatics with dramatic visuals "traditional"—in that it has only a loose semblance of narrative, whereas *KÀ* actually has a plot. Both are dazzling and, given the extremely high production values, seem worth the extremely high ticket prices.

o **Best Small Show:** Only the space in which *Absinthe* (p. 205) is performed can be called small; the over-the-top acrobatics, stunts, dance, comedy, and mind-blowing originality of each certainly can't be.

o **Best Classic Show:** Fare thee well, big, huge stage sets; pointless production numbers; showgirls; nipples on parade; and Bob Mackie headdresses.

If you want more than just a musty blast from the past, check out *Vegas! The Show* (p. 219), which celebrates multiple eras of classic Sin City entertainment in one spectacular package.

○ **Best Magic Shows:** This town isn't good enough for **Penn & Teller** (p. 215) and their master class in the art and artifice of illusion taught by guys who will both amuse and amaze. Meanwhile, mixing traditional illusions (big sets and big shocks) with a rock-'n'-roll aesthetic, **Criss Angel's** *Mindfreak Live!* (p. 209) will make you rethink everything you thought about magic shows.

○ **Best Music Shows:** Fans of '80s metal, big hair and all the fun that came with it flock to *Rock of Ages* (p. 217) for a night of head-banging, hilarious nostalgia, while **Human Nature's** *Jukebox* (p. 212) will shock you with how well four white Australian dudes can sing classic Motown songs, boy-band hits, and pop classics.

○ **Best Daytime Shows:** It's almost as much of a comedy show as it is a magic show, but the set done by **Mac King** (p. 214) will leave you astounded with some great close-up tricks while laughing your head off at the same time. A similar mix of laughs and gasps can be found at the comedy juggling show done by **Jeff Civillico** (p. 212).

THE best OUTDOOR EXPERIENCES IN LAS VEGAS

○ **Best Pools:** There are acres of water park fun at **Mandalay Bay** (p. 48), including a wave pool, lazy river, beach, regular swimming pools, and even its own open-air casino. Meanwhile, the lush landscaping, fountains, and water slides at **The Mirage** (p. 63) will make you feel like you're in a tropical paradise. For more picks for our favorite pools, see p. 64.

○ **Best Golf:** The greens fees are outrageously high, but the course at **Wynn Las Vegas** (p. 189) is one of the most lush in town. "Real" golfers head to **TPC Las Vegas** (p. 188) for its challenging holes, eye-candy scenery, and occasional Justin Timberlake sightings.

○ **Best Drives:** The 13-mile **Red Rock Scenic Drive** (p. 250) provides a way to enjoy the colorful rocks and canyons without leaving the air-conditioned comfort of your car. On the other hand, you could get a good breeze going at about 140 mph in one of the race or exotic cars you can drive yourself at the **Las Vegas Motor Speedway** (p. 169).

○ **Best Retreat:** If you need a respite from the hustle and bustle of Las Vegas, head north to **Mount Charleston** (p. 252) for a relaxed mountain retreat, or to work up a sweat while hiking or snowboarding.

○ **Best Man-Made Wonder:** One of the greatest engineering feats in history is the 726-foot-tall **Hoover Dam** (p. 243). You can take tours of the mighty facility and learn how it made Las Vegas (and much of the American Southwest) possible.

SUGGESTED LAS VEGAS ITINERARIES

2

The Strip alone has hundreds of restaurants, dozens of shows, and more attractions, sights, and sounds than can easily be catalogued, much less visited. So yes, when you come to Las Vegas, you certainly won't be lacking in things to do. But the sheer enormity of the city and its laundry list of items to add to your daily to-do list could leave even the most intrepid traveler feeling a little overwhelmed.

The itineraries in this chapter are designed to help narrow down the big list a little while maximizing your time. This way you can spend less energy planning and more having fun. Each itinerary has a theme, but you can always mix and match to create your perfect Las Vegas getaway.

Instead of a step-by-step tour, the itineraries are broken down by morning, afternoon, and nighttime activities with multiple suggestions for each, again allowing you to customize your vacation in a way that makes sense for you.

ICONIC LAS VEGAS

There are many things with which Las Vegas has become synonymous: gambling and all things excess are probably at the top of the list, but there's also the dancing waters, the dolphins, the buffets, the Cirque du Soleil shows, the steakhouses, the offbeat museums, the wild nightlife, and much more. This itinerary will guide you to the must-see and must-do, all of which are fun for first-timers or repeat offenders. Have your cameras ready!

Mornings

Start your day with a photo opportunity at the **Welcome to Fabulous Las Vegas Sign,** perhaps the city's most iconic symbol. Then keep your "say cheese" smile in place as you take a driving tour past the only-in-Vegas, postcard-worthy exteriors of hotels like the pyramid-shaped **Luxor,** the castle-themed **Excalibur,** the Gotham re-creation of **New York–New York,** the modern wonder of **City-Center,** the Italian villa charm of **Bellagio,** the Gallic splendor of **Paris Las Vegas,** and the Roman decadence of **Caesars Palace.**

If you started early enough and still have time before lunch, check out one (or preferably both) of the city's more colorful attractions with the glorious botanical gardens at the **Bellagio Conservatory** or the majestic animals at the **Mirage Secret Garden & Dolphin Habitat.** Both are fun to look at, but more importantly, offer a bit of a peaceful respite from the madness that is Las Vegas. Trust us, you'll need a break every now and then!

Afternoons

You can go one of two ways for lunch, either with a classic Vegas buffet or a view of the throngs of humanity that crowd the Strip. For the former, check out the **Spice Market Buffet** at Planet Hollywood or **Bellagio Buffet.** Both offer a seemingly endless array of well-prepared food; while they may not be the cheapest buffets in town, neither are they the most expensive, so you can have your proverbial—or literal—cake and eat it, too.

The other way to go would be to have a nosh at a Strip-side cafe so you can do some people-watching. The best of the bunch are **Mon Ami Gabi** for Americanized twists on classic French bistro cuisine at Paris Las Vegas, and **Tom's Urban** at New York–New York, which serves up a diverse menu from burgers to steaks with eclectic salads and one giant eggroll.

After you have refueled, head to one of the city's offbeat, unique museums. Tops on our list are the **National Museum of Organized Crime and Law Enforcement,** aka the Mob Museum, which takes a look at the Mafia and its influence on the country and Vegas in particular; or the **National Atomic Testing Museum,** which explores the history of the nuclear age with a special focus on the nearby Nevada Testing Site.

Close out your afternoon with some shopping, window or otherwise. Even if you can't afford to buy, a stroll through the highly themed malls like **The Forum Shops** (ancient Rome) or **Grand Canal Shoppes** (Venice canals complete with gondoliers) is a hoot.

Nights

If you didn't eat the buffet at lunch you may want to consider one for dinner, but our preference would be to send you to a steakhouse. The best of the bunch are **StripSteak** at Mandalay Bay, Michael Mina's version of a modern steakhouse, which not only serves some of the best Japanese beef on the Strip but also has a really exciting non-steak menu; don't confuse this with **Strip House** at Planet Hollywood, which has fantastically flavorful cuts of meat and a peek-a-boo bordello theme; and the simply named **The Steakhouse** at Circus Circus, which has an old-school charm, terrific food, and affordable prices.

We hope you didn't eat too much, because your night is just getting started. Next, it's on to one of the shows by Cirque du Soleil, the French-Canadian circus troupe that reinvented and now rules the Las Vegas entertainment scene. There are many to choose from, but our favorites include the dreamy wonder of *Mystère* at Treasure Island, the martial arts spectacle of *KÀ* at MGM

Suggested Las Vegas Itineraries

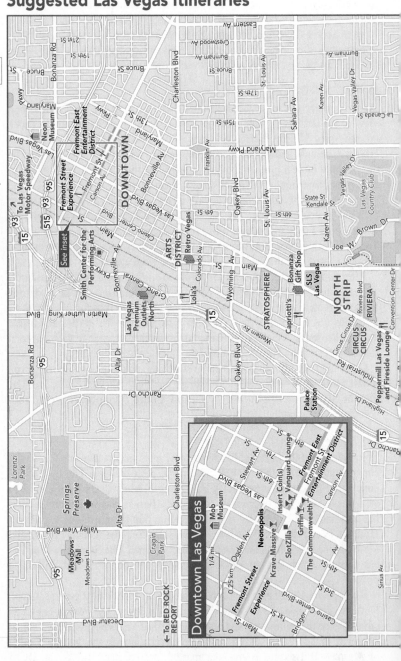

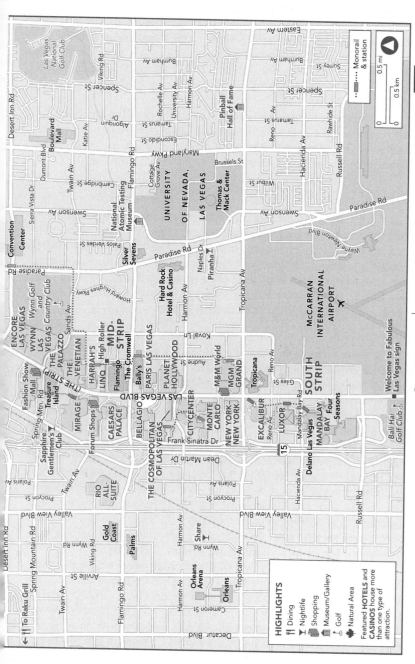

HIGHLIGHTS

🍴 Dining
🍸 Nightlife
🛍️ Shopping
🏛️ Museum/Gallery
⛳ Golf
🌿 Natural Area

Featured **HOTELS** and **CASINOS** house more than one type of attraction.

Monorail & station

0   0.5 mi
0   0.5 km

13

Grand, the water ballet of *O* at Bellagio, or the King of Pop spectacle that is *Michael Jackson ONE* at Mandalay Bay.

From there it's on to the truly iconic Las Vegas experiences, which are all best viewed at night. The dancing waters of the **Fountains of Bellagio** are worth visiting no matter how many times you have seen them; the **Mirage Volcano** is still a lava-spewing delight; and the **Fremont Street Experience** in Downtown Las Vegas will immerse you in the neon-lit glory that is Glitter Gulch.

End your day dancing the night away at one of the city's hot nightclubs like the technologically innovative, LED-laden **Light** at Mandalay Bay or the world's largest nightclub **Hakkasan** at MGM Grand. Or put some money down in the casino. It certainly doesn't get more iconic Vegas than that.

OVER-THE-TOP LAS VEGAS

Las Vegas was built on the idea that "average" and "normal" were adjectives that should never be used to describe the city. They don't just build hotels here; they build the biggest hotels in the world. And then they throw a roller coaster, a volcano, a $500-per-person golf course, or a $400-per-meal restaurant into the mix. Vegas is all about extravagance, so this itinerary will help you find the biggest of the big, the wildest of the wild, and the most outrageous, over-the-top experiences the city has to offer.

Mornings

You're going to have a busy day of excess, so it's important to start out with an ample breakfast to keep your energy level high. Room service is always an option—there's nothing quite as extravagant as having servers bring you food without ever getting out of bed—but if you feel like getting out and about, try the sumptuous **brunch buffets at Wynn Las Vegas** or **Caesars Palace.** Both offer a mind-boggling number of food choices (Caesars Bacchanal Buffet claims over 500 individual dishes at any time), all of which are a cut above your standard buffet. Handmade omelets and crepes, freshly baked breads, and heaping mounds of bacon, sausage, and even steak will go well with your unlimited mimosas. At more than $45 per person (for the weekend champagne brunch), the price will remind you that this is no pedestrian all-you-can-eat experience. **The Sterling Brunch at BLT at Bally's** will set you back nearly $100 for the weekend meal, but with all-you-can-eat caviar, lobster tails, and free-flowing Perrier-Jouet champagne, it's worth every penny.

The morning hours are the best time to schedule your outdoor activities. Not only are crowds often lighter, as a lot of people sleep in (it is a vacation, after all), but temperatures are also more moderate. This is especially true in the summer, when an afternoon stroll down the Strip can emulate a trek across the desert. So use this time to catch some rays poolside or, if you are recreationally minded, work up a moderate sweat with a round of golf. If you are a guest of **Wynn Las Vegas** or **Encore,** you can play the links at the **Wynn Las Vegas Golf Club** for a princely sum of $300 per person.

End your morning with a visit to a spa for some pampering and luxuriating. The **Qua Baths & Spa at Caesars Palace** offers virtually every massage, aromatherapy, skin-care treatment, and relaxation technique known to man—some of which will cost you more per 30-minute session than your hotel room. Soak in the jacuzzi or sit in the unique ice room before heading out for the rest of the day.

Afternoons

You may still be full from breakfast, but that doesn't mean you can't have a little dessert to tide you over. Stop by **Serendipity 3** at Caesars Palace and order the Golden Opulence Sundae, made with rare ice cream and chocolate that's topped with edible 23-carat gold leaf. It's only $1,000—so get two!

Then it's off to the shopping malls, where the true excess can really begin. **The Forum Shops at Caesars Palace,** the **Grand Canal Shoppes at The Venetian, The LINQ, Grand Bazaar Shops, Crystals at CityCenter, Fashion Show,** and the **Miracle Mile at Planet Hollywood** are all filled with high-end retailers designed to drain your checking account and max out your credit cards. If those are a little out of your price range, consider going the completely opposite direction at the **Bonanza Gift and Souvenir Shop.** Billed as the largest souvenir shop in the world, this is the place where you can find pretty much anything—from tacky to, well, *more* tacky—emblazoned with the words "Las Vegas" on it. The kitsch factor here is off the charts.

Finally, experience some of the quintessential, only-in-Vegas attractions, such as riding a gondola through a shopping mall at **The Venetian,** or watching the water ballet at the **Fountains of Bellagio.**

Nights

Start your evening with a meal at **Joël Robuchon,** the multi-Michelin-star-winning darling of the foodie world—and with good reason. The degustation menu will only cost you a mere $445 a person (and that's before wine) to find out why. Or if your extravagance knows no bounds, try the FleurBurger at **Fleur by Hubert Keller.** Made from Wagyu beef, topped with foie gras truffle and accompanied by a bottle of 1996 Chateau Petrus, it costs a measly $5,000.

Next, you'll want to see a show, and you should focus on those that can only be seen here. If **Mariah Carey** or **Jerry Seinfeld** is in town, you should seize the opportunity to catch one of their performances at Caesars Palace, because these shows are exclusive to Vegas. Or check out any of Cirque du Soleil's Vegas-only productions, the best of which are *O* at Bellagio and *KÀ* at MGM Grand. Each is set in its own multimillion-dollar theater, with stage sets—a giant pool and an enormous revolving platform, respectively—unlike anything you've seen before.

Nighttime is the best time for getting the true Strip experience, so how about renting a limousine (maybe one of those superstretch Hummers, if you are feeling really crazy) and instructing the driver to just cruise Las Vegas

VEGAS BY air

Most people are satisfied with the views of Las Vegas from terra firma. Walking or driving up the Strip, especially at night, is a requirement for the first-time Vegas visitor. But, for some, there is no better way to see Sin City in all its neon glamour than from the air. If you are one of these intrepid souls, then look for a helicopter tour of Las Vegas.

There are more than a dozen competing companies offering tours of the city and surrounding areas, and most offer the same type of services at very similar prices. We're including a few of the more well-known companies below, but comparison shopping is highly encouraged.

Maverick Helicopters (www.maverick helicopter.com; ✆ **888/261-4414**) is one of the most well-known tour operators in Las Vegas. Its large fleet of ECO-Star

helicopters has one of the best safety records in the business, and a variety of packages are available, including twilight and night flights over the Strip. If you want to venture farther, Hoover Dam and Grand Canyon packages are available. Rates start at around $119 per person and go up from there, depending on the length and distance of the tour you choose. Most include transportation to and from your hotel.

VegasTours.com (www.vegastours. com; ✆ **866/218-6877**) features a similar list of air adventures, including a nighttime flight over Vegas and several to the Grand Canyon, while **Papillon Tours** (www.papillon.com; ✆ **888/635-7272**) not only offers helicopter tours, but airplane and ground excursions as well.

Boulevard? Hanging out of the sunroof with a cocktail in your hand is discouraged, but people do it anyway.

An after-dark stop at the **High Roller** is in order to give you a bird's-eye view of Las Vegas from the top of the world's tallest observation wheel, and then it's off to the party spots.

Most of the Vegas club scene starts late (11pm or midnight), so have your driver take you to one of the hip hot spots, such as **XS** at Encore, **Light** at Mandalay Bay, or **Marquee** at the Cosmopolitan of Las Vegas. These are see-and-be-seen places, so dress to impress and be on the lookout for a celebrity or three hanging out in the VIP areas. You can easily drop a grand if you want to sit at a table with bottle service.

If it's more of the classic Las Vegas vibe you're looking for, try **Peppermill's,** with its retro-'70s/'80s interior. So cheesy—it's hip again.

Your final destination should be in the spot that makes Vegas tick, the casino. Yes, there are casinos all over the country now, but there's nothing quite like tossing the dice at a craps table at **Caesars Palace** or spinning the reels in the high-limit lounge at **Wynn Las Vegas.**

GUYS' GETAWAY

Not every trip to Vegas with the guys needs to get as crazy as the movie *The Hangover,* but if you're looking for a real man's-man experience, no other city does it quite like this one. Whether it's a bachelor blowout weekend or just an excuse to blow off steam without your significant other's disapproving glances, this itinerary is designed to explain why they call this place "Sin City."

Mornings

You were probably out late the night before and there may have been alcohol involved, so start your morning with a hearty guy's breakfast at **Hash House a Go Go.** Its huge portions of reimagined farm food are chest-poundingly substantial, and there is even a specialty called O'Hare of the Dog—a Budweiser served in a paper bag with a side of bacon.

To get your body in shape for the day ahead, spend the morning taking advantage of the various sports and recreation options available around town. Nearly every hotel has a fitness center, and some, such as Bally's, offer full tennis courts. If you're a fan of the fairway, head over to **Bali Hai golf course,** located conveniently on the Strip, for 18 holes and some wheeling around in their GPS-enabled golf carts. Or, if you need something more extreme, a visit to **Red Rock Adventures** at Red Rock Resort, where you can arrange everything from rock climbing to horseback riding to river rafting. Need something even *more* extreme? Take a few laps around the track with the **Richard Petty Driving Experience** at the Las Vegas Motor Speedway, an interactive attraction that puts you behind the wheel of 600 horsepower NASCAR car at speeds of 155 mph.

Afternoons

Continue your guys-gone-wild day with a stop at **Gilley's** for some great down-home grub and even a ride on the mechanical bull if you feel like proving your machismo.

Daytime is playtime in Las Vegas, where the big trend is to have nightclub-worthy experiences during the afternoon at some of the hotel pools. **DAY-LIGHT Beach Club** at Mandalay Bay, **Wet Republic** at MGM Grand, and **Encore Beach Club** at Encore Las Vegas are all open to the general public (for a cover charge) and include everything from live DJs to fully stocked bars, and certainly a bevy of bikini-wearing partiers. If that's not enough to appeal to the guy in you, **Sapphire Gentleman's Club** now has its own daytime pool party complete with strippers.

Next, head back to the casino for a little sports-book action. You can place a wager on just about any type of sporting event in existence (cricket, anyone?), and depending on the season and the day of the week, you might be able to catch a game in action. The **sports books** at the Mirage and Caesars Palace are always good options for their huge screens and high energy, but you may want to consider the M Resort, the Venetian, or the Palazzo, which offer in-running betting. Popular in the U.K., this means that you can not only wager on the outcome of the game, but place bets during the action as well.

If that isn't enough to get your adrenaline flowing, consider one of the serious thrill rides in town, such as the extreme adventures atop the 1,000-foot

Stratosphere Tower at the Stratosphere Hotel. You can play a little game and make whichever friend screams the loudest while on **Insanity: The Ride** or **SkyJump** buy the first round of drinks later that night. Or take a run at **Slot-Zilla,** a zip-line attraction in Downtown Las Vegas that features both seated and superhero flying position rides.

Nights

We know. We already sent you to some sports books, but you should go back to the only one that is a real restaurant. The 45,000-square-foot **Lagasse's Stadium** at the Venetian is a sports bar on steroids, with 100 flatscreen TVs and a menu crammed with highlights from Emeril's American and Creole cuisine.

Now for some nighttime entertainment. Topless revues are becoming an endangered species around Vegas—which you can probably blame on the Internet—but there are still a couple left that will allow you to get your (not so cheap) thrills. Sadly, you won't catch too many of the traditional showgirl headdresses anymore, save for street buskers and the occasional appearances with former Mayor Goodman, but their modern, equally topless counterparts are still shimmying away at **Fantasy** at Luxor or **X Burlesque** at Flamingo.

The party gets started late in Vegas, and you might want to start at a bar or two, such as **The Commonwealth** on Fremont Street or **Gold Spike**, both in Downtown Las Vegas. Then it's time to hit the dance floor. **Marquee** at the Cosmopolitan is an obvious place to start, but give newcomers **Jewel** at Aria or **Intrigue** at Wynn a shot.

What's that? You haven't had enough gambling? Well, head over to Planet Hollywood's **Passion Pit,** complete with lingerie-clad dealers at the blackjack tables and go-go girls.

And if you want more girly action, Vegas has **strip clubs** aplenty. The best of the best are detailed in chapter 8.

GIRLS' GETAWAY

With the plethora of strip clubs and showgirls in this town, you'd think that Vegas is a man's world. Not so! There are plenty of activities and attractions for the ladies—from wild, bachelorette-style craziness to relaxing, leave-your-cares-at-home-style getaways. Here are just a few suggestions.

Mornings

If you dream of going to Paris, skip the hotel of the same name and go more or less across the street to Caesars Palace and **Payard Patisserie & Bistro** for breakfast. The chef is from the City of Lights, and you'll know it when you taste his croissants. The food is not cheap, but it is high quality, generously portioned, and just plain delightful. (It's also worth an evening stop for the amazing desserts.)

Vegas is retail heaven, and you could spend your whole day going to branches of pretty much every designer name you can think of in the major hotel malls (**Crystals** at CityCenter, **The Forum Shops** at Caesars Palace, **The Grand Canal Shoppes** at Venetian/Palazzo, **Miracle Mile** at Planet Hollywood, and shops at Bellagio and Wynn Las Vegas). Bargain shoppers will want to check out the **Las Vegas Premium Outlets North** near Downtown. Truth be told, there are not a lot of bargains there; but it's an outlet, so something will turn up.

Afternoons

You can have a fabulous girly lunch at the elegant **Bouchon** at The Venetian. Thomas Keller's brasserie is tucked away into a private tower so you don't have to be inundated with the dinging of the casino floor as you tuck into your eggs Benedict and mimosas.

Okay, it's time for some serious pampering. You could just stretch out by the pool (didn't you just buy a new bikini this morning?), but it's hot outside. So make your way to the spas at **Encore, Bellagio,** or **The Venetian** (which is a branch of the Canyon Ranch) for a full menu of massages, facials, weird treatments imported from countries you've never heard of, and lots more—all designed to make you feel as relaxed and limp as an al dente noodle.

Nights

If your girls' getaway weekend is of the rowdy bachelorette variety, have dinner at **STK** at Cosmopolitan. It's kind of like eating a steak in a loud nightclub, surrounded by really beautiful people. If it's a more sultry, femme fatale atmosphere you're after, get a big table at **Red Square** at Mandalay Bay and drink cold vodka while noshing on upscale Russian fare.

Hey, speaking of getting rowdy, if you're tired of all those signs with scantily clad women all over Vegas, equal time can be attained at such shows as the male-stripper review *Thunder From Down Under,* at Excalibur or the tried-and-true *Chippendales* at Rio. Or, if that's not risqué enough, try the delightfully profane circus of *Absinthe* at Caesars Palace. Just don't allow the host to pull you up on stage for audience participation. You'll thank us later.

Fizz bar at Caesars Palace is a calm, sophisticated spot to have a tipple to gear up for the rest of your evening. Check out their outlandish champagne cocktails and the art on the wall from Elton John's private collection (his husband co-created the joint). A somewhat more gearing-up-for-the-clubs atmosphere is across the way at **Hyde Bellagio,** which in addition to having fun cocktails (is that a Belini cart? Why, yes, it is!) has the best view of the Bellagio Fountains from its lakeside patio.

Finally, strap on that pair of Christian Louboutins you bought earlier today (lucky you), because it's time to go dancing. If you're single and looking to mingle (or whatever, we don't judge), the scenes at **Light** at Mandalay Bay, **XS** at Encore Las Vegas, and **Omnia** at Caesars Palace are such that people will stand in line for hours (and pay outrageous cover charges) just to get inside. We have to admit they are awfully fun.

Wanna just go dance and not be bothered by the meat-market scene? Consider going to gay clubs, such as **Piranha** or **Share,** both just off the Strip.

They welcome women, but remember that you aren't going to be the priority.

UNLIKELY LAS VEGAS

It's really hard to overlook the Strip—after all, a number of people have spent billions and billions of dollars to ensure that you don't—but there are still some surprisingly unusual and captivating sights to see in and around Las Vegas. This itinerary is designed to help you discover them. You will need a car to do this tour.

Mornings

Those pricey buffets at the casinos may offer you truckloads of food, but even the ones at the out-of-the-way hotels are the very definition of "discovered." Instead, go down home for the delightful Southern cooking at **M&M Soul Food Café.** Chicken and waffles, biscuits and gravy, or anything with grits is a great way to start the day as far as we're concerned.

Walk off that breakfast by exploring the nearby **18b Arts District,** home to a number of art galleries and studios, bravely taking a stance against prefab, soulless Vegas. You might take special note of **Retro Vegas,** a fun and funky store celebrating Sin City and mid-century modern furnishings (they work remarkably well together). If it's the first Friday of the month, you could come back and stroll here in the evening, as that's when the galleries come into the streets for a food, art, and entertainment festival.

Springs Preserve is a remarkable destination, focused on nature and eco-logical concerns. The interpretive center examines the history of the region as related to water consumption, which sounds "dry" but really isn't. Need proof? Try the so-real-you-are-there flash flood exhibit or the 3-D movie theater that puts you atop the Hoover Dam being built. Outside are trails through the wetlands, animal habitats, and other exhibition halls dealing with the environment and recycling. The place is informative, entertaining, and absolutely vital in this day and age, and you can't believe that something of this quality and social significance is anywhere near Vegas.

Afternoons

Although Las Vegas is obviously our favorite city, New York comes in a close second and a lot of that has to do with the food. Downtown is becoming Brooklyn-esque, with great independent restaurants such as **F. Pigalle** and **Glutton** becoming the new neighborhood hangouts. Great for the residents of Downtown, even better for you since you get a taste of what you'd be eating if this were your town.

From there, we recommend a duo of only-in-Las Vegas museums. Begin with the **National Atomic Testing Museum.** It's about more than just the 5 minutes when the bomb was awesome (apparently people really thought that—they have photos that you won't believe, like the one of Miss Atomic

Bomb), instead tracing the history of the atomic age and focusing specifically on the aboveground nuclear testing that occurred just outside of Las Vegas. It's a fascinating and sobering experience.

Then you're off to the **Pinball Hall of Fame,** where you can not only appreciate, but actually play, classic machines and arcade games from the 1960s to the present day.

If you want to skip the latter, consider taking in the afternoon show by **Mac King** or **Jeff Civillico** at Harrah's Las Vegas and Flamingo, respectively. Both are considered among the best shows in Vegas and are good values for the money. King is an illusionist and comedian of great personal charm who still practices magic that doesn't require computer technology, while Civillico is a comic-juggler with a family-friendly and very funny patter. You can often get discounted (or even two-for-one) tickets for both shows in local magazines or online.

Nights

Now we'll send you far west to a place only foodies tend to know: **Raku Grill,** a Japanese *robata* (charcoal grill) restaurant that is a hangout for many of the chefs in town when they're off the clock. Alternately, you could try **Omae,** another off-Strip restaurant that features an all-*omakase* menu of pristine, Japanese fare touched with French techniques. The chef guides you through the predetermined menu based on what's best that day.

After dinner, why not do something completely "unlikely," like perform on the Las Vegas Strip? There are several hotel lounges that offer karaoke, but the sing-along fun at **Ellis Island** is probably the best. Or, instead of a show in one of the casinos, see what's playing at **The Smith Center for the Performing Arts** in Downtown Las Vegas. You might be able to catch a Broadway touring show, a big-name concert, or a jazz set in one of the many theaters at the complex.

End your night exploring the booming bar scene of Downtown's **Fremont East Entertainment District** or the **Main Street Arts District** with funky taverns like **Downtown Cocktail Room, The Commonwealth, Vanguard Lounge,** and **Velveteen Rabbit, Hop Nuts** and more, all within steps of each other. Each has its own vibe and is mostly populated by locals, so try each on for style and see what fits.

EATING LAS VEGAS

Las Vegas is a mecca for food lovers, offering endless opportunities to gorge oneself on virtually every type of cuisine, from cheap eats to gourmet meals. This itinerary presumes you are very hungry and want to at least sample as much of it as you can, throwing waistlines, cholesterol counts, and common sense to the wind. You'll need a car to do this tour, although you may want to consider walking as much of it as you can . . . to give the illusion that you're getting a little exercise in between binges.

Mornings

There are plenty of ways to overdo it from a food perspective first thing in the morning. You could go big with the super decadent and deliriously over-the-top selections at **The Pantry** at Mirage, or get an entire day's worth of calories at an inexpensive buffet like the **Main Street Garden Court** in Downtown Las Vegas—but let's be reasonable, shall we? After all, you don't want to get too full before the day has really even started.

So instead, go for something a little lighter but still packed with flavors, like the sumptuous quiche or croque madame at **Payard Patisserie.** Both come in very satisfying portions, yet they'll keep you from getting too loaded down.

If you decided to sleep in a bit (and really, who could blame you?), then you could go for brunch at **Verandah** at Four Seasons, which offers its own crepes and quiches.

Otherwise, the rest of your morning could be spent exploring various sweet shops, so you can stock up on quick hits of sugar to get you through the rest of the day. **M&M World** allows you to mix and match your own selection of candy, while local favorite **Ethel M Chocolates** serves a finer brand of confections. Or you could visit the new **Hexx Kitchen and Bar,** which, in addition to having a full-service restaurant, boasts its own line of chocolate, ice cream, and confections.

Afternoons

For lunch, we're going to suggest something a little more serious and substantial. The inspired grub at **Todd English P.U.B.** is a terrific choice, especially if you go for the "carvery" part of the menu, which allows you to mix and match meats, breads, cheeses, and toppings to create a sandwich.

Speaking of sandwiches, we'd be totally remiss if we didn't mention **Capriotti's** as a perfect place to have lunch. Their divine submarine sandwiches (we're partial to the Bobby, which is like Thanksgiving on a bun) will make you consider getting the epic 20-inch size and calling it a day.

Burgers are another way to go, and there are lots of options in Vegas including the fantastic offerings at **Bobbys' Burger Palace, Gordon Ramsay BurGR, Holstein's Shakes and Buns,** and the nationally beloved **Shake Shack.**

As you are digesting, take a stroll over to Bellagio to visit the **Jean-Philippe Patisserie** and sample the finest chocolate available in Las Vegas, or go to Monte Carlo and check out **The Cupcakery** for their mouth-watering temptations. Regarding the latter, if you can only choose one, go for the Oh My Gosh, Ganache, which has chocolate ganache baked *into* the cake!

If you're lucky enough to be visiting on the first Friday of the month, be sure to go to the **First Friday** street festival in the Arts District, where you'll find a parking lot's worth of food trucks and vendors serving everything from pizza to sushi to barbecue and more. Don't miss the state fair–style selections, including the genius deep-fried chocolate chip cookie dough. Missing this will haunt you—trust us.

Nights

Finally, we're going to go whole hog, or cow as the case may be, by sending you to dinner at one of the city's steakhouses. **The Steakhouse** at Circus Circus is a local favorite, offering full meals at the same prices that others charge for an a la carte selection. **Strip House** at Planet Hollywood puts a modern spin on things with a charming peek-a-boo bordello theme and fantastic cuts of meat. But for our money you can't beat **Old Homestead Steakhouse** at Caesars Palace, a sister of the legendary New York City restaurant. The portions here are huge, which is appropriate since this is the restaurant that claims to have invented the doggie bag.

If a steak seems like too much of a commitment to you, you could try one of the growing number of restaurants that serves small bites instead of full meals. Chief among them would be **L'Atelier** at MGM Grand by master chef Joël Robuchon, where you can get various-size tasting menus or order small plates on your own, each of which will be better than the last. **La Cave** at the Wynn has fantastic gourmet small plates and a fun environment in which to eat them. Another great choice in this category would be **Raku Grill,** where you can get fantastic skewers of meat, vegetables, seafood, and more cooked over a Japanese charcoal grill. Just be warned that even though the portions are small, you'll wind up ordering a lot of them, and it could end up costing you more than just a standard meal.

But wait, we're not done. This is a 24-hour town, and lots of restaurants are open all night to satisfy those 2am cravings. **The Peppermill Lounge** is an institution for late night/early morning bites, with a massive menu and fun takes on classic diner food, or you could head back to **The Pantry** for the 24-hour restaurant's night shift of food.

CITY LAYOUT

Located in the southernmost precincts of a wide, pancake-flat valley, Las Vegas is the biggest city in the state of Nevada. Treeless mountains form a scenic backdrop to hotels awash in neon glitter. Although bursting with residents and visitors, the city is quite compact, geographically speaking.

There are two main areas of Las Vegas: the **Strip** and **Downtown.** The former is probably the most famous 4-mile stretch of road in the nation. Officially called Las Vegas Boulevard South, it contains most of the top hotels in town and offers almost all the major showroom entertainment. First-time visitors will, and probably should, spend the bulk of their time on the Strip.

Downtown, meanwhile, is where Vegas started its Glitter Gulch fame, complete with neon ambassadors Vegas Vic and Sassy Sally watching over the action.

For many people, that's all there is to Las Vegas. But there is actually more to the town than that: Paradise Road, just east of the Strip, and Boulder Highway on the far-east side of town, are home to quite a bit of casino action; Maryland Parkway boasts mainstream shopping; and there are different

Help for Troubled Travelers

The **Travelers Aid Society** is a social-service organization geared to helping travelers in difficult situations. Its services include reuniting families separated while traveling, feeding people stranded without cash, and even providing emotional counseling. If you're in trouble, seek them out. In Las Vegas, services are provided by **Help of Southern Nevada,** 1640 E. Flamingo Rd., Ste. 100, near Maryland Parkway (www.helpsonv.org; ☏ **702/369-4357**). Hours are Monday through Thursday 7am to 5pm.

restaurant options all over the city. Many of the "locals' hotels," most of which are off the regular tourist track, offer cheaper gambling limits plus budget food and entertainment options. Confining yourself to the Strip and Downtown is fine for the first-time visitor, but repeat customers (and you will be) should get out there and explore. Las Vegas Boulevard South (the Strip) is the starting point for addresses; any street that crosses it starts with 1 East and 1 West at its intersection with the Strip (and goes up from there).

All major Las Vegas hotels provide comprehensive tourist information at their reception and/or sightseeing and show desks.

Other good information sources are the **Las Vegas Convention and Visitors Authority,** 3150 Paradise Rd. (www.lasvegas.com; ☏ **877/847-4858** or 702/892-7575), open Monday through Friday 8am to 5:30pm; the **Las Vegas Metro Chamber of Commerce,** 6671 Las Vegas Blvd. S., Ste. 300 (www.lvchamber.com; ☏ **702/735-1616**), open Monday through Friday 8am to 5pm; and, for information on all of Nevada, including Las Vegas, the **Nevada Commission on Tourism** (www.travelnevada.com; ☏ **800/638-2328**), open 24 hours.

NEIGHBORHOODS IN BRIEF

South Strip

For the purposes of organizing this book, we've divided the Strip into three sections. The **South Strip** can be roughly defined as the portion of the Strip south of Harmon Avenue, including the MGM Grand, Mandalay Bay, the Monte Carlo, New York–New York, Luxor, CityCenter, and many more hotels and casinos. First-timers should consider staying here or in the Mid-Strip area simply because this is where the bulk of the stuff you're going to want to see, do, and eat are located.

Mid-Strip

The **Mid-Strip** is a long stretch of the Las Vegas Boulevard South between Harmon Avenue and Spring Mountain Road, which includes such big-name casinos as Planet Hollywood, the Cosmopolitan of Las Vegas, Bellagio, Caesars, the Mirage, Treasure Island, Bally's, Paris Las Vegas, Flamingo Las Vegas, Harrah's, and more. As mentioned above, this is a great area for newbies, and it's also the preferred location for people with mobility issues since fewer steps will get you to more places.

North Strip

The **North Strip** stretches north from Spring Mountain Road all the way to the Stratosphere and includes SLS, Wynn/Encore, Stratosphere, and Circus Circus, to name a few. Although there are certainly things to see along this chunk of the Strip, development has mostly stalled, so you'll see more things closed or partially constructed in this area than you will see open and completed. With the exception of Wynn/Encore SLS, it is the lower-rent part of the Strip, with all of the good and bad that comes along with it.

Downtown

Also known as **"Glitter Gulch"** (narrower streets make the neon seem brighter), Downtown Las Vegas, which is centered on Fremont Street between Main and 9th streets, was the first section of the city to develop hotels and casinos. With the exception of the Golden Nugget, which looks like it belongs in Monte Carlo, this area has traditionally been more casual than the Strip. But between the **Fremont Street Experience** (p. 160), the **Fremont East Entertainment District** (p. 164), and a general resurgence, Downtown offers a more affordable yet still entertaining alternative to the Strip.

The area between the Strip and Downtown is a seedy stretch dotted with tacky wedding chapels, bail-bond operations, pawnshops, and cheap motels. However, the area known as the **18b Arts District** (roughly north and south of Charleston Blvd. to the west of Las Vegas Blvd. S.) is making a name for itself as an artists' colony. Studios, galleries, antique stores, bars, small cafes, and the fun **First Friday Las Vegas** festival (p. 164) can be found in the vicinity. Eventually it may warrant its own neighborhood designation, but for now we include it in the Downtown category.

Just Off the Strip

With land directly on the Strip at a premium, it isn't surprising that a veritable cottage industry of casinos, hotels, restaurants, nightclubs, attractions, and services have taken up residence in the areas immediately surrounding the big megaresorts. Within a mile in any given direction, you'll find major hotels such as the Rio, the Orleans, the Westgate (formerly the Las Vegas Hilton), and the Hard Rock, to name a few, as well as important visitor destinations such as the Las Vegas Convention Center. You'll also find many smaller chain/ name-brand hotels and motels offering reliable service at rates that are usually cheaper than you'll pay in a big casino-hotel on the Strip.

South & East of the Strip

Once you get a little bit of distance between you and the Strip, you'll start getting into the types of neighborhoods that will look much more familiar to you—except, perhaps, with a lot more desert landscaping. Shopping centers and housing tracts dominate the landscape of the bedroom community of Henderson, while lower-priced motels and chain restaurants take up a lot of space along the Boulder Highway corridor on the far-east side of town. In addition to the luxurious Green Valley Ranch Resort, sprinkled throughout are other fun, low-cost casino-hotels, and some out-of-the-way restaurants and attractions worth knowing about.

North & West of the Strip

The communities of Summerlin and North Las Vegas are where many of the people who work on the Strip live, shop, eat, and play. Yes, there are some major casino-hotels in the area, including the stunning Red Rock Resort, and a few notable restaurants, but for the most part what you'll find here are dependable chain stores and eateries that offer comfort shopping and food at better-than-Strip prices.

LAS VEGAS IN CONTEXT

The global recession hit Vegas hard, but like the rest of the world, Sin City is recovering with improved visitation numbers, the most new development projects in years, and a little bit less red on the balance sheets at the major casino corporations. That recovery, though, is creating a Las Vegas that looks different than it used to, with more of a focus on value and a renewed sensibility that the city is open to more than just the traveler willing to blow $400 per night on a hotel room.

LAS VEGAS TODAY

No major city in America has reinvented itself as many times, especially in such a short period, as Las Vegas. Just look at the recent decades. In the '80s, it was a discount afterthought. In the '90s, it was family and theme heaven. The new millennium brought in ultra-luxury and sky-high prices on everything from rooms to shampoo in the sundry stores.

For the better part of the new millennium, the watchword was "expensive." The average room rate soared to over $200 a night, significantly higher than what visitors, once lulled by lower double-digit bargains, were used to paying. It was not unusual for the high-end hotels to charge $400 or even $500 for a standard room.

And why not? The crowds kept coming. Occupancy rates in Vegas were well over 90%, nearly 30% higher than the national average. Flush with big returns on their stock investments, equity in their home, or simply easy-flowing credit, those who could afford it flocked to the city in record numbers, generating record profit for the casinos. Vegas became hip, drawing a younger, more affluent demographic that lined up to pay for the fancy hotel rooms, the exclusive nightclubs, the celebrity-chef restaurants, and the high-limit gaming tables.

The Average Joe, on the other hand, got priced right out of town. For a lot of people—the people whose money helped build those massive hotels and casinos—the idea of a Vegas vacation became cost-prohibitive.

But then came the global economic meltdown and Vegas was hit hard. The number of visitors coming to the city dropped dramatically, and those who came spent a lot less money in the casinos. By 2010, the average room rate plunged to the lowest level in nearly a decade and more rooms were going empty, with occupancy rates in the low 80% range—still good when compared to the national average, but scary for a city that depends on filling those rooms to keep its economy going.

Many gaming companies fell into bankruptcy, and while their casinos have remained open, their bank accounts have slammed shut. Just like many Americans who ran up too much credit-card debt, the gaming companies are operating under obligations that run into the billions, and they are having a hard time paying the bills.

As the national economy improved and we moved into the second decade of the new millennium, so did the Las Vegas economy. Visitation and occupancy rates perked up, and people seemed to be willing to spend money again. As importantly, Vegas reinvented itself once again, becoming a major venue for music festivals, and drawing younger crowds than it had in decades.

In the long run, this could wind up being good news for the Average Joe tourist and the music lover. Room rates have remained lower, and most of the new stuff planned for the city—attractions, shows, concert venues, restaurants, and so on—is aimed squarely at the midmarket crowd. While rates will certainly go up as the economy improves, the hotel companies are skittish about the idea of returning them to their sky-high levels because they are worried that the national mood of extravagant spending has changed.

Welcome back, Joe. Las Vegas has missed you.

Adapting to Las Vegas

Las Vegas is, for the most part, a very casual city. Although there are a few restaurants that have a restrictive dress code, most of them—and all of the showrooms, casinos, and attractions—are pretty much come as you are. Some people still choose to dress up for their night on the town, resulting in a strange dichotomy where you might see a couple in a suit and evening gown sitting next to a couple in shorts and sandals at a show or in a nice restaurant.

Generally speaking, spiffy-casual (slacks or nice jeans, button-up shirts or blouses, or a simple skirt or dress) is the best way to go in terms of what to wear, allowing you to be comfortable in just about any situation. Go too far to one extreme or the other and you're bound to feel out of place somewhere.

The only exception to this rule is the nightclubs, which often have very strict policies on what you can and cannot wear. They vary from club to club, but, as a general rule, sandals or flip-flops, shorts, and baseball caps are frowned upon. Think "business casual," but your business is getting into the club: that nice pair of jeans or slacks, a collared, pressed shirt, and leather dress shoes will get you in the door; fancier clothes (jackets, cocktail dresses) may get you past the velvet rope a little faster.

Yes, it does get hot in Las Vegas, so you really should factor that in when you're planning your wardrobe for your trip. It's important to note that every enclosed space (casino, showroom, restaurant, nightclub, and so on) is heavily air-conditioned, so it can actually be chilly once you get inside. Think light layers and you should be okay.

Las Vegas is a 24-hour town, so you can find something to eat or drink all the time; but many of the nicer restaurants open only for dinner, with 5 or 6pm to 10 or 11pm the standard operating hours. Nightclubs usually open around 10pm and go until dawn, with the bulk of the crowds not showing up until midnight at the earliest. There are a few afternoon shows, but most are in the evenings and often run two shows a night with start times that range from 7 until 10:30pm. Casinos and most regular bars are open 24 hours a day.

LOOKING BACK: LAS VEGAS HISTORY

The Early 1900s: Las Vegas Takes Shape

For many years after its creation via a land auction in 1905, Las Vegas was a mere whistle-stop town. That all changed in 1928 when Congress authorized the building of nearby Boulder Dam (later renamed Hoover Dam), bringing thousands of workers to the area. Although gambling still happened in the backrooms of saloons after it became illegal in 1909, the lifting of those prohibitions in 1931 is what set the stage for the first of the city's many booms. Fremont Street's gaming emporiums and speakeasies attracted dam workers and, upon the dam's completion, were replaced by hordes of tourists who came to see the engineering marvel (it was called "the Eighth Wonder of the World"). But it wasn't until the early years of World War II that visionary entrepreneurs began to plan for the city's glittering future.

The 1940s: The Strip Is Born

Contrary to popular lore, developer Bugsy Siegel didn't actually stake a claim in the middle of nowhere—his Flamingo opened in 1946 just a few blocks south of already-existing properties.

The true beginnings of what would eventually become the Las Vegas Strip started years earlier. According to lore, Thomas Hull was driving toward Downtown's already-booming Fremont Street area when his car broke down just outside of the city limits. As he stood there sweating in the desert heat, he envisioned, or perhaps just wished for, a cool swimming pool in the scrub brush next to the highway. Luckily, Hull was a hotel magnate, and he put his money where his mirage was. El Rancho Vegas, ultraluxurious for its time and complete with a sparkling pool facing the highway, opened in 1941 across the street from where the upcoming SLS Las Vegas (formerly the Sahara) now stands. Scores of Hollywood stars were invited to the grand opening, and El Rancho Vegas soon became the hotel of choice for visiting film stars.

Beginning a trend that continues today, each new property tried to outdo existing hotels in luxurious amenities and thematic splendor. Las Vegas was on its way to becoming America's playground.

Las Vegas promoted itself in the 1940s as a town that combined Wild West frontier friendliness with glamour and excitement. Throughout the decade, the city was Hollywood's celebrity retreat. The Hollywood connection gave the town glamour in the public's mind—as did the mob connection, which became clear when notorious underworld gangster Bugsy Siegel built the fabulous Flamingo, a tropical paradise and "a real class joint."

While the Strip was expanding with major resorts like the Frontier, Bugsy's Flamingo, and the Thunderbird, Downtown kept pace with new hotels such as the El Cortez and casinos like the Golden Nugget. By the end of the decade, Fremont Street was known as "Glitter Gulch," its profusion of neon signs proclaiming round-the-clock gaming and entertainment.

The 1950s: Building Booms & A-Bombs

Las Vegas entered the new decade as a city (no longer a frontier town), with a population of about 50,000. Hotel growth was phenomenal, with legendary names like the Sahara, the Dunes, the Sands, and the Tropicana all gaining neon-lit fame.

The Desert Inn, which opened in 1950 with headliners Edgar Bergen and Charlie McCarthy, brought country-club elegance (including an 18-hole golf course and tennis courts) to the Strip.

In 1951, the Eldorado Club Downtown became Benny Binion's Horseshoe Club, which would gain fame as the home of the annual World Series of Poker.

In 1955, the Côte d'Azur–themed Riviera became the ninth big hotel to open on the Strip. Breaking the ranch-style mode, it was, at nine stories, the Strip's first high-rise. Liberace, one of the hottest names in show business, was paid the unprecedented sum of $50,000 a week to dazzle audiences in the Riviera's posh Clover Room.

Elvis appeared at the New Frontier in 1956 but wasn't a huge success; his fans were too young to fit the Las Vegas tourist mold.

In 1958, the $10-million, 1,065-room Stardust upped the stakes by importing the famed *Lido de Paris* spectacle from the French capital. It became one of the longest-running shows ever to play Las Vegas. Two performers whose names have been linked to Las Vegas ever since—Frank Sinatra and Wayne Newton—made their debuts there.

Mae West not only performed in Las Vegas, but also cleverly bought up a half-mile of desolate Strip frontage between the Dunes and the Tropicana.

In the 1950s, the wedding industry helped make Las Vegas one of the nation's most popular venues for "goin' to the chapel." Celebrity weddings of the 1950s that sparked the trend included singer Dick Haymes and Rita Hayworth, Joan Crawford and Pepsi chairman Alfred Steele, Carol Channing and TV exec Charles Lowe, and Paul Newman and Joanne Woodward.

On a grimmer note, the '50s also heralded the atomic age in Nevada, with nuclear testing taking place just 65 miles northwest of Las Vegas. A chilling 1951 photograph shows a mushroom-shaped cloud from an atomic bomb test visible over the Fremont Street horizon. Throughout the decade, about one bomb a month was detonated in the nearby desert (an event, interestingly enough, that often attracted loads of tourists).

The 1960s: The Rat Pack & the King

The very first month of the new decade made entertainment history when the Sands hosted a 3-week "Summit Meeting" in the Copa Room that was presided over by "Chairman of the Board" Frank Sinatra, with Rat Pack cronies Dean Martin, Sammy Davis, Jr., Peter Lawford, and Joey Bishop (all of whom happened to be in town filming *Ocean's Eleven*). The series of shows helped to form the Rat Pack legend in Vegas and, in many ways vice versa, making the town hip and cool—the ultimate '60s swinging retreat.

It needed the help. After nearly a decade of almost constant building and expansion (no fewer than 10 major resorts opened in the 1950s), a crackdown on the Mafia and its money, which had fueled the city's development, brought construction to a halt. Only two major properties opened during the decade—the Road to Morocco–themed Aladdin in 1963 and the Roman Empire bacchanalia that was Caesars Palace in 1966. Perhaps trying to prove that the mob was gone for good, Las Vegas became a family destination in 1968, when Circus Circus burst onto the scene with the world's largest permanent circus and a "junior casino" featuring dozens of carnival midway games on its mezzanine level.

Elvis officially became part of the Vegas legend with the release of the film *Viva Las Vegas* in 1964, which not only furthered the city's "cool" quotient but also gave it an enduring theme song that remains a part of the city's identity more than 60 years later. But it was not until 1969 that the King's place in Sin City history would be cemented with his triumphant return to Las Vegas at the International's showroom with a series of concerts that made him one of the city's all-time legendary performers. His fans had come of age.

The 1970s: The Glamour Fades

The image of Las Vegas that emerged in the 1970s was one that would take decades to shed: a tacky tourist trap with aging casinos, cheap restaurants, and showrooms filled with performers whose careers were on their last legs. With a few exceptions, investment had slowed to a crawl and Vegas didn't seem as exciting anymore, especially when it was forced to compete with the sparkling newness of Atlantic City, where gambling was legalized in 1976.

There were some bright spots. In 1971, the 500-room Union Plaza opened at the head of Fremont Street on the site of the old Union Pacific Station. It had what was, at the time, the world's largest casino, and its showroom specialized in Broadway productions.

THE mob IN LAS VEGAS

The role of the Mafia in the creation of Las Vegas is little more than a footnote these days, but it isn't too bold of a statement to suggest that without organized crime, the city would not have developed in the ways that it did and its past would have certainly been less colorful.

Meyer Lansky was a big name in the New York crime syndicate in the 1930s, and it was largely his decision to send Benjamin "Bugsy" Siegel west to expand their empire. Although the Strip had already begun to form with the opening of El Rancho in 1941 and the Frontier in 1942, it was Bugsy's sparkling Flamingo of 1946 that began a Mafia-influenced building boom and era of control that would last for decades. Famous marquees, such as the Desert Inn, the Riviera, and the Stardust, were all built, either in part or in whole, from funding sources that were less than reputable.

During the '60s, negative attention focused on mob influence in Las Vegas. Of the 11 major casino hotels that had opened in the previous decade, 10 were believed to have been financed with mob money. Then, like a knight in shining armor, Howard Hughes rode into town and embarked on a $300-million hotel and property-buying spree, which included the Desert Inn itself (in 1967). Hughes was as "Bugsy" as Benjamin Siegel any day, but his pristine reputation helped bring respectability to the desert city and lessen its gangland stigma.

During the 1970s and 1980s, the government got involved, embarking on a series of criminal prosecutions across the country to try to break the back of the Mafia. Although not completely successful, it did manage to wrest major control of Las Vegas away from organized crime, aided by new legislation that allowed corporations to own casinos. By the time Steve Wynn built the Mirage in 1989, the Mafia's role was reduced to the point where the most it could control were the city's innumerable strip clubs.

These days, strict regulation and billions of dollars of corporate money keep things on the up and up, but the mob's influence can still be felt even at the highest levels of Las Vegas government. Former Mayor Oscar B. Goodman, first elected in 1999, was a lawyer for the Mafia in the 1960s and 1970s, defending such famed gangsters as Meyer Lanksy and Anthony "Tony the Ant" Spilotro. The popular and colorful Goodman cheerfully refers to his Mafia-related past often, joking about his desire to settle conflicts in the desert at night with a baseball bat like "in the good old days."

As if to bring things full circle, Goodman championed **The Mob Museum** (p. 161), a stunning facility that examines the history and influence of the Mafia in America and Las Vegas in particular. It is located in a former courthouse that was the site of the Mafia-related Kefauver hearings of the 1950s.

The year 1973 was eventful: Over at the Tropicana, illusionists extraordinaire Siegfried & Roy began turning women into tigers and themselves into legends in the *Folies Bergere.* Meanwhile, just up the street, the original MGM Grand (now Bally's) trumped the Plaza as the largest hotel and casino in the world, with Dean Martin as the opening evening's host.

Las Vegas made its way into America's living rooms with two very different television programs. Merv Griffin began taping his daytime talkfest in 1971 at Caesars Palace, taking advantage of a ready supply of local headliner guests. Then, in 1978, *Vega$* debuted, instantly emblazoning the image of star Robert Urich cruising down the Strip in his red Thunderbird convertible on the minds of TV viewers everywhere.

As the decade drew to a close, an international arrivals building opened and turned McCarran Field into McCarran International Airport, and dollar slot machines caused a sensation in the casinos.

The 1980s: The City Erupts

As the '80s began, Las Vegas was suffering an identity crisis. The departure of the mob and its money, combined with a struggling economy and Reagan-era conservatism, put a damper on the shining star of the desert. There was little new development, and a lot of the "classic" hotels became rundown shadows of their former selves.

A devastating fire in 1980 at the original MGM Grand killed more than 80 people, and just a few months later a fire at the Las Vegas Hilton killed eight more. In some ways these tragedies helped to further the transformation of the public's view of the entire city. Las Vegas became tacky, desperate, and possibly unsafe.

Even the showrooms, once the magnificent Elvis/Sinatra klieg light that lured people from around the world, had become something of a joke. For entertainers, Vegas was where you played when your career was over, not when you were on top.

What Las Vegas really needed was a white knight, and they got one in the form of Golden Nugget owner Steve Wynn and his $630-million gamble on the Mirage. Financed mostly through the sale of junk bonds, the hotel's construction would eventually change the course of Las Vegas history.

The hotel opened in 1989, fronted by five-story waterfalls, lagoons, and lush tropical foliage—not to mention a 50-foot volcano that dramatically erupted regularly! Wynn gave world-renowned illusionists Siegfried & Roy carte blanche (and more than $30 million) to create the most spellbinding show Las Vegas had ever seen, and he brought in world-class chefs to banish the idea that all you could eat in the town were all-you-can-eat spreads and $4.99 prime rib.

It was an immediate success; financially, of course, but more importantly as a matter of perception. Almost overnight, Las Vegas became cool again and everyone wanted to go there.

The 1990s: King Arthur Meets King Tut

The 1990s began with a blare of trumpets heralding the rise of a turreted medieval castle, fronted by a moated drawbridge and staffed by jousting knights and fair damsels. Excalibur reflected the '90s marketing trend to promote Las Vegas as a family-vacation destination.

Was that trend successful? Well, Chevy Chase did take his family on a *Vegas Vacation* in 1997, but the city kept the Sin part of its name alive, at least in popular culture, with Robert Redford making an *Indecent Proposal* (1993); Nicholas Cage hitting rock bottom in *Leaving Las Vegas* (1995); and Elizabeth Berkley strutting her stuff in the widely derided *Showgirls* (1995).

Canadian circus/theater group Cirque du Soleil transformed the entertainment scene in Las Vegas with the 1993 debut of *Mystére* at the newly opened Treasure Island. It would be the first of no fewer than eight Cirque shows that would launch over the next 2 decades.

The era of megahotels continued on the Strip, including the *new* MGM Grand hotel, backed by a full theme park (it ended Excalibur's brief reign as the world's largest resort), Luxor Las Vegas, and Steve Wynn's Treasure Island.

In 1993, a unique pink-domed 5-acre indoor amusement park, Grand Slam Canyon (later known as Adventuredome), became part of the Circus Circus hotel. In 1995, the Fremont Street Experience was completed, revitalizing Downtown Las Vegas. Closer to the Strip, rock restaurant magnate Peter Morton opened the Hard Rock Hotel, billed as "the world's first rock-'n'-roll hotel and casino." The year 1996 saw the advent of the French Riviera–themed Monte Carlo and the Stratosphere Las Vegas Hotel & Casino—its 1,149-foot tower makes it the highest building west of the Mississippi. The unbelievable New York–New York arrived in 1997.

But it all paled compared with 1998 to 1999. As Vegas hastily repositioned itself from "family destination" to "luxury resort," several new hotels opened, once again eclipsing anything that had come before. Bellagio was the latest from Vegas visionary Steve Wynn, an attempt to bring grand European-style to the desert, while at the far southern end of the Strip, Mandalay Bay charmed. As if this weren't enough, the Venetian's ambitiously detailed re-creation of everyone's favorite Italian city came along in May 1999 and was followed in short order by the opening of Paris Las Vegas in the fall of 1999.

The 2000s: The Lap of Luxury

The 21st century opened with a bang as the Aladdin blew itself up and gave itself a from-the-ground-up makeover (which in turn only lasted for a handful of years before Planet Hollywood took it over and changed it entirely), while Steve Wynn blew up the Desert Inn and built a new showstopper named for himself. Along the way, everyone expanded, and then expanded some more, ultimately adding thousands of new rooms. The goal became "luxury," with a secondary emphasis on "adult." Little by little, wacky, eye-catching themes were phased out (as much as one can when one's hotel looks like a castle), and generic sophistication took its place. Gaming was still number one, but the newer hotels were trying to top each other in terms of other recreations—decadent nightclubs, celebrity chef–backed restaurants, fancy spas, and superstar shows.

"More is more" seemed to be the motto, and its embodiment was the massive CityCenter, perhaps the most ambitious project in Las Vegas yet. Composed of a 4,000-room megaresort, two 400-room boutique hotels, condos, shopping, dining, clubs, and more, it covers more than 60 acres and, as such, is a city-within-the-city. Gone are the outrageous themes, replaced by cutting-edge modernism—all sleek lines of glass and metal designed with the future in mind, not only from an architectural standpoint but from an ecological one as well. Sure, building the massive CityCenter probably made the earth shudder a bit, but its advanced green building and sustainable operating systems helped to ensure that the planet didn't just collapse in on itself from the weight of it all.

The excess of Vegas was spotlighted in popular culture as well. *Ocean's Eleven* got a new millennium makeover in 2001 with a cast of superstars like George Clooney, Brad Pitt, and Julia Roberts. Then in 2009, *The Hangover* took it all to a new level with a raunchy morality tale of a Vegas bachelor party gone horribly awry. The 2013 *Hangover 3* brought the action back to Vegas to close out the trilogy.

Even the city's motto, which became a popular part of the American lexicon, was a winking nod to the seemingly endless ways to satisfy the id: "What happens in Las Vegas, stays in Las Vegas."

Once known solely as an outpost of all-you-can-eat buffets and $4.99 prime rib specials, Las Vegas became one of the top dining destinations in the world. Every celebrity chef worth his or her sea salt had a restaurant here, and the level of culinary quality rose almost as fast as the prices. Take a look at some of the famous names attached to Vegas restaurants: Emeril Lagasse, Wolfgang Puck, Gordon Ramsay, Bobby Flay, Todd English, Hubert Keller, Mario Batali, Joël Robuchon, Thomas Keller, and Julian Serrano. It's a veritable who's who of the culinary world. Dining in Las Vegas has become one of the top reasons people want to visit the city.

And proving that Las Vegas really is a 24-hour town, the nightlife scene exploded in Vegas. Megaclubs such as XS (p. 233) at Encore Las Vegas, Marquee (p. 231) at the Cosmopolitan, and Hakkasan (p. 230) at MGM Grand (billed as the largest nightclub in the world) pull in droves of the young and beautiful (or people who think they are, or who just want to be around them) who do not seem to be deterred by the eye-popping high prices ($20–$50 cover, $10–$15 drinks), long lines (expect to wait at least an hour), and lack of personal space. It's a see-and-be-seen scene, where you better dress to impress or expect to be relegated to the darker corners.

Céline Dion made it safe to be a Vegas headliner again as she kicked off a 5-year residency at Caesars Palace in 2003 (and came back in 2011). She would be followed by big-ticket names like Elton John, Bette Midler, Cher, and Garth Brooks, all of whom made Vegas their performing home for a while.

Clearly, no one can rest on their laurels in Vegas, for this is not only a town that never sleeps, but also one in which progress never stops moving, even for a heartbeat.

WHEN TO GO

Most of a Las Vegas vacation is usually spent indoors, so you can have a good time here year-round. The most pleasant seasons are spring and fall, especially if you want to experience the great outdoors.

Weekdays are slightly less crowded than weekends. Holidays are always a mob scene and come accompanied by high hotel prices. Hotel prices also skyrocket when big conventions and special events are taking place. The slowest times of year are parts of January and February; late June through August; the week before Christmas; and the week after New Year's.

If a major convention is to be held during your trip, you might want to change your date. Check the box on p. 38 for convention dates.

Climate & Current Weather Conditions

First of all, Vegas isn't always hot, but when it is, it's *really* hot. One thing you'll hear again and again is that even though Las Vegas gets very hot, the dry desert heat is not unbearable. We know this is true because we spent a couple of days there in 104°F (40°C) weather and lived to say, "It wasn't all that bad, not really." The humidity averages a low 22%, and even on very hot days, there's apt to be a breeze. Having said that, once the temperature gets into triple digits, it is wise to limit the amount of time you spend outdoors, and to make sure you are drinking plenty of water even while you are inside enjoying the blessed air-conditioning (which is omnipresent). Dehydration and heatstroke are two of the most common ailments that affect tourists—don't be a victim of one of them. Also, except on the hottest summer days, there's relief at night, when temperatures often drop by as much as 20 degrees.

Las Vegas' Average Temperatures (°F & °C) & Rainfall

		JAN	FEB	MAR	APR	MAY	JUNE	JULY	AUG	SEPT	OCT	NOV	DEC
Average	(°F)	49	54	60	67	78	87	93	91	83	70	57	48
	(°C)	9	12	16	19	26	31	34	33	28	21	14	9
High Temp.	(°F)	58	63	70	78	89	99	104	102	94	81	67	57
	(°C)	14	17	21	26	32	37	40	39	35	27	19	14
Low Temp.	(°F)	39	44	49	56	66	75	81	79	71	59	47	39
	(°C)	4	7	9	13	19	24	27	26	22	15	8	4
Rainfall	(inches)	0.6	0.8	0.4	0.2	0.1	0.1	0.4	0.3	0.3	0.3	0.4	0.5

But this is the desert, and it's not hot year-round. It can get quite cold, especially in the winter, when at night it can drop to 30°F (−1°C) and lower. Although rare, it does snow occasionally in Las Vegas. The winter of 2008 to 2009 dropped nearly 3 inches of snow on the Strip. There's nothing quite like the sight of Luxor's Sphinx covered in snow. The breeze can also become a cold, biting wind of up to 40 mph or more. And so there are entire portions of

wild WEATHER

Las Vegas rests in the middle of a desert, so how wacky can the weather possibly get? A lot crazier than you think. Although Las Vegas's location results in broiling-hot temperatures in the summer, many people tend to forget that deserts get cold and rainy, while wind is also a potential hazard.

Winter temperatures in Las Vegas have been known to dip below 30°F (–1°C), and when you toss in 40 mph winds, that adds up to a very chilly stroll on the Strip. And snow is not an unheard-of occurrence. Most years see a flurry or two falling on Las Vegas, and since 1949, a total of 12 "storms" have resulted in accumulations of 2 inches or greater, with the largest storm dropping 9 inches on the Strip in January 1949. In December 2003, parts of Las Vegas got 6 inches of the white stuff, and although it didn't stick around too long on the Strip, the sight of the famous "Welcome to Fabulous Las Vegas" sign in the middle of a driving blizzard was quite a spectacle. And more recently (the winter of 2008–09), Vegas received nearly 3 inches of snow on the Strip itself, with nearly 10 inches accumulating in other areas of town. Locals usually find the snow a charming addition to the city (and the stuff melts completely in a day or two, so they don't have to shovel it—lucky them).

Though snow is a novel quirk that many Vegas residents and visitors welcome, rain isn't always as well received. The soil in Las Vegas is parched most of the year, making it difficult for the land to absorb large amounts of water coming down in a short time. Between June and August, when most of the area's rainfall takes place due to the Southwest's monsoon season, there is a good possibility of flash flooding.

At times, the skies just open up, resulting in flooding that wreaks havoc on Sin City. On July 9, 1999, Mother Nature unleashed more than 3 inches of rain *in just a few hours* on a city that averages about 4 inches of rain a year. The deluge killed two people, swamped hundreds of cars, and destroyed millions of dollars in property. A 2013 storm caused havoc up and down the Strip with collapsed ceilings in the Mirage, a flooded casino at Caesars Palace, and a waterfall inside Gilley's at Treasure Island (go look it up on YouTube). This kind of storm (and rain in general) is rare, but even a light shower can make things treacherous on the roads, the sidewalks, and the slippery marble walkways that front almost every casino in town.

The topography of the Las Vegas region also makes it prone to high, often damaging winds. Situated at the bottom of a bowl ringed by mountains, 15 to 20 mph steady winds are not uncommon, and gusts of 70 to 80 mph have been recorded. In 1994, a brief windstorm knocked down the massive sign at the Las Vegas Hilton, and in 2010 a storm tore apart the Cloud 9 balloon, billed as the largest tethered helium balloon in the world.

the year when you won't be using that hotel pool at all (even if you want to; most of the hotels close huge chunks of those pool areas for "the season," which can be as long as the period from Labor Day to Memorial Day). If you aren't traveling in the height of summer, bring a jacket. Also, remember sunscreen and a hat—even if it's not all that hot, you can burn very easily and very fast.

MAJOR convention DATES FOR 2017

Listed below are Las Vegas's major annual conventions, with projected attendance figures for 2017; believe us, unless you're coming for one of them, you probably want to avoid the biggies. Because convention schedules frequently change, contact the **Las Vegas Convention and Visitors Authority** (www.vegasmeansbusiness.com) to double-check the latest info before you commit to your travel dates.

Event Attendance	Dates	Expected
Consumer Electronics Show	Jan 5–8	176,000
Shooting, Hunting & Outdoor Trade Show	Jan 17–20	61,000
World of Concrete	Jan 17–20	48,000
Adult Entertainment Expo	Jan 18–21	50,000
Las Vegas Market Furniture Show	Jan 22–26	50,000
Int'l Air-Conditioning, Heating, Refrigerating Expo	Jan 30–Feb 1	60,000
Safari Club International	Feb 1–4	21,000
National Association of Broadcasters	Apr 22–27	96,000
National Hardware Show	May 3–5	32,000
Int'l Esthetics Cosmetic and Spa Conference	Jun 24–26	25,000
Las Vegas Market Furniture Show	July 30–Aug 3	750,000
SEMA/Automotive Aftermarket Industry Week	Oct 31–Nov 3	130,000

Holidays

Banks, government offices, post offices, and many stores, restaurants, and museums are closed on the following legal national holidays: January 1 (New Year's Day), the third Monday in January (Martin Luther King, Jr., Day), the third Monday in February (Presidents' Day), the last Monday in May (Memorial Day), July 4 (Independence Day), the first Monday in September (Labor Day), the second Monday in October (Columbus Day), November 11 (Veterans Day/Armistice Day), the fourth Thursday in November (Thanksgiving Day), and December 25 (Christmas).

Any holiday, especially ones that involve a day off work for most people, will mean big crowds in Vegas. This includes "holidays" like St. Patrick's Day, Cinco de Mayo, and Spring Break.

Las Vegas Calendar of Events

You may be surprised that Las Vegas does not offer as many annual events as most other tourist cities. The reason is Las Vegas's very *raison d'être:* the gaming industry. This town wants its visitors spending their money in the casinos, not at Renaissance fairs and parades.

When in town, check the local paper and contact the **Las Vegas Convention and Visitors Authority** (www.lasvegas.com; ✆ **877/847-4858** or 702/892-7575) or the **Las Vegas Chamber of Commerce** (www.lvchamber.com; ✆ **702/735-1616**) to find out about other events scheduled during your visit.

FEBRUARY

The Super Bowl. Granted, the actual game is not held in Las Vegas, but the numbers of people it brings to the city rival those that go to wherever the big game is being held. Sports fans and sports bettors come out in droves to watch the action on the big screens around town and to lay down a wager or two on the outcome. It usually takes place on the first Sunday in February.

Valentine's Day. This is the marriage (and possibly divorce) capital of the world, so the betrothed line up to exchange their vows all across town on Cupid's day. As on other days of the year, the city's Marriage Bureau stays open until midnight, and some chapels perform dozens of weddings. February 14.

MARCH

USA Sevens. Not a rugby fan? No matter, a day at the Sevens tourney is an experience. The largest attended rugby event in the country welcomes some 75,000 visitors to the **Sam Boyd Stadium,** 7000 E. Russell Rd. (samboydstadium.com; © **702/895-3761**), located about 20 minutes from the Strip. Teams from 16 countries compete in some 45 matches and fans travel from all around the world to cheer on their home countries or teams, dressed in jerseys, war paint, and outlandish costumes. Though the games are on the weekend, leading up to the tournament is a full week of events, including pep rallies, a beer festival, and a Parade of Nations. Held in early March. For more information, visit www.usasevens.com.

NASCAR. The **Las Vegas Motor Speedway,** 7000 Las Vegas Blvd. N. (www.lvms.com; © **800/644-4444**), has become one of the premier facilities in the country, attracting races and racers of all stripes and colors. The biggest races of the year are the Boyd Gaming 300 and the Kobalt Tools 400, held in early March.

March Madness. Remember everything we just said about the Super Bowl? Apply it here for the NCAA college basketball championships throughout the second half of the month.

MAY

Rock in Rio USA. The hugely popular music concert with roots in Brazil, Spain, and Portugal held its inaugural Las Vegas fest in May 2015. The events are a partnership between Rock in Rio, MGM Resorts, and Cirque du Soleil, and take place every other year at its permanent festival ground on the North Strip (across from the former Sahara hotel, now SLS). It features five stages, a cityscape, carnival rides, and more. The first year featured performances by Taylor Swift, Bruno Mars, Metallica and No Doubt, and concerts in other cities have drawn the likes of Beyoncé, Justin Timberlake, and Stevie Wonder, to name a few, and have drawn upwards of 700,000 people. For more information, visit www.rockinrio.com. May 2017.

JUNE

World Series of Poker. When Harrah's Entertainment bought the legendary Binion's Horseshoe in Downtown Vegas out of bankruptcy, it quickly turned around and sold the hotel, but kept the hosting rights to this famed event, moving its location and place on the calendar. Now held at the **Rio All-Suite Hotel and Casino,** 3700 W. Flamingo Rd. (© **800/752-9746**), in June and July (with the final table held in November for some incomprehensible reason), the event features high-stakes gamblers and showbiz personalities competing for six-figure purses. There are daily events, with entry stakes ranging from $125 to $5,000. To enter the World Championship Event, players must pony up $10,000 but could win a fortune (the 2013 top prize was $8.3 million). It costs nothing to crowd around the tables and watch the action, but if you want to avoid the throngs, you can catch a lot of it on TV. For more information, visit www.wsop.com.

Electric Daisy Carnival. One of the biggest annual Electronic Dance Music (EDM) events in the world draws upwards of 400,000 people to the city with a multi-day series of concerts from the biggest DJs and club music stars in the business. Past festivals saw EDM megastars like Tiesto, Avicii, Afrojack, Eric Prydz, Richie Hawtin, Carl Cox, and Adam Beyer in front of the dancing mobs. If you don't know who any of those acts are, it's probably best to consider a different weekend, as rooms are scarce. Usually held the third weekend in June at the Las Vegas Motor Speedway. For more information, visit www.electricdaisycarnival.com.

SEPTEMBER

Life is Beautiful Festival. Started in 2013, this festival takes over a huge chunk of Downtown Las Vegas with music from bands both big (Beck, Imagine Dragons, Janelle Monae) and small; food and cooking demonstrations from celebrity chefs; art projects and displays; a speaker series; performances from Vegas shows including Cirque du Soleil; and more. The friendly neighborhood vibe, terrific organization (at least so far), and endless array of things to see, do, and eat make this a favorite for more than 65,000 people.

OCTOBER

Halloween. Las Vegas gets even scarier than normal on and around Halloween, with "spooky" twists to many of the major attractions (Adventuredome becomes "Fright Dome," with haunted houses and more), debaucherous costume parties at the nightclubs, and a parade and festivities in Downtown Las Vegas. October 31.

DECEMBER

National Finals Rodeo. This is the Super Bowl of rodeos, attended by about 200,000 people each year and offering more than $6 million in prize money. Male and female rodeo stars compete in everything from calf roping to steer wrestling, bull riding, team roping, saddle bronc riding, bareback riding, and barrel racing. In connection with this event, hotels book country stars into their showrooms, and a cowboy shopping spree—the **NFR Cowboy Christmas Gift Show,** a trade show for Western gear—is held at the convention center. The NFR runs for 10 days, during the first 2 weeks of December, at the 17,000-seat Thomas & Mack Center of the University of Nevada, Las Vegas (UNLV). Order tickets as far in advance as possible (*©* **866/388-3267**). For more information, see www.nfrexperience.com.

New Year's Eve. Between 300,000 and 400,000 people descend on Las Vegas to ring in the New Year, making it one of the largest gatherings for the holiday outside of New York's Times Square. Fireworks are the dominant entertainment, with pyrotechnics launched from the roofs of many hotels on the Strip and under the canopy at Fremont Street in Downtown Las Vegas. The Strip is closed to vehicles for the night, so traffic and parking are a nightmare, as is booking a room (expect to pay a hefty premium), which should be done well in advance. December 31.

WHERE TO STAY

There are about 150,000 hotel rooms in Las Vegas. If you stayed in a different room every night, it would take you 411 years to get through them all. You could give one to every single resident of Dayton, Ohio, and still have enough left over for you and about 10,000 of your closest friends.

The point is, finding a hotel room in Las Vegas is not hard; it's finding the right one for *you* that can be challenging. Do you want a luxurious suite where you can lounge in bed and order room service, or basic accommodations where you'll dump your luggage and then not see the room again until you stumble back to it as the sun is coming up the next morning? Do you want classic Glitter Gulch glitz or contemporary Sin City glamour? High tech or low cost? Las Vegas has all of the above and just about everything in between.

4

PRACTICAL INFORMATION
The Big Picture

With a few exceptions in the very expensive category, most hotel rooms in Las Vegas are pretty much the same. After you factor in location and price, there isn't that much difference between rooms, except perhaps for size and the quality of their surprisingly similar furnishings.

Hotel prices in Vegas are anything but fixed, so you will notice wild price fluctuations. The same room can routinely go for anywhere from $60 to $250, depending on demand. So use our price categories with a grain of salt and don't rule out a hotel just because it's listed as "Expensive"—it's very common to get great deals on pricey hotels. On the negative side, some hotels start with their most typical lowest rate, adding "and up." Don't be surprised if "up" turns out to be way up. Just look online or call and ask.

Yes, if you pay more, you'll probably (but not certainly) get a "nicer" establishment and clientele to match (perhaps not so many loud drunks in the elevators). On the other hand, if a convention is in town, the drunks will be there no matter how upscale the hotel—they'll just be wearing business suits and/or funny hats. And frankly, the big hotels, no matter how fine, have mass-produced rooms; at 3,000 rooms or more, they are the equivalent of '60s tract housing. Consequently, even in the nicest hotels, you can (and probably will) encounter plumbing noises, notice scratch marks on the walls or furniture, overhear conversations from other rooms, or be woken by the maids as they knock on the doors that don't have the DO NOT DISTURB sign up.

Cancellation policies vary hotel to hotel, but generally speaking you can usually back out of your booking anywhere from 24 to 48 hours ahead of your check-in date without penalty. Exceptions to both of these general rules are often found on major holidays like New Year's Eve, or during big event weekends like the Super Bowl.

Getting the Best Deal

Here are some tips for landing a low rate:

- **Remember the law of supply and demand.** Las Vegas hotels are most crowded and therefore most expensive on weekends. So the best deals are offered midweek, when prices can drop dramatically. If possible, go then. You should also check the convention calendar run by the **Las Vegas Convention and Visitors Authority** (www.vegasmeansbusiness.com; ⓒ **877/ 847-4858**) to find out whether a big trade show is scheduled at the time of your planned visit; if more than 50,000 conventioneers are descending on Vegas, *change your dates* as one-third or more of the beds will be booked and prices will soar. The most popular conventions are listed under "When to Go" on p. 36; use it as a guide for when to avoid the city. Remember also that planning to take your vacation just a week before or after official peak season can mean big savings.

- **Book online.** This is such a smart way to book that we've devoted an entire box to it. See p. 43.

- **Be social.** Almost every major resort in town has some presence in the social media world, including Facebook pages, Twitter feeds, and smartphone apps. Connect with them and you may find yourself getting exclusive offers that the luddites out there won't be hearing about.

- **Don't be afraid to bargain.** Get in the habit of asking for a lower price than the first one quoted. Always ask politely whether a less expensive room is available than the first one mentioned, or whether any special rates apply to you. If you belong to the players' club at the hotel-casino, you may be able to secure a better deal. Of course, you will also be expected to spend a certain amount of time and money gambling there.

- **Beware of fees.** So-called "resort fees" have become very common in Vegas and they can add up, ranging anywhere from $3 to $29 per night. Although the specifics vary from property to property, they usually cover amenities like Internet service, health club access, newspapers, printing of boarding passes, maybe a bottle of water or two, and the like. So what if you're not going to use any of that? Too bad—you still have to pay (at most hotels—some make it optional). Many hotels include this in their totals when you book your room, but a few wait and sock it to you at checkout, so be sure to ask ahead. (We have noted those hotels with resort fees in the listings, but do note that they change often.)

online SAVINGS

Before going online, it's important that you know what "flavor" of discount you're seeking. Currently, there are three types of online reductions:

1. **Extreme discounts on sites where you bid for lodgings without knowing which hotel you'll get.** You'll find these on such sites as Priceline.com and Hotwire.com and they can be money-savers, particularly if you're booking within a week of travel (that's when the hotels resort to deep discounts to get beds filled). As these companies use only major chains, you can rest assured that you won't be put up in a dump. For more reassurance, visit the website BetterBidding.com. On it, actual travelers spill the beans about what they bid on Priceline.com and which hotels they got. You'll be pleasantly surprised by the quality of many of the hotels that are offering these "secret" discounts.

2. **Discounts on the hotel's website itself.** Sometimes these can be great values, especially if you're a member of a loyalty program. In 2016, a number of major chains announced that they would be giving up to 10% off the lowest going rates to those who booked directly, through special membership areas of the hotel's website. Before biting, though, be sure to look at the discounter sites below.

3. **Discounts on online travel agencies, such as Hotels.com, Booking.com, Expedia.com, and Vegas specialist Travelworm.com.** Some of these sites reserve rooms in bulk and at a discount, passing along the savings to their customers. But instead of going to them directly, I'd recommend looking at such dedicated travel search engines as **Hipmunk.com, HotelsCombined.com, Momondo.com**, and **Trivago.com**. These sites list prices from all the discount sites as well as the hotels directly, meaning you have a better chance of finding a deal. **Note:** Sometimes the discounts these sites find require advance payment for a room (and draconian cancellation policies), so double-check your travel dates before booking.

Tingo.com is another good source, especially for luxury hotels. Its model is a bit different: users make a pre-paid reservation through it, but if the price drops between the time of booking and the date of arrival, the site refunds the difference in price.

You might also try the app **Hotel Tonight** (www.hoteltonight.com). It works best for day-of bookings, though it now allows users to book a few days in advance and for multiple day stays. Occassionally, it can get the best prices for procrastinators (up to 70% off if you book on the day of travel, 40% on average if you book a few days in advance), but again, check around to make sure you're getting a real deal.

It's a lot of surfing, I know, but in the hothouse world of Sin City hotel pricing, this sort of diligence can pay off.

○ **Beware of hidden extras.** The hotels that don't charge resort fees (which are few and far between these days) charge extra for things that are always free in other destinations, such as health-club privileges. Expect to pay anywhere from $15 to $35 to use almost any hotel spa/health club. Wi-Fi also doesn't come free; usually there is a $12-to-$20 charge per 24-hour period. (We've noted when there is a fee in the listings so that you won't be taken by surprise.)

○ **Consider a suite.** If you are traveling with your family or another couple, you can pack more people into a suite (which usually comes with a sofa bed) and thereby reduce your per-person rate. Remember that some places charge for extra guests and some don't.

What Am I Looking for in a Hotel?

If gambling is not your priority, what are you doing in Vegas? Just kidding. But not 100% kidding. Vegas's current identity as a luxury, and very adult, resort destination means there are several hotels that promise to offer you all sorts of alternatives to gambling—lush pool areas, fabulous spas, incredible restaurants, lavish shopping. But if you look closely, much of this is Vegas bait-and-switch; the pools are often chilly (and often partially closed during non-summer months), and it will be years before there is more foliage than concrete in these newly landscaped environments; the spas cost extra (sometimes a whole lot extra); the best restaurants can require a small bank loan; and the stores are often the kinds of places where average mortals can't even afford the oxygen. So what does that leave you with? Why, that's right—gambling.

The other problem with these self-proclaimed luxury hotels is their size. True luxury hotels do not have 3,000 rooms—they have a couple of hundred, at best, because you simply can't provide first-class service and Egyptian-cotton sheets in mass quantity. But while hotels on the upper end of the price spectrum (Wynn, Encore, Bellagio, the Venetian, and so on) have done their best to offer sterling service and to make their rooms more luxurious than those at other Vegas hotels, there's only so much that any place that big can do. Don't get us wrong—these places are absolutely several steps up in quality from other large hotels, and compared to them, even the better older hotels really look shabby. But they are still sprawling, frequently noisy complexes.

If the hubbub of a casino makes you itch, there are a few non-gaming hotels and even non-gaming towers within casino-hotels that could help reduce your stress level. Check out Mandarin Oriental at CityCenter or the Delano at Mandalay Bay.

Casino hotels, by the way, are not always a nice place for children. It used to be that the casino was a separate section in the hotel, and children were not allowed inside. (We have fond memories of standing just outside the casino line, watching Dad put quarters in a slot machine "for us.") But in almost all the new hotels, you have to walk through the casino to get anywhere—the lobby, the restaurants, the outside world. This makes sense from the hotel's point of view; it gives you many opportunities to stop and drop $1 or $100 into a slot. But this often long, crowded trek gets wearying for adults—and it's far worse for kids. The rule is that kids can walk through the casinos, but they can't stop, even to gawk for a second at someone hitting a jackpot nearby. The casino officials who will immediately hustle the child away are just doing their job—but, boy, it's annoying.

Price Categories	
Expensive	$150 and up
Moderate	$100–$150
Inexpensive	Under $100

So, take this (and what a hotel offers that kids might *like*) into consideration when booking a room. Again, please note that those gorgeous hotel pools are often cold (and again, sometimes closed altogether) and not very deep. They look like places you would want to linger, but often (from a kid's point of view) they are not. Plus, the pools close early. Hotels want you inside gambling, not outside swimming.

Finally, the thing that bothers me the most about this latest Vegas phase: It used to be that I could differentiate between rooms, but that's becoming harder and harder. Nearly every major hotel has changed to more or less the same effect; gone is any thematic detailing and in its place is a series of disappointingly similar (if contemporary and sleek) looks. Expect clean-lined wood furniture, plump white beds, and monochromes everywhere you go. All that may distinguish one from another would be the size of the room or the quality of the furnishings.

Ultimately, though, if it's a busy time, you'll have to nab any room you can, especially if you get a price you like. How much time are you going to spend in the room anyway?

SOUTH STRIP

The southern third of the Strip, from roughly Russell Road to Harmon Avenue, is home to some of the biggest and most extravagant hotels in the world.

Best for: First-time visitors who want to experience all of the Vegas insanity they have read about and seen on TV.

Drawbacks: Prices are higher here than in non-Strip locations; the sheer number of people can cause major traffic jams (and we're not just talking about on the street).

Expensive

Aria Las Vegas ★★★ The first time I drove into the CityCenter complex at night, it was so dazzling, with its Gehry-esque jagged front (of the shops at Crystals), sleek skyscrapers towering over the Strip, and bullet-like tram coasting between the buildings, I distinctly remember thinking, "So this is what the future is like." And to this extent, Aria, at the center of this faux urban block, exemplifies the future of Las Vegas: imposing and on the cutting edge of design.

Though its glass and steel exterior may seem sterile from afar, once you get up close and personal with Aria, you'll see that it's actually quite a vibrant space. The entire property is awash with imaginative visual details, even near the entrance, where a waterfall quietly cascades down a ridged wall on the outside of the building. Obviously, gaming is the main focus of the 150,000-square-foot casino, but there are plenty of other elements to catch

Las Vegas Hotels

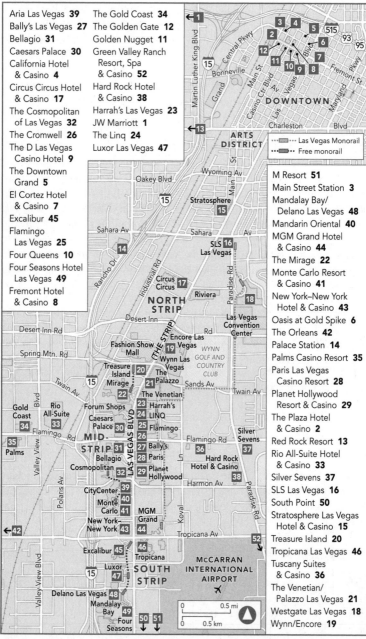

4

WHERE TO STAY | South Strip

your eye, whether it's a hand-carved wooden mural, Maya Lin's *Silver River* installation "flowing" behind the front desk, or the array of enormous, colorful butterflies suspended from the ceiling in the lobby. One of my favorite art works is a series of smoky prints by actor Christopher Walken that lines a corridor of the casino. If that doesn't make this hotel cool, I don't know what does.

The resort is enormous, with some 4,000 rooms, all with their own distinct character. The "standard" rooms are hardly standard, starting out at 520 square feet, with rich, warm tones and floor-to-ceiling windows that bathe the room in abundant sunlight. Should you want to shut out the sun without getting out of bed, that isn't a problem—the blackout curtains, along with pretty much everything electronic in your room, can be controlled by the in-room tablet located on the nightstand next to the bed. I love the spacious bathrooms with their plush robes (to keep guests warm amid all the cold granite). Some might consider it a design flaw that getting to the deep-soaking tub means you have to first pass through the frosted-glass shower, but a few extra steps won't kill you.

Aria also offers an even more VIP experience in its Sky Suites, where the smallest accommodation is a one-bedroom at 1,050 square feet. Suite guests enjoy such niceties as a private entrance and elevator, a pool exclusively for Sky Suites guests, and a lounge with a daily wine and cheese reception, not to mention front-of-line passes for the buffet.

Aria's collection of restaurants on the main and second floors feature cuisine from some of the best chefs in the country—when was the last time you had a James Beard Award-winner make your pizza? Venture out of the hotel to see the rest of CityCenter, which includes more hotels, shopping, and more dining options at Crystals.

If Aria is any indication of what Vegas is going to be like for the next 50 years, we're happy to jump on board.

3730 Las Vegas Blvd. S. www.arialasvegas.com. (?) **866/359-7757** or 702/590-7757. 4,004 units. $149 and up double; $289 and up suite. Resort fee $35. Extra person $50 No discount for children. Parking 1 hr. free, self-parking $7–$10, valet $13–$18; prices vary during special events. **Amenities:** 15 restaurants; casino; concierge; executive-level rooms; health club; heated outdoor pools; room service; spa; showroom; free property-wide and in-room Wi-Fi (included in resort fee).

Four Seasons Hotel Las Vegas ★★★ Before Nobu, the Cromwell, and Mandarin Oriental, if you wanted a true boutique hotel in Las Vegas, your only option was the Four Seasons. Not that that was a bad thing—Four Seasons' reputation for luxury and attentive service is unrivaled worldwide. Except now there are a few more rivals on the Strip. The increasingly crowded market means that Four Seasons has had to up its game, and so in 2012 it underwent a total overhaul of the property, from the picturesque lobby to all 424 rooms located on the top five floors of Mandalay Bay.

Today, those rooms are even more handsome and contemporary. Cool, mod-style patterns on the walls plus well-placed mirrors make the standard rooms feel bigger than their allotted 500 square feet, while retro lamps and jacquard-patterned footstools at the end of the bed provide contrasting industrial and lush textures. And the bathrooms! Shiny chrome finishes, backlit mirrors, and a lack of frame around the shower glass make the space feel seamless, and therefore bigger. Somehow the beauty of the space rubs off: I don't know how they do it, but the lighting in them makes every guest look 10 years younger. The hotel's high perch allows for sweeping views; those rooms directly overlooking the Strip command a steeper price.

One of the best things about Four Seasons is that, despite its connection to the massive resort next door, it's as secluded as they come, perfect for its discerning, and often celebrity guests. It has its own pool, two restaurants (the Verandah serves afternoon tea), and an excellent bar in the lobby. The private driveway and cul-de-sac are surrounded by palm trees and other tropical foliage, shielding guests from the typical Vegas loudness (in volume and garishness). This sense of calm carries throughout the entire resort, from the pleasant check-in, until you arrive in your beautiful room. But if guests want to leave this serene space to immerse themselves in the true Vegas experience, they can simply bop next door to the Mandalay Bay.

3960 Las Vegas Blvd. S. www.fourseasons.com. © **877/632-5000** or 702/632-5000. 424 units. $224 and up double; $399 and up suite. Resort fee $35 per night. Extra person $35. Children 17 and under stay free in parent's room. Valet parking $22; no self-parking. Pets under 25 lb. accepted. **Amenities:** 2 restaurants; concierge; executive-level rooms; fitness center; heated outdoor pool; room service; spa; free Wi-Fi.

Mandalay Bay/Delano Las Vegas ★★★ Mandalay Bay has anchored its end of Las Vegas Boulevard since 1999 and has managed to stay fresh and relevant by undergoing a series of facelifts the past few years. First it revamped the casino floor to make it less campy and more modern. Then it added a new nightclub, as well as a couple of new restaurants and upgrades to existing ones, followed by the addition of a resident Cirque du Soleil show. You'll be hard-pressed to find a resort this large that's as upscale and exciting, with as many amenities.

The original Mandalay Bay Tower boasts 3,211 rooms, which, thanks to the building being so tall, offer great views of the Valley. (Request one of the 550 "DR View Rooms" to ensure you've got the lights of the Strip outside your window, not the highway). The resort recently completed its $100 million remodel of its suites, taking the spacious rooms into the 21st century with new color palettes. Resort Kings are now decked out in white and cobalt, while Resort Queens stay warm with combinations of either rich ruby and latte shades or lavender and mocha. Cushy seats right against the window are a nice touch. Bathrooms are large, with shower and tub separated by lots of cold marble, but that's a first world problem.

The adjoining Delano has taken the place of THEhotel and infused it with South Beach spirit, a welcome change. The Miami touch has lightened everything up, though it includes nods to Las Vegas' natural landscape. In the now neutral-colored foyer between valet and the lobby is an impressive,

126,000-pound, 150 million-year-old, split metaquartzite boulder hauled in from the surrounding Nevada desert. Pass between the smoothed halves to enter the lobby, where you'll encounter a number of smaller rocks before registration. A piece by Korean artist Jaehyo Lee features hundreds of them strung along pieces of wire stretched from the tall ceiling to the ground. A recent installation showcased works derived completely from wood and other natural materials from the Mojave, including a sculpted bench composed of concrete and desert sandstone.

All of the hotel's 1,117 suites were re-done as well, with lots of white and neutral tones and touches of gold. Ultra-plush beds with white tufted headboards can be difficult to part with in the morning, while gigantic bathrooms feature black marble around the separate tub and glass-enclosed shower. And there are cute touches, like postcards left on the bed with cheeky sayings like "My life has a superb cast, I just can't figure out the plot."

A little less secluded than the Four Seasons, there's still a sense of exclusivity at Delano, with its own beach club, reserved for guests, right off of Mandalay Beach. Also, the new addition is non-gaming, but it's just a quick walk down the hallway to the Mandalay Bay's loud, 135,000-square-foot casino, one of the largest on the Strip.

As a whole, Mandalay Bay hosts some of the finest restaurants on the Strip, including **Strip Steak, RM Seafood, Aureole, Border Grill,** and more (see chapter 5). Beer aficionados take note: the resort's beverage director is the first female *cicerone* (the beer equivalent of a sommelier) in the country, and she has made sure that craft beers are featured prominently on many menus.

The resort has managed to maintain a good balance of grown-up and family fun by including in its arsenal a massive arena for live performances; **Shark Reef** aquarium (p. 154); and Mandalay Beach, an impressive pool complex that features a wave pool, lazy river, and bona fide sand on a beach that sometimes hosts live concerts. **Light** nightclub (p. 231) has its own pool component, Daylight, set to an electronic music soundtrack.

Mandalay Place, the retail-lined walkway that connects Mandalay Bay and neighbor Luxor is a convenient way to traverse the two indoors (and to shop).

3950 Las Vegas Blvd. S. (at Hacienda Ave.). www.mandalaybay.com. © **877/632-7800** or 702/632-7108. 4,429 units (including Delano). $60 and up double; $225 and up suite. Resort fee $33. Extra person $40. Children 14 and under stay free in parent's room. Parking 1 hr. free, self-parking $7–$10, valet $13–$18; prices vary during special events. **Amenities:** 24 restaurants; aquarium; casino; concierge; 12,000-seat events center; executive-level rooms; health club; showroom; 5 outdoor pools w/lazy river and wave pool; room service; sauna; spa; watersports equipment/rentals; free Wi-Fi.

Mandarin Oriental ★★★

As part of the dazzling CityCenter, Mandarin Oriental has the advantage of being the smallest venue in the complex. Having only 400 rooms allows for a more intimate Vegas experience. It also means that the high level of customer service—something the Mandarin Oriental chain is known for in the rest of the world—is felt immediately, right from the moment you take the elevator up 23 floors to check in.

Even though you're likely paying a premium price to stay in this exclusive hotel, the rooms aren't enormous, starting at around 500 square feet. What you're paying for is the luxury of the space, done in subtle, but modern Asian decor, beautifully furnished with great attention to design details, like the dark woods and chrome finishes throughout, mother-of-pearl headboards, and vases of fresh cut flowers. A frosted panel of glass separates the open tub from the rest of the room, allowing natural light to bathe you while you soak away. It's certainly one of the most serene rooms I've ever stayed in, perhaps thanks to good feng shui. Or maybe because I feel like I'm not in Las Vegas when I'm here.

That 23rd-floor lobby also serves traditional tea service in the afternoons, in both Chinese and European styles, though you can Vegas-ize your experience to include champagne. The Mandarin Bar, occupying the corner of that floor, offers romantic views of the Strip through floor-to-ceiling panoramic windows, and is a delightfully fancy-schmancy place to have a cocktail in the evenings. Add to this the temple of fine dining by French chef Pierre Gagnaire and you've got a floor you don't have to leave for an entire night.

The more casual Mozen Bistro features both Asian and continental cuisine, while the secluded pool deck oasis also has its own cafe.

But if you want to do anything else, like see a show or gamble, you'll have to step outside of the Mandarin Oriental bubble. Fortunately, with Aria and the **Shops at Crystals** (p. 192) just outside your door, you won't have to go far.

3752 Las Vegas Blvd. S. www.mandarinoriental.com. © **888/881-9578** or 702/590-8888. 392 units. $229 and up double; $409 and up suite. Resort fee $32 per night. Extra person $50. Children 11 and under stay free in parent's room. Valet parking only at a cost of $30, prices vary during special events. **Amenities:** 4 restaurants; concierge; executive-level rooms; health club; heated pool; room service; spa; free Wi-Fi.

MGM Grand Hotel & Casino ★★   MGM Grand is a big green monster. When you combine this megaresort with its two auxiliary accommodation

Resort Fees

Even though Las Vegas is back on its economic upswing, room rates have stayed a tad lower than in other cities in order to stay competitive. Hotels, however, have found new ways to increase their bottom line, mainly through the addition of nefarious "resort fees." These extra charges are tacked on top of the nightly room rate and variously include things like Internet access, entry to the fitness center, printing of boarding passes, local and toll-free phone calls, and the like. Some hotels throw in extra goodies like bottles of water, discounted cocktails or meals, and credits for future stays. So try to take advantage of all the fee covers, because even if you don't, you still have to pay the fee. We indicate which hotels charge resort fees in the listings in this chapter and include their current prices, but do note that the amount, and what they include, changes *often*; ask when booking your room or take some time to read the fine print if making arrangements online.

towers, Signature Suites and Skylofts, it's the second largest hotel in the world and the largest hotel on the Strip. You might think a property this enormous would feel like it's too big for its own britches, treating visitors like they're numbers rather than guests. But MGM Grand has a surprisingly high standard for customer service on all levels.

It helps that a $160-million renovation in 2012 updated all of the rooms with bold strokes, placing pleasantly contrasting geometric patterns on everything from the padded headboards to carpets, while jewel tones on the accessories add nice pops of color.

With the exception of the West Wing, rooms tend to be oversized; standard king and queen rooms are even large enough to have a couch in a seating area, plus a writing desk and chair. Modern touches include 40-inch flatscreens and media hubs brimming with electrical outlets. If you want to start getting into real space, there are the residential spots at the Signature, the tall white buildings behind the MGM. If you've got the money to burn and need a palace, there's always the Skylofts, the mind-blowing, multi-bedroom villas that feature their own Strip-view balconies with hot tubs, 24-hour butler service, and other spiffy amenities. A final room category are the "Stay Well" rooms dedicated to the health-conscious Vegas visitor (yes, there is such a thing), and designed in conjunction with Cleveland Clinic and Deepak Chopra. Set on one entire floor, they feature vitamin C-infused showers, specialized lighting to suppress melatonin and fight jetlag, and welcome HEPA air filtration to rid your atmosphere of the very Vegas toxins of smoke, allergens, and pollen.

Getting from your room to most anywhere else in the hotel is relatively easy, unless you're headed to megaclub and restaurant **Hakkasan** (p 230). Then, you have to navigate most of the maze-like 170,000 square feet of casino—but follow the path (and the crowds) and you will be at one of the biggest nightlife hot spots in town. The club has a day party at the pool known as Wet Republic, where you get to hear the DJs you usually see at night in broad daylight.

If being crammed into the club isn't your scene, resident Cirque du Soleil show *KÀ* (p. 206) is one of the most breathtaking on the Strip, and the other non-party pools have a lazy river running through them.

MGM boasts one of the more exciting restaurant lineups on the Strip, including two restaurants from highly acclaimed French chef Joël Robuchon, Emeril's **New Orleans Fish House,** and sake-lover's **Shibuya,** all of which are reviewed in chapter 5.

3799 Las Vegas Blvd. S. (at Tropicana Ave.). www.mgmgrand.com. ℰ **800/929-1111** or 702/891-7777. 5,044 units. $125 and up double; $215 and up suite. Resort free $33. Extra person $40. Children 13 and under stay free in parent's room. Parking 1 hr. free, self-parking $7–$10, valet $13–$18; prices vary during special events. **Amenities:** 23 restaurants; nightclub; cabaret theater; casino; concierge; events arena; executive-level rooms; large health club; Jacuzzi; 5 outdoor pools w/lazy river; room service; salon; shopping arcade; spa; wedding chapel; free Wi-Fi.

Moderate

Excalibur ★   Kitsch is still king at this elaborate castle on the Strip. Excalibur fulfills that "adult Disney" mentality that the city was trying to go after in the early '90s. It's enormous, it's loud, and it's often crowded, but despite a few updates to the decor, it still doesn't take itself too seriously.

If you're on a budget, the standard rooms should suit you just fine; they're comfortable, if a bit outdated. The Contemporary Tower rooms are worth the extra price upgrade for more modern (as the name implies) touches and decor, as well as nicer bathrooms. Both come with 21st-century amenities like flatscreen TVs, Internet, and cable access. Come prepared with earplugs, however, as the walls are woefully thin, so you can hear exactly what your neighbors are saying and doing (and vice versa). For the price though, you won't find any better location on the Strip.

A medieval wedding isn't a rare request these days, and should you decide at the last minute you want to do a themed wedding, you can rent your own Guinevere and Lancelot (or Arthur, whoever fits) attire from the Canterbury Wedding Chapel (though one representative told us that requests lately have been more *Game of Thrones* than Arthurian legend).

For those fair maidens who aren't getting married just yet, the hunky Aussies from *Thunder From Down Under* are ready to show you what the fuss is all about. A totally different group of Aussies, The Australian Beegees, are a surprisingly accurate tribute act that put on a fun, disco-filled, nostalgic show.

Excalibur is still one of the only kid-friendly resorts on the Strip (we suppose it's hard to get away from that reputation when you're in the shape of a giant castle). The **Fun Dungeon** arcade features more than 150 carnival and arcade games, and is perfect for those bored kids and teens who have nothing else to do in town.

Following the trend of buffets being reborn, Excalibur's underwent its own $6 million overhaul, revealed in late 2014. The remodel included transforming the dining room to more modern digs—all traces of the old Round Table

Pet-Friendly Hotels

Up until recently, if you wanted to bring Fido or Fluffy to Vegas with you, your options for lodging were fairly limited, with only one major hotel on the Strip allowing pets (the Four Seasons). Now, more hotels are jumping on the pet-friendly bandwagon, including all of the Caesars Entertainment properties. Their popular *PetStay* program allows dogs up to 50 pounds to get a taste of Sin City. There are fees associated, of course ($25–$40), and there are plenty of restrictions, but you get amenities like food and water dishes, recommended dog walking routes, and more. The program is offered at Caesars Palace, Paris Las Vegas, Planet Hollywood, Harrah's, the Flamingo, Bally's, Rio Suites, and the LINQ. For more information on *PetStay*, check out www.caesars.com/petstay. You can also contact the Las Vegas Convention and Visitors Authority (www.lasvegas.com; ℓ **877/847-4858**) for info on other pet-friendly accommodations.

theme have been erased—and updating the menu so that you and your knights have more international choices.

3850 Las Vegas Blvd. S. (at Tropicana Ave.). www.excalibur.com. ✆ **800/937-7777** or 702/597-7700. 3,981 units. $45 and up double. Daily resort fee $29. Extra person $25. No discount for children. Parking 1 hr. free, self-parking $5–$8, valet $8–$13. **Amenities:** 5 restaurants; buffet; food court; casino; concierge; outdoor pools; room service; showrooms; wedding chapel; free Wi-Fi.

Luxor Las Vegas ★ Though it was never as grand as the ruins at Giza, the black, bold Luxor pyramid that punctuates the Strip has lost its original kitschy glory. Sure, the exterior hasn't changed, and the 315,000-watt beam of light that shoots from the top of the Luxor is still so powerful you can see it from outer space. But inside, the dynasty has definitely fallen. Gone are the once-unavoidable faux Egyptian monuments (save for Cleopatra's Needle and the Sphinx in the front, as well as the ominous Ramses statues still guarding the main entrance) in favor of a toned-down environment. It's a shame, really. The little details were what made Luxor so fun to explore. Today it's known only for its reasonable room rates and connection to Mandalay Bay.

Most believe that the Pyramid Rooms are the best to stay in, if only for the inclinator (not an elevator) ride that guests must take to get to their abode. It's a jolting, not-smooth ride at a 39-degree angle up the side of the building, but a novel way to change floors. But beyond that elevator ride, I don't recommend the Pyramid for stays; the angled windows in it make the rooms in that tower feel smaller than they are. And if you need a tub, you're out of luck in the pyramid. Bottom line: request a room in one of the other twin, 22-story cubes.

The casino feels enormous even by Las Vegas standards at 120,000 square feet, but ever since the stripping of the Egyptian kitsch, it's pretty banal. Maybe the artifacts were too distracting from the clanging of more than 2,000 slot machines.

Luxor's five-acre pool is divided into four sections. An oasis of faux Egyptian decor, it boasts one of the largest pool decks on the Strip. During the summer, there's an LGBT-friendly pool party (one of the few on the Strip) Temptation Sundays, with a live DJ and lots of hot, sculpted eye candy.

What Luxor lacks in personality these days, it makes up for in entertainment options. Prop comedian Carrot Top's long-running show is still a hit, while Cirque du Soleil-produced **Criss Angel:** *Mindfreak* (p. 209) is a hit with Angel's loyal fans. Things can get educational as well, with visits to the popular Bodies and well-regarded *Titanic* exhibits, both of which are reviewed in chapter 6.

Though the restaurant collection is more diverse at neighbor Mandalay Bay, Luxor has a few of its own gems, such as modern **Mexican Tacos & Tequila,** and game-meat oriented **Tender Steakhouse,** covered in chapter 5.

3900 Las Vegas Blvd. S. (btw. Reno and Hacienda aves.). www.luxor.com. ✆ **888/777-0188** or 702/262-4000. 4,400 units. $63 and up double; $150 and up whirlpool suite; $249–$800 other suites. Resort fee $29. Extra person $35. No discount for children. Parking 1 hr. free, self-parking $5–$8, valet $8–$13. **Amenities:** 6 restaurants; buffet; food court; nightclub; casino; concierge; executive-level rooms; health club; 5 outdoor pools; room service; showrooms; spa; free Wi-Fi.

Monte Carlo Resort & Casino ★ As far as moderate, middle-of-the-road Strip resorts go, Monte Carlo is probably the king of them all. It's not all hoity-toity like Bellagio, but it's not exactly the Riviera, either (R.I.P.). Yet, it's quietly survived, making changes when needed, but, like its decor, remaining bland. Dependable and consistent in service and amenities, but bland.

There's nothing wrong with bland or beige, the *de rigeur* color of Monte Carlo. It's easy on the eyes. Classic lines and furnishings welcome you into the rooms, which offer respectably comfortable beds, granite bathrooms, and faux European wood furniture. And it's one of the few hotels on the Strip where you can get from the reception area to your room without walking through the casino, making it a favorite of families. Feel like getting a little crazy? The 700-square-foot spa suites have oversize hot tubs smack dab next to the bed. Why Monte Carlo, you old devil you.

The addition of boutique **Hotel 32** on the top floors has also spiced things up, offering a limo pickup, private elevator, personal suite assistant (are they not called butlers anymore?), and all the rest of the perks that come with being a VIP (and paying the VIP price). At the very least, the rooms are swankier, if not more colorful.

In the past year, Monte Carlo started taking advantage of its Strip-front property by opening a pedestrian plaza right on the Strip. It now connects to the 2-acre open air entertainment and retail space known as **The Park,** and you're now within spitting distance of the new 20,000-seat T-Mobile Arena, plus there's a new theater in the works as we write. With restaurants such as **Yusho** (p. 106), **800 Degrees Pizza, Double Barrel Roadhouse,** and local coffeehouse **Sambalatte** at the front of the hotel, passing tourists don't even have to set foot into the casino for a drink or bite to eat. Indoors, **Andre's** is still elegant French fare, and **The Pub** boasts a great craft beer selection, both of which are discussed in chapter 5.

The pool is fun, but even with the lazy river it isn't the best on the Strip, having dropped in ranking behind those at Mandalay Bay and MGM Grand.

3770 Las Vegas Blvd. S. (btw. Flamingo Rd. and Tropicana Ave.). www.montecarlo.com. ⓒ **800/311-8999** or 702/730-7777. 3,002 units. $69 and up double; $145 and up suite. Daily resort fee $33. Extra person $35. No discount for children. Parking 1 hr. free, self-parking $5–$8, valet $8–$13 **Amenities:** 7 restaurants; food court; casino; concierge; executive-level rooms; fitness center; Jacuzzi; outdoor pool w/wave pool and lazy river; room service; showroom; spa; watersports equipment/rentals; wedding chapel; free Wi-Fi.

New York–New York Hotel & Casino ★★ The hotel that's so-nice-they-named-it-twice is really good at detail (at least on the exterior). Even though the one-third-size replica of the New York skyline seems all crammed into the facade, it covers it all in 2.4 million square feet: the 150-foot Statue of Liberty, the 300-foot-long Brooklyn Bridge, the Chrysler Building, the Empire State Building. It's like looking at a live-action cartoon postcard. And it's these aesthetic touches that make this one of the quintessential Las Vegas resorts. People still want a hotel that has a roller coaster wrapped around it.

family-friendly HOTELS

We've said it before and we'll say it again: Vegas is simply not a good place to bring kids. Most of the major hotels no longer offer babysitting, and fewer offer discounts for children staying in a parent's room (many others have lowered the age for children who can stay for free). But if you must bring them, you'll be best served at the hotels below or in a non-casino hotel, particularly a reliable chain, and a place with kitchenettes.

- **Circus Circus Hotel & Casino** (p. 71) Centrally located on the Strip, this is our first choice if you're traveling with the kids. The hotel's mezzanine level offers ongoing circus acts daily from 11am to midnight, dozens of carnival games, and an arcade. And behind the hotel is a full amusement park.

- **Excalibur** (p. 52) Though the sword-and-sorcery theme has been considerably toned down, Excalibur features an entire floor of midway games and a large video-game arcade. It also has some child-oriented eateries and shows, but there's a heavily promoted male-stripper show, too, so it's not perfect.

- **Four Seasons** (p. 47) For free goodies, service, and general child pampering, the costly Four Seasons is probably worth the dough. Your kids will be spoiled!

- **Mandalay Bay** (p. 48) Mandalay Bay certainly looks grown up, but it has a number of factors that make it family-friendly: good-size rooms to start—which you do not have to cross a casino to access; a variety of restaurants; a big ol' shark attraction; and, best of all, the swimming area—wave pool, sandy beach, lazy river, lots of other pools—fun in the Vegas sun!

- **The Orleans** (p. 83) Considered a "local" hotel, its proximity to the Strip makes it a viable alternative, especially for families seeking to take advantage of its plus-size pool area, kid's activity area, bowling, and movie theaters.

- **Stratosphere Casino Hotel** (p. 70) For families looking for reasonably priced, if not particularly exciting, digs, this is a good choice. Plus, it's not in the middle of the Strip action, so you and your kids can avoid that. Thus far, it's not moving in the "adult entertainment" direction, and it has thrill rides at the top.

Along with Monte Carlo, New York–New York has been pushing its offerings more to its front on the Strip, adding busy restaurants such as **Shake Shack** (there's always a line, but worth it) and **Tom's Urban**, along with candy-land **Hershey's World.**

But while the outside of New York–New York is still exciting, the inside has been toned down, with less "New York-ness" to the casino floor and the rooms. Sure the rooms are sleek, with plush padded headboards, 40-inch flatscreen TVs, and marble in the bathrooms, but we miss the Chrysler Building-like Art Deco pizazz they once had. Call it gentrification.

One thing that hasn't changed? It's a long, looooonng slog from registration to your room, no matter which tower you're in. But if you can make it there, you'll make it anywhere . . . else in the hotel. (I'm sorry.)

The risqué resident Cirque du Soleil show *Zumanity* (p. 209) underwent a few show changes in the past year, but is still adult-oriented, a little less cheesy, and best for those who are really comfortable with the sensuality of the human body.

3790 Las Vegas Blvd. S. (at Tropicana Ave.). www.newyorknewyork.com. © **800/693-6763** or 702/740-6969. 2,024 units. $79 and up double. Daily resort fee $33. Extra person $35. No discount for children. Parking 1 hr. free, self-parking $7–$10, valet $13–$18; prices vary during special events. **Amenities:** 13 restaurants; food court; buffet; casino; executive-level rooms; fitness center; Jacuzzi; outdoor pool; room service; showroom; spa; free Wi-Fi.

Tropicana Las Vegas ★ Sadly, the Tropicana has lost its soul and its way. A number of restaurants and attractions have come and gone as the resort's new owners (Doubletree by Hilton, believe it or not) have attempted to define the iconic resort's new identity. Luxurious? Sure. But there isn't much memorable about it anymore, which is a bummer. They attempted to transport the Miami feel to its dining and pool parties, to minimal success, so the powers that be have kept things at status quo (reasonable rates, middle-of-the-road dining, active casino) until they discover the magic formula to make this once legendary property relevant again. It maintains its spectacular location, right on the corner of Las Vegas Boulevard and Tropicana, at great value to guests, and that remains its saving grace.

If you do stay here, you'll find that the $200 million spent on renovations transformed the main floor from a dark, dingy casino into a bright, white gambling palace. The rooms, which were completely gutted, follow suit in terms of brightness. Plantation-style shutters on the windows allow just the right amount of light in to highlight the bleach-white, high thread count linens; bamboo and rattan furniture makes you feel like you've checked into a beach house rather than a Strip hotel room. Our favorites are the Bungalow Deluxe Rooms, located just off the pool in two-story buildings, which feel very exclusive, and offer potent eye candy from their private balconies.

3801 Las Vegas Blvd. S. (at Tropicana Ave.). www.troplv.com. © **888/826-8767** or 702/739-2222. 1,375 units. $89 and up double. Resort fee $29. Extra person $25. No discount for children. Free self- and valet parking. **Amenities:** 3 restaurants; food court; casino; executive-level rooms; health club; 3 outdoor pools; showroom; wedding chapel; free Wi-Fi.

MID-STRIP

The middle of the Strip is from Harmon Avenue to Spring Mountain/Sands Road and features many of the grand Vegas gambling destinations you have seen in the movies.

Best for: People without transportation who want to be able to walk to everything they want to see.

Drawbacks: Peak times bring out massive crowds and higher prices.

Expensive

Bellagio ★★★ The Bellagio has come to exemplify everything that's recognized as luxury in Las Vegas. It was opened in 1989 by Steve Wynn (along with the Mirage), setting the standard for Las Vegas elegance. Nearly 2 decades later, the Lake Como-inspired resort is still at the top of its game.

Just walking into the Bellagio is a thrill. First you pass the aquatic spectacle of the **Fountains of Bellagio** (p. 158) outside, then enter into the lobby under a stunning ceiling garden of artist Dale Chihuly's hand-blown flowers (p. ii). Follow your nose to the wafting scents from the lush Conservatory and **Botanical Garden** (p. 158), which changes its displays seasonally five times a year (the fifth, in case you're wondering, is in celebration of Chinese New Year).

The handsome accommodations are available in two different color palettes, inspired by the attractions downstairs. The blue and platinum scheme, contemporary and relaxing, is meant to evoke the Fountains of Bellagio; while the serene green and plum pairing offers the earthy warmth of the Conservatory. The decor straddles the line between funky and elegant. Bathrooms are larger than most Brooklyn apartments, with marble vanities and large soaking tubs.

Most of the upscale restaurants that were part of the opening team are still here, including **Michael Mina, Fix,** and **Le Cirque,** with a few newcomers that reflect Las Vegas' changing appetites, like **Yellowtail** and **Lago,** which are all reviewed in chapter 5. Vodka and tea drinkers alike flock to **Petrossian,** while nightlife beats on at lounges such as **Hyde Bellagio** and **Lily,** all covered in chapter 8. Resident Cirque du Soleil show *O* (p. 208) is still an aquatic and acrobatic masterpiece.

The price points are pretty steep all around the hotel, and not just at the gaming tables. Weekend cabana rentals next to one of the six pools in its Mediterranean oasis are $300; head to the more-exclusive Cypress Pool, and just sitting in a chair will cost you a whopping $50—or more.

3600 Las Vegas Blvd. S. (at the corner of Flamingo Rd.). www.bellagio.com. © **888/987-6667** or 702/693-7111. 3,933 units. $169 and up double; $450 and up suite. Resort fee $35. Extra person $50. No discount for children. Parking 1 hr. free, self-parking $7–$10, valet $13–$18; prices vary during special events. **Amenities:** 14 restaurants; buffet; nightclubs; casino; concierge; executive-level rooms; large health club; 6 outdoor pools; room service; showrooms; spa; wedding chapel; free Wi-Fi.

Caesars Palace ★★★ Caesars dips its toes into old Vegas and new Vegas, maintaining that kitschy, over-the-top cheesiness that was associated with the city for a long time (Roman columns and statues), while at the same time embracing all the modern elegance that's become expected.

There are six towers of varying degrees of luxury. The most basic rooms are in the Roman and Forum towers, which are the oldest, but have been recently renovated with modern touches like mirrored headboards, sleeker lines, and in-mirror TVs in the bathroom. As the name implies, Palace Tower rooms (the closest to the convention space) are decidedly more regal, and larger, with wood and gold finishes. The Laurel Connection is a boutique hotel experience comprised of the Augustus and Octavius Towers, which not only have their own line of luxury amenities, but also a private valet on Flamingo, so guests don't have to navigate the casino floor to get to their rooms. Floor-to-ceiling windows admit plenty of light into the big sleeping areas, which come complete with plush sofas that hug the corner of the room.

And yes, you can even book the Hangover Suite. The one in the film, however, isn't an actual suite in the hotel, but a set modeled after the Emperor's Suite in the Forum Tower. Just don't end up on the roof.

The old Centurion Tower took on a new identity as **The Nobu Hotel Las Vegas,** named for the restaurants by modern Japanese pioneer Nobu Matsuhisa. Everything about it departs from the Caesars aesthetic: it's appointed with contemporary and traditional Japanese decor such as mini-teak stools and black stone tile in the open showers. Exclusive amenities include sleep oils, Nobu's own brand of tea in the mini-bar, and priority seating in the Nobu restaurant downstairs. You can even order Nobu fare as room service. Since the boutique essentially operates as its own entity, the smaller guest-to-staff ratio allows for more personalized service.

There are almost as many pools at the **Garden of the Gods** complex as there are hotel towers. Named for various Roman gods, each caters to its own niche of clientele based on its moniker. The Venus pool is European style (as in bikini top optional) and often has a DJ soundtrack, while you can play swim-up blackjack at Fortuna. Tucked away in the corner, Jupiter pool is the most secluded and quiet, but Bacchus is secluded in its own way, reserved for the high rollers, invited guests, and celebrities.

Dining options at Caesars Palace are diverse and renowned, including Italian favorite Rao's, French gastronomic temple **Restaurant Guy Savoy,** and Bobby Flay's first Vegas restaurant, **Mesa Grill,** as well as others reviewed in chapter 5.

Shoppers love wandering around the massive **Forum Shops** (p. 195) for high end retail. The **Colosseum** (p. 216) hosts resident acts such as Elton John, Mariah Carey, and Rod Stewart. Head outdoors to the big tent for *Absinthe* (p. 205), the most outrageous show on the Strip.

3570 Las Vegas Blvd. S. (just north of Flamingo Rd.). www.caesarspalace.com. © **877/427-7243** or 702/731-7110. 3,960 units. $119 and up double; $440 and up suite. Resort fee $32. Extra person $30. No discount for children. Free self- and valet parking. **Amenities:** 11 restaurants; buffet; food court; nightclubs; casino; concierge; executive-level rooms; health club; 8 outdoor pools; room service; spa; 3 wedding chapels; free Wi-Fi.

The Cosmopolitan of Las Vegas ★★★

When the Cosmopolitan opened in 2010, it was the start of a brand new era in Las Vegas. The town was slowly climbing out of the recession, and this was likely to be the last new resort to be built from the ground up for a long time. So it broke the mold.

What you'll notice first about the Cosmopolitan is that there are so many things to notice. Crisp LED screens on the columns near check-in display fluid, moving graphics that keep guests entranced. A 9-foot, metallic Lucky Cat art installation in the pop-up exhibition space beckons those seeking good fortune (and who isn't, in Vegas?). At one point, Liberace's Rhinestone Roadster was even parked near the Strip entrance. There's no shortage of visual stimulation in the 100,000-square-foot casino or the floors above, and that's even without the frenetic slot machines.

They especially love their chandeliers at the Cosmopolitan. The three-story specimen in the middle of the casino floor is made of 2 million crystals and houses the multi-level Chandelier Bar. It joins the Bond Bar on the Strip side, which has live DJs and girls dancing in boxes above the crowd; and the more subdued Vesper Bar near registration (a spot where you'd likely find casino execs having a drink). Each has its own dedicated cocktail program to match the vibe.

The most basic rooms are quite swank, done up in relaxing blues and metallics, starting at around 500 square feet. Each features a giant, marble-tiled bathroom. The direct view from the bed right into the shower is . . . cool? (If you're not feeling modest.) If it's reasonable, upgrade to at least the terrace studio. In these, you also get the benefit of 200 more square feet and a kitchenette, plus a private terrace, a rarity on the Strip. The one-bedroom suites have even better amenities, like deep Japanese soaking tubs that look out the window, separate seating areas that can be closed off from the bedroom, and terraces that wrap around the corner of the building.

The Cosmopolitan's restaurant collection also ushered in a new era for Vegas' culinary scene. It helped move appetites away from celebrity chef-driven spots to more urban, real-food-city fare. Its **Wicked Spoon Buffet** reset the bar for the all-you-can-eat-experience (it, along with some of the other dozen restaurants at Cosmo, are reviewed in chapter 5).

Entertainment-wise, Cosmopolitan has made a name for itself as a stop for indie bands and big name artists. Sometimes they play the intimate Chelsea showroom, sometimes they'll play outdoors to standing room only at the Boulevard Pool. The pool also serves as the daylife part of **Marquee,** one of the biggest nightclubs on the Strip. In winter, the pool gets covered, faux snow gets piped into the air, and the space becomes a skating rink.

The clientele here, whether they're guests or not, tend to run on the younger side. This isn't a quiet hotel, that's for sure, nor does it ever aim to be.

3708 Las Vegas Blvd. S. www.cosmopolitanlasvegas.com. © **877/551-7778** or 702/698-7000. 2,995 units. $140 and up double. Resort fee $30 per night. Extra person $30. Children under 17 stay free in parent's room. Free self- and valet parking. **Amenities:** 13 restaurants; buffet; casino; concierge; executive-level rooms; health club; heated outdoor pools; room service; spa.; free Wi-Fi.

The Cromwell ★★   At 188 rooms, this is probably the only hotel that can truly call itself "boutique," which is exactly what The Cromwell was going for when it transformed the old, tired Bill's Gamblin' Hall into this handsome newbie.

Yes, the casino is still pretty dark inside, but now it's the kind of sophisticated dark that you want to be caught in. Warm, sultry colors and textures decorate the casino floor, starting at the modern vintage (if there is such a thing) Bound Bar at the front, which allows guests to have a drink in the lobby without feeling overwhelmed by the casino. They kept the original red chandeliers of Bill's, which fit in perfectly with the new, sexy digs.

The rooms tend to run a little smaller, but make up for it in luxurious appointments. Influenced by modern Paris (down to the French phrases elegantly scrawled on the carpets in the hallways), the accommodations feature dark, hardwood floors (practically unheard of in Las Vegas), antique trunks as furniture, tufted leather headboards, and deep, luscious berry hues. Bathrooms are definitely small, but pack a visual punch, with tall showers, handheld showerheads, and readable tile that offers more life coaching quotes. On the tech front, you no longer need a key to open your room. Opt for the eKey app that allows you to wave your iPhone over the pad on the door, *et voila!* Access granted. Perfect for those of us who have a habit of misplacing keycards.

While it's dark in the casino, **Giada** (p. 115) de Laurentiis' namesake restaurant on the second floor is a bright airy space awash in natural light. We review her first eatery in chapter 5.

The Cromwell is definitely aiming at a younger demographic—but those with disposable incomes; guests also receive admission to the party scene of the hotel. Nightclub mainstay **Drai's** (p. 229) emerged from its basement lair to take over the rooftop and its pool for a nightlife and daylife component (though Drai's Afterhours still operates 'til the wee hours of the morning down in the depths of the hotel).

3595 Las Vegas Blvd. S. www.thecromwell.com. ℂ **844/426-2766** or 702/777-3777. 188 units. $99 and up double. Resort fee $32. Extra person $35. No discount for children. Free self- and valet parking. **Amenities:** Restaurant; nightclubs, casino; concierge; heated outdoor pool; room service; free Wi-Fi.

The Venetian/Palazzo Las Vegas ★★   When Las Vegas was going through its period of building hotels in homage to other cities (New York-New York, Luxor, Paris Las Vegas), there was a tendency to create these hotels as more of a caricature of the real deal. Somehow, Venetian managed to escape that campy, kitschy feel; it is, without a doubt, one of the most beautiful and luxurious properties to come out of that trend.

The exterior, much like Paris Las Vegas, crams a lot of the actual city's landmarks into one small footprint. There's the canals and Campanile right at the front, and the Doge's Palace facade—where the plaza sometimes gets shut down for private, hoity-toity events. Indoors, right at Venetian's registration, guests are treated to Michelangelo's work on the ceiling of the Sistine Chapel, recreated in the type of gorgeous detail that carries through the rest of the property.

St. Mark's Place is another masterful fake, an actual square within the **Grand Canal Shoppes** (p. 196), ringed by retailers and restaurants with "patio" seating. Wandering minstrels treat crowds to live performances. It's a nice nod to the city, with less worry of pickpockets.

Both Venetian and Palazzo are proper all-suite hotels, with the smallest rooms starting at a generous 650 square feet. The suites are bi-level, with sunken living rooms that have full-size sleeper sofas on request, and even enough room to fit in two more comfortable chairs and a dining table with three seats. Colors are rich and royal, the entire space has a warm, relaxing glow, perfect for when you fall into one of the plush beds tucked with soft, high thread count sheets. Bathrooms are downright palatial, complete with deep, marble-encased Roman tubs, separate enclosed shower, and double vanities. Three TVs—one each in the bedroom and living rooms, and of course one in the bath—make sure that you're always entertained.

Venetian also has boasting rights in the culinary realm: its arsenal of restaurants has more James Beard Award-winners (Wolfgang Puck, Thomas Keller, Mario Batali and Daniel Boulud) than any other property on the Strip, as well as celebrity chefs such as Buddy Valastro and Emeril Lagasse. See chapter 5 for a more detailed discussion.

The Grand Canal Shoppes meander between the Venetian and Palazzo, featuring faux canals which snake through them, complete with singing gondoliers. The Palazzo's atrium features seasonal floral displays, as well as a waterfall. The Chinese New Year display is often one of the most elaborate on the Strip (the year of the dragon featured a giant, mechanical, fire-breathing one). Created with feng shui in mind, guests are encouraged to walk around it three times, clockwise, in order to bring good luck for the lunar new year.

3355 Las Vegas Blvd. S. www.venetian.com. © **888/283-6423** or 702/414-1000. 7,093 units. $159 and up double. Resort fee $32. Extra person $35. Children 12 and under stay free in parent's room. Free self- and valet parking. **Amenities:** 39 restaurants; casino; concierge; executive-level rooms; health club; outdoor pools; 24-hr. room service; extensive shopping mall; showrooms; spa; wedding chapels; free Wi-Fi.

Moderate

Bally's Las Vegas ★ The obvious reason to stay at Bally's: its prime, center-Strip location. The less obvious reason? Some of its suites are darn nice (something that few visitors know).

What was originally the MGM Grand when it opened in 1973, Bally's has pretty much stayed the same, as the rest of the Strip grew bigger and more opulent. It's only in the past couple of years that we've been seeing more grand changes throughout the property, first inside, then out.

The Jubilee Tower rooms were the first to be completely renovated and are worth spending an extra $20 above the price of the standard rooms. If Bally's feels a little dated on the outside, these spaces say otherwise, with polished wood furnishings, tufted headboards, pillow top beds, and lots of marble in the bathrooms. The colors are a little tame, but everything feels new and clean and swanky. Should you decide to go a little bigger—and you should—a suite here will run at least $100 less per night than you'll find at Bellagio right across the street. The Jubilee Grand Suites will surprise you; they're twice the size of the regular rooms, with lots of red, more amenities, and why, yes, that IS a whirlpool right in the middle of your room. The other non-Jubilee Tower rooms and suites are serviceable, but if you can afford to stay somewhere prettier, why not?

Most visitors who aren't bedding down here stop by for the famed **Sterling Brunch** (p. 14) which runs nearly $100 a pop. **BLT Steak** replaced the classic Bally's Steakhouse, but retained the brunch in the transition, so now you get to eat your endless caviar and lobster tails in a much more contemporary setting. It's only a quick walk through the corridor connecting Bally's and Paris Las Vegas next door to get to more dining options.

Finally, the front of Bally's got a facelift early in 2015 with the addition of **Grand Bazaar Shops** (p. 195), an outdoor retail and dining experience with lots of tiny boutiques you won't find elsewhere in Las Vegas.

3645 Las Vegas Blvd. S. (at Flamingo Rd.). www.ballyslv.com. © **800/634-3434** or 702/739-4111. 2,814 units. $36 and up double; $199 and up suite. Resort fee $29. Extra person $30. No discount for children. Free self- and valet parking. **Amenities:** 4 restaurants; buffet; food court; casino; concierge; health club; outdoor pool; room service; showrooms; spa; 8 night-lit tennis courts; free Wi-Fi.

Flamingo Las Vegas ★   Aside from the Tropicana, Flamingo is probably the most recognizable hotel name in Las Vegas, mainly because it's the longest survivor on the Strip. Bugsy Siegel opened the 105-room (it would be considered "boutique" today) Flamingo in 1946, and 7 decades later, despite the fact that the original bones are completely gone, he'd probably still recognize the place.

The pink neon that has been burned into our collective memories still streams through the hotel, especially when you check into the FAB rooms and retro-inspired GO rooms. The main difference between the two? The GO rooms are prettier to look at, having been remodeled more recently, and come standard with showers only (FAB rooms do have tubs). The Flamingo embraces its Rat Pack history, with the GO rooms attempting to throw you back into all its mod glory, with vinyl padded headboards, black and white photos of Vegas days of yore, and pops of color on the striped wallpaper, all with modern amenities like electronic window treatments, and TVs built into the mirrors.

Shows such as *Donny and Marie* (p. 211) and *Legends in Concert* (p. 213) have been chugging along to sold-out crowds in search of nostalgia, while Olivia Newton-John recently threw her hat in the Vegas headliner ring.

The pool is one of the hotel's biggest draws. Lush foliage covers 15 acres of lagoons, waterfalls, and streams, as well as five pools and whirlpools. The GO pool features DJ-driven pool time, but the other swimming spots are more family-friendly. You can find the flocks of the namesake bird on Flamingo Island, part of the property's famed **Wildlife Habitat,** as well as other animals such as ducks, ibis and turtles, all part of this carefully maintained ecosystem. These species might not be native to Nevada, but they're definitely a part of the Las Vegas landscape.

3555 Las Vegas Blvd. S. (btw. Sands Ave. and Flamingo Rd.). www.flamingolv.com. © **800/732-2111** or 702/733-3111. 3,517 units. $85 and up double; $122 and up suite. Resort fee $29. Extra person $30. No discount for children. Timeshare suites available. Free self- and valet parking. **Amenities:** 4 restaurants; buffet; food court; casino; executive-level rooms; health club; 5 outdoor pools; room service; showrooms; spa; wedding chapels; free Wi-Fi.

Harrah's Las Vegas ★   What Harrah's lacks in panache, it makes up for in location, and for the non-stop action on its casino floor. It's not exactly the most luxurious or sophisticated on the Strip, but it is smack dab in the middle of it, and for that it's worth a stay if you're planning on a) doing stuff at lots of other hotels or b) gambling here the whole time.

Accommodations are forgettable-looking, with the expected amenities, but roomier than other hotels you'll find at this price point. In a word, they're just fine, with the exception of a handful of basic rooms that haven't been updated yet—don't be afraid to ask for more modern digs in the Carnaval South tower if you get stuck with one of them.

The casino is a gambler's paradise, with more than 80 table games and 1,200 slot machines hungry for your money. Entertainment options are about right for the demographic: There's the famous Improv Theater, where up-and-coming comedians take the stage, as well as headliners **The Righteous Brothers** and afternoon-favorite **Mac King** (p. 214) comedy show. *Million Dollar Quartet* (p. 214) is an underrated show that should be checked out if you're a fan of Elvis, Johnny Cash, Jerry Lee Lewis, and/or Carl Perkins.

Restaurant wise, **Ruth Chris'** is a good standby for steak, with a primo view of the Strip, while the new **Fulton Street Food Hall** (p. 121) is a nice recent addition. It's not a food court, but you know those big market-like eating emporiums we're seeing pop up around the country? This is Las Vegas' version.

3475 Las Vegas Blvd. S. (btw. Flamingo and Spring Mountain rds.). www.harrahslas vegas.com. © **800/427-7247** or 702/369-5000. 2,526 units. $65 and up double; $270 and up suite. Resort fee $29. Extra person $30. No discount for children. Free self- and valet parking. **Amenities:** 5 restaurants; buffet; casino; concierge; executive-level rooms; health club; outdoor pool; room service; showroom; spa; free Wi-Fi.

The Mirage ★★   What we know of Las Vegas today—the over-the-top offerings, the temples of excess, all with the notion that luxury can be attainable even by regular folks—all started with The Mirage when it opened in 1989. Since then, hotels have only been getting bigger and more extravagant.

SO YOUR TRIP GOES swimmingly . . .

Part of the delight of the Vegas resort complexes is the gorgeous pools—what could be better for beating the summer heat? But there are pools and there are *pools*, so you'll need to keep several things in mind when searching for the right one for you.

During the winter, it's often too cold or windy to do much lounging, and even if the weather is amenable, the hotels often close part of their pool areas during winter and early spring. Also, the pools are not heated for the most part, but in fairness, they largely don't need to be.

Most hotel pools are shallow, chest-high at best, only about 3 feet deep in many spots (the hotels want you gambling, not swimming). Diving is impossible—not that a single pool allows it anyway.

Although the stories about the "Death Ray" at CityCenter's Vdara hotel were overblown (where the sun reflecting off the mirrored hotel exterior reportedly caused plastic to melt), be warned that sitting by pools that offer scant shade requires diligent application of sunscreen.

At any of the pools, you can rent a cabana (which often includes a TV, special lounge chairs, and—even better—poolside service), but these should be reserved as far in advance as possible, and most cost a hefty fee. If you are staying at a chain hotel, you will most likely find an average pool, but if you want to spend some time at a better

one, be aware that most of the casino-hotel pool attendants will ask to see your room key. If they are busy, you might be able to sneak in, or at least blend in with a group ahead of you.

When it comes to our favorites, we tend to throw our support to those that offer luxurious landscaping, plenty of places to lounge, multiple dipping options, and some shade for those times when the desert sun gets to be too much. This is a good description of the pools at both **The Mirage** and the **Flamingo,** which offer acres of veritable tropical paradises for you to enjoy. Ditto the renovated pool area at the **Tropicana,** serving up a sunny Miami Beach-feeling among lush grounds.

If you're looking for something a little more adventurous, try the epic facility at **Mandalay Bay,** complete with a wave pool, a lazy-river ride, and good old-fashioned swimming holes, along with a sandy beach. **MGM Grand** has a similar facility, although not as big and without the waves.

Partying is not confined to the night-clubs these days. Many of the hotels offer pool-club experiences (p. 237), but even when they aren't in full-on party mode, the pools at **Hard Rock** (sandy beaches, swim-up blackjack), the Palms (multilevel, high-end cabanas), **Aria Las Vegas** (acres of sexy modernity), and **The Cosmopolitan of Las Vegas** (not one but two party pools overlooking the Strip) serve up high-energy frolicking.

But not all of them have an exploding volcano in front it.

It's not just the volcano that's set to explode every hour to music, but also the lush foliage in the domed atrium, the 20,000-gallon aquarium behind the check-in desk, and **Siegfried and Roy's** (yes, they're still around) **Secret Garden Habitat,** that keep the Mirage top-of-mind to would-be visitors. Even if you've never been here before, you know that volcano. You know Siegfried and Roy.

And beyond the fake lava, this is a darn nice place to stay. Accommodations are downright luxurious for the price point, with clean lines, bold colors and natural wood furnishings surrounding a great pillow top mattress on the bed. Neutral-colored marble in the bathroom is a nice touch, and the hotel is vocal about its ADA-accessible rooms.

Dining options in the past few years have gotten on par with the rest of the Strip: Tom Colicchio's **Heritage Steak** focuses on good, properly-sourced meat cooked over an open fire; the new **Portofino** is inching its way into becoming one of the best Italian restaurants in town; **The Pantry** serves as the 24-hour coffee shop, but feels more like you're eating in your mom's kitchen; **Carnegie Deli** still serves some of the best football-sized, New York–style pastrami sandwiches in town.

The pool is open and heated all year, and considered one of the best on the Strip thanks to a lagoon-like setting, waterfalls, and waterslides. The adult-oriented Bare Pool Lounge allows for European-style sunbathing (read: topless) and is a nice oasis in its own right.

3400 Las Vegas Blvd. S. (btw. Flamingo and Spring Mountain rds.). www.mirage.com. © **800/627-6667** or 702/791-7111. 3,044 units. $79 and up double; $160 and up suite. Resort fee $33. Extra person $35. No discount for children. Parking 1 hr. free, self-parking $7–$10, valet $13–$18; prices vary during special events. **Amenities:** 14 restaurants; buffet; casino; concierge; executive-level rooms; health club; outdoor pools; room service; showrooms; spa; free Wi-Fi.

Paris Las Vegas Casino Resort ★★★   If visiting Paris, France is at the top of your bucket list—the Vegas version won't let you cross it off, but it *will* give you a snapshot of what you'll encounter in the real deal. The Eiffel Tower in front is half the size of the original, but is exact in detail, right down to the number of rivets that hold it all together and the glass elevator that takes you to the top observation deck.

Inside, you're transported to Vegas' idea of the City of Light, with the legs of the Eiffel Tower coming through the ceiling—painted with clouds—to give you the illusion that you are directly under it. The rooms, while clean, proficient, and larger than most standard accommodations, look only vaguely inspired by the French countryside. There are a few Empire-style furnishings, but they're not fooling anyone. Buck up to stay in one of the Red Rooms, which are sexier than standard rooms and have cute, lip-shaped sofas to remind you of that French kiss. Considering you're basically center-Strip, you won't mind that the rooms aren't that fancy for the price.

The **Eiffel Tower Restaurant** (p. 154) is still voted one of the most romantic spots in town. A meal at **Gordon Ramsay Steak** (p. 110) will set you back a bit, but is the best of his three restaurants on the Strip; make a reservation as soon as you can. French bistro **Mon Ami Gabi** (p. 118) seats you right in the front terrace of the hotel, offering some of the best people watching and a killer view of the Bellagio Fountains, but there's better French food to be had in town, and all of this is covered in chapter 5.

Nightclub **Chateau's** rooftop perch makes it one of the few clubs in town that lets you hang outdoors while celebrity hosts have parties indoors, and *Jersey Boys* is still going strong.

3655 Las Vegas Blvd. S. www.parislv.com. © **888/266-5687** or 702/946-7000. 2,916 units. $75 and up double; $170 and up suite. Resort fee $32. Extra person $30. No discount for children. Free self- and valet parking. **Amenities:** 12 restaurants; buffet; casino; concierge; executive-level rooms; health club; outdoor pool; room service; showrooms; spa; 2 wedding chapels; free Wi-Fi.

Planet Hollywood Resort & Casino ★★

The giant, continuous LED screens that lead down to the corner of Las Vegas Boulevard and Harmon Avenue might evoke the frenetic video boards of Times Square; they're definitely just as bright! That amazing stretch of signage is one of the most dazzling on the Strip, and reminds us that this truly is still one of the most electrifying (if not electrified) places on earth.

Once inside, your senses get a break from the constant flash—the interior is modern and elegant, and even the usually frenetic casino floor feels glamorous. Every room has a similar earthy color palette of purple, green, and mustard, and velour-tufted headboards crown all the beds—but each room has its own theme, which is a swell use of the property's insane amount of memorabilia. So you might have Laurel and Hardy or Marlon Brando's Vito Corleone peering down at you in the tub. The separate tub in the bathroom, incidentally, is a nice place to soak. If you're staying in one of the tony Panorama Suites, corner rooms with sweeping views of the Strip, your tub is basically in the middle of the room so you can enjoy the view from your bubbles.

In addition to the PH rooms proper, we're also including in this review a few thousand more from the adjoining Elara, a timeshare/hotel by Hilton Grand Vacations that you have to book through Hilton directly, though you don't need to own a timeshare to stay there. But that type of property means that all units have kitchens, whether they're in studios or four-room suites, making this quite kid-friendly.

Check-in tip: For some reason valet parking is always full here, even if you're a guest. Unfortunately this means you have to self-park in the garage at the Miracle Mile Shops, then schlep your gear through the mall, which is a giant circle—so whether you go right or left from the garage doesn't really matter. Some of the floor of the mall is still surfaced with cobblestone, so it's a bumpy schlep at times.

Planet Hollywood has numerous dining options including **Gordon Ramsay BurGR** and the vegetarian-friendly **Spice Market Buffet** (discussed in chapter 5) and serious shopping opportunities (covered in chapter 7). For entertainment, Britney Spears headlines in the 4,000-seat **Axis Theater** a few times a month, at least through 2017.

3667 Las Vegas Blvd. S. www.planethollywoodresort.com. © **877/333-9474** or 702/785-5555. 3,768 units. $79 and up double. Resort fee $32. Extra person $30. No discount for children. Free self- and valet parking. **Amenities:** 11 restaurants; buffet; bars/

lounges; casino; concierge; executive-level rooms; health club; 2 Jacuzzis; performing arts center; 2 outdoor pools; room service; showroom; spa; wedding chapel; free Wi-Fi.

The LINQ ★

Formerly the pseudo-Asian-themed Imperial Palace, it took a few name changes before the powers that be settled on The LINQ—if only so it wouldn't be so confusing when people were talking about The LINQ Promenade, a new shopping and retail space that extends straight from the Strip between The LINQ and Flamingo hotels.

The rebirth of IP into The LINQ meant a total overhaul of the property: brand spankin' new casino floor, total gutting of the rooms, and a beautiful new facade to match. The new rooms are small, starting at 250 square feet (the 47-inch flatscreen TVs seem almost comically large in such a tiny space), but pack a punch visually. Deluxe rooms feature white linens, natural wood furnishing and Vegas-oriented wallpaper behind the beds, from mod patterns to huge macro images of old Las Vegas signs. Brand new poolside rooms double as cabanas, with patio access direct to the pool, if you're interested in creating your own dayclub experience. If you're lucky, you'll have a great view of the **High Roller** (p. 155), the observation wheel that now marks the center of the Vegas skyline.

The pool itself now matches all the other beautiful pools you'll find on the Strip, located on the second floor of tower 3. It's 21-and-over, which obviously makes this not suitable for families, but ideal for young adults who are looking for a good time during the day.

There are plenty of dining options in the LINQ Promenade next door, but you can get your own celebrity chef fix at **Guy Fieri's Vegas Kitchen & Bar** (p. 117) right at the front of the hotel.

3535 Las Vegas Blvd. S. www.caesars.com/linq. © **800/634-6441** or 702/794-3366. 2,553 units. $61 and up double; $193 and up suite. Resort fee $29. Extra person $30. No discount for children. Free self- and valet parking. **Amenities:** 8 restaurants; casino; concierge; health club; heated outdoor pool; room service; spa; showrooms; salon; auto museum; wedding chapel; free Wi-Fi.

Treasure Island ★★

Though it's called Treasure Island (TI to locals), the pirate theme that gave this hotel its name is no longer as obvious. Recent renovations have toned down the property almost to a fault. Gone from the front is the swashbuckling Sirens of TI ship, once home to an innuendo-laden (and pretty stupid) show, to give way to a proposed shopping mall that is yet to open. Seems odd, with Fashion Show mall across Spring Mountain and the Shoppes at Palazzo right across the Boulevard, you'd think there are enough stores already to feed that fix. The hideous brown building that anchors the hotel at the corners of Spring Mountain and Las Vegas Boulevard houses a CVS and looks out of place, appearing more like a medical center than what should be a welcoming first sight for the formerly-fun property.

TI rooms, while pleasant enough, aren't that exciting to look at. Don't get us wrong, they're cozy, with warm, earthy tones, but the TI-branded ("Sensa-TIonal") pillow top mattresses are probably the best part of the deal.

Mystére (p. 208) is the longest running Cirque du Soleil show in town and is still considered one of the best.

3300 Las Vegas Blvd. S. (at Spring Mountain Rd.). www.treasureisland.com. ✆ **800/944-7444** or 702/894-7111. 2,885 units. $59 and up double; $99 and up suite. Resort fee $30. Extra person $30. Free for children 14 and under in parent's room. Free self- and valet parking. **Amenities:** 9 restaurants; buffet; casino; concierge; executive-level rooms; health club; outdoor pool; room service; showroom; spa; wedding chapels; free Wi-Fi.

NORTH STRIP

The northern end of the Strip, from Spring Mountain/Sands Road to Charleston Avenue, is not quite as densely populated with major casinos, but still has enough Vegas flair to make it worth your while.

Best for: Visitors who want to be on the Strip but want a slightly more manageable experience from a crowd-and-congestion perspective.

Drawbacks: It's a longer walk to most of what you'll want to see; some of the hotels here are past their prime.

Expensive

Wynn/Encore ★★★   The guy who basically invented the notion that Las Vegas could become a luxury destination for discerning guests? Steve Wynn. He's credited with opening the Mirage and Bellagio and transforming Las Vegas into the high-service capital we know it as today. That's the guy whose name is up on top of the hotel. He even signed the thing to let you know it's his.

His eponymous hotel and sister property Encore (because he did it again . . . duh) are the epitome of modern luxury. Breathe in the lovely (quite possibly pumped in, but we don't care) floral scent as you walk through the doors, and appreciate the lush red, gold, and green that accents the decor; it's like walking through one big manufactured, Wynn-branded garden. These resorts are also humongous. No matter if you walk into Wynn or Encore, it's a winding road through and around the casino floor, wherever you need to go. But there's so much to visually take in, you won't mind the trek.

The Wynn Tower features the hotel's standard rooms, but they're far from ordinary. Floor-to-ceiling windows let in lots of light, and, with a nice touch of feng shui, the beds face the windows as opposed to the walls, so you can wake up to a gorgeous view of the mountains or golf course. In fact, you won't even have to get out of the ultra-plush bed to open the curtains in the morning. With a touch of a button on the panel on the bedside table, you can cast them open and say "hello, Las Vegas!" Rooms are awash in creamy tones, and the gorgeously appointed bathrooms are encased in plenty of marble, including the oversize bathtub next to the gloriously powerful shower. Soak it up, this is as glamorous as it gets.

Wynn Tower Suites offer slightly larger accommodations, but also have the benefit of a private entrance for check-in. It's a higher price point, but the rate includes one ticket to **Steve Wynn's Showstoppers,** a Vegas-style revue with a 30-piece orchestra and just as many performers who sing iconic Broadway numbers that also happen to be favorite tunes of Wynn himself. They also kick in access to the Tower Suites' own pool.

The rooms of younger sister Encore next door are comparatively elegant and luxurious, following the same calming aesthetic, but with a few subtle, chic differences. Encore is all suites, with separate sitting and sleeping areas divided by a half wall. The black upholstery also makes the rooms seem far more contemporary. The pillow top Wynn Dream Bed lives up to its name (I had one of most restful sleeps I've ever had on the Strip on one). Bathrooms are downright palatial, with a giant tub next to the glass-enclosed shower, dual sinks and a 13-inch flatscreen TV, because feeling like you're rich means having a TV in your bathroom.

The Moroccan hammam that is Encore's spa is one of the most opulent on the Strip. The ornate mosaic tile in the lobby alone had me so entranced that it felt like the massage treatment was simply a nice bonus.

"Daylife" is a major component to Wynn and Encore, centered around three different pool areas, plus the clandestine digs of the Tower Suites pool. The Wynn and Encore pools are both calm and low-key, each with multiple bodies of water, Jacuzzis, and cabanas. The Encore European pool allows for topless sunbathing. **Encore Beach Club,** however, is another animal entirely: a day-time party on the weekends for guests more concerned with the live DJ than they are with their tans.

Eating at both these hotels will run up a bill, but high-end culinary options such as **Costa di Mare** (p. 123), **Sinatra** (p. 124), **Botero,** and **Wing Lei,** are totally worth the splurge.

3131 Las Vegas Blvd. S. (corner of Spring Mountain Rd.). www.wynnlasvegas.com. ℂ **888/320-9966** or 702/770-7100. 4,750 units. $259 and up double. Resort fee $32. Extra person $50. No discount for children. Free self- and valet parking. **Amenities:** 19 restaurants; buffet; casino; concierge; executive-level rooms; health club; outdoor pools; room service; showrooms; spa; wedding chapels; free Wi-Fi.

Moderate

SLS Las Vegas ★ What's old becomes new again in Las Vegas. The iconic Sahara Hotel shuttered in 2011, and with it, one of the last outward vestiges of vintage Vegas disappeared. In its place, the sleek, sophisticated SLS ushered in the new guard of Vegas resorts, as well as made everyone take notice of the new things happening north of Wynn.

SLS is part of a chain of hotels that also have outposts in Los Angeles and Miami—if that tells you how trendy this place wants to be. They have big guns behind that mandate: power designer Philippe Starck was at the helm transforming the formerly kitschy Sahara into a temple of modern aesthetics, with edgy design, ornate chandeliers, and plenty of metallic colors throughout the casino floor.

But what they didn't take into account is the hotel's location. Sure, if you build it they will come, but the visitors SLS wants to come—the hip, L.A.

weekenders, millennials with disposable income, the young and rich who aren't necessarily celebrities—aren't filling the place up as fast as management would like. SLS's nearest neighbors are Circus Circus, Stratosphere, the World's Largest Gift Shop and the abandoned Fontainbleu resort project. As a result, the SLS is the swankiest spot on that end of the Strip, but still offers rooms at near-budget prices.

That's good news for budgeteers as the 325-square-foot rooms (small for the Strip, but average for the area) are as hip as you'd find in any modern boutique hotel in a big city. Platform beds give the illusion that sleepers are floating off the ground. Well-placed, wall-size mirrors—on the walls and the ceilings—make the room feel bigger, while cold metal and white bathroom features make good use of little space, with infinity sinks, and dual-head, glass-enclosed showers. In the "Lux Rooms" the designer juxtaposed classic French chandeliers and wall coverings featuring drawn-on trim, with modern furnishings and a stark white palette.

Many of the restaurants came under culinary director chef José Andrés, whose **Bazaar Meat** (p. 122) quickly became one of the most talked-about restaurants in town. Los Angeles imports **Cleo** (p. 122) and **Umami Burger** have also been a big hit with guests.

SLS owner SBE Entertainment is also in the nightlife business, so it's got a few clubs to pay attention to as well, including **Foxtail** (p. 230), **The Sayers Club,** and daylife party **Foxtail Pool Club.**

Now that SLS is built, it just needs some time for everyone to come.

2535 Las Vegas Blvd. S. (corner of Sahara Ave.). www.slslasvegas.com. © **888/991-0887** or 702/761-7757 1,600 units. $55 and up double; $143 and up suites. Resort fee $30. Extra person $30. Free self- and valet parking. **Amenities:** 8 restaurants; executive-level rooms; fitness center; outdoor pools; room service; free Wi-Fi.

Stratosphere Las Vegas Hotel & Casino ★

One of the best ways to get your bearings when you're in Las Vegas: look for the Stratosphere. It's at the very north tip of the Strip, and whatever you do, don't call it the Space Needle (the Stratosphere Tower, the tallest freestanding tower in the United States, is twice the size, dammit!).

Beyond its size and the whiz-bang rides at the top, the Stratosphere has failed, in recent years at least, to make much of an impact on Las Vegas' tourist market. So it finally stopped trying, and today, it's a a no-muss, no-fuss budget accommodation.

Which is perfectly fine because heaven knows there's an army of budget-conscious visitors just looking for a clean, inexpensive place to sleep. And Stratosphere fits that bill. So what if the exterior is dated and the standard rooms are so bland you'll have trouble remembering what they look like as you exit them? They're just fine. And for those who want slightly better than that, but still at an impressively reasonable price (usually) the "Select" category digs are surprisingly contemporary, with a warm color palate of red and brown, and such essentials as flatscreen TVs, and alarm clocks with MP3 docks. Bathrooms run small, but at these rates, who's complaining?

And you'll be within spitting distance of the best perch from which to see the entire Las Vegas Valley. At the top of the tower the elegant continental restaurant, **Top of the World** (p. 125) is in motion, giving guests a 360-degree view of the surrounding area, making one full revolution every 80 minutes. Thrill seekers climb up even higher to hang out (literally) on crazy rides that are discussed more on p. 157.

The big downside to staying here? The immediate area surrounding the hotel is a little shady. At night, take a cab or car if you're leaving the hotel.

2000 Las Vegas Blvd. S. (btw. St. Louis and Baltimore aves.). www.stratospherehotel. com. © **800/998-6937** or 702/380-7777. 2,444 units. $52 and up double; $146 and up suite. Resort fee $25. Extra person $15. Children 12 and under stay free in parent's room. Free self- and valet parking. **Amenities:** 8 restaurants; buffet; several fast-food outlets; arcade; casino; concierge; executive-level rooms; large pool area w/great views of the Strip; room service; showrooms; wedding chapel; fitness center; Wi-Fi (for a fee).

Inexpensive

Circus Circus Hotel & Casino ★

Cheap? Check. Cheesy? Check. The last-standing reminder of when Vegas tried to go family-friendly? You betcha and thank goodness. This is one of the few places in Vegas where cash-strapped families can come without worry, knowing they won't mortgage the house for a vacation, and that they can let their kids loose to be entertained (or entertain themselves). They do the latter on the midway level, with its hundreds of carnival games and non-stop circus performers. And we don't mean a couple of sad jugglers or cut-rate clowns honking their noses—there is a permanent circus with serious athletes, from jaw-dropping trapeze artists and high wire acts, to acrobats, magicians, and yes, even some truly fantastic jugglers. It's this free, delightful spectacle that keeps Circus Circus the best option for traveling families.

Sure, Circus Circus is a budget resort/casino in the sense that it's way cheaper than anything new on the Strip, but you'll be hard-pressed to find another that's as massive and accommodating to all ages. There are almost 4,000 rooms over the three towers and five low-rise, motel-like Circus Manor buildings that sit on the property's 68 acres. Circus Circus is also home to the only RV park on the Strip. If you're going to be a stickler for modern appointments, the West and Casino towers were the most recently remodeled, with flatscreen TVs, Wi-Fi, and comfy pillow top mattresses. Standard room sizes are all comparable, averaging about 360 square feet, so the only thing that sets these two towers apart from the Skyrise Tower is that the latter feels slightly less blah and dated.

The enormous hotel also sports a casino to match its size, clocking in at 101,000 square feet, for when parents want to play a few games of their own. The dining options are mostly kid-friendly, with pizza, sandwiches, and a buffet to satisfy everyone's taste. **The Steakhouse** (p. 124) is the hotel's culinary diamond in the rough, a bona fide classic Vegas red meat joint with white tablecloths, good cuts of dry-aged beef, and stellar service.

coming ATTRACTIONS

Heavily themed hotels faded away in the 1990s, but may make a return with the proposed **Resorts World Las Vegas.** The Asian-inspired, $7-billion project from Malaysia-based gambling giant Genting Gaming will have at least 3,500 rooms, a 175,000-square-foot casino (the biggest in Vegas), a 4,000-seat show-room, an indoor waterpark, a panda habitat, and replicas of the Great Wall of China and the Terra Cotta Warriors. It will be located on the North Strip in place of the old Stardust and should open by late 2017.

We did say this place was family-friendly right? Indoor amusement park **Adventuredome** (p. 157) pleases kids of all ages—even the grown-up ones.

2880 Las Vegas Blvd. S. (btw. Circus Circus and Convention Center drives). www.circus circus.com. © **877/434-9175** or 702/734-0410. 3,767 units. $26 and up double. Resort fee $23 per night. Extra person $20. Children 17 and under stay free in parent's room. Free self-parking, valet $8–$13. **Amenities:** 7 restaurants; buffet; several fast-food outlets; casino; circus acts and midway-style carnival games; executive-level rooms; outdoor pools; room service; wedding chapel; free Wi-Fi.

DOWNTOWN

The original Las Vegas, with classic and historic hotels, is Downtown; the glare of Glitter Gulch has become the must-see tourist destination of the Fremont Street Experience.

Best for: Budget-minded tourists; those looking for a friendlier atmosphere than the snooty Strip.

Drawbacks: Harder-to-find upscale experiences; the surrounding neighborhoods can be a bit rough.

Moderate

The D Las Vegas Casino Hotel ★ Why is this place called "The D"? Well, it's a nod to Detroit, the hometown of the property owners; or it could reference to the nickname of CEO Derek Stevens. Final guess: an homage to the neighborhood of Downtown Las Vegas. Nah, scratch that. With all the Detroit references, this may well be the only hotel in the United States, outside of Detroit itself, that uses Motor City as its inspiration. (Non-Detroit related, but just as quirky, a large-scale, bronze replica of Brussels' Mannekin Pis statue also greets guests outside the main valet, an homage to the Stevens' Belgian roots.)

And you know what? That downright-weird homage works. The two-level casino floor is far more airy than when it had its Irish theme (under the old management). The 638 rooms all got a nice refresher too, with bold red and black accents throughout.They're not the fanciest hotel rooms you'll find in town, but for Downtown, and for the price, these are veritable sanctuaries.

The aptly named Longbar—the longest bar in Nevada, naturally—is one of the few bars left in Vegas where flair bartenders whip bottles about their heads before they make you a drink. Detroit exports **American Coney Island** (open 24 hr., like the original) and **Joe Vicari's Andiamo Steakhouse** make The D a favorite stop for Motor City natives, but both are tasty enough to warrant a trip even if you've never been there.

Final fun (or perhaps odd fact): The D is one of two hotels in town (the other is Golden Gate, see below) to accept crypto-currency Bitcoin as payment at its front desk, restaurants and retail shop.

301 Fremont St. (at 3rd St.). www.thed.com. ✆ **800/274-5825** or 702/388-2400. 638 units. $29 and up double. Resort fee $20. Extra person $20. Children 11 and under stay free in parent's room. Free self- and valet parking. **Amenities:** 3 restaurants; lounge; casino; concierge; unheated outdoor pool; room service; free Wi-Fi.

The Downtown Grand ★★　We said good-bye to Lady Luck Casino in order to welcome the Downtown Grand, and to be fair, we think Lady Luck is okay with it. Because now she's been reborn as a hipster hotel with a trendy, industrial aesthetic. Reclaimed factory space? Exposed brick walls? Funky chandeliers and framed artwork on the ceilings? Are we still in Vegas? The 25,000-square-foot casino floor reminds us, of course, yes.

There are five different room types to choose from, the smallest a respectable 350 square feet, which is fine if you don't want to move around a whole lot. The next level up, Premium, are usually corner rooms at 450 square feet, with room for extra seats. All come equipped with conventional and USB plugs near the beds, 46-inch flatscreens, and are decorated straight out of the Crate & Barrel's CB2 catalog.

There were a few hiccups with the restaurants as the Downtown Grand tried to forge a culinary identity. It started with eight eateries, but now only four remain (three of which are across the street from the hotel proper): **S+O,** its 24-hour restaurant, plus **Pizza Rock** and old-timer **Triple George Grill,** all of which serve Downtown Grand guests.

The pool on the roof is a nice touch. It's big enough that it doesn't feel jam packed, even when non-guest locals hang out on a Sunday afternoon, which happens often, and means the scene here has a definite cool-neighborhood feel. Guests enjoy meeting the locals and vice-versa.

206 N. 3rd St. (btw. Stewart and Ogden aves.). www.downtowngrand.com. ✆ **888/384-7263.** 680 units. $31 and up double. Resort fee $22. Free self- and valet parking. **Amenities:** 4 restaurants; 6 bars; rooftop pool; fitness center; casino; room service; free Wi-Fi.

Golden Nugget ★★　One of the most iconic facades of Downtown, the white and gold sparkling face of the Golden Nugget may seem like it's a throwback, but the interior is light years ahead. Since 2005, the Golden Nugget has spent $300 million on upgrades to keep the hotel in step with Las Vegas' ever-changing zeitgeist. The Gold Tower boasts lots of gold and black mod decor, thanks to a recent $15 million redo, plus the spa and salon just saw $800,000 worth of upgrades. The Rush Tower rooms were unveiled in 2009 and are just as comfortable and plush, but bigger, and with a more sedate color palette. Both offer cloud-like pillow top mattresses, 42-inch plasma TVs and excellent views. Hopefully the Carson, the last of the towers, will get a redo in the near future.

But why are we talking rooms? It's the pool area that's made this place justly famous. At **The Tank,** you can swim (kind of literally) with sharks, or at the very least, go screaming down a tube that cuts through the live shark aquarium. The three-story pool complex also features waterfalls and a bar that stays open year-round, even when the pool isn't.

If you've come to see the Hand of Faith, the world's largest gold nugget, unfortunately you'll have to travel to the Laughlin, Nevada Golden Nugget, where it is currently on display.

129 E. Fremont St. (at Casino Center Blvd.). www.goldennugget.com. ⓒ **800/846-5336** or 702/385-7111. 2,419 units. $69 and up double; $259 and up suite. Resort fee $25. Extra person $20. No discount for children. Free self- and valet parking (with validation). **Amenities:** 8 restaurants; buffet; bars, lounges, and nightclub; casino; executive-level rooms; health club; outdoor pool; room service; showroom; spa; Wi-Fi (for a fee).

Inexpensive

California Hotel & Casino ★ Las Vegas is sometimes referred to as the "Ninth Island," in that so many people from Hawaii end up here. And those trading in their own paradise for ours, just for a visit, like to stay at the California, which has manufactured its own brand of "Aloha." A Hawaiian theme touches all the public areas of the hotel, from casino dealers decked out in gaudy Hawaiian shirts to restaurant menus heavy with Island faves such as saimin, moco loco, and the ever-popular oxtail soup.

Guestrooms depart from "island style" (thankfully, I'd say). Like sister properties the Downtown Fremont Hotel and Main Street Station, rooms are understated, but comfortable (to be honest, they appear to be cookie cutters of each other) with standard amenities all at decent prices. Other than the Hawaiian theme, staying at one of these hotels is just like staying at any of the others in the same family. But for the value, and if you really need to get your spam sushi fix, the California does in a pinch.

12 Ogden Ave. (at 1st St.). www.thecal.com. ⓒ **800/634-6255** or 702/385-1222. 781 units. $55 and up double. No resort fee. Extra person $10. Children 13 and under stay free in parent's room. Free self- and valet parking. **Amenities:** 5 restaurants; casino; small rooftop pool; Wi-Fi (for a fee).

El Cortez Hotel & Casino ★ With the revitalization of the Fremont East Entertainment District (that's at the other end of the Fremont Street Experience tunnel), El Cortez managed to dust itself off, revamp and renew with the area, which is now teeming with new, trendy bars and restaurants. Touting itself as the "longest continuously operating hotel-casino in Las

Vegas," El Cortez's rich history began in 1941, and is peppered with names like Meyer Lansky and Bugsy Siegel (two of the "businessmen" who purchased it in 1945), and Jackie Gaughan (who bought it in 1963, selling it to corporate interests in 2008). The hotel is now on the National Register of Historic Places, and the sign that sits atop the corner of Fremont Street and Seventh Streets has been the same since the 1940s.

Ten Designer Suites are the result of collaboration between the hotel and Las Vegas Design Center, where four lucky winners showcase their take on the city's iconic aesthetic: live out your Sin City fantasy in a mob-themed suite, in 1950's glam chic, or in digs reminiscent of vintage Vegas, among others. Revealed in 2009, the tony Cabana Suites are in a separate tower entirely, a new batch of 64 boutique rooms that straddle both vintage decor and ultra-contemporary design. The original rooms may pale in comparison to all the new additions. They're vintage as in "traditional" not "hipster," but run larger than plenty of other rooms Downtown, and are usually priced quite affordably.

During Downtown's home-grown autumn music, food, and arts festival, *Life is Beautiful,* El Cortez is smack dab in the middle of it all. If you're planning on attending, staying here is a fantastic idea. But thanks to being set right in the heart of the now-gentrifying Downtown, it's still one of the coolest places to stay, even when there's not a festival going on.

600 Fremont St. (btw. 6th and 7th sts.). www.elcortezhotelcasino.com. ℭ **800/634-6703** or 702/385-5200. 428 units. $28 and up double; $55 and up suite. Resort fee $9. Extra person $10. No discount for children. Free self- and valet parking. **Amenities:** 2 restaurants; casino; free Wi-Fi.

Four Queens ★   Old school Vegas is alive and well at Four Queens, which has been open since 1966. It's a popular spot for those serious about gambling, who don't need all the frills of a Strip casino and are fine with camping out in one spot as their stacks of chips rises and falls.

The rooms won't be winning interior design awards anytime soon, thanks to the garishly striped drapes and non-descript standard hotel art, but they serve their purpose as a clean, comfortable place to rest your head and gather yourself for a night of braving the Fremont Street Experience, which is right outside Four Queens' door. The South Tower's rooms are bigger, but the North Tower offers views of the hubbub of FSE, so choose wisely.

In-house Chicago Brewing Company serves a satisfying bar menu, as well as a selection of its own microbrews, which you can get in a 64-ounce to-go jug known as a growler, though it may be cumbersome to tote around as you walk Downtown. Local prom favorite **Hugo's Cellar** (p. 126) is one of the last examples you can find of vintage Vegas dining, a proficient gourmet room that still greets ladies with long-stemmed red roses.

202 Fremont St. (at Casino Center Blvd.). www.fourqueens.com. ℭ **800/634-6045** or 702/385-4011. 690 units. $39 and up double; $110 and up suite. No resort fee. Extra person $15. Children 11 and under stay free in parent's room. Free self- and valet parking. **Amenities:** 3 restaurants; 2 bars; casino; room service; Wi-Fi (for a fee).

Fremont Hotel & Casino ★   You know those Vegas movie montages where the camera gives a 360-spinning view from the overwhelmed traveler who is visually assaulted by the flashing lights and activity of old Vegas? That's usually filmed right in front of the Fremont Hotel, under the $70 million LED canopy that is the Fremont Street Experience. The Fremont is pretty much Ground Zero if you plan on spending the majority of your time in the area. With rooms that start at around 280 square feet, you're paying (not a lot) for location here. Rooms are clean, comfortable, and decorated with serene, low-key and modern furnishings to give your mind a rest from the constant activity that's just outside.

Food isn't a focus here, with a couple of chain restaurants and obligatory buffet (though we'd hardly call eight stations a decent buffet by Vegas standards), but you're close enough to all the new culinary delights opening Downtown that it won't matter. Also those looking for a day at the pool will be disappointed; you'll have to go across the street to sister hotel California if you want to catch some pool time.

200 E. Fremont St. (btw. Casino Center Blvd. and 3rd St.). www.fremontcasino.com. ✆ **800/634-6182** or 702/385-3232. 447 units. $48 and up double. No resort fee. Extra person $10. No discount for children. Free valet parking; no self-parking. **Amenities:** 3 restaurants; buffet; casino; access to outdoor pool at nearby California Hotel; Wi-Fi (for a fee).

The Golden Gate ★   Las Vegas just celebrated its sesquicentennial this year, and the only spot that's been around nearly as long is The Golden Gate, formerly known as The Nevada Hotel, which opened in 1906. Even then it was at the forefront of modern technology. The hotel was the site of the first telephone in the state in 1907. Its number was 1.

The hotel survived all attempts to outlaw fun in Nevada—gambling from 1910 to 1931, and Prohibition from 1920 to 1933—and became a mainstay in Las Vegas lore, through the roaring '20s, the Rat Pack era, and the whispered days of the Vegas mob. Frank Sinatra used to sit at the Casino Bar before and after performances. The bar still serves his signature Frankie Two Fingers: two fingers of Jack Daniels, splash of water, and four ice cubes.

In 2012, Golden Gate finally underwent a much-needed renovation after stagnating for 50 years, remodeling 106 of the rooms that had been there since 1906, and adding a new, five-story luxury tower, including two showgirl-inspired penthouses, complete with giant feather motifs in the carpet, vintage photographs on the walls of beautiful girls in ornate headdresses, and black and whites of Marilyn Monroe. These suites take over the entire fifth floor. The new, and pretty fab, non-suite rooms give a nod to the design aesthetic of *Mad Men:* some swinging '60s mod patterns on the curtains and furnishings; black, brown, and red leather touches and Art-deco accents, plus requisite vintage photos of Vegas celebrities who frequented the hotel in its heyday. The rooms and bathrooms are tiny, but well-appointed, with queen beds and 32-inch flatscreen TVs; suites have wet bars and sectional couches.

The 99-cent shrimp cocktail was allegedly born here, and, for what we can only assume is nostalgia, is still a draw at the 24-hour coffee shop Du-Par's, despite it now being $3.99.

Golden Gate's longevity also means it embraces the trappings of the 21st century. This, along with The D, is one of the first hotels to accept cryptocurrency Bitcoin as payment (though you still can't gamble with Bitcoin—they're not that progressive).

1 Fremont St. www.goldengatecasino.com. © **800/426-1906** or 702/385-1906. 120 units. $25 and up for up to 4 people. Resort fee $20. Free self- and valet parking. **Amenities:** 2 restaurants; casino; bars; free Wi-Fi.

Main Street Station ★★ The Victorian-themed Main Street Station is an underrated hotel and one of the great bargains in the city.

Taking a walk through the casino is like being in a well-organized, less-dusty antique shop; the chandeliers come from the Coca-Cola building in Austin and the Figaro Opera House in Paris, France, and the ornate hammered-tin ceilings are also vintage. Men get a more modern glimpse of history in the restroom off the casino floor, where there's a bona fide chunk of the Berlin Wall on display.

The rooms run a little small at 400 square feet, but are adequate for a Downtown stay. Sadly their contemporary decor is a departure from all the historical artifacts downstairs. Suites are slightly larger, but their color schemes and furnishings are more dated than in the rooms. The amenities are all up-to-date, though, including flatscreen TVs, cable TV, Internet for purchase, and refrigerators. *Tip:* The noisier part of the tower is the north side, nearer the freeway, so light sleepers should opt for the south side.

You can head right over to Fremont Street Experience for a full-on Vegas experience, but if you crave something more low-key, **Triple 7 Brewery** is right inside the hotel. Its catch-all menu (steaks, seafood, pizza, and even sushi) is fine, but the surprise comes from the decent selection of microbrews. There's a seasonal selection, including a rotating IPA on draft. The **Garden Court Buffet** remains a favorite in town and is described in chapter 5.

200 N. Main St. (btw. Fremont St. and I-95). www.mainstreetcasino.com. © **800/465-0711** or 702/387-1896. 406 units. $36 and up double. No resort fee. Extra person $10. No discount for children. Free self- and valet parking. **Amenities:** 2 restaurants; buffet; casino; access to outdoor pool at nearby California Hotel; free shuttle to Strip and sister properties; Wi-Fi $9.99 for 24 hr.

Oasis at Gold Spike ★★ When Zappos CEO Tony Hsieh moved his company into Las Vegas' old town hall and invested $350 million of his own money into buying properties and backing small businesses who promised to move into Downtown, it looked like the area was on the verge of a total turn-around. That initiative, called the Downtown Project, hasn't yet created the promised Las Vegas utopia (in fact, the success of the endeavor is still being hotly debated), but one of the results is that the "Project" went into the hotel business. Oasis is the hotel portion of Gold Spike, a formerly sketchy hotel and casino that was transformed into a trendy bar and playground (the Living Room offers pool tables and shuffleboard, while the Backyard features giant Jenga blocks and boards to play cornhole).

I have to say: the Oasis lives up to its name. It's a serene, 44-room getaway from all millennial-oriented fun downstairs. Look past the fact that the rooms are referred to as "crash pads" and appreciate that they're custom designed with beautiful minimalist art, comfy furnishings, and solid walls to keep them quiet. Ultra-contemporary touches include co-working space in the lobby, bike rentals, and turntables with a selection of vinyl. The bathrooms are more spacious than normal, with spa showers, but no tubs. The pool courtyard is a bit on the small side, but not too small for a hotel with less than 50 rooms. It's latest claim to fame is that the Oasis was home to the 31st (!) season of MTV's *The Real World* (yes, that show is apparently still running). Should you want to start being "real" yourself, the decked-out, 5,000-square-foot, 3-bedroom penthouse is available for a stay.

Note: This place is so modern, it doesn't have in-room phones or alarm clocks (since most guests simply use smartphones). But they will furnish them upon request.

217 Las Vegas Blvd. www.oasisatgoldspike.com. ☏ **702/768-9823.** 44 units. $39 and up double; $69 and up suite. Resort fee $20. No discount for children. Free self- and valet parking. **Amenities:** Restaurant; room service; fitness center; business center; pets welcome (for a fee); outdoor pool; free Wi-Fi.

The Plaza Hotel & Casino ★★ How the Plaza, which has stood on Main Street since 1971, got so darn nice looking is one of those only-in-Vegas tales. We can thank the Fontainebleu, a luxury property that was supposed to go up on the north end of the Strip, for going bankrupt halfway through construction. When it couldn't be finished, all of its "soft goods"—furniture, upholstery, carpets, beddings—had to go, and it all went to pretty-up the Plaza as part of its $35 million renovation.

And with the Fontainebleu's new furnishings (cushy beds and sheets, fab vintage photos for the walls, Keurig coffeemakers in the suites), you'd never guess that the Plaza had once been one of Downtown's dingiest properties. Today, guests feel they've snagged a luxurious Strip experience at rock-bottom Downtown prices.

The hotel anchors the Fremont Street Experience, so you can walk right out the front door under the neon canopy, but make it a night in taking dinner at **Oscar's** (p. 126)—the namesake restaurant of former Las Vegas mayor Oscar Goodman—or gorge yourself on the obscenely large plates of food from **Hash House A-Go-Go** (p. 117).

The notion of "you get what you pay for" doesn't apply at the Plaza; you'll get so much more than you expect.

1 Main St. www.plazahotelcasino.com. ☏ **800/634-6575** or 702/386-2110. 1,003 units. $29 and up double. Resort fee $15. Extra person $15. No discount for children. Free self- and valet parking. **Amenities:** 4 restaurants; food court; casino; showrooms; bars and lounges; wedding chapel; salon; fitness center; outdoor pool; tennis courts; free Wi-Fi.

JUST OFF THE STRIP

Within about a mile east, west, and south of the Strip are dozens of hotels, many of which offer the same kind of casino-resort experience but usually at significantly cheaper rates.

Best for: People with a car at their disposal; those who want to be near the action but not in the thick of it.

Drawbacks: Traffic to and from the Strip can be a nightmare, even if you are only driving a mile.

Expensive

Hard Rock Hotel & Casino ★★
For visitors seeking to achieve a certain level of "cool," the Hard Rock is the place. The off-Strip hotel advertises itself as where celebrities party when they're in town (and to be fair, sometimes they do), selling the notion that if you stay here, you'll be as groovy as the stars whose memorabilia decorates the casino floor and walls, or maybe even a . . . Kardashian? They're still cool, right?

Even if you haven't had your 15 minutes of fame, the rooms will make you feel like a big shot. Original Casino Tower rooms boast ultramodern furnishings, a steely color palette, and French doors that fully open onto a railing, but no balcony (just don't channel your inner Keith Richards and throw anything out the window). Paradise Tower rooms run slightly larger and are warmer in color, but have the same amenities, including fully stocked mini-bars, 40-inch TVs, and extra-large showers. The newest, HRH Tower features all suites, but departs from the color scheme and goes with clean white all around, from the linen and furnishings to the TV hutch that separates the sleeping and living rooms. Open-minded guests might be interested in the fetish-themed Provocateur Penthouse, enhanced with furniture custom made for more risqué activities.

Notorious weekend pool party **Rehab** is now more than 10 years old and just as debauched as ever, with plenty of hard, barely-clad bodies jamming themselves into the pool for all-day booze and DJ-fueled revelry. If you're in your early 20s and are trying to spend your entire Vegas trip drunk and wet, you'll be at Rehab. That's not to say if you fall outside of that demographic, you'll have a bad time. **The Joint** welcomes huge-named rock acts, and the nightclubs are a steady stream of hip hop and EDM acts each weekend. There's enough varying levels of cool that everyone can leave feeling like they're the rock star.

4455 Paradise Rd. (at Harmon Ave.). www.hardrockhotel.com. ℂ **800/473-7625** or 702/693-5000. 1,489 units. $48 and up double; $177 and up suite. Resort fee $28. Extra person $35. Children 12 and under stay free in parent's room. Free self- and valet parking. **Amenities:** 6 restaurants; casino; concert venues; concierge; fitness center; spa; executive-level rooms; outdoor pools w/lazy river and sandy-beach bottom; room service; free Wi-Fi.

Palms Casino Resort ★★
The Palms first planted its stake in pop culture as the home to seven strangers in the first installment of *Real World: Las*

RELIABLE CHAIN alternatives

Most people who come to Las Vegas want to stay in one of the big megaresorts on the Strip. But sometimes budget, timing, or having points useable for a free stay may steer you to a more traditional lodging. Just about every hotel chain has at least one outlet in the city, and all offer the kind of reliable, comfortable, and often affordable accommodations that they are known for. Here are some examples, all of which are located within a mile or two of the Strip, so you can have the best of both worlds.

Best Western Mardi Gras, 3500 Paradise Rd.; mardigrasinn.com; (C) 800/634-6501
Best Western McCarran, 4970 Paradise Rd.; bwvegas.com; (C) 800/275-4743
Candlewood Suites, 4034 Paradise Rd.; ihg.com/candlewood; (C) 877/226-3539
Clarion Hotel, 305 Convention Center Dr.; choicehotels.com; (C) 702/952-8000
Courtyard by Marriott, 3275 Paradise Rd.; marriott.com; (C) 800/661-1064
Courtyard by Marriott, 5845 Dean Martin Dr.; marriott.com; (C) 800/321-2211
Embassy Suites, 3600 Paradise Rd.; lasvegasembassysuites.com (C) 800/362-2779
Embassy Suites, 4315 Swenson St.; embassysuites.com; (C) 800/362-2779
Fairfield Inn by Marriott, 3850 S. Paradise Rd.; marriott.com; (C) 702/791-0899

Fairfield Inn Suites, 5775 Dean Martin Dr.; marriott.com; (C) 702/895-9810
Hampton Inn, 4975 S. Dean Martin Dr.; hamptoninntropicana.com; (C) 702/948-8100
Holiday Inn Express, 5760 Polaris Ave.; hiexpress.com/lasvegas; (C) 888/465-4329
Hyatt Place, 4520 Paradise Rd.; lasvegas.place.hyatt.com; (C) 702/369-3366
La Quinta Inn and Suites, 3970 Paradise Rd.; laquintalasvegasairportnorth.com; (C) 800/753-3757
Las Vegas Marriott, 325 Convention Center Dr.; marriott.com; (C) 702/650-2000
Renaissance Las Vegas, 3400 Paradise Rd.; renaissancelasvegas.com; (C) 702/784-5700
Residence Inn, 3225 Paradise Rd.; marriott.com; (C) 800/677-8328
Residence Inn, 370 Hughes Center Dr.; marriott.com; (C) 702/650-5510
Staybridge Suites, 5735 Dean Martin Dr.; staybridge.com/lasvegas; (C) 800/238-8889
Super 8, 4250 Koval Lane; super8.com; (C) 800/454-3213
Travelodge, 3735 Las Vegas Blvd. S.; travelodgevegasstrip.com; (C) 800/525-4055

Vegas, then as a constant backdrop on E! reality show *The Girls Next Door* when Hugh Hefner–mates visited the Playboy-branded tower, now known as the Fantasy Tower. These days, Palms has maintained its cool factor without needing any camera time, with a recent multi-million dollar renovation that included all the rooms in the Ivory Tower, nightclubs, and new restaurants.

You've got to be a serious high roller to even think about staying in the insane suites of the Fantasy Tower, which include the two-floor, Hardwood Suite, complete with basketball court, or the sensually charged Erotic Suite, which features a huge rotating bed and mirrored ceiling among other, ahem, amenities. For us mere mortals, there's the Ivory Tower (home of the still-pimped-out Real World Suite). The original building of the Palms, with its

428 guest rooms, even at 440 square feet, is still super swank. Warm wood furnishings nicely play off the fuchsia, teal, and silver of the throw blanket and chaise lounge. A stark-white bathroom is meant to evoke being in the spa, and it's pretty close, with open showers (no tubs, sorry), frosted glass and lots of marble. If you really need to stretch out, upgrade to the Superior Room with its Jacuzzi, or if you're feeling especially fancy, a 1,200-square-foot one-bedroom at Palms Place, which features a state-of-the-art whirlpool bathtub.

But tub or not, you won't have a problem cooling down when you've got the sprawling pool deck just below. **Ditch Fridays,** a massive 21-and-over pool party, remains a rowdy way for visitors and hotel guests to kick off their weekends—though if you'd prefer to relax on Friday afternoons, you may want to request a room that doesn't overlook the pool. Also, there is lots more skin both in and around the pool now that world's largest Hooters (seriously) has set up shop on the perimeter.

The nightlife scene is going through a little facelift right now; only **Ghostbar** remains as a club option. But Palms' restaurant game has remained strong. The addition of Chicago Chinese restaurant **Lao Sze Chuan** has been met with great fanfare, while **Alizé** and **N9NE Steakhouse** have remained consistently good dining options. Brunch favorite Simon at Palms Place has been replaced by burger-centric **Café 6,** but still offers the same serene views of the Palms Place pool.

4321 W. Flamingo Rd. (just west of I-15). www.palms.com. © **866/942-7777** or 702/942-7777. 1,300 units. $79 and up double. Resort fee $29. Extra person $30. No discount for children. Free self- and valet parking. **Amenities:** 9 restaurants; buffet; food court; casino; concierge; executive-level rooms; movie theaters; nightclubs and bars; showroom; outdoor pool; room service; spa; fitness center; free Wi-Fi.

Moderate

Rio All-Suite Hotel & Casino ★★   The multi-towered Rio stands in all its purple and red-striped glory just off the main drag of the Strip on Flamingo. Though it's technically off-Strip, it's got all the excitement of the storied Boulevard. This is definitely a rowdy spot geared towards revelers, so if you're looking for a quiet getaway, the Rio might not be your cup of tea.

The other selling point here is the (usually) moderate price of the digs, but I must insert one warning: though it's a self-billed "all-suite" hotel, don't be misled. Instead of separate sleeping and living spaces, the rooms are merely bigger, clocking in starting at 600 square feet, with couches and coffee tables across from the beds. The newly-renovated Samba Suites add a much needed splash of teal to the otherwise neutral colors of the original rooms, as well as upgraded, dark-wood furniture and chrome finishes.

No matter which room you go with, floor-to-ceiling windows and a high floor choice offer spectacular views of the area.

There's a vast array of entertainment options at the Rio, from long-running magicians *Penn & Teller,* to eye candy performances by the *Chippendales,* not to mention rooftop nightclub and lounge **VooDoo.** You won't go hungry either, with its sprawling **Carnival World & Seafood Buffet,** Chinese favorite **KJ Kitchen and Dimsum** and Guy Fieri's newest Mexican spot, **El Burro Burracho.** Just make sure you wait a spell after you eat if you're going to take a ride on the **VooDoo Zipline** that suspends you 490 feet in the air and, well, zips you back and forth between the two towers. If a few rounds of golf is on your agenda, the Rio features access to tee times at **Rio Secco** and **Cascata Golf** courses.

3700 W. Flamingo Rd. (just west of I-15). www.riolasvegas.com. ✆ **888/752-9746** or 702/777-7777. 2,582 units. $39 and up suite. Resort fee $29. Extra person $30. No discount for children. **Amenities:** 11 restaurants; 2 buffets; multiple fast-food outlets; casino; concierge; executive-level rooms; golf course; health club; spa; outdoor pools; showrooms; room service; free Wi-Fi.

Tuscany Suites & Casino ★
While you're not exactly transported to Italy when you're at Tuscany Suites, you're definitely transplanted to a more laid-back Sin City (and one that's less costly than a Strip hotel).

The all-suite hotel offers a high level of customer service and generous rooms that start at 650 square feet of space. They're nothing to write home about in the looks department, though they do boast separate dining areas, and come equipped with refrigerators and wet bars, which make this a family-friendly option. Each has either two queens or one king bed alongside a living room with full-size couch and chair. A small casino is also on site.

The immense conference and banquet space brings in most of Tuscany Suites' clientele, so many revelers carry on their event from their hall straight to the Piazza Lounge for after-parties before retiring to their rooms. The lounge is often bumping with great live entertainment, and packed with guests having a fantastic time.

255 E. Flamingo Rd. www.tuscanylv.com. ✆ **877/887-2261** or 702/893-8933. 700 units. $79 and up suite. Resort fee $24. Extra person $20. Children 12 and under stay free in parent's room. **Amenities:** 3 restaurants; lounge; casino; concierge; fitness center; outdoor pool; room service; free Wi-Fi.

Westgate Las Vegas Resort and Casino ★
Formerly the Las Vegas Hilton—and briefly, LVH—Westgate has taken over the hotel most convenient to the Convention Center. The developers are best known for their time-share properties around the country. They treated the 40-year-old hotel and casino to a multi-million-dollar facelift, hoping to make the iconic property near the north of the Strip relevant once again. Though they converted some of the rooms into timeshares while they were at it, it still operates primarily as a hotel, so you don't need to own one to reserve a night here.

The premium rooms are still efficient, but since it's a new hotel, try to stay in one of the updated rooms or 300 suites. The Signature Rooms reveal some much-needed color and pizzazz, and Hollywood-inspired touches like black tufted-leather headboards and red-leather pullout sofas in the king suites. Marble floors, Keurig coffeemakers, 60-inch TVs, and sateen linens have guests relaxing in style.

The hotel has a lot of dining options, including the country's largest **Benihana,** Park City, Utah transplant **The Edge Steakhouse** and a 24-hour American comfort food spot, **Sid's Café,** named for Westgate Las Vegas owner David Siegel's father, Sid Siegel.

Close proximity to the Las Vegas Convention Center make this an easy choice if you're attending a show there, but a convenient Monorail spot on-property also makes the rest of the Strip just as accessible.

There's 95,000 square feet of gaming space, so this isn't the biggest casino floor in town, but nearly 5,000 square feet of it constitutes the world's largest race and sportsbook called the "SuperBook" (bonus: it's totally non-smoking).

3000 Paradise Rd. (at Riviera Blvd.). www.westgatelasvegasresort.com. ℂ **800/732-7117** or 702/732-5111. 3,000 units. $67 and up double. Resort fee $33. Extra person $35. Children 17 and under stay free in parent's room. Free self- and valet parking. **Amenities:** 11 restaurants; buffet; food court; casino; executive-level rooms; health club; spa; outdoor pool; room service; showrooms; 6 tennis courts; free Wi-Fi.

Inexpensive

The Gold Coast ★ Close proximity to the Strip, as well as having the more upscale Rio and Palms within throwing distance, makes this budget-friendly hotel a contender for those who want to be near the action without necessarily paying for it. Definitely a locals favorite thanks to cheaper room rates and well-prepared, well-priced drinks and meals, Gold Coast isn't the most glamorous of hotels, but it gets the job done.

The rooms start on the small side, at about 320 square feet, but they're appointed as nicely as anywhere else. What they lack in space they make up for in style, with contemporary furniture and textures throughout a space that won't for a second make you think you've opted for a second-rate hotel room. Flatscreen TVs, in-room coffeemakers, hair dryers, and ironing boards are among the amenities; bathrooms are a little tight, but are efficient with the space available, and spotless.

The 86,000-square-foot casino is always teeming with locals who know the right places to make their bets, with nearly 2,000 slot and video poker machines at the ready. There's also a 70-lane bowling alley should you want to throw a few rocks, and **Ping Pang Pong** (p. 137), long considered one of the best Chinese restaurants in Las Vegas.

Shuttle service takes you where you want to go on the Strip, as well as to sister property The Orleans (see below).

4000 W. Flamingo Rd. www.goldcoastcasino.com. ℂ **800/331-5334** or 702/367-7111. 711 units. $45 and up double. Resort fee $16. Extra person $20. Children under 15 stay free in parents' room. Free self- and valet parking. **Amenities:** 4 restaurants; buffet; fast-food outlets; bowling alley; casino; executive-level rooms; fitness center; heated outdoor pool; room service; barber shop; free Wi-Fi.

The Orleans ★ Unless you're really into faux New Orleans decor, The Orleans probably hasn't hit your radar. But in all fairness, it's a reasonably priced, if oddly placed, hotel and casino that serves its purpose. Set on Tropicana Avenue a non-walkable distance from the Strip (though shuttles run continuously between it and sister properties Gold Coast near the Strip, Sam's Town to the far east, and Suncoast on the west side of town), The Orleans is a self-contained resort with an 18-screen movie theater, bowling alley, massive arena, and a showroom that hosts well-established comedians and throwback artists that make you think, "Oh. Don McLean is still alive."

In the midst of a $30 million renovation, The Orleans has updated the hotel, abandoning the previous beige color scheme for warmer tones and more upscale decor. They've played up the all-suite moniker they've given themselves, keeping the separate sitting areas set off from the sleeping space. The second phase of the upgrade includes new dining options, including the sleek **Alder & Birch,** a modern steakhouse whose clean lines stick out like a sore (but pretty) thumb off of The Orleans' Mardi Gras-laden casino floor and **Ondori Asian Kitchen,** with more to come.

If you've rented a car or don't mind cabbing it down to Las Vegas Boulevard, you'll be satisfied with your choice to stay here. What it lacks in authenticity it definitely makes up for in value.

4500 W. Tropicana Ave. (west of the Strip and I-15). www.orleanscasino.com. © **800/ 675-3267** or 702/365-7111. 1,886 units. $50 and up double; $185 and up suite. Resort fee $16. Extra person $20. Children 15 and under stay free in parent's room. Free self- and valet parking. **Amenities:** 8 restaurants; buffet; food court; 9,000-seat arena; 70-lane bowling center; casino; children's center offering amusements and day care for kids 3–12; concierge; executive-level rooms; health club; 18-screen movie theater; outdoor pools; room service; showroom; spa; free Wi-Fi.

Palace Station ★   When the Fertitta family started their chain of casinos dedicated to locals, they opened the first, interestingly enough, as close as possible to the Strip. In business since 1976, but known then as simply "The Casino," Palace Station has stood proud over I-15 near Sahara as a reminder to those hotels located on Las Vegas Boulevard that the locals have a stake in this town, too. Palace's proximity to the Strip is definitely an advantage, but those looking for a truly luxurious experience might be let down. The rooms are adequate, clean, and comfortable, but basic in terms of amenities and size. In other words, should you take selfies in the room, you won't be using #highroller as a hashtag unless you're being ironic.

Though the Courtyard Rooms are lighter on the wallet than the Tower Rooms, they definitely show it (though they have the advantage of being non-smoking). If you can afford it, opt to stay in the 21-floor Luxury Tower, if only because it's much more comfortable, with pillow top mattresses, 42-inch flatscreen TVs, modern decor, and better views of the Strip.

Palace Station is a required stop for serious players who want to get their money's worth out of a night of gambling, with lower limits than those a few blocks away on the Strip. More than 100,000 square feet of casino holds the most baccarat and pai gow tile games off the Strip, and an always-busy Asian gaming section. There are more than 1,700 one-armed bandits and video poker machines to chunk your change into (just kidding, machines don't take or give coins anymore), 44 table games and a 307-seat bingo hall—the closest to the Strip—that runs from 9am to 11pm 7 days a week.

The Oyster Bar remains a popular eatery for both locals and visitors, the 10-seat bar often has long lines of hungry regulars who are there for dozens of raw, plump oysters and giant, seafood-filled pan roasts made to order. This spot, like the rest of Palace Station, is no-frills Las Vegas, but will fill you up.

2411 W. Sahara Ave. www.palacestation.com. © **800/678-2846** or 702/367-2411. 1,011 units. $35 and up for up to 4 people. $17 resort fee. Free self- and valet parking. **Amenities:** 7 restaurants; buffet; food court; airport and Strip shuttle; arcade; casino; executive-level rooms; fitness center; outdoor pools; room service; free Wi-Fi.

Silver Sevens ★ When this low-slung hotel near the airport was called Terrible's—named after a local chain of gas stations—a common question arose: "Why would I go someplace called Terrible?" To be fair, it never really lived up to its unfortunate moniker, and under its recent name and management change, things have certainly taken a turn for the better. It's the ultimate in budget Vegas vacation properties—low-limit gaming, easy-on-the-wallet accommodations and dining—without any hint of sketchiness.

The rooms in the newer tower feature calm blue and brown decor, and perfunctory amenities: flat-panel TVs, decent beds, and a smaller-than-average bathroom, but you get what you pay for. One bonus is that all of the rooms are non-smoking, so you don't have to deal with the scent of the last guest's habit. And while you may not like the idea of the daily resort fee, this one is only $17 and includes access to the fitness center, free Wi-Fi both in the rooms and at the Corona Cantina, and transportation to and from the Strip and McCarran International Airport.

The pool is nice little surprise in the middle of the hotel's courtyard, an oasis away from the loud traffic from the surrounding Paradise and Flamingo Roads. If you're really watching your pennies, there's also a buffet, 24-hour coffee shop, and a passable steak house, but you're close enough to the Strip that you can eat better if you just take a little walk.

4100 Paradise Rd. (at Flamingo Rd.). www.silversevenscasino.com. © **877/773-4596** or 702/733-7000. 330 units. $29 and up double. Resort fee $17. Extra person $12. Children 17 and under stay free in parent's room. Free self- and valet parking. **Amenities:** 4 restaurants; buffet; outdoor pool; fitness center; room service; free Wi-Fi.

SOUTH & EAST OF THE STRIP

The main areas worth knowing about are the Boulder Highway strip on the far east side of town, the bedroom community of Henderson, and Lake Las Vegas—all of which offer a range of casino and non-casino hotels that can save you money and/or provide a unique Vegas experience.

Best for: Repeat visitors who want to try something new; value hunters.

Drawbacks: You'll have to drive to get to most of the major tourist attractions; upper-end restaurants and shows are harder to find.

locals' HOTELS

Most residents of Las Vegas—the locals—never go anywhere near the Strip. They prefer to play, eat, be entertained, and occasionally stay, at casino-hotels in their own neighborhoods, partly because of convenience, but mostly because it usually costs a lot less money. All of the following hotels are, admittedly, located away from the main tourist areas, but if you have a car at your disposal, you can save yourself some dough by trying them. Several offer free shuttles to other sister properties.

Just south of the Strip along I-15 is **Silverton,** 3333 Blue Diamond Rd. (www.silvertoncasino.com; ✆ **866/946-4373** or 702/263-7777), a delightful ski lodge–themed hotel and casino with a warm casino, surprisingly stylish rooms (considering how cheap they usually are; figure in the $40–$75 range), and several affordable restaurants. The sports-minded may want to stop here just for the massive Bass Pro Shops attached to the complex, offering everything from skis to the boats with which to pull people wearing them.

About 5 miles west of the Strip along Boulder Highway are several locals' hotel options. The biggest and best known is **Sam's Town,** 5111 Boulder Hwy. (www. samstownlv.com; ✆ **866/897-8696** or 702/456-7777). In addition to the second-biggest casino in town (behind only MGM Grand), the western-themed property has a 56-lane bowling alley, an 18-screen movie theater, more than a dozen restaurants, bars and lounges, and a big indoor atrium with a silly light-and-laser show. The rooms are nothing to write home about, but they are fine, especially for the bargain-basement prices they go for. Another favorite is **Boulder Station** ★, 4111 Boulder Hwy. (www.boulderstation.com; ✆ **800/683-7777** or 702/432-7777), which has more than 300 guest rooms, a 75,000-square-foot casino, movie theaters, restaurants, bars, and a concert venue. Rates usually run from $75 to $125 a night, but rooms can be had for as little as $49 per night.

Arizona Charlie's East ★, 4575 Boulder Hwy. (www.arizonacharlies.com; ✆ **888/236-9066** or 702/951-5900) features 300 minisuites, a 37,000-square-foot casino, several restaurants, and a casino lounge. It's only a step or two above budget accommodations, but priced similarly, and still very well maintained. Lastly, the **Eastside Cannery** ★, 5255 Boulder Hwy. (www.arizonacharlies.

Expensive

Green Valley Ranch Resort, Spa & Casino ★★★   Green Valley claimed its title as the posh side east of the Strip when this opulent hotel opened its doors in 2005. Part of the Stations Casinos family of properties dedicated to giving locals the same luxurious experience as its Strip counterparts, Green Valley Ranch set the ever-raising bar for amenities and restaurants that we continue to see today in spots such as Red Rock in Summerlin and Aliante on the north side, at incredibly reasonable prices.

The tiled eaves, exposed stone walls, vaulted ceilings, and mosaic stone walls of the registration and lobby area that scream Mediterranean decor continue into the expansive, 95,000-square-foot casino floor that's jam-packed with locals and visitors alike. Lower limits and a bingo room draw in plenty com; ☎ **866/999-4899** or 702/856-5300) has a casino, several restaurants, bars and lounges, and 300 very stylish rooms that rival the Strip for amenities and decor, but are miles away in terms of price.

Just down the street, you'll find locals' favorite **Sunset Station** ★, 1301 W. Sunset Rd., Henderson (www.sunsetstation. com; ☎ **888/786-7389** or 702/547-7777), with 450 fairly basic hotel rooms, but a host of amenities like a bowling alley; movie theaters; an outdoor amphitheater; a really nice, low-limits casino; lots of restaurants; a very good buffet; and more. Meanwhile, nearby **Fiesta Henderson** ★, 777 W. Lake Mead Dr., Henderson (www.fiestahendersonlas vegas.com; ☎ **888/899-7770** or 702/558-7000) is a Southwestern-themed joint with basic yet comfortable lodgings, plus plenty of gaming options, restaurants, bars, movie theaters, and more. Things are cheap here, with rooms going for as low as $30 a night during the week.

On the north and west sides of town are several smaller properties popular with locals. **Fiesta Rancho** ★, 2400 N. Rancho Rd. (www.fiestarancholasvegas. com; ☎ **888/899-7770** or 702/631-7000) is similar in concept and execution to its sister property mentioned above. In addition to the 100 rooms, there is a big casino and a regulation-size ice-skating rink, complete with equipment rentals and lessons (p. 185). Prices go as low as $40 a night. Right across the street is **Texas Station,** 2101 Texas Star Lane, North Las Vegas (www.aliantecasino hotel.com; ☎ **800/654-8888** or 702/631-1000), which (unsurprisingly, owing to its name) has a "Yeehaw!" theme covering its basic motel rooms, bowling alley, movie theaters, big casino, and one of the best steakhouses in town, **Austins.** If you continue north—about as far north as you can go without running into a mountain—you'll find **Aliante Casino and Hotel** ★★, 7300 Aliante Pkwy., North Las Vegas (www.aliante casinohotel.com; ☎ **877/477-7627** or 702/692-7777), a beautifully done resort with smallish rooms that are gorgeously decorated with all of the latest amenities. The facility boasts several restaurants, bars and lounges, a Strip-worthy pool, and a big casino, all wrapped up in warm design elements. It's a solid 25-minute drive from the Strip without traffic, but with prices as low as $29 a night for rooms this nice, it might just be worth it.

of habitual players, but there isn't that sense of desperation that you might catch a whiff of at other off-Strip slot factories.

Casino guests and locals get to take full advantage of the lagoon-like pool that offers 17 private cabanas, as well as one of the most posh spas off the Strip, complete with 22 treatment rooms, co-ed steam rooms, Jacuzzis, and a private outdoor lap pool.

The 495 guest rooms are as nice as the public areas, starting at 5,000 square feet—generous for an off-Strip hotel. And when you upgrade to one of 80 luxury suites, your square footage increases immensely, from 695 square feet to the behemoth 4,000-square-foot Penthouse, all of which have ultra-comfortable beds, marble bathrooms, and in-room martini bars.

The caliber of dining has also improved over the years. **Hank's Fine Steak and Martinis** has held strong since opening, with great cuts of meat and ice cold martinis, while on Fridays at **Feast Buffet,** the buffet's best kept secret, "Mama" Sarah Jamerson, a beloved line cook from New Orleans, prepares crab legs to order for a long line of in-the-know guests.

Green Valley Ranch is a perfect spot to become a regular when you visit. They know the true meaning of customer service.

2300 Paseo Verde Pkwy. (at I-215). www.greenvalleyranchresort.com. © **866/782-9487** or 702/617-7777. 495 units. $140 and up double. Resort fee $32. Extra person $35. Children 17 and under stay free in parent's room. Free self- and valet parking. **Amenities:** 7 restaurants; buffet; food court; casino; concierge; executive-level rooms; spa; health club; lounge; movie theaters; outdoor pools; room service; free shuttle service to the airport and the Strip; free Wi-Fi.

Moderate

M Resort ★★ If you're making the trek from California on I-15, The M Resort is your first indication that you're about to enter Sin City proper, but your last chance if you want the Las Vegas experience without being inundated with the Vegas *experience.* About 10 miles to the south of Mandalay Bay, M Resort has the luxury, sophistication, and swank design that are hallmarks of many of today's Vegas properties; but with much better value, a low-key clientele of locals, and a lower threshold for sensory overload from throngs of visitors.

Built by the Marnell family (the "M" in M Resort), who are also responsible for such iconic hotels as The Mirage, Caesars Palace and Wynn, the hotel's casino relies on its natural surroundings to accent its beauty. Skylights above the casino floor allow abundant light in, so there's no casino-cave feeling; decor is in natural materials such as wood, crystal, stone, and mother-of-pearl.

In each of the nearly 400 rooms, dark wood paneling combined with ample natural light make everything seem airy, and the contemporary touches abound. Foreign travelers will be familiar with inserting the key in the holder next to the door to power the room up; remove it and everything shuts down. Windows from the bedroom into the bathroom might make you feel exposed, but once you're soaking in the tub, with a killer view of the desert, you won't even notice (and no, they probably can't see you from outside the hotel).

Some 30,000 square feet of the hotel is kitchen space devoted to food and beverage, including **Anthony's Prime Steak and Seafood** (named for M Resort president Anthony Marnell) and his namesake Gourmet Burgers and Brews, as well as the hugely popular **Studio B Buffet,** which puts out a legendary seafood spread on weekends.

Oenophiles can spend time in the property's own wine cellar, or catch some rays on the glorious pool deck, where most of the restaurants also have patio seating. On weekends, Daydream Pool is a DJ-driven pool party where locals who have worked hard all week take some leisure time without having to deal with over-zealous partiers from the Strip.

It might be a good hike from the Strip, but the vibe and value make this a serious contender for a relaxing getaway.

12300 Las Vegas Blvd. S. (at St. Rose Pkwy.). www.themresort.com. ℂ **877/673-7678** or 702/797-1000. 390 units. $135 and up double. No resort fee. Extra person $30. Children 17 and under stay free in parent's room. Free self- and valet parking. **Amenities:** 8 restaurants; buffet; casino; concierge; executive-level rooms; health club; spa; salon; heated outdoor pool; room service; shuttle service to the airport and Strip; Wi-Fi (for a fee).

Inexpensive

South Point ★★   The gold, gleaming towers that stand apart from the Strip are bound to catch your eye, making you wonder, who stays all the way out there when the main attraction is close enough to touch? The answer: budget-conscious travelers who still fulfill their need for expensive-feeling accommodations. And they also probably like horses.

Similar in caliber to The Orleans and Gold Coast, South Point offers decent rooms at reasonable prices. You can spend what you save on lodgings right at South Point, either on the sprawling casino floor or at its myriad entertainment options, such as the bowling alley, cinema, or, during the right time of year, at the 500,000-square-foot Arena and Equestrian Center.

Super old-school continental restaurant **Michael's Gourmet Room** is alive and well at South Point, after being transported there from Barbary Coast many years ago—stained glass dome and all. There's a perfunctory steak house, old school oyster bar, and a Mexican spot, but one of the most pleasant surprises is finding Midwestern favorite **Steak 'n Shake** flipping burgers until late at night.

The rooms are spacious for the area, starting at about 500 square feet, with all the amenities you'd find in rooms further north on Las Vegas Boulevard: 42-inch plasma screen TVs and comfy beds, all in a subdued color palate. And let's face it, for those who just want a place to store their stuff and lay their head at night (or morning), the price at South Point—often a whole $100 less than its Strip counterparts on any given night—is always right.

9777 Las Vegas Blvd. S. www.southpointcasino.com. ℂ **866/796-7111** or 702/796-7111. 2,163 units. $79 and up double. Resort fee $14. Extra person $20. Children 16 and under stay free in parent's room. Free self- and valet parking. **Amenities:** 11 restaurants; buffet; several fast-food outlets; 70-lane bowling center; casino; concierge; 4,400-seat equestrian and events center; 16-screen movie theater; outdoor pool; room service; spa; fitness center; free Wi-Fi.

NORTH & WEST OF THE STRIP

Summerlin, on the far west side of town, and North Las Vegas (north of the city, appropriately enough) are suburbs that have pockets of casino-hotel options ranging from budget to luxury, and lots of outdoor opportunities from golf to hiking and beyond.

Best for: The recreation-minded; people who want a more relaxing Vegas vacation.

Drawbacks: Long drives to the Strip and fewer entertainment options.

Expensive

JW Marriott ★★   If the whole point of staying off the Strip is so you can feel like you're not in Las Vegas, then JW Marriott has your name written all over it. A mere 15 minutes from Las Vegas Boulevard, through the cul-de-sacs and fancy plaza shopping of Summerlin, JW Marriott sits on 54 acres of a pristinely landscaped grounds. A lot of the resorts that go up in town seem to be all steel and glass, but this 500-room hotel stays very West Coast with its Spanish mission-style buildings.

Part of JW Marriott's charm is that it's literally an oasis away from the Strip's madness. A large, resort-style pool features waterfalls, and Spa Aquae allows guest to tune out in serene lounges, cold dipping pools, and soothing steam rooms. Yet while you're away from the Strip, you're not missing out on any of its luxurious appointments. JW Marriott's rooms are stacked with visually bland but plush furnishings, big screen TVs, rainfall showers, and marble throughout the bathrooms. Ground-floor rooms offer outdoor patios—something relatively unheard of for standard rooms—and a nice perch to have when the weather permits.

This may be a non-gaming hotel, but most visitors aren't here to put their money on red. Rather, they come to see how they do on the greens. The TPC Las Vegas course is one of the most prestigious golf courses in the state, complete with babbling brooks and quaint foot bridges over 18 holes, making this one of the few hotels in town where you can actually enjoy the grounds where it sits.

And in the event you decide you do want that casino experience, the adjacent Rampart Casino will bring you right back.

221 N. Rampart Blvd. www.jwlasvegasresort.com. © **877/869-8777** or 702/869-7777. 500 units. $124 and up for up to 4 people. Resort fee $19. Free self- and valet parking. **Amenities:** 9 restaurants; buffet; casino; concierge; fitness center; outdoor pool; room service; spa; free Wi-Fi.

Red Rock Resort ★★★   When the far-west property opened in 2006, many assumed it would be a close facsimile to sister property Green Valley Ranch, which is pretty tony in its own right. The 800-room hotel and casino Red Rock Resort proved to be the swankier sister, even giving Strip contenders a run for their money.

Set right against the **Red Rock Canyon National Conservation Area** (see chapter 9), it's one of the most picturesque places you can stay, with red-tinged mountains just to the west and the lights of the Strip about 10 miles away to the east. Whichever side you decide to stay on, there's no such thing as a bad view.

It's perfect for those who want the Vegas experience without the craziness of the Strip, complete with an 80,000-square-foot casino that is like a maze through the subdued, gorgeous main floor, with 3,000 slot and video poker machines. And unlike many of the Strip casinos, Red Rock's bingo hall is popular with visitors and locals alike—of all ages. There tends to be a lot of locals coming through Red Rock Resort and many bring their families, as it's not just for gambling, with options such as a luxury bowling alley, and even a day care center. Pool-wise, there's the three-acre water feature, complete with beach, Jacuzzis, and even a stage for outdoor concerts by big-name acts. Downtown Summerlin, a new shopping mecca, just opened next door.

The Red Rock has seen a recent renaissance in its recent dining offerings, going beyond the standard proficient buffet, coffee shop, and food court that is typical of locals' casinos. Its stellar steak house, **T-Bones,** is chugging along nicely, but they've also recently added **8 Noodle Bar** for those who prefer to slurp Asian fare, the Italian cuisine resto **Salute,** and **Hearthstone,** the hotel's attempt at a trendy, neighborhood comfort-food eatery—which they manage to pull off with success. Lovely outdoor patio seating is available at all these spots (a nice option for those who want to get away from the casino).

The rooms take their cue from the natural landscape surrounding the resort and are done in earthy colors, with such niceties as 42-inch plasma TVs, sound systems you can jack your iPod into, and enormous bathrooms. Pair all that with the views and you might just forget that you're in Sin City.

11011 W. Charleston Rd. www.redrocklasvegas.com. © **866/767-7773** or 702/797-7777. 816 units. $160 and up (up to 4 people). Resort fee $32. Extra person $35. Children 15 and under stay free in parent's room. **Amenities:** 10 restaurants; buffet; food court; bars and lounges; casino; concierge; day-care center; health club; 16-screen movie theater; outdoor pools and beach area; room service; spa; free Wi-Fi.

WHERE TO EAT

For a long time, Vegas was considered an epicurean wasteland, a place where prime rib that cost more than $4.99 was considered haute cuisine, and all-you-can-eat buffets dominated the landscape. Then the pendulum swung in the opposite direction. It got to the point where you couldn't swing a delicately seasoned roast leg of lamb with a honey-mint jus without hitting a celebrity chef and their fancy, very expensive restaurants. Wolfgang Puck, Emeril Lagasse, Joël Robuchon, Thomas Keller, Julian Serrano, Gordon Ramsay, Alain Ducasse, Charlie Palmer . . . the list goes on and on, and so did the bills that came at the end of the meals.

Now, things have sort of settled in the middle. Fine dining continues to be more than fine in Vegas, but the good news for folks with less adventurous palates, or less extravagant budgets, is that there is plenty to eat here for everyone. All-you-can-eat buffets still abound, cheap eats can still be found if you know where to look, and moderately priced restaurants are making a big comeback. We hope you're hungry!

5

RESTAURANTS BY CUISINE

AMERICAN
Bier Garten ★★, p. 129
Carson Kitchen ★★★, p. 130
Culinary Dropout ★★, p. 135
Dick's Last Resort ★, p. 100
Eat ★★★, p. 131
Guy Fieri's Vegas Kitchen ★, p. 117
Hash House a Go Go ★★★, p. 117
Holstein's Shakes & Buns ★★, p. 117
Lagasse's Stadium ★, p. 118
Serendipity 3 ★, p. 119
Stewart + Ogden ★★, p. 128

ASIAN
Red 8 ★★, p. 125
Fú ★★, p. 135
Flock & Fowl ★★, p. 138

BARBECUE
Big Ern's BBQ ★★, p. 129
Gilley's ★★, p. 116
Memphis Championship Barbecue ★★, p. 141

BISTRO
Bouchon ★★★, p. 108
db Brasserie ★★★, p. 109
Mon Ami Gabi ★★, p. 118
Payard Patisserie & Bistro ★★★, p. 119

BUFFETS
Bellagio Buffet ★★, p. 144
The Buffet at Aria ★, p. 143
The Buffet at TI ★, p. 146
Caesars Palace Bacchanal Buffet ★★★, p. 145
Excalibur's Buffet ★, p. 143

5

WHERE TO EAT | Restaurants by Cuisine

PIZZA

Pizza Rock ★★, p. 128
Naked City Pizza ★, p. 136

PUB

Gordon Ramsay Pub & Grill ★, p. 116
Pub 1842 ★★, p. 101
The Pub at Monte Carlo ★, p. 103
Todd English P.U.B. ★★★, p. 104

SANDWICHES

Capriotti's ★★★, p. 137
Goodwich ★, p. 131

SEAFOOD

Emeril's New Orleans Fish House ★,
p. 96
Estiatorio Milos ★★★, p. 110

SOUL FOOD

M&M Soul Food ★★, p. 141

SOUTHWESTERN

Mesa Grill ★★, p. 111

SPANISH

Julian Serrano ★★, p. 101

STEAK

Alder & Birch ★★, p. 134
Andiamo Steakhouse ★★, p. 125
Bazaar Meat ★★★, p. 122
Delmonico Steakhouse ★★, p. 109
Gordon Ramsay Steak ★, p. 110
Old Homestead Steakhouse ★★★,
p. 111
Oscar's Beef Booze Broads ★★,
p. 126
The Steakhouse ★, p. 124
Strip House ★★, p. 113

THAI

Chada Thai ★, p. 138
Lotus of Siam ★★★, p. 139

VENEZUELAN

Viva Las Arepas ★★, p. 132

SOUTH STRIP

Expensive

Andre's ★★ FRENCH   The namesake of this restaurant is often considered the first "big name" chef to arrive in Las Vegas. Andre Rochat's original Downtown outpost—essentially a renovated cottage—closed in 2008 after 40 years. But its current fancy digs at Monte Carlo uphold his reputation. The emphasis here is still on classic French dishes like escargot de Burgogne, Dover sole *grenobloise* and lamb Provençal, all of which are in rotation on his current menus, all with deliciously *haute* presentations. Who serves lobster Thermidor anymore these days? More often than not, Andre's does. The round jewel box dining room is warm and intimate, accented in earthy browns and light blue. Should you get overwhelmed by having to choose from the more than 1,000 wines, the capable sommelier will help. A secret cognac and cigar lounge upstairs is a perfect spot for a nightcap.

Price Categories	
Expensive	Main courses $30 and up
Moderate	Main courses $15–$30
Inexpensive	Main courses under $15

In Monte Carlo, 3770 Las Vegas Blvd. S. www.andrelv.com. © **702/798-7151.** Main courses $26–$78. Tues–Sun 5:30–10pm.

Aureole ★★★ NEW AMERICAN   Even if you have no idea what kind of food Aureole serves, you definitely know about its wine tower. The four-story, gleaming glass and steel structure in the middle of the main dining room not

South Strip Restaurants

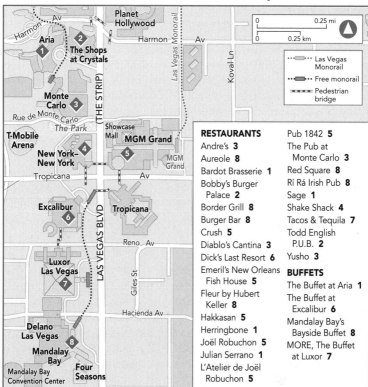

RESTAURANTS

Andre's **3**
Aureole **8**
Bardot Brasserie **1**
Bobby's Burger Palace **2**
Border Grill **8**
Burger Bar **8**
Crush **5**
Diablo's Cantina **3**
Dick's Last Resort **6**
Emeril's New Orleans Fish House **5**
Fleur by Hubert Keller **8**
Hakkasan **5**
Herringbone **1**
Joël Robuchon **5**
Julian Serrano **1**
L'Atelier de Joël Robuchon **5**

Pub 1842 **5**
The Pub at Monte Carlo **3**
Red Square **8**
Rí Rá Irish Pub **8**
Sage **1**
Shake Shack **4**
Tacos & Tequila **7**
Todd English P.U.B. **2**
Yusho **3**

BUFFETS

The Buffet at Aria **1**
The Buffet at Excalibur **6**
Mandalay Bay's Bayside Buffet **8**
MORE, The Buffet at Luxor **7**

only houses one of the best wine collections in the city, but also has an added bonus of stunning "Wine Angels" who gracefully rappel up and down the wine racks on wires to secure your bottle of wine from the 50,000 available. They've ditched their black Mission Impossible-style catsuits in favor of sparkly, red and muted-orange numbers, but don't worry, they're just as form fitting as the previous uniforms. After witnessing this very Vegas spectacle, you get to enjoy one of the city's great fine dining experiences. The seasonal menu focuses on American, responsibly sourced ingredients treated with the most delicate of touches. Mainstays include a dense, double cut pork chop with collard greens and bacon bits, and roasted king salmon brightened with mint cucumber sauce and a heart of palm salad. Pick and choose according to your tastes from an a la carte menu, a seasonal, prix fixe tasting menu, a selection of small plates for noshers, and even happy hour offerings (for those on limited budgets). The best seats in the house are by the Swan Court, where you can observe the resident paired swans through the floor-to-ceiling windows. Though chef Palmer only stops in every once in awhile, his kitchen, run by chef Arnaud Masset, is as exacting as it would be if Palmer were running service himself.

In Mandalay Bay, 3950 Las Vegas Blvd. S. www.aureolelv.com. *877/632-1766.* Small plates $8–$18, main courses $32–$72. Mon–Sat 5:30–10:30pm.

Crush ★★ CONTINENTAL   This long and narrow eatery from local restaurateurs Michael and Jenna Morton—who also own **La Comida** (p. 128) Downtown—is always busy, especially when there's an event at the MGM Grand Garden Arena. Large steel doors (with text from the epic of Gilgamesh etched into them) separate the rustic front from the more private dining areas and another bar in the back, but if you want to be where the action is, sit near the front bar. On this "small plates"–heavy menu, the flatbreads are tops, with intriguing topping combinations like date and artichoke or wild mushroom with Fontina cheese. I also like the sea scallop "benedict" topped with quail eggs and chorizo. For bigger appetites, I'd recommend the hearty lobster pot pie or crab risotto. There are also options for those with dietary restrictions, including gluten-free, dairy-free and shellfish-free foods.

At MGM Grand, 3799 Las Vegas Blvd. S. www.crushmgm.com. *702/891-3222.* Small plates $9–$18, main courses $16–$45. Sun–Thurs 5:30–10:30pm; Fri–Sat 5:30–11:30pm.

Emeril's New Orleans Fish House ★ CREOLE/SEAFOOD   Few names in the American culinary world are as recognizable as Emeril Lagasse, thanks to his many shows in the early days of the Food Network. Before TV stardom, his original Fish House in New Orleans was his claim to fame. This outpost at the MGM Grand isn't as good as the original, but it's still one of the best representations of Crescent City cuisine on the Strip. Grab a seat at the raw bar to watch as your oysters are shucked just for you, or go for the full monty in the dining room and order all the Creole classics: barbecue shrimp, shrimp etouffée, and the tastiest gumbo in town. To get the full "bam!" effect, Emeril's signature banana cream pie is a must for dessert.

In MGM Grand, 3799 Las Vegas Blvd. S. www.emerils.com. *702/891-7374.* Main courses lunch $19–$36, dinner $18–$44 (more for lobster). Daily 11:30am–10pm.

Fleur by Hubert Keller ★★★ CONTINENTAL   What used to be chef Hubert Keller's fine dining Fleur de Lys has been dialed down to a more relaxed establishment, though we wouldn't call it "casual," per se. The dining room remains elegant, while the faux patio seating features leather club chairs, perfect to lounge in for lunch bites like pulled pork sandwiches or a bacon and onion-heavy *tarte flambée.* Like many other restaurants, small plates are now the norm. Little bites here take you around the world, from beef tartare tacos and kushi oysters, to Japanese gyoza and Peruvian crudo, all meant to be shared before you embark on your own entree. You can get a burger from Keller's Burger Bar, also located in Mandalay Bay, or you can order a Fleur Burger here, made of Wagyu beef with caramelized onions and mushrooms, served on toasted brioche. Just be sure you're not ordering the Fleur Burger 5000, which is pretty much the same thing, except topped with more extravagant ingredients like truffles and foie gras, and served with a bottle of 1996 Petrus to wash it down. Oh, and that one costs $5,000.

In Mandalay Bay, 3950 Las Vegas Blvd. S. www.hubertkeller.com. © **702/632-9400.** Main courses lunch $19–$22, dinner small plates $10–$25, dinner full plates $32–$95. Mon–Fri 11am–10pm; Sat–Sun 11am–10:30pm

Hakkasan ★★★ CHINESE All those bright, hole-in-the-wall Chinese restaurants you've been to? This is the complete opposite of them. Hakkasan's first floor (above it is a dance club) is all about cutting-edge design: high ceilings and tall black lacquer lattices that evoke the feeling of walking in a maze. The meals are as pleasantly puzzling. While you'll encounter familiar dishes like dim sum, Mongolian beef, and crispy chicken in lemon sauce, they're elevated with elegant presentation and delicate flavors and ingredients (the prices are elevated in turn). The Peking duck, for example, is served with traditional accoutrement of thin crepes, scallion and cucumbers, but also with a healthy dose of reserve caviar. Less familiar Chinese dishes on the menu are aimed at the high-roller Asian clientele, but adventurous diners will find them exciting, as well.

Hakkasan first served its brand haute Chinese cuisine in London, where Chef Ho Chee Boon won a Michelin star before expanding the empire here and adding the nightclub that has become one of the MGM's biggest draws.

In MGM Grand, 3799 Las Vegas Blvd. S. www.hakkasanlv.com. © **702/891-3838.** Main courses $18–$255. Sun–Thurs 5–11pm; Fri–Sat 5pm–midnight.

Joël Robuchon ★★★ FRENCH There are fancy French meals in Las Vegas, and then there are meals at Joël Robuchon. Nearly every culinary accolade in the world has been bestowed on Robuchon: He has 28 Michelin stars under his toque—more than any other chef in the world. He's won the *Meilleur Ouvrier de France* for culinary arts, the highest honor given to French craftsmen. European guidebook Gault-Millau even created a title just for him, naming him Chef of the Century. All this is to say that the meal you have here will be worth the sticker shock.

The jewel box of a dining room features plenty of regal purple, fresh flowers, and a stunning crystal chandelier. It's so formal that it can feel like eating at church, but once you get started on the exquisite, 18-course tasting menu, the over-the-top decor begins to feel appropriate. Each dish is a study in pristine ingredients and impeccable technique, combining flavors and textures in ways that only a chef of this caliber can imagine. Where else would you even consider eating a crab gelee or foie gras carpaccio? Having had the good fortune of witnessing the kitchen during service, I can tell you that the chefs back there are working silently, paying attention to the most painstaking details. This is how a chef earns three Michelin stars over and over again.

In MGM Grand, 3799 Las Vegas Blvd. S. www.joel-robuchon.com. © **702/891-7925.** Reservations strongly recommended. Jacket recommended. Prix-fixe tasting menus $127–$250, 18-course tasting menu $445, a la carte main courses $85–$235. Daily 5:30–10pm.

L'Atelier de Joël Robuchon ★★★ FRENCH   Compared to its buttoned-up sister restaurant next door, the *l'atelier* (French for workshop) of Chef Robuchon is downright casual. Make no mistake, it's still very much a fine dining experience, but one where you're not afraid to use the wrong fork or laugh really loud. The best seats are at the counter around the open kitchen, where you can watch the choreography of the chefs preparing your meal on a black box stage, and chat with fellow patrons.

The food here is as meticulously constructed at the big Robuchon, but approaches the realm of comfort food, if your idea of comfort includes the fancy Spanish ham *jamon Iberico* sliced right off the leg and placed onto tomato toast. The signature foie gras-stuffed quail is tiny, but rich and satisfying, especially when accompanied by Robuchon's famed *pommes purée*—the silkiest, creamiest mashed potatoes you'll ever eat, reportedly made with a pound of butter for each pound of potatoes. The multi-course seasonal discovery menu will set you back (but not nearly as much as Robuchon next door), though there are a couple of three-course prix fixe menus at around $100 pop, and one pre-theater offering of $50, so it's possible to experience a meal here without breaking the bank.

In MGM Grand, 3799 Las Vegas Blvd. S. www.joel-robuchon.com. ℂ **702/891-7358.** Reservations strongly recommended. Main courses $41–$95, 9-course discovery menu $168, small plates $18–$40. Daily 5–11pm.

Sage ★★ NEW AMERICAN   This restaurant, from chef Shawn McClain, often flies under the radar because while McClain has won James Beard

Awards and owned a number of successful restaurants in Chicago, outside of culinary circles, he's not a household name. As such, this is one of the most underrated restaurants in the city, but one that serious food lovers need to discover for themselves. You could do so at the bar, which not only offers innovative cocktails, but also features one of the few absinthe programs in the city. But I'd recommend heading into the dining room for a more relaxing meal of innovative dishes like Wagyu beef tartare, prepared with a crushed caper aioli and topped with a poached egg and little chocolate bits that create texture and bitterness. Sage's signature foie gras custard Brûlée is a savory take on the creamy dessert, and it's just as rich and creamy. The menu changes seasonally, with emphasis on organic, sustainable ingredients, often foraged for Sage itself. Dishes that stay on the menu, like a Wagyu short rib braised for 36 hours, only change up in accompaniment; you might have white asparagus one month, or horseradish-smoked potatoes another. Lighter options include pan-roasted halibut or butter poached salmon.

In Aria Las Vegas, 3730 Las Vegas Blvd. S. www.aria.com. © **877/230-2742.** Main courses $37–$59. Daily 5–11pm.

Moderate

Bardot Brasserie ★★ FRENCH   Chef Michael Mina's take on a bistro is as classic as they come, down to the dark wood paneling, brass railings, and low lighting. If you've encountered a dish in a Paris neighborhood bistro, it's on the menu here. Charcuterie and pâté are popular ways to begin dinner, as well as buttery escargot Bardot-style, served in puff pastry. Duck *a l'orange* is such an old school dish that even most French restaurants don't serve it anymore. But here, translated onto the wings of the duck with a delicate sauce, you'll be happy it made a comeback. Other traditional offerings, such as steak frites, mussels in white wine, and roasted bone marrow feature rustic presentations in copper pans or on plain white plates, so you can feel like you're eating real food rather than a contrived piece of art.

Weekend brunch is increasingly one of the most popular meals here, thanks to well-executed preparations of *Croque Madames* and ample eggs Benedicts served on croissants rather than boring old English muffins, not to mention a reasonably priced, bottomless glass of rosé. The concise, French-heavy wine list is meant to pair with the dishes, while a really strong cocktail program encourages guests to hang out at the bar and make a night of it there.

In Aria Las Vegas, 3730 Las Vegas Blvd. S. www.arialasvegas.com. © **877/230-2742.** Brunch courses $14–$19, main courses $24–$59. Daily 5–10:30pm; brunch Sat–Sun 10am–2pm.

Border Grill ★★ MEXICAN   The Food Network made chefs Susan Feniger and Mary Sue Milliken into household names as the *Two Hot Tamales* with a contemporary take on authentic Mexican fare. Outside of Chicago chef Rick Bayless, there are few other gringos who understand the soul and flavors of the cuisine as well as they do. I'm talking home-cooked, regional Mexican dishes, all executed with modern flair. Yucatan-style pork is slow roasted with crimson *achiote* and in banana leaves, simple grilled skirt steak needs nothing more than charred corn relish and a warm, house-made flour tortilla as a vehicle to your mouth. Yes, they have tacos too, but forget about your plain ol' carne asada. Here you want them filled with Wagyu beef and grilled pineapple salsa, or shredded brisket with a zesty, crunchy slaw. The Forum Shops outlet features a raw bar where you can pull up a seat to watch as fresh ceviche is made to order, beach-style. Border Brunch, offered on weekends at both locations, is an all-you-can eat extravaganza that is not a buffet. Rather, items are cooked to order for optimum freshness. This is a Mexican restaurant after all, so *cervezas* are cold, and margaritas, in flavors like pineapple vanilla or mango cilantro, are strong. ***Warning:*** No matter which Border Grill you head to—there are locations in Mandalay Bay and the Forum Shops at Caesars—be prepared for a hike. You'll find the Mandalay Bay outpost on the way to the Shark Reef, far away from the casino, while at the Forum Shops it's tucked under the spiral elevator—also clear on the other side of the mall from the Caesars Palace casino.

In Mandalay Bay, 3950 Las Vegas Blvd. S. www.bordergrill.com. ℂ **702/632-7403.** In Forum Shops at Caesars, 3500 Las Vegas Blvd. S. ℂ **702/854-6700.** Main courses lunch $10–$26, dinner $16–$36, Border Brunch $35. Mon–Fri 11:30am–10pm; Sat–Sun 10am–10pm.

Diablo's Cantina ★★ MEXICAN   Outside of Border Grill, Las Vegas doesn't have that many great authentic Mexican restaurants, but the ones we do have are fun. Located Strip-side of Monte Carlo, Diablo's open first floor and second floor balcony offer great people watching and solid taqueria fare: burritos, quesadillas and tacos, as well as a few north-of-the-border specialties like burgers and chicken wings. If you're inclined to go full Diablo, there's a chicken wing challenge: eat 20 of the buggers coated in habanero and ghost chili peppers, and you are placed on the Wall of Fame. On the less stomach-searing side are the chili verde enchiladas, with hunks of pork in a sauce of roasted green tomatillos. At night, the music gets louder and the margarita-fueled masses get rowdier, and the upstairs features live bands or a DJ.

In Monte Carlo, 3770 Las Vegas Blvd. S. www.diabloslasvegas.com. ℂ **702/730-6615.** Main courses $14–$21. Mon–Wed 11am–11pm; Thurs 11am–1am; Fri–Sat 11am–2am; Sun 11am–10pm; bar open later.

Dick's Last Resort ★ AMERICAN   A frat bro's paradise, Dick's is beer and beef-fueled, and it doesn't pretend to be anything else, which is refreshing for those who don't want to think too hard about dinner. You'll be hard pressed to find any other restaurant serving entrees like barbecue half-racks of ribs and honey-glazed chicken from a bucket, among other artery-clogging (but totally worth it) specialties like chicken-fried steak and battered fish and chips. Servers are deliberately rude to customers (it's part of the schtick here), they can get a little vulgar at times, but tend to be good at reading how far they can push people's buttons. Plus, they can take it as well as they can dish it out, so feel free to sass back.

In Excalibur, 3850 Las Vegas Blvd. S. www.dickslastresort.com. © **702/597-7791.** Main courses $15–$23. Sun–Thurs 11am–11pm; Fri–Sat 11am–midnight.

Herringbone ★★ NEW AMERICAN *Top Chef* alum Brian Malarkey opened Herringbone as his second restaurant on the Strip (the first was Sear-sucker at Caesars Palace, but we like this one better). The restaurant, which has original outposts in La Jolla and San Diego, specializes in what he calls Southern California coastal cuisine, but really means a lot of small shareable plates. In the Vegas kitchen is local favorite chef Geno Bernardo, who adds in a bit of his Italian influence, like in his killer rendition of grilled octopus, or whole-grilled branzino with shaved fennel salad. Cocktails are fun and inno-vative, so they might take a few minutes to be made, but worth the wait. You could even conceivably get away with just ordering a dozen oysters and a few of glasses of wine and still get the full Herringbone experience. There is indoor lounge seating with large windows, but the best seats are on the out-door patio overlooking the Aria's pool. Umbrellas and pergolas over the tables offer much-needed shade from the sun during the day, especially during the popular weekend brunch.

In Aria Las Vegas, 3730 Las Vegas Blvd. S. www.herringboneeats.com. © **702/590-9898.** Brunch courses $18–$33, main courses $34–$62. Sun–Thurs 11:30am–10pm; Fri–Sat 11:30am–11pm; brunch Sat–Sun 10am–4pm.

Julian Serrano ★★ SPANISH   After years of being known as one of the first fine dining titans in Las Vegas (thanks to his restaurant Picasso at Bella-gio), Serrano went back to his Spanish roots when he opened this restaurant at Aria. Definitely more relaxed and casual than its haute cuisine French sister, it offers Spanish fare as it was meant to be eaten: as tapas, shared with others and over lots of sangria. While it's definitely a Vegas version of what you'd find in Barcelona, it's as authentic as possible, with dishes like a classic torti-lla with eggs and potatoes (not the wrap), crusty tomato bread topped with thin slices of Serrano *jamon* (no relation to the chef), and fried chicken *cro-quetas,* crunchy on the outside, creamy with béchamel inside. There is also a selection of traditional paella, the Spanish rice dish cooked with meats and seafood until a *soccarat* (crunchy, charred brown crust) forms at the bottom of the pan. While the tapas are all reasonably priced on their own, you might be ordering quite a few of them to get a full meal, which can get pricey.

In Aria Las Vegas, 3730 Las Vegas Blvd. S. www.arialasvegas.com. © **877/230-2742.** Reservations recommended. Main courses lunch $12–$50, main courses dinner $24–$50, tapas $7–$39. Sun–Thurs 11:30am–11pm; Fri–Sat 11:30am–11:30pm.

Pub 1842 ★★ PUB FARE   Chef Michael Mina has three other spots in town, and this is his most casual, not to mention the most affordable. The 1842 in the name refers to the year that the pilsner was invented, and so Mina built this restaurant as a gastropub, where the brews are as important as the food.

YOU GOTTA HAVE A theme

It shouldn't be too surprising to learn that a town devoted to gimmicks has just about every gimmick restaurant there is. No matter your interest, there is probably a theme restaurant here for you, from sports to pop culture and back again. Fans should have a good time checking out the stuff on the walls, but for the most part the memorabilia is usually more interesting than the food. Here are some of the best of the bunch.

The House of Blues ★★, in Mandalay Bay, 3950 Las Vegas Blvd. S. (www.hob. com, ✆ **702/632-7600**, Sun–Thurs 7am–11pm, Fri–Sat 7am–midnight), has a Mississippi Delta blues theme complete with frequent concerts and a gospel brunch. The food is down-home Southern and there is lots of it for pretty decent prices.

Southern staples are also on tap at the **Harley-Davidson Café ★**, 3725 Las Vegas Blvd. S., at Harmon Avenue (www. harley-davidsoncafe.com, ✆ **702/740-4555**, Sun–Thurs 8:30am–11pm, Fri–Sat 9am–midnight), alongside shrines to the easy-rider lifestyle evoked by the motorcycle brand.

The Hard Rock Cafe ★, 3771 Las Vegas Blvd. S. (www.hardrock.com, ✆ **702/733-7625**, daily 8:30am–11pm), has decent burgers and all of the requisite music memorabilia you have come to expect packed in a massive, 42,000-square-foot, three-level behemoth with a gigantic gift shop, a 1,000-seat concert venue, and more.

Note: There is a second Hard Rock Cafe at the Hard Rock Hotel, 4475 Paradise Rd., at Harmon Avenue (✆ **702/733-8400**).

Parrot Heads, as fans of Jimmy Buffet refer to themselves, like to party it up at **Margaritaville ★**, at the Flamingo, 3555 Las Vegas Blvd. S. (www.margaritavillelas vegas.com, ✆ **702/733-3302**, Sun–Thurs 11am–1am, Fri–Sat 11am–2am), the singer's tropical-themed cafe/bar/club. The menu runs a range from Mexican to something sort-of-Caribbean-themed to basic American, and it's not all that bad, considering. Partaking in lots of fruity tropical drinks doesn't hurt, either.

If the rodeo is more your style, the Pro Bull Riding organization has its own place at the **PBR Rock Bar & Grill ★** at Planet Hollywood, 3663 Las Vegas Blvd. S. (www.pbrrockbar.com, ✆ **702/750-1685**, daily 8am–late). It serves up down-home American food in a country-western environment complete with a mechanical bull and tire swings above the tables.

You would think the celebrity shrine and memorabilia factory that is the **Planet Hollywood** restaurant would be in the Planet Hollywood Resort. But you'd be wrong. Instead, it's at Caesars Palace in the Forum Shops, 3500 Las Vegas Blvd. S. (www.planethollywood. com, ✆ **702/791-7827**, Sun–Thurs 11am–11pm, Fri–Sat 11am–midnight).

Which is fantastic, because a menu that includes foodie-friendly bar food like lobster corn dogs with crème fraîche mustard, and burgers topped with peanut butter, bacon jam, and potato chips (it works—really!). Each dish looks as beautiful as it tastes. In addition to more than 30 craft and imported beers on tap, there's a section of the bar menu dedicated to different variations of the Moscow Mule. Mina's wine programs in all his other restaurants are exceptional—that rings true for here as well, including wines by the glass.

In MGM Grand, 3799 Las Vegas Blvd. S. www.pub1842.com. ✆ **702/891-3922**. Main courses $18–$47. Sun, Mon, Thurs 11:30am–10pm; Fri–Sat 11:30am–11pm.

The Pub at Monte Carlo ★ PUB FARE   The term "gastropub" gets bandied a lot in Vegas. It refers to beer-centric bars that serve elevated food. But let's be real: Sometimes all you want is a really good selection of suds and some food to keep you from getting too tipsy. Which is what you get at this two-story pub: It has 200 beers on tap, from the usual suspects to more interesting craft and local selections, including the pub's own brews. Beers are categorized by flavor profiles, which comes in handy when you know what you like, but aren't sure how to branch out. The menu itself features bar-fare greatest hits like sandwiches, pizzas, and burgers. Don't be fooled by the "Gus' Small Bites" moniker—Gus being the whale mascot of The Pub—the appetizers (like loaded potato skins and wedges served with Amberbock chili and cheese) are big enough to be meals themselves. *Perk:* Sports junkies won't miss any action thanks to the bar's many TVs, and live bands set the soundtrack on weekend nights in the large warehouse setting.

In Monte Carlo, 3770 Las Vegas Blvd. S. www.montecarlo.com. ✆ **702/730-7420.** Main courses $12–$28. Sun–Thurs 7am–11pm; Fri–Sat 7am–1am.

Red Square ★★ CONTINENTAL/RUSSIAN   The headless statue of Stalin outside the restaurant notwithstanding, Red Square doesn't *actually* serve Russian cuisine. Its menu is made up of American cuisine with Russian ideas, and hey, that's pretty fun. Like a starter of "Siberian Nachos" that pairs smoked salmon, wasabi cream, and fish roe on top of fried wonton chips, or short rib dumplings, a nod to *pelmeni,* served with horseradish sour cream. The caviar service is of fine domestic varieties (that happily won't break the bank), with proper accompaniments of egg whites, shallots, and crème fraîche, to be piled extravagantly on blini or toast points. There are also dishes of Russian extraction, like the beef Stroganoff and the chicken Kiev, and they're tasty but not all that authentic. The Kiev, for example, is a roulade of the chicken that's crusted on the outside, but lacks the best part of a true Kiev, which is cutting into it to let the melted butter spill out. This all may seem beside the point if you decide to go full fantasy here, donning a (loaner) fur coat and Cossack's hat to dine in the vodka locker, an icy chamber near the front of the bar where one can drink vodka, and shiver at the same time—like they do in the old country.

In Mandalay Bay, 3950 Las Vegas Blvd. S. www.redsquarelasvegas.com. ✆ **702/632-7407.** Main courses $27–$65. Sun–Thurs 4–11pm; Fri–Sat 4pm–midnight.

Rí Rá Irish Pub ★★ IRISH   How authentic is this Irish pub? It was imported piece by piece from West Cork in Ireland, along with a number of the servers and bartenders (you can't fake a brogue that thick), who've lucked out on a great work exchange program. The Guinness flows freely—not to mention properly, and at the right temperature—to accompany traditional Irish pub fare like bangers and mash, fish and chips and shepherd's pie. The menu also encompasses contemporary Irish-fusion cuisine, like the potato cake starter that's topped with sour cream and balsamic oil, and a fantastic meatloaf made with pork, veal, and beef, and served with Guinness ketchup, cheddar, and onion rings. Take a tour of the space, it looks narrow from the front but goes much deeper than you expect, to include three more bars—one Victorian-themed bar and watched over by a 500-pound statue of St. Patrick, a Whiskey room, and a live music venue which hosts bands direct from, where else, Ireland.

At Mandalay Place, 3930 Las Vegas Blvd. S. www.rira.com. © **702/632-7771.** Main courses lunch $11–$22, dinner $11–$28. Mon–Thurs 8am–3am; Fri 8am–4am; Sat 9am–4am; Sun 9am–3am.

Shake Shack ★ BURGERS   As the first West Coast outpost of the New York burger institution, Shake Shack opened up with great fanfare outside, appropriately enough, New York-New York Hotel and Casino. At heart, it's a simple burger joint, but the lines snaking out the door suggest that it's more than that. All the Angus beef burgers are cooked to medium, and if you get the most-plain iteration, it would simply be tucked into the soft brioche bun with lettuce, tomato, cheese, and their secret Shack Sauce. And in a town when you can get a burger topped with foie gras and truffles and a side of Chateau Petrus, sometimes all you want is a plain, but really good, burger. For those already indoctrinated into the Shake Shack menu, there are a couple of only-in-Vegas bites that might interest you, like the ShackMeister burger, topped with ShackMeister ale-marinated onion rings, cheese, and Shack Sauce, along with the Shack-a-palooza, a sundae monstrosity with three scoops of each frozen custard flavor, made to be split between four to six people, or just two if you're feeling especially gluttonous.

In New York–New York, 3790 Las Vegas Blvd. S. www.shakeshack.com. © **725/222-6730.** Main courses $5–$10. Sun–Thurs 11am–midnight; Fri–Sat 11am–2am.

Tacos & Tequila ★★ MEXICAN   Though its open-air dining room in the middle of the hotel makes Tacos & Tequila feel oddly exposed, the only real downside to dining here is that you'll have to talk a bit louder. That will cease to be a problem once you dive into one of their margaritas, all made with fresh-squeezed lime juice and agave nectar, before other luscious ingredients—like prickly pear, pomegranate, mango, or pineapple—are added to the mix. Like your tequila straight? T&T has an extensive tequila list along with flights of unique *añejos, reposados* and even mezcals. On the "tacos" side of the enterprise (the menu also has fajitas, quesadillas and burritos, by the way), the food is enlivened by a dozen traditional and off-the-beaten-path fillings: grilled steak, bacon, poblano chilies of the Alambre, carnitas and light, summery vegetables. Dedication to high quality and organic products ensure the food tastes fresher than what you'd get from your neighborhood taco joint, and the higher-than-average check prices reflect that.

In Luxor, 3900 Las Vegas Blvd. S. www.tacosandtequilalv.com. © **702/262-5225.** Main courses $11–$22. Daily 11am–11pm.

Todd English P.U.B. ★★★ PUB FARE   Out of the two restaurants of chef Todd English's on the Strip (the other being his Mediterranean-inspired Olives at Bellagio up the Strip), we like this one better because, for some time

quick BITES

Food courts are a dime a dozen in Vegas, but the one in **New York–New York**, 3790 Las Vegas Blvd. S. (*C* **702/740-6969**), deserves a mention for two reasons. First, it's the nicest setting for this sort of thing on the Strip, sitting in the Greenwich Village section of New York–New York, which means scaled replica tenement buildings, steam rising from the manhole covers, and more than a little (faux, naturally) greenery, a nice change from unrelentingly shrill and plastic mall decor. Second, the selections are better-than-average food court, with a deli and pizza (as befitting an ode to NYC), and excellent if expensive (for this situation) double-decker burgers, plus **Ben & Jerry's** ice cream. Hours vary by outlet.

The **Monte Carlo**, 3770 Las Vegas Blvd. S., between Flamingo Road and Tropicana Avenue (*C* **702/730-7777**), has traditional offerings like **McDonald's** and **Subway,** which can be comforting if you need it. The food court is open daily from 6am to 3am.

The food court at **Flamingo Las Vegas,** 3555 Las Vegas Blvd. S.

(*C* **702/733-3111**), has a couple of interesting outlets like **Pan Asian Express** and **Johnny Rockets** hamburgers, among others. Hours vary, but it's usually open from 8am until 2am.

If you head farther down the Strip, to **The Grande Canal Shoppes** at the Venetian, 3355 Las Vegas Blvd. S. (*C* **702/414-4500**), you can find another decent food court, with a **Panda Express,** a good pizza place (despite the confusing name of **LA Italian Kitchen**), and more. Plus, it's right by the canals of this faux Venice, one of our favorite places in Vegas. Hours are Sunday through Thursday from 10am until 11pm, and Friday and Saturday from 10am until midnight.

And of course, it should come as no surprise that the biggest mall in Vegas has the biggest food court as well. **The Fashion Show Mall,** 3200 Las Vegas Blvd. S. (*C* **702/369-8382**), has more than a dozen outlets from **KFC Express, Nathan's Famous, Subway, Wendy's,** and more. Hours are Monday through Saturday from 10am until 9pm, and Sunday from 11am until 7pm.

now, it's felt like English has forgotten about Olives, and therefore we have too. Absent chef notwithstanding, the pub is still a fine place to eat, drink, watch sports and, overall, be merry. The menu is a mix between classic English pub fare (bangers and mash, shepherd's pie, fish and chips) and American bar food (brown butter lobster rolls, grilled bologna sandwiches, fried chicken and waffles), that are complemented by a fantastic beverage program. The beer list alone is worth the trip, with selections from all of the great beer-producing regions in the world, and more obscure ciders and sours. When's the last time you saw bona fide mead on a beer list? Speaking of beers, there is one challenge that you can face here, but it's a good one. The Pub's 7-Second Challenge dares you to pound a beer in seven seconds or less, and it's free. (Not that we would endorse binge drinking, but here's a pro-tip: Don't pick a really fizzy beer).

In The Shops at Crystals, 3720 Las Vegas Blvd. S. www.toddenglishpub.com. *C* **702/489-8080.** Reservations recommended. Main courses $13–$24. Mon–Fri 11am–late; Sat–Sun 9:30am–late.

Yusho ★★ JAPANESE   It's nice to see that the ramen craze has finally made it to the Strip, especially front and center on the Strip where Yusho is. But there's more on the menu than just noodle soup at this bright shop with anime-inspired decor, including smaller snacks you'd find at any good night market in Asia. Grilled meats on skewers are among the typical street food dishes, like the boneless, Thai chile-spiced chicken wings, or the Chinese-style chunks of lamb dusted with cumin. If you want to go with the signature dishes: The Logan Poser Ramen is named for the neighborhood of the original Yusho in Chicago and features chewy noodles in a creamy *tonkatsu* broth with a poached egg, Thai chilies, and a skewer of crispy pork. But that demonstration of excess is nothing compared to the Monster Ramen, a near bathtub of soup with grilled shrimp and pork on skewers, maitake mushrooms, butter(!), and three eggs. Be sure to ask your server if there's anything off-menu that you need to try, but be warned that the chef is a mad genius who likes to offer very, um, unusual specials. The last time I went I was duped—er, pleasantly surprised—into eating "Quacky Mountain Oysters." They were tasty, but I was glad they didn't tell me until the end that I was chomping down on deep-fried duck testicles.

In Monte Carlo, 3770 Las Vegas Blvd. S. www.yusholv.com. ℂ **702/730-6888.** Small plates $8–$45. Wed–Thurs, Sun 5–11pm; Fri–Sat 5pm–1am.

Inexpensive

Bobby's Burger Palace ★★ BURGERS   Though he's best known for Southwest flavors (like those at his Mesa Grill at Caesars Palace), Food Network old guard Bobby Flay decided to go the more pan-American route for his second restaurant in town. Though the menu at the walk-up counter is almost exclusively stuff that goes between two buns, he's maintained his reputation for big, bold flavors in just about every version. Flay takes a regional

Great Meal Deals

We've already alluded to the rock-bottom budget meals and graveyard specials available at casino hotel restaurants, quality not assured and Pepto-Bismol not provided. As prices and deals can change without notice, we don't want to list examples, but finding a full prime-rib dinner for around $10 is not rare (pun definitely intended).

Your best bet is to keep your eyes open as you travel through town, as hotels tend to advertise their specials on their marquees. Or you can go to www.vegas.com and click on **"Dining"**

and then **"Dining Bargains,"** though the tips and prices may be somewhat out-of-date. Following are three examples of current options for late-night munchies: **Coronado Café** at the South Point offers a $3.95 steak-and-eggs meal, while $2.95 gets you a hearty breakfast at **The Sundance Grill** at the Silverton. At the Hard Rock Hotel, **Mr. Lucky's 24/7** is a particularly good diner, with particularly good people watching. Ask your server about the $7.77 steak, three grilled shrimp, and sides, it's not on the menu, so you have to know about it.

approach to the burger, which you can build on standard beef, turkey, or chicken breast; offering varieties like the Philadelphia, which is a play on its native cheese steak, with grilled onions, provolone cheese, and hot peppers; and the Miami, served Cubano-style, pressed with ham, Swiss cheese, mustard, and pickles. He's also a fan of putting potato chips in his sandwiches, like the Crunchburger with double American cheese and house-made chips. Shakes are fun, with out-of-the-ordinary flavors like pistachio and blueberry pomegranate, but you can't beat the classic dark chocolate.

At The Shops at Crystals, 3750 Las Vegas Blvd. S. www.bobbysburgerpalace.com. ⓒ **702/598-0191.** Main courses $10–$12. Daily 11am–midnight.

Burger Bar ★ DINER   At the original fancy burger restaurant on the Strip, chef Hubert Keller encourages diners to get creative. Everyone starts with patty options that range from Angus beef to lamb to buffalo, then diners pile on toppings that range from the usual bacon and cheddar cheese to the extravagant, like foie gras, truffle mayo, or jalapeno bacon. Be careful though, enough of those high-ticket items, plus the cost of a side of fries, and you might be wondering why you didn't just go out for a steak instead. If you feel like leaving it up to the experts, there are "pre-determined" burgers as well, like the Keller special made with buffalo, caramelized onions, baby spinach, and blue cheese, or the Hangover Burger; which will remind you of a certain fast food burger that also has special sauce, lettuce, and cheese on a sesame seed bun—but this one is way better.

In Mandalay Place, 3930 Las Vegas Blvd. S. www.burger-bar.com. ⓒ **702/632-9364.** Main courses $10–$60 (burgers start at $10, depending on kind of meat, toppings start at 45¢ and go way up). Sun–Thurs 11am–11pm; Fri–Sat 11am–1am.

MID-STRIP
Expensive

B&B Ristorante ★★ ITALIAN   Mario Batali, one of the other original Food Network alums on the Strip, has an exorbitantly priced steak house as well as a wine bar in town, but this is our favorite of the bunch. It isn't your red-sauce-Italian kind of place. Here you'll eat the kind of food you'd eat at someone's house in Rome. At B&B, less is more, with many dishes having five ingredients or less. Batali's home-style, rustic menu is heavy on handmade pastas, like the long strands of *chitarra* with cherry tomatoes, cured fish roe and breadcrumbs, and bucatini all'Amatriciana tossed with *guanciale,* hot peppers, and pecorino. There's a bit of offal as well, as in the tripe served Roman-style, and lamb's tongue with chanterelle mushrooms. The restaurant is also the base for his Las Vegas charcuterie program, where antipasto standards like prosciutto, coppa, and soppresatta are cured in-house.

In The Venetian, 3355 Las Vegas Blvd. S. www.bandbristorante.com. ⓒ **702/266-9977.** Main courses $29–$135. Daily 5–11pm.

Mid-Strip Restaurants

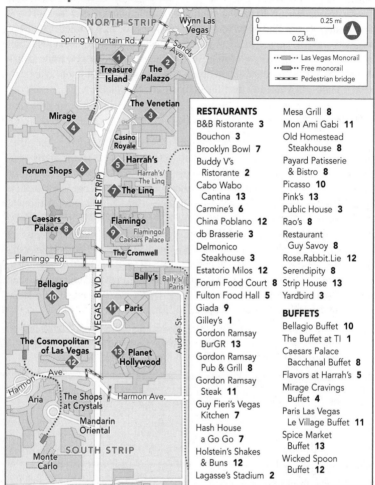

RESTAURANTS

B&B Ristorante **3**
Bouchon **3**
Brooklyn Bowl **7**
Buddy V's Ristorante **2**
Cabo Wabo Cantina **13**
Carmine's **6**
China Poblano **12**
db Brasserie **3**
Delmonico Steakhouse **3**
Estatorio Milos **12**
Forum Food Court **8**
Fulton Food Hall **5**
Giada **9**
Gilley's **1**
Gordon Ramsay BurGR **13**
Gordon Ramsay Pub & Grill **8**
Gordon Ramsay Steak **11**
Guy Fieri's Vegas Kitchen **7**
Hash House a Go Go **7**
Holstein's Shakes & Buns **12**
Lagasse's Stadium **2**

Mesa Grill **8**
Mon Ami Gabi **11**
Old Homestead Steakhouse **8**
Payard Patisserie & Bistro **8**
Picasso **10**
Pink's **13**
Public House **3**
Rao's **8**
Restaurant Guy Savoy **8**
Rose.Rabbit.Lie **12**
Serendipity **8**
Strip House **13**
Yardbird **3**

BUFFETS

Bellagio Buffet **10**
The Buffet at TI **1**
Caesars Palace Bacchanal Buffet **8**
Flavors at Harrah's **5**
Mirage Cravings Buffet **4**
Paris Las Vegas Le Village Buffet **11**
Spice Market Buffet **13**
Wicked Spoon Buffet **12**

Bouchon ★★★ BISTRO   When Thomas Keller, one of the greatest chefs in the American pantheon, decided to open a restaurant in Las Vegas, rather than try to replicate his famed French Laundry in Napa Valley in a field already crowded with 4-hour fine dining experiences, he brought his relaxed bistro instead. "Relaxed" is a term we use loosely, as there are still white tablecloths and impeccable service to go along with the stellar food. The classic French brasserie setting, with brass rails and dark woods, is lightened up by natural sunlight that streams in through the big windows that open to a private courtyard. Set in the exclusive Venezia tower, it's one of the few places where you can eat on the Strip and not feel like you're eating on the Strip. The fare is straightforward, traditional French bistro dishes, like roasted chicken with seasonal vegetables, steak frites with herbed hotel butter, and trout almandine. But you don't have to necessarily go big to enjoy a meal here. Grab a seat at the raw bar along the side to slurp down some of the most pristine oysters you'll find anywhere in the city, or dive into a selection of hors d'oeuvres like the lovely salmon rillettes served from a jar, or a classic quiche du jour. Though the food is seemingly simple, you're paying for the painstaking attention to detail that goes into making the most humble of dishes taste divine.

In The Venetian, 3355 Las Vegas Blvd. S. www.bouchonbistro.com. © **702/414-6200.** Reservations strongly recommended. Main courses dinner $19–$59, brunch $12–$34. Mon–Thurs 7am–1pm, 5–10pm; Fri–Sun 8am–2pm (brunch), 5–10pm; Oyster bar daily 3–10pm.

db Brasserie ★★★ BISTRO   When chef Daniel Boulud decided to return to Las Vegas with his own bistro, he had the chutzpa to place it in the Venetian, despite the fact that Thomas Keller's Bouchon (see above) is in another wing of the same building. Which leads to the question: Can Venetian support two brasseries? The answer is apparently yes. More easily accessible in the resort's Restaurant Row (in good company with Delmonico Steakhouse and Yardbird) Boulud's restaurant feels more relaxed, with a more contemporary take on French classics. But they each have their strengths. While Bouchon is ideal for an evening spent at the raw bar, sucking down oysters and quaffing champagne, I'd head to db Brasserie to tear into Boulud's smoked salmon deviled eggs topped with steelhead roe, then the signature Frenchie burger, topped with cheese and pork belly. Oh yeah, and I'd wash that burger down with a well-mixed cocktail.

In The Venetian, 3355 Las Vegas Blvd. S. www.dbbrasserie.com. © **702/414-6200.** Main courses dinner $18–$75. Open nightly 5–11pm; brunch Sat–Sun 11:30am–3pm; happy hour daily 3–6pm, 10pm–close.

Delmonico Steakhouse ★★ CREOLE/STEAK   Though Emeril Lagasse is best known for his Creole fare at the original Delmonico in New Orleans, he's fine-tuned the menu here to focus on meat. (If you want to sample his NOLA fare exclusively, you're better off heading to the Fish House at MGM Grand.) The front lounge is a popular place to grab a pre-dinner or pre-show drink, though you can order most of the dining room menu here, like the potato chips dressed with parmesan cheese and truffle sauce, or his famed gumbo. But guests at Delmonico's are far more likely to go for meat, and rightly so; we're big fans of the dry-aged, bone-in rib eye for its deep flavor, the fine chateaubriand for two, and the double cut Kurobuta pork chop. Sides are ample, like the enormous twice-baked potato, or the Southern-inspired grits with cheddar and bacon. An extensive whiskey library is worth a gander; they actually have one of those sliding ladders found in real libraries to pull down some of the more interesting vintages from the top bar shelf.

In The Venetian, 3355 Las Vegas Blvd. S. www.emerils.com. © **702/414-3737.** Main courses lunch $15–$51, dinner $36–$95. Daily 11:30am–2pm; Sun–Thurs 5–10pm; Fri–Sat 5–10:30pm.

Estiatorio Milos ★★★ GREEK/SEAFOOD   Those who have been to an actual fish market in Greece or Tokyo might be familiar with this sight as your server gives you a tour past the kitchen: varying species and sizes of fish and shellfish all waiting on ice to be plucked and cooked. Much like those markets, the fish here have only been out of the water about 24 hours, having been caught in the regional waters of the Mediterranean specifically for Milos before catching the first flight to Vegas. If words like *lavraki, fagri,* and *barbouni* are literally all Greek to you, your server will explain each fish—from where they came from, down to their flavor profiles. Pick the one that sounds good, and they're grilled with nothing more than olive oil and a bit of lemon juice. If you have a non-seafood lover with you, there are options like grilled lamb chops and a filet mignon, both served with fried Greek potatoes. You'll both be able to enjoy a starter of the Milos special: a pile of light, deep fried zucchini and eggplant so beautifully stacked you might not want to disturb its construction.

Dinner is insanely expensive here (flying fish in from the Mediterranean every day ain't cheap!) but the lunch special is one of the best deals on the Strip, hands down. For $25.17 (the price goes up one penny each year), you can taste your way through three courses of Milos' most popular dishes, with choices that include Greek mezze of various yogurt-based dips, whole-grilled Mediterranean sea bass, a side dish, and dessert.

In The Cosmopolitan of Las Vegas, 3708 Las Vegas Blvd. S. www.milos.ca. ⓒ **702/698-7930.** Lunch 3-course prix fixe $25, dinner main courses $28–$68. Sun–Thurs noon–11pm; Fri–Sat noon–midnight.

Gordon Ramsay Steak ★ STEAK/SEAFOOD   Though his TV persona on shows like *Hell's Kitchen* and *Kitchen Nightmares* make chef Gordon Ramsay seem like a terror, in reality he's just a passionate chef who earned many accolades before he ever became famous. Out of his three restaurants in town, this is his finest. Enter via the tube-like "Chunnel" structure, which is meant to "transport" guests from "Paris" to "London." On the ceiling is a Union Jack, and a neon sculpture that looks like a bunch of random squiggles, but the lines actually represent Ramsay's hand motions when he's making a beef Wellington. The Wellington, one of the dishes feared most by contestants on *Hell's Kitchen,* is done really well here, in the classic manner, with a filet wrapped in prosciutto and cooked with a mushroom *duxelle* inside pastry dough (and we can't imagine why the TV chefs have such a hard time with it). Steaks are a must, and they're presented to guests on a multi-tiered mirrored cart, so you can decide if you'd like one of the 28-day dry aged cuts or the more marbled American Wagyu. The Wagyu rib cap is pricey, but terrifically luscious and tender. The other Gordon Ramsay restaurants on the Strip have a version of the sticky toffee pudding, but it's best at the steak house. The traditional English dessert cake comes soaked in brown sugar toffee sauce, with a side that looks like a whole stick of butter, but is really brown butter ice cream.

In Paris Las Vegas, 3655 Las Vegas Blvd. S. www.gordonramsay.com. ⓒ **877/346-4642.** Main courses $41–$104. Daily 5–10:30pm.

Mesa Grill ★★ SOUTHWESTERN   One of the first Food Network chefs (after Emeril) to set up shop in Vegas, Flay has proved that his reputation, and his Mesa Grill, has some longevity. He's known for creating strong Southwestern flavors, but with a delicate touch. The tiger shrimp and tamale is a mainstay at all his restaurants, a combination of sweet shrimp and mildly pungent garlic. While I'd normally never put anything on a steak besides salt and pepper, the chipotle-glaze on the rib eye works like gangbusters. The rest of the menu features dishes that are "ancho-chile glazed" or "New Mexico spice-rubbed," but in each, the spice is applied with great balance so that flavors never become overwhelming.

In Caesars Palace, 3570 Las Vegas Blvd. S. www.mesagrill.com. ℂ **877/346-4642.** Main courses brunch and lunch $16–$24, dinner $25–$52. Mon–Fri 11am–2:30pm, 5–11pm; Sat–Sun 10:30am–3pm, 5–11pm.

Old Homestead Steakhouse ★★★ STEAK   Though the steak house is a mainstay of Las Vegas dining, New York has been doing steak waaaay longer. Case in point: Old Homestead, which opened in 1868 in the Big Apple. When Old Homestead finally made it out West, they knew they didn't have to mess with what's been working for the past 150 years. The same giant steaks, direct from famed butcher Pat LaFrieda, are all here: the New York Strip, a porterhouse for two, and even the Gotham rib eye, a cut so big that the bone that remains in it makes you feel like Fred Flintstone. Homestead does well by veggies, too, especially the Kitchen Sink Salad, chock full of shrimp, salami, bacon, avocado, and hearts of palm. The rest of the menu is classic steak house fare with insane upgrades, such as shrimp cocktail with some of the biggest shrimp we've ever seen, lobster mac and cheese, and duck fat fries.

In Caesars Palace, 3570 Las Vegas Blvd. S. www.theoldhomesteadsteakhouse.com. ℂ **877/346-4642.** Main courses $37–$90. Sun–Thurs 5–10pm; Fri–Sat 5–10:30pm.

Restaurant Guy Savoy★★★ FRENCH   In 2006, at the height of the dining revolution in Las Vegas, there was an influx of French chefs to land on the Strip. Guy Savoy, who was a star in Paris, was recruited by the president of Caesars Palace based on one dish: the artichoke black truffle soup. Once you've tasted it yourself, you can understand why someone would use their executive powers to bring the person responsible for it to another country. The soup, and Savoy's other signature dishes, are far from the ultra-modern, deconstructed dishes that come from other French chefs in town. Rather this is French fare elevated to its most elegant form. Colors of Caviar is a shot-glass parfait of expensive roe in layers of black and green, topped tableside with white vinaigrette sabayon. In the fall, during white truffle season, the restaurant gets some of the biggest specimens and creates an entire menu around the expensive tuber—but the best dish in that series is a simple risotto topped with a few delicate shavings of the truffle. These dishes, along with a roaming bread cart (to pair bread with each course, naturally) and dessert cart (the chocolate mousse is Savoy's own grandmother's recipe) are ideal introductions for those who want to leap into fine French dining, without being completely lost.

In Caesars Palace, 3570 Las Vegas Blvd. S. www.caesars.com. © **702/731-7286.** Reservations required. Signature Menu $26–$90; Innovation Menu $375; main course $80–$110. Wed–Sun 5:30–9:30pm.

Picasso ★★★ FRENCH As one of the original fine dining restaurants in Las Vegas when Bellagio opened in 1989, Picasso, like the priceless artwork that hangs in it, is timeless. Chef Julian Serrano has been in command since the beginning, and he's still spinning haute French fare like no other. There are several prix fixe menus to choose from, though they all change often, reflecting the season and whatever looks best that day. Does Serrano's artful cuisine complement the millions of dollars of artwork or is it the other way around? With dishes like the warm quail salad with sautéed artichokes and pine nuts, roasted milk-fed veal chops, or pigeon and torchon of foie gras, all beautifully presented and arranged by nimble hands in the kitchen, it's a toss-up. Though we feel that you can see Picasso's paintings in Vegas more often than you can experience a meal this exceptional.

In Bellagio, 3600 Las Vegas Blvd. S. www.bellagio.com. © **866/259-7111.** Reservations required. Prix-fixe 4-course dinner $115, 5-course degustation $125. Sun–Wed 5:30–9:30pm.

Rao's ★★★ ITALIAN The original Rao's in Harlem, New York City is purportedly the hardest reservation in the world to get. With only 13 tables, all of which are claimed with standing reservations, you've got to know somebody who knows somebody to eat there. When Rao's finally decided to expand to Las Vegas, lovers of their classic Southern Italian cuisine rejoiced. The Caesars Palace outpost is an exact replica of the original, complete with Christmas decorations hung up over the bar year-round, portraits of celebrities who have joined them for dinner all along the walls, and the working Wurlitzer jukebox, except *this* space has the good fortune of having an outdoor patio and being three times the size. The food is essentially the same as it has been for decades, and no one would want that to change. The meatballs are the thing here, made from "Aunt Anna" Rao's original recipe of pork, beef, and veal, tender and swimming in tangy marinara sauce. Uncle Vincent's Lemon Chicken, with the right amount of char on the skin to soak up the tart lemon vinaigrette, is mandatory as well. The seafood salad, chock full of calamari, shrimp, crab, and lobster, is tossed in an acidic citronette dressing so bright, we contemplated drinking it right from the plate. For dessert, the tiramisu is one of the booziest in the city.

In Caesars Palace, 3570 Las Vegas Blvd. S. www.caeasarspalace.com. © **702/731-7267.** Main courses $29–$57. Sun–Thurs 5–10pm; Fri–Sat 5–10:30pm.

Rose.Rabbit.Lie ★★★ CONTINENTAL Billing itself as a supper club, this haphazardly punctuated restaurant does a good job of straddling the lines between fancy dining room, weird entertainment space, and speakeasy. There used to be a show in the performance space next door, which was supposed to bleed into the restaurant, but once the show closed, the restaurant had to figure out how to make use of the random stages throughout the dining room. So if you're eating in the main room or drinking away in the library bar, you'll get treated to random lounge musicians with performances just avant garde enough to pique your interest. The focus here is small plates that are small in size, but not in price. Though with dishes like caviar "tacos" on Yukon gold potato shells, duck confit pasta, and crispy oysters Rockefeller, Rose.Rabbit. Lie. can be forgiven. For dessert, don't miss the chocolate terrarium; a garden served under a glass cloche that features chocolate "dirt" as well as other cocoa-enhanced delights.

At The Cosmopolitan of Las Vegas, 3708 Las Vegas Blvd. S. www.roserabbitlie.com. © **877/667-0585.** Small plates $9–$38, main courses $24–$56. Wed–Thurs 6pm–midnight; Fri–Sat 6pm–1am.

Strip House ★★ STEAK   Tucked away into the mezzanine of Planet Hollywood, Strip House is dark and definitely romantic, though the low lighting isn't the only thing contributing to the intimate atmosphere. The red-flocked walls are dressed with vintage burlesque and borderline naughty photos of barely clad girls (by today's standards, they seem downright tame). Talk your way into one of the corner booths so you have a view of the rest of the room; the close seating allows you and your dining companion to whisper sweet nothings in each other's ears. The meat program is concise, offering favorite cuts like a New York Strip and dry-aged rib eyes, all served with a bulb of roasted garlic so mild it won't put a damper on your evening. A side of potatoes crisped up in goose fat is small, but packed with flavor and crunch, while creamed spinach offers a hint of black truffles. And if chocolate is your aphrodisiac, the towering 24-layer chocolate cake should be your sweet finish.

In Planet Hollywood Resort & Casino, 3667 Las Vegas Blvd. S. www.striphouse.com. © **702/737-5200.** Main courses $29–$54. Sun–Thurs 5–11pm; Fri–Sat 5–11:30pm.

Moderate

Brooklyn Bowl ★★ ECLECTIC   You got one-stop shopping at this multi-purpose venue: a two-story concert hall at The LINQ, a 32-lane bowling alley,

---

kid-friendly DINING STRATEGIES

Buffets   Cheap meals for the whole family. The kids can choose what they like, and there are sometimes make-your-own sundae machines. See "Buffets" (p. 142) for buffet reviews. Those with reduced prices for kids are noted.

Food Courts   Yes, you can get a Subway sandwich at home, but there is something comforting about the safe array of choices that kids will recognize and probably not complain about. In

addition to those listed in the Quick Bites box on p. 105, check out Forum Food Court (p. 120) at Caesars, which has few recognizable names but better quality.

Theme Restaurants   Although the cuisine usually won't win any awards, theme restaurants are often great places to take kids for their wide-ranging menus and plenty of distractions to keep them entertained. See "You Gotta Have a Theme" (p. 102).

and a restaurant that serves fantastic comfort food. Start on one floor and head to the rest in any order you like. The menu alone might just keep you in the restaurant all night though, thanks to a huge selection that includes hummus, pork rinds, French bread pizzas, and barbecue. For having such a diverse menu, Brooklyn Bowl surprisingly does a good job with all of it. The fried chicken is particularly stellar, and available by the platter or as a dinner. It can even be prepared gluten-free. Oh, and if you do decide to go bowling, definitely keep that separate from eating, as fingers greasy from fried chicken don't belong in bowling balls.

In The LINQ, 3545 Las Vegas Blvd. S., Suite 22. www.brooklynbowl.com. ✆ **702/862-2695.** Main courses $14–$28. Sun–Thurs 11am–2am; Fri–Sat 11am–4am.

Buddy V's Ristorante ★★ ITALIAN   Though he's best known as the *Cake Boss* on TLC, Buddy Valastro has a savory side too, which he thankfully has decided to share at this restaurant at the front of the Shoppes at Palazzo. The menu is rooted in his family's original recipes, with favorites like a deep, hearty lasagna, steak pizzaiola, and his mother-in-law's shrimp scampi with angel hair pasta. It doesn't have to be Sunday to enjoy the gravy, a rich, chunky red sauce chock full of sausage, lamb, and meatballs, that tastes like it's been simmering on the stove all day, served in a bowl over rigatoni. Go full on family-style for brunch, for an all-you-can-eat extravaganza that includes salumi, frittatas, eggs *al forno,* carbonara, and traditional chicken parmesan. As you can imagine, desserts are strong here, with bites like warm Nutella cake, and traditional cannolli crusted with pistachios and filled with sweet pastry cream. But half the fun of the showcase bakery across the hall is the windows into the pastry kitchen, where crowds watch cooks make and fill Valastro's signature "lobster tail" puff pastry cone with custard cream and fruit.

In The Grand Canal Shoppes at The Palazzo, 3325 Las Vegas Blvd S. www.buddyvlasvegas.com. ✆ **702/607-2355.** Main courses lunch $14–26, dinner $14–$46. Sun–Thurs 11:30am–10pm; Fri–Sat 11:30am–11pm.

Cabo Wabo Cantina ★ MEXICAN   Sammy Hagar not only has his own brand of tequila, but a Mexican restaurant from which to serve it. Celebrity backer notwithstanding, Cabo Wabo has a fun party atmosphere that's amplified when it spills out on the Strip-front patio. An offshoot of the original Cabo San Lucas location, it's spring break year-round here, fueled, naturally, with margaritas laden with Hagar's tequila, that can be slammed by the glass or by the pitcher. Watch out for the "Can't Drive 55," a mind-eraser with tequila, Sammy's Beach Bar rum, vodka, gin, and a couple of mixers—you shouldn't be driving anything after this. The menu features perfunctory Mexican fare. Though no one's really expecting it to be Border Grill caliber, it does the job, with tacos, burritos, and enchiladas laying the base for a long night of drinking. The Red Rocker has a residence in Las Vegas, so chances are good you might actually run into him here.

In Planet Hollywood Resort & Casino, 3663 Las Vegas Blvd. S. www.cabowabocantina.com/vegas. ✆ **702/385-2226.** Main courses $14–$35. Daily 8am–11pm.

Carmine's ★ ITALIAN   The menu for this family-style Italian restaurant is plastered against the wall, and when you look at the prices—averaging $40 a pop for entrees—you will experience some sticker shock. But the blow is softened when you realized that each order is meant for at least four people (or two really gluttonous ones). With high ceilings and two stories, it feels like a banquet hall, but the servers have a knack for making you feel like you're the only people there. The chicken wings Scarpariello-style, with hot and sweet cherry peppers, are a great starter before you get into plate-sized veal scaloppine and enough pasta to feed an Italian army. Whether you're in a big group or a four top (seriously, you want to go with at least three other people), these massive dishes still taste like they were made in a home kitchen. And there's no shame in asking for a doggy bag.

In The Forum Shops at Caesars Palace, 3500 Las Vegas Blvd. S. www.carminesvegas. com. ℭ **702/473-9700.** Family-style main courses $28–$86. Sun–Thurs 11am–11pm; Fri–Sat 11am–midnight.

China Poblano ★ CHINESE/MEXICAN   Pronounced "CHEEna poBLAno," this is chef José Andres' unlikely mash-up of two popular cuisines. The menu explains that they are related thanks to the Spanish galleons that brought Asian spices and fruits to Mexico and chilies to China. The best part? It's not really fusion fare, as evidenced by the two different walk-up windows in front: one for tacos, one for dumplings. While we have successfully avoided learning what a ma-po tofu taco would taste like, ultimately China Poblano is a study in regional street food, which you are welcome to mix and match as you please. From the Chinese section (where all the prices end in 88¢ for good luck), we're fans of the *har gow,* a standard on dim sum menus; the *rou jia mo,* the Chinese version of a hamburger with braised red pork on a sesame bun; and When Pigs Fly, steamed barbecue pork buns. Speaking of pigs flying, Andres is the only chef we'd allow to charge us $5 to $10 for one taco, reasonable for fillings like langoustine and slow-cooked Oaxacan-style beef. Also noteworthy are the super-cheesy chilaquiles in a bright green tomatillo salsa.

In The Cosmopolitan of Las Vegas, 3708 Las Vegas Blvd. S. www.chinapoblano.com. ℭ **702/698-7900.** Small plates $5–$22. Daily 11:30am–11:30pm.

Giada ★★★ ITALIAN   Chefs usually have a restaurant or two under their belts before they are elevated to "celebrity chef" status, but Food Network staple Giada de Laurentiis did it the other way around. After finding success through showcasing her easy-breezy, California Italian cuisine on TV for many years, she finally has a brick-and-mortar to her name. And her name is everywhere in this bright, airy restaurant at The Cromwell that overlooks the Strip. Embroidered on the napkins, embossed on the plates, stitched into backs of the chairs, Giada wants you to know you're in *Giada's* house. Antipasti platters are a great way to start, mixing and matching bites like eggplant caponata, bacon-wrapped dates, cheese and salumi from the market-style deli in the front. Not in the mood for a full-on Italian feast? Skip the dining room, take a seat at the bar and make a meal of the antipasti alone. You'll save a little money too. Whatever you do, make sure to try at least one of her signature dishes—the lemon spaghetti, or the chicken cacciatore for two. A cute footnote: when Giada refers to Italian dishes in her show, she suddenly turns on her Italian accent, enunciating words like "spah-GEH-ti" and "ree-gah-TOH-ne." In order for guests to fully channel her, the menu includes phonetic spellings of how she says them aloud. We told you she wants you to know where you're eating.

In The Cromwell, 3595 Las Vegas Blvd. S. www.thecromwell.com. ℭ **702/777-3777.** Main courses $25–$81. Daily 8am–11pm.

Gilley's ★★ BARBECUE   There's really only one spot serving real barbecue on the Strip, and it's this honky-tonk at Treasure Island. Don't be discouraged if you don't know how to two-step or are lacking cowboy boots, Gilley's 'cue is loved by all. There's a namesake beef and bean chili on the menu, but it was the award-winning green chili that had us wanting another bowl. A rich, tomatillo sauce enhanced with Hatch and poblano chilies, making it tangy and only slightly spicy, it is studded with big chunks of pork, topped with Mexican sour cream, and served with fresh tortillas. Barbecue is done properly here, smoked over a mesquite pit. St. Louis spare ribs get finished with a Southern Comfort barbecue sauce glaze, while the baby back ribs also take a glaze at the end, though you're more than welcome to order them naked (the ribs, not you) if all you need for flavor is smoke. The combos are the best way to go here, with choices of two to six meats, so you can sample a little bit of everything. Should you want to take a ride on the mechanical bull, make sure you do it before you eat, or wait a good period after—it's definitely not fun when you're as stuffed as you'll get here. Line dancing to help digest is always a good idea.

At Treasure Island, 3300 Las Vegas Blvd. S. www.gilleyslasvegas.com. ℭ **702/894-7111.** Main courses $9–$35. Sun–Thurs 11am–2am; Fri–Sat 11am–4am.

Gordon Ramsay Pub & Grill ★ PUB/BRITISH   If you want to leave Vegas being able to brag you ate at one of Gordon Ramsay's restaurants, yet aren't into paying an arm and a leg for it (as you would at his steakhouse at Paris), and want more than just a burger to show for it (as you'd get from BurGR at Planet Hollywood), this is your best compromise. During the day it's a casual pub, comfortable enough to down a few pints from the 36 beers on tap, and perhaps a Scotch egg (traditionally this bar snack would be a hard-boiled egg encased in sausage, but this one is delicate, silky and soft-boiled). At night, when the lights dim in the dining room, the mood shifts and the vibe becomes (slightly) more elegant. I'm particularly fond of the fish & chips: flaky cod dressed in a crunchy Yorkshire ale batter with thick cut chips and mushy peas. A suggested pairing of Innis & Gunn is right on, and also happens to be one of Ramsay's favorite pints. The front of the bar and dining room are open to the casino floor, which is great for people watching, terrible for intimate conversations.

In Caesars Palace, 3570 Las Vegas Blvd. S. www.gordonramsay.com. ℭ **877/346-4642.** Main courses lunch $14–$27, dinner $21–$67. Sun–Thurs 11am–11pm; Fri–Sat 11am–midnight.

Guy Fieri's Vegas Kitchen ★ AMERICAN   Even if his name wasn't emblazoned (literally, with flames on the sign, much like the flames often found on his shirts) on the front of the restaurant, when dishes have names like bacon mac and cheese burger, the Tatted-up turkey burger, and Dragon's Breath Chili cheese fries, it's obvious that this restaurant belongs to Food Network favorite Guy Fieri. He's made his reputation out of showcasing outrageous dishes that fit his ebullient personality. While the food may sometimes feel overwrought (Does wing sauce really need to be infused with Fireball whiskey? Does an Italian deli salad really need a crown of prosciutto-wrapped provolone?), you can't deny that some of his Franken-flavor combinations work. Like the Guy-talian fondue dippers, which are crunchy breadsticks wrapped with pepperoni, served with an awesome provolone and sausage dip; and The Mayor of Flavortown, a towering pastrami and Swiss sandwich. Fieri attended UNLV before he went on to build his celebrity chef empire, so he's included a dish that was one of his staples when he was a poor college student: crispy, spiral-cut potatoes tossed Buffalo-style with hot sauce and topped with blue cheese. Fieri's second Vegas restaurant, El Burro Burracho is at the Rio and features his take on Mexican fare, which means lots more flare but *en Español*.

In The LINQ, 3535 Las Vegas Blvd. S. www.guyfieri.com. ✆ **702/734-3139.** Main courses $16–$32. Sun–Thurs 8am–midnight; Fri–Sat 8am–2am.

Hash House a Go Go ★★★ AMERICAN   If you're going to actually pay for breakfast in town, please don't do it at a buffet (brunch is another story, though). Your first meal of the day deserves to be a good one. This is Vegas, after all, you need to be properly fueled. Enter Hash House a Go Go (either at The LINQ, Plaza, Rio, or its original location on the West side) known for 1) "twisted farm food," and 2) obscenely large portions. For example, the crispy pork tenderloin (used in a sandwich) is pounded out to the size of a Frisbee. When it arrives, eclipsing a tiny bun, it's comical. Farm Scrambles are served not on plates, but platters, with a thick foundation of griddled mashed or crispy potatoes. The omelets have salmon, tomato, pesto, and brie; or ham, spinach, and cheddar folded in. One of the biggest hits is the fried chicken Benedict, dressed with a reduction of sweet maple syrup, and two eggs on bacon-studded mashed potatoes . . . and there's a split biscuit somewhere underneath all of that. Lunch and dinner feature more of the same home-style fare, from meatloaf to one-pound burgers, all way bigger than most can finish. *Note:* Check the website for contact info and directions for other locations.

In The LINQ 3535 Las Vegas Blvd. S. www.hashhouseagogo.com. ✆ **702/254-4646.** Main courses $10–$39. Daily 24 hr.

Holstein's Shakes & Buns ★★ AMERICAN   Who knew pigs dressed as cows could be this cute? That's the motif at Holstein's, created by local artist Juan Muniz, and it's part of the appeal of this fancy burger joint, obviously meant to draw in a younger crowd, perhaps even luring in those waiting in line for Marquee right outside. Vegas has many gourmet burger spots to choose from, but Holstein's is my favorite; they kept it classy, yet funky and cool, which is great when you've got burgers like the Gold Standard, made with dry-aged beef sirloin and topped with aged goat cheddar, tomato confit, and garlic-chive aioli. The Steakhouse Burger, a black peppercorn-crusted patty with steak sauce, onion jam, wild mushrooms, and Swiss is also primo. If that sounds too fancy for your tastes, there are plainer options, like the classic with the usual toppings; or the Nom Nom, which, while built on a Kobe beef patty, is dressed with cheddar cheese, potato chips, and thousand island dressing. As far as shakes go, the grown-up Bamboozled varieties are fun (drink more than one of these and you'll definitely feel it later).

In The Cosmopolitan of Las Vegas, 3708 Las Vegas Blvd. S. www.holsteinslv.com. ℗ **702/698-7940.** Main courses $12–$30. Sun, Tues–Thurs 11am–midnight; Fri–Sat, Mon 11am–2am.

Lagasse's Stadium ★ AMERICAN   Emeril himself is a self-proclaimed sports guy, so he transformed this space (a former nightclub) into the best man cave ever. You can't look anywhere without having an HDTV in your line of sight, as there are about 100 of them, broadcasting every sport imaginable. The draw here is the stadium seating, all facing a wall of giant screens, that you have to reserve for big sporting events (table minimums can be hefty, but the comfy couches and personalized service is worth it for a large group). The Super Bowl, as you can imagine, is nuts, as is March Madness. But you'll also see grown men legitimately interested in women's college softball—a step forward (or maybe they had bets down). Friendly rivalries all play out in the dining room, with the kitchen rolling out specials that relate to the teams at stake in big games (sometimes they're reaching, but that's fine). For the Patriot-Seahawks matchup during Super Bowl XLIX, for example, New England clam chowder and Fanny Bay oysters from Puget Sound were on the menu. The daily offerings are a mix of Emeril's classic NOLA cuisine, including a shrimp po' boy, shrimp and grits, and his fantastic etouffee; and pub fare like pizza, burgers, and sandwiches, all with that special "bam" for which Emeril is known.

In The Palazzo, 3325 Las Vegas Blvd. S. www.emerils.com. ℗ **702/607-2665.** Main courses $14–$37. Mon–Fri 11am–10pm; Sat–Sun 8:30am–10pm.

Mon Ami Gabi ★★ BISTRO   In a town full of faux French bistros, it can be difficult to figure out how they differ from one another. They all serve roasted chicken and steak frites; they all have quiche and charcuterie boards as starters. While Mon Ami Gabi might not have the caliber of chef behind it like **Bouchon** (p. 108) or **Bardot** (p. 99), what it lacks in celebrity-affiliation, it makes up for in location. Occupying prime real estate center-Strip at Paris, under the shadow of the Eiffel Tower, with patio seating and a perfect view of the Fountains of Bellagio, it offers what is quite possibly the best perch for people watching in the city. So what does it matter that the frisee salad with poached egg, the buttery escargot, and the delicate crepes aren't groundbreaking or original? They're all done exceptionally well and they charge lower prices than the other Strip bistros. Take note that at dinner the prices do go up a dollar or two, but remember that you're paying for bigger portions, as well as the view.

In Paris Las Vegas, 3655 Las Vegas Blvd. S. www.monamigabi.com. ☎ **702/944-4224.** Main courses $10–$26 lunch, $13–$40 dinner. Sun–Thurs 7am–11pm; Fri–Sat 7am–midnight.

Payard Patisserie & Bistro ★★★ BISTRO   Parisian Francois Payard is best known for his buttery, sugary confections. His coveted chocolate croissants are available from the express line, but those who take the time for a full meal here are amply rewarded. There are few places on the Strip that match this elegant, ladies-who-lunch environment, with barely a dozen tables and an exhibition kitchen in the middle. And the food! The croque madame, one of the best in the city, is a toasted ham-and-cheese sandwich laden with béchamel cheese and two fried eggs; while the Benedicts, stacked high with salmon or lobster, rest on buttery, flaky croissants. Lunch offerings are even more substantial, with pressed sandwiches and burgers, and the Niçoise salad will take you right back to Lyon. If you have a minute, take a look at the ornate clock at the front of the cafe; it's called the Chocolate Clock not because it's made of chocolate (though that would be worth seeing), but because it dispenses free petit fours when it chimes several times a day.

In Caesars Palace, 3570 Las Vegas Blvd. S. www.caesarspalace.com. ☎ **702/731-7972.** Breakfast $16–$22, lunch $16–$28, dinner $16–$30. Daily breakfast 7–11am; lunch Mon–Thurs 11am–1:30pm; Fri–Sun 11am–3pm

Public House ★ GASTROPUB   Not to be confused with the venue of the same name at Luxor—that one is more sports bar than gastropub—this temple of spirits has one of the most extensive beer programs on the Strip. There are 24 taps alone, but that doesn't include the more than 200 IPAs, lagers, and stouts that come in bottles and cans, all of which you can see through the front window in cold storage. Don't miss out on the true cask ales, which are transported to the bar through lines along the ceiling. And I'm happy to report that they didn't dumb down the menu to simple pub grub. Sure, burgers and steaks are on offer, but so are more unusual choices, like a duck confit *poutine,* roasted bone marrow, crispy pig ears, and potatoes Spanish-style with a spicy aioli. If you find the beer list daunting, there's an in-house cicerone—the beer version of a wine sommelier—who can walk you through and make suggestions. *Warning:* Since it's so close to Venetian's convention space, lunch gets really crowded when there's a big show in town.

In The Palazzo, 3327 Las Vegas Blvd. S. www.publichouselv.com. ☎ **702/407-5310.** Main courses $14–$44. Daily 11am–11pm.

Serendipity 3 ★ AMERICAN   Foot-long hot dogs? Sure. An omelet stuffed with bacon and French fries specifically for hangovers? Why not? Just as the savory items are huge here, so are the sweets, which is Serendipity's forte. You'll spot the whimsical space outside of Caesars Palace from a mile away, thanks to its pink striped awning. Inside, the Tiffany lampshades will remind you of the original Serendipity 3 in New York City. One of the most ridiculous items we've ever seen here is the Saints and Sinners French toast, which is not simply a couple of slices of Texas toast, but a full loaf of white bread topped with a savory side of bacon and eggs, next to a sweet side with berries and whipped cream. Don't worry, they've cut the crusts off the bread because they're classy like that. Chocoholics rejoice at the Frrrozen Hot Chocolate, a Serendipity signature that combines 20 different types of chocolate to ice-slushy consistency. At a time when so many places are trying to move away from the kitsch of excess in Las Vegas, it's nice to find spots like this that still embrace it.

In Caesars Palace, 3570 Las Vegas Blvd. S. www.caesarspalace.com. ⓒ **877/346-4642.** Reservations not accepted. Main courses $10–$20, desserts $10–$1,000. Sun–Thurs 9am–11pm; Fri–Sat 9am–midnight.

Yardbird ★★ ECLECTIC   Miami probably isn't the first place you'd think of for Southern comfort food, yet it's the birthplace of Yardbird, a spot that nails down-home cooking. At first glance, it's one of those trendy places with exposed filament lighting and reclaimed wood panels on the walls, but that pretention doesn't harm the food. (They also serve drinks in mason jars, but since they're from the south we'll give them a pass.) The key dish here is the fried chicken, named for Llewelyn, one of the grandmothers of the original Yardbird owners, and it's purported to be her recipe. We don't care if they invented it in a lab, frankly, it's that good. The chicken brines for about 27 hours before anybody even thinks about cooking it; then it gets covered in cayenne pepper and deep-fried. You can order the bird alone as a half chicken, or get the whole shebang; it's served with golden brown, cheddar cheese waffles, honey hot sauce, and chow-chow, a sweet and tangy Southern relish. Besides the chicken, they've got a fab version of shrimp and grits, topped with crispy ham; and country-style pate served with pickles that are made in-house. The perfect starter? A set of old school hors d'oeuvres like toast with chicken liver mousse, and a fun BLT stacked with thick-cut bacon and fried green tomatoes. For cocktails, they've created an ice program like no other, infusing cubes with herbs like rosemary and thyme, and freezing the sprigs inside; or adding mustard so that as the ice melts, it adds a savory aspect to smoky drinks. It's weird, but I like it. Even if it is served in a mason jar.

In The Venetian, 3355 Las Vegas Blvd. S. www.runchickenrun.com. ⓒ **702/297-6541.** Main courses lunch $13–$28, dinner $14–$55. Mon–Thurs 11am–11pm; Fri–Sun 11am–midnight.

Inexpensive

Forum Food Court ★★ FOOD COURT   You might wonder why we'd include a food court in a Vegas guide book when there are plenty of food courts in malls around the country. To put it mildly: decision fatigue. Sometimes you just want to eat, and not think too hard about it, or you just have a taste for one thing but don't want to pay through the nose or sit through a whole experience to get it. Formerly the Cypress Street Marketplace, this assortment of casual eateries got a facelift, then a name change, and added a few nationally recognized brands: Earl of Sandwich, Graeter's Ice Cream, Smashburger, DiFara Pizza from Brooklyn, even Philip's Seafood all the way from Maryland. Sure it's fast food, but at least it's not your usual suspects.

In Caesars Palace, 3570 Las Vegas Blvd. S. www.caesarspalace.com. ✆ **702/731-7110.** Most items under $15. Daily 11am–11pm.

Fulton Street Food Court ★★ FOOD COURT
This one *looks* like a food court at first glance, but it's not. And while you order and collect your food yourself, it's also not a buffet since you pay for each dish a la carte. This is Las Vegas' first food hall, one of those vast marketplaces that are popping up all over the country that focus on quality-prepared food (rather than mass volume fare). Here, there are nine distinct stations specializing in sushi, pizza, noodles, and comfort food. If you're on the go, there are options prepared fresh daily, ready for hungry guests to eat and run. Or stay awhile and build your own meal, like custom pizzas and bento boxes, all made to order.

In Harrah's Las Vegas, 3475 Las Vegas Blvd. S. www.harrahs.com. ✆ **800/214-9110.** Most items start at $9. Daily 24 hr.

Gordon Ramsay BurGR ★★ BURGERS
Gordon Ramsay's got a high-priced steakhouse, a more casual (but still pricey) pub, and then there's BurGR, his take on the classic American comfort food. It's set in a Hell's Kitchen–themed dining room, with lots of colorful booths and a wall of glass-enclosed fire near the front. The menus feature a glossy shot of Ramsay, with flames behind him, his arms raised, and mouth open as if he's shouting one of his feared epithets from the show (be glad you're not in the kitchen!). The menu comprises more than a dozen burgers, which run from the traditional, like the American, to the uber cheesy—topped with Fontina, raclette and goat cheeses. The Brittania burger features a fun mix of English sharp cheddar, mango chutney and arugula; but we're partial to the Hog Burger, with a patty made of sustainably raised Mangalitsa pork, topped with more sharp cheddar, apple chutney, and greens. Shakes are layered concoctions of multiple flavors, and you order those by number; the #1 includes caramel pudding, chocolate shake, and a toffee cookie. The sticky toffee pudding gets a new treatment as well, served in a tube as a push pop with salted-peanut ice cream. No matter what you think of Ramsay's persona on TV, this is as fun as his food gets.

In Planet Hollywood Resort & Casino, 3667 Las Vegas Blvd. S. www.gordonramsay.com. ✆ **702/785-5462.** Main courses $13–$18. Sun–Thurs 11am–midnight; Fri–Sat 11am–2am.

Pink's ★★★ DELI
If you've been to the iconic Pink's in Los Angeles, you know how special this hot dog stand is. It's stood near Hollywood for 7 decades, serving A-list celebrities right along with regular Joes who just want one of their all-beef dogs with the perfect snap. The Planet Hollywood location, right on Las Vegas Boulevard, is the right fit for this legendary shack, even though the celebrity count isn't as high. But you can still order the same

hot dog, with unusual toppings like mushrooms, Swiss, and mayo. The "Vegas Strip" dog features two links in one bun, smothered with mustard, onions, chili, and guacamole; the "Showgirl" is crowned with bacon, onions, relish, tomato, kraut, and sour cream. Come to think of it, we'd like to see an actual showgirl eat one of these, headdress and all. Fortunately, here you don't have to line up around the block, as you would in L.A.

At Planet Hollywood Resort & Casino, 3663 Las Vegas Blvd. S. www.planethollywood resort.com. © **702/405-4711.** Main courses $6–$10. Sun–Thurs 11am–midnight; Fri–Sat 11am–1am.

NORTH STRIP

Expensive

Bazaar Meat ★★★ STEAKHOUSE   Chef Jose Andres is one of the most avant-garde chefs of his generation, yet he manages to translate his whimsy into approachable food for the masses. Bazaar Meat, an offshoot of his Bazaar in Los Angeles, is his take on a Vegas steakhouse. The massive room feels like a hipster hunting lodge, with mounted animal heads on the wall and hanging tapestries. Seating is a mix and match of chairs and love seats, all leather, but not all the same. The centerpiece of the main dining room is an open kitchen with a wood-burning grill, where you can watch the cooks searing off big hunks of meat for guests. But there are other counters where guests can dine and interact with chefs, like the charcuterie bar where whole legs of *jamon* hang from the window. Interaction is a big concept here—you don't just order oysters, for example, you request them, and a roving oyster server comes to you, pulls one out with a gloved hand, and shucks it right there for you. A starter of a pork skin chicharron—a popular snack in Andres' native Spain— isn't simply placed on the table for you to pick at. It's presented as one large sheet of puffed-up skin; you're handed a mallet and instructed to smash it to bits. One of our favorite starters is the Wagyu beef carpaccio, served wrapped around a breadstick with Parmesan cheese and an onion dipping sauce. Andres' meat menu focuses on sustainably sourced cuts, most of them from Angus or Wagyu cows, which explains the exorbitant prices. But there are a few, like a flat iron or skirt steak, that won't break the bank.

In SLS Las Vegas, 2535 Las Vegas Blvd. S. www.slslasvegas.com. © **702/761-7757.** Main courses $38–$125. Sun–Thurs 5:30–10pm; Fri–Sat 5:30–11pm.

Cleo ★ MEDITERRANEAN   Another Los Angeles transplant, Cleo gives a nod to the former Sahara hotel by retaining the slanted ceiling, an original design feature of the space, but updating it with a glamorous black-and-white portrait of Cleopatra. The big open room is narrow and long, with more booths than two- or four-top tables. The main event for diners is the *mezze,* a small plate of food meant to be shared and in a specific way: fresh, warm flat bread is delivered to the table in paper bags so that eaters can tear a piece and dip it into perfect baba ghanoush or creamy lebneh cheese salty with feta. Other stars among the little plates are crispy, deep-fried Brussels sprouts

North Strip Restaurants

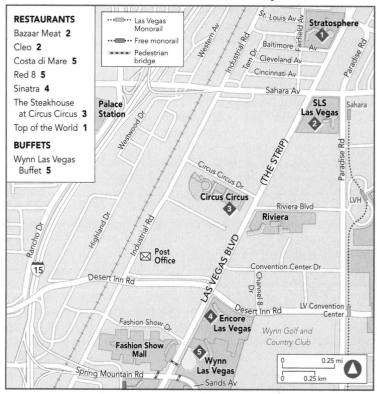

RESTAURANTS

Bazaar Meat **2**
Cleo **2**
Costa di Mare **5**
Red 8 **5**
Sinatra **4**
The Steakhouse at Circus Circus **3**
Top of the World **1**

BUFFETS

Wynn Las Vegas Buffet **5**

···◼··· Las Vegas Monorail
···◼··· Free monorail
▭▭▭ Pedestrian bridge

tossed with chili, hazelnuts, and a spritz of lemon. Flatbreads are another popular item, the Middle Eastern version of pizza, topped with powerful ingredients like merguez sausage, or wild mushrooms with arugula and gruyere cheese. Once you're done sharing, from the open kitchen in the middle come main entrees like lamb cooked in a *tagine* (a traditional Moroccan clay pot), or a hearty eggplant *moussaka,* layered with béchamel and Bolognese sauces.

In SLS Las Vegas, 2535 Las Vegas Blvd. S. www.slslasvegas.com. ✆ **702/761-7612.** Small plates $9–$10, main courses $8–$18. Sun–Thurs 6–10:30pm; Fri–Sat 6–11pm.

Costa di Mare ★★★ ITALIAN/SEAFOOD   People used to joke about being afraid to eat seafood in the desert until James Beard Award-winner Paul Bartolotta proved there was nothing to laugh about. He has since left, and his namesake Bartolotta Ristorante di Mare was handed over to chef Mark LoRusso, and the biggest change was apparently only to the name. The seafood at this two-story restaurant is flown in daily from the Italian Mediterranean, caught by regional fishermen whom the chef has met and recruited himself; some of them only catch for him. When the server swings the glass cart around to your table to show you what's available, you'll be introduced to specimens like dorade, purple snapper, and scorpion fish, all of which have been out of the water for only about 24 hours. Sweet, giant langoustines come from a very specific region near Italy, and even after much pestering, chefs will not divulge its location. If you choose one of the whole fish, or the langoustines, you can opt to have it grilled simply with olive oil and lemon, or you can go more extravagant and have the fish baked under a salt crust. With the latter treatment, they bring the finished dish out to you on a cart and crack the hardened mound, releasing the fish to filet it for you at the table. Don't be put off by all the sea salt, the cooking process results in a perfectly seasoned, perfectly cooked fish. Pastas are as divine as the bounty from the sea, and they aren't all dressed with seafood. The ravioli filled with sheep's milk ricotta and served with pecorino and Marsala wine glaze, and the pappardelle, wide ribbons of pasta with earthy porcini mushrooms, are both eye-rolling good. Like Milos above, the price for seafood this fresh and pristine is exorbitant. But, if you're going to have one Las Vegas dining splurge in a truly gorgeous setting with impeccable service, this is one of those times where "you get what you pay for" is mandatory.

In Wynn Las Vegas, 3131 Las Vegas Blvd. S. www.wynnlasvegas.com. © **888/352-3463** or 702/248-3463. Main courses $21–$150. Daily 5:30–10pm.

Sinatra ★★★ ITALIAN   As the name suggests, this restaurant is an homage to Ol' Blue Eyes, with giant portraits of him on the wall, and other memorabilia, like his Grammy and his Academy Award for his role in *From Here to Eternity*. The man behind the menu, Theo Schoenegger was a longtime personal chef for the singer, so he is acutely familiar with what he liked to eat. (Interestingly, Sinatra himself was an avid home cook. He'd often toil all day on Sundays for a large family dinner, offering dishes like the ones you'd find here.) The fare is homey, with dishes like veal Milanese (crusted and pan-fried, topped with arugula), and simple pastas like fusilli with tomato sauce, taking center stage. Should you want to eat "his way," Frank's personal favorites were spaghetti and clams in a fragrant tomato broth, and osso buco with creamy risotto Milanese. The soundtrack here, as you'd expect, comes exclusively from the crooner's catalog, but with contemporary covers here and there; you can even purchase a CD of the piped-in music.

In Encore Las Vegas, 3121 Las Vegas Blvd. S. www.wynnlasvegas.com. © **702/248-3463.** Main courses $27–$55. Daily 5:30–10:30pm.

The Steakhouse ★ STEAK   Despite the unimaginative name, this mainstay at Circus Circus is one of the most underrated steakhouses on the Strip. Open for more than 3 decades, this place is about as retro as they come—no renovations here, we're guessing. Probably the only difference between now and when this place opened is that you can't smoke in the dim dining room anymore. As you enter, you're greeted by the dry-aging lockers, where you can peer into the windows to see big hunks of meat aging, creating intensely flavored beef. While many steakhouses on the Strip have a wide variety of options as far as appetizers, starters, and accouterment—at this classic spot you don't have to make many decisions. You pick your cut of meat, how you want it prepared on the mesquite grill, and you get a choice of potato, and soup or salad. If you feel like you'll want more, there are other starters available, like the hearty French onion soup, or the shellfish tower. The prices, unfortunately, didn't stay in the '70s, but dropping around $100 on a full steak dinner for two is one of the best deals you'll find on the Strip these days.

In Circus Circus, 2880 Las Vegas Blvd. S. www.circuscircus.com. © **702/794-3767.** Main courses $32–$77. Sun–Fri 4–10pm; Sat 4-11pm.

Top of the World ★★ CONTINENTAL   At nearly 850 feet above the Las Vegas Strip, this revolving restaurant is one of the best perches from which to see the city. The food used to come second, but has, of late, caught up with the lures of the view. As for the cuisine, Top of the World falls somewhere between a steakhouse (there are ample cuts of meat to choose from, like Wagyu skirt steak, or the 60-day aged bone-in Kansas City strip) and a fusion joint (rack of lamb marinated with the zesty herbs of the Moroccan condiment called *charmoula* is a specialty, as is the succulent pork belly served with bright chimichurri sauce). It takes nearly 90 minutes for one full revolution of the restaurant. Try to score a table right next to the window so you get the full experience, and are able to watch the daring souls drop off from the Sky Jump platform above.

In Stratosphere Casino Hotel, 2000 Las Vegas Blvd. S. www.topoftheworldlv.com. © **702/380-7777.** Main courses lunch $25–$34, dinner $40–$80. Daily 11am–11pm.

Moderate

Red 8 ★★ ASIAN   This Asian eatery at Wynn is much easier on the wallet than just about every other eatery in the resort (including the other Chinese restaurant, the upscale Wing Lei). Dressed in red, the luckiest color in Asian mythology, it's a funky, intimate spot overlooking the casino floor (undoubtedly with many players hoping the crimson luck reaches them). The menu is predominantly Chinese, with delicate dim sum, roasted ducks, barbecue, and hearty congee, but you can find other regions of Asia represented as well, with Thai-style vermicelli and Malaysian charred rice noodles also on offer. It's not fast food, but it is laid back, casual, and quick, so you can have a satisfying meal before you head back to the tables.

In Wynn Las Vegas, 3131 Las Vegas Blvd. S. www.wynnlasvegas.com. © **702/770-3380.** Main courses $19–$35. Sun–Thurs 11:30am–midnight; Fri–Sat 11:30am–1am.

DOWNTOWN

Expensive

Andiamo Steakhouse ★★ STEAK/SEAFOOD   When the Detroit-based chain arrived, it fit right in with the other steakhouses in town, perhaps because it "went native." The outposts in its hometown are more modern and chic; here, they went all-in on the old-school, but upscale, Vegas vibe. The brick-lined hallway evokes walking through a grotto, while tall, high-backed leather booths make cozy date spots. It's a place Dean and Frank would have headed to after a show, had this place been around. (It opened in 2013.) In those 2 years, the focus has shifted from the Italian *trattoria* fare to steaks from butchers like Pat LaFrieda, each served with a selection of sauces. (I think the signature Zip Sauce, a tangy, herby butter whose exact ingredients the staff won't divulge, is the best choice to go with big cuts like the rib eye and the enormous 32-ounce Tomahawk steak, served with the long rib bone still attached so you can pretend you're a caveman.) And who features a chopped steak on a menu anymore? This throwback dish, made with the house blend of minced meat, mushrooms, onions, and red wine, brings back more than a few loving waves of nostalgia. If you go Italian, you'll understand why this chain has been so popular in Detroit for the past 20 years. With dishes like hearty veal ragu with wide ribbons of pappardelle, and potato gnocchi tossed with wild mushroom and Madeira wine sauce, Andiamo has quickly became one of my favorites too.

In The D Las Vegas, 301 E. Fremont St. www.thed.com. ℰ **702/388-2220.** Main courses $43–$83. Daily 5–11pm.

Hugo's Cellar ★ CONTINENTAL   Among Downtown restaurants, there are those that want to be cutting edge and cool . . . and then there are places like Hugo's, which will never change. Nor does anyone want it to. As they've been doing since they opened, all women receive a red rose when they descend into the below-street-level restaurant, and the rest of the night includes many other rituals, all of which are orchestrated by the affable, well-mannered, and devoted waitstaff. Their duties extend beyond taking and bringing your orders; salads are prepared from a cart they roll up to your table, with choices like shrimp, marinated artichokes, hearts of palm, and chopped eggs, to be tossed with romaine lettuce. Watch as they deftly prepare one to your specifications. They'll also carefully recommend mains, which aren't as exciting as the salad, but come with grandiose names like "chicken *champignon*" and "duckling anise *flambé*"—it's nice to know these continental standards of a bygone era have somehow survived here. Desserts are included with your entree, so you must have the bananas foster or cherries jubilee, which is also prepared tableside, and set ablaze (hooray!). Considering how the Las Vegas culinary scene has evolved in the last decade, it's not a bad idea to see where it all started.

In the Four Queens, 202 Fremont St. www.hugoscellar.com. ℰ **702/385-4011.** Main courses $44–$67. Daily 5–10pm.

Oscar's Beef Booze Broads ★★ STEAK   What does a former mob lawyer and mayor of Las Vegas do after he retires? Hizzoner Oscar Goodman opens a steak house, of course. And it's like a shrine built to a person who hasn't died yet, including memorabilia and photographs from the 12 years he ruled this city. It also has all the elements of a classic Vegas experience. The beef: cuts of meat like Joe C's filet and the Spilotro steak (nods to former

Downtown Restaurants

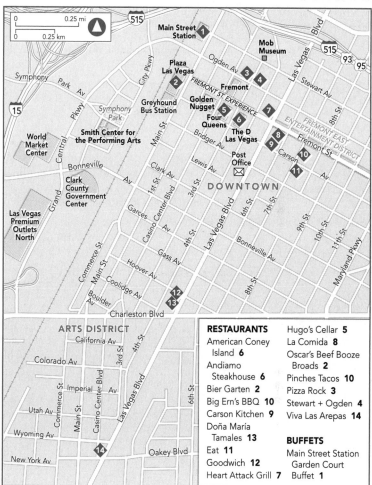

RESTAURANTS

American Coney Island **6**	Hugo's Cellar **5**
Andiamo Steakhouse **6**	La Comida **8**
Bier Garten **2**	Oscar's Beef Booze Broads **2**
Big Ern's BBQ **10**	Pinches Tacos **10**
Carson Kitchen **9**	Pizza Rock **3**
Doña María Tamales **13**	Stewart + Ogden **4**
Eat **11**	Viva Las Arepas **14**
Goodwich **12**	**BUFFETS**
Heart Attack Grill **7**	Main Street Station Garden Court Buffet **1**

clients when Goodman was a lawyer) are cooked over 600-degree grills for a nice crust on the outside. The booze: Do as Oscar does and drink a cold, stiff martini with dinner. The broads: The introvert in us had a hard time wrapping our head around this, but Goodman wanted to evoke the memory of the old days, when showgirls would sit and socialize with guests. Here, ladies come up and chat with you, and are capable of carrying on real conversations about sports and history and offer tips on Las Vegas. That's it. No ulterior motives, just a nice chat with a pretty girl. I gotta say: you'll be hard-pressed to find such a truly Vegas-dedicated experience elsewhere in the city.

In The Plaza, 1 Main St. www.oscarslv.com. ✆ **702/386-7227.** Main courses $25–$45. Daily 5–11pm.

Moderate

La Comida ★★ MEXICAN   After passing on ownership of N9NE Steakhouse at the Palms, local restaurateurs Michael and Jenna Morton set their sights on Downtown and their first Mexican restaurant. It's a very Downtown Las Vegas sort of place, in that Downtown restaurants don't want to appear like they're in Las Vegas at all. The dim restaurant opens to a rustic dining room, featuring dark woods, plaster, brick-exposed walls, and Day of the Dead-Santaria-inspired decor. A walk-up window outside allows bartenders to serve guests who don't have the time to stop in. The menu goes above and beyond what you'd expect from a neighborhood Mexican joint, including full-roasted sea bass prepared Veracruz-style with onions, olives. and chiles, and marinated beef steak with nopales, or prickly pear fruit and roasted poblano peppers. Of course there are also tacos on the menu, with toothsome fillings like chicken with salsa verde and avocado, or carnitas with pickled red onions. The margarita list is worth noting here, thanks to an impressive selection of tequilas on which to base the fresh fruit flavors.

100 Sixth Ave. (btw. Fremont St. and Carson Ave.). www.lacomidalv.com. © **702/463-9900.** Main courses $15–$25. Mon–Thurs 11:30am–11pm; Fri–Sat 11:30am–2am.

Pizza Rock ★★ PIZZA   Las Vegas used to be a not-very-good pizza town, but that's slowly changing. When Tony Gemignani brought his California-based Pizza Rock to Las Vegas, he didn't just bring one style of pizza with him, he brought all of them. Gemignani, who is also an 11-time World Pizza Champion, installed five different types of electric, gas, and wood-burning ovens to be able to prepare 10 different regional styles of pizza. There's the proper Napoletana-style pizza, with a chewy, blistered crust (this is the one that earned him a few awards); they only make a set amount of dough for this pizza each day, so when they're out, they're out. The rectangular Roman pies are long enough to warrant three different sections of toppings on them. New York pizza lovers are represented as well, along with Detroit and the underrated New Haven, CT-style of pizza. And we like that instead of trying to tackle Chicago deep dish, he went the opposite direction, making cracker-thin crust that can be topped with traditional ingredients like fennel-laced sausage. As for the ambiance: the music is loud, and as the name suggests, rock-heavy, and there's a curious half-cab of a semi truck that anchors one side of the dining room, which also serves as the DJ booth. A second Pizza Rock location recently opened at Green Valley Ranch, with Little Tony's at Palace Station for a closer slice.

201 N. Third St. (at Ogden Ave.). www.pizzarocklasvegas.com. © **702/385-0838.** Main courses $10–$25. Sun–Thurs 11am–midnight; Fri–Sat 11am–2am.

Stewart + Ogden ★★ AMERICAN   After a few hiccups with its dining program, Downtown Grand finally settled on keeping S+O (its shorthand name) as its main restaurant. Open 24 hours, it's got all the makings of a classic Vegas coffee shop, but with funky, colorful decor that matches the artful design of the Downtown Grand. While you've got classics like two-egg breakfasts, and chicken and waffles, there are also more eclectic selections, from a Hawaiian-style loco-moco of a hamburger patty with gravy over rice, to oxtail soup, perfect for hangovers. Comfort food rounds out the rest of the menu, with servings of thick slabs of meatloaf, fried chicken, and the ultra-hearty braised short rib. Compared to what you'd be paying for food this good on the Strip, a meal here is always a steal.

At the Downtown Grand, 206 N. 3rd St. (at Ogden Ave.) www.downtowngrand.com. ℰ **702/719-5100.** Main courses breakfast $9–$12, lunch $5–$14, dinner $11–$20. Daily 24 hours.

Inexpensive

American Coney Island ★ DELI/HOT DOGS   Despite its name, this legendary restaurant came from Detroit, not New York, though the hot dog-heavy menu does suggest boardwalk fare. The original was opened in 1917 by a Greek immigrant who put chili, onions, and mustard on a griddled link, thereby creating a regional style of hot dog. The descendants of this gentle-man finally expanded their brand to Las Vegas and the hotel that is closely associated with its hometown. The menu is small, but so is the one in Detroit; it includes the namesake hot dog, topped with the classic, no-bean chili that has a hint of cinnamon, and Midwestern-style lamb gyro, with proper, home-made tzatziki yogurt sauce as dressing. Being happily fed for under $10 makes the grub all that much more tasty. FYI, Detroit natives, there is not a competing Lafayette Coney Dog next door like in Motor City.

In The D Las Vegas, 301 E. Fremont St. www.thed.com. ℰ **702/388-2400.** Main courses under $5. Daily 24 hr.

Bier Garten ★★ AMERICAN   The whole point of a beer garden is to sit outside and drink all day, so don't bother with the indoor seating of this Plaza restaurant; you'll be subjected to watching people eat McDonald's from the food court. Grab a seat at one of the picnic tables in the gorgeous backyard—complete with grass, pergola for a little shade, and outdoor TVs—and you're set. It's a pleasant change from the attempted urbanization of Downtown. That beer washes down a large selection *Wursts* (sausages) named after fallen Las Vegas casinos. The Stardust is a favorite, a German brat with caramelized onions, kraut, and sweet mustard, while those who like their sausage more avant garde—and messy—will enjoy the Golden Slipper, made with Andou-ille, bacon, cream cheese, and a fried egg. The selections also come with listed beer pairings so you can make sure you're getting all the right flavors. If sausage isn't your game, there are German-style pretzels and French fries that are meant to be dressed with an assortment of dipping sauces, like sriracha ketchup and Cheese Whiz.

At The Plaza Hotel & Casino, 1 S. Main St. (at Fremont St.). www.biergartenlv.com. ℰ **702/386-2110.** Main courses all under $10. Daily 11am–midnight.

Big Ern's BBQ ★★ BARBECUE   Barbecue is such a divisive topic that true connoisseurs refuse to believe that it can be properly made outside of the South. Add to that the fact that Big Ern himself is from California, and 'cue aficionados grow even more skeptical. But once you smell the smoke from his brisket or pulled pork, you'll know this is the real deal. Ern's shop in Downtown Container Park is small, but packs 'em in. Diners clamor not only for the brisket here, but also for chicken, hot links, and ribs, all served with a sweet sauce that's more molasses than Kansas City. Carolinans might take offense at the sauce, but they won't be able to resist the meats on their own. It's also rare to find a BBQ joint outside the Midwest that serves rib tips, but here they can be added on to any rib dinner. Complete your meal with classic sides like pork and beans, cole slaw, or a baked potato, make your way to a spot in the park, and enjoy a barbecue feast that won't make you miss the South.

In the Downtown Container Park, 707 Fremont St. (at 7th St.). www.bigernsbbq.com. © **702/834-7845.** Main courses $7–29. Sun–Thurs 11am–11pm; Fri–Sat 11am–1am.

Carson Kitchen ★★★ AMERICAN   Chef Kerry Simon built his culinary empire all over Vegas, starting at Hard Rock, then the Palms, and a few other spots here and there, but this is his crowning achievement. It's a two-story, relaxed, neighborhood restaurant—something that restaurateurs all over the city are desperately trying to replicate—serving up contemporary, seasonal, and addictive, comfort food. A starter of crispy chicken skins—yes, just the skins—comes with a small dose of smoky honey, and you'll eat them like potato chips. The "butter burger" is just as fun, served with creamy boursin and cheddar cheese, and yes, cooked in a healthy dose of butter. But don't worry, the menu's not all calorie bombs. One of the best dishes we've ever eaten was Carson Kitchen's spicy ragu of rabbit, served with spaghetti squash—something that healthy should never be that delicious. The cocktail program includes thoughtful, multi-faceted drinks that run the gamut from clean and fruity to smoky and masculine. Grab a seat at the counter so you can watch the chefs in the open kitchen, and keep an eye on the "swear jar" to see how they're doing.

124 S. 6th St. (at Carson Ave.). www.carsonkitchen.com. © **702/473-9523.** Main courses $12–$19. Sun–Wed 11:30am–10pm; Thurs–Sat 11:30am–11pm.

Doña María Tamales ★ MEXICAN   For more than 30 years, this standalone restaurant has been the house that tamales built. Situated between the Strip and Downtown, it's a convenient location when you need a proper Mexican fix. Its expansive menu that features all of Mexico's greatest hits: ample platters of tacos, burritos, enchiladas and, my favorite, handmade tamales (unwrap the corn husk to reveal packets of masa filled with pork, chicken, cheese, or beef, or in the dessert version, pineapples, and raisins). The chili rellenos are dauntingly big, but getting every bite down won't be a problem because they're so good. Dinners come as full-on meals, complete with rice, beans, soup or salad, and tortillas.

910 Las Vegas Blvd. S. (at Charleston Blvd.). www.donamariatamales.com. © **702/382-6538.** Main courses breakfast and lunch $8–$15, dinner $9–$15. Daily 8am–10pm.

Eat ★★★ AMERICAN   Eat was one of the first restaurants to open during the recent period of gentrification Downtown, and fortunately, has managed to stay open, unlike others in its class. Chef Natalie Young cut her teeth at restaurants on the Strip for many years before finding this opportunity. She created a restaurant she knew the area needed; a place that doesn't seem like it belongs in Las Vegas at all. The storefront features funky decor, local art, and a tiered herb garden near the front, welcoming guests in to dine. Only open for breakfast and lunch, the place always seems to be bumping with guests there for her Southern-influenced fare. Shrimp and grits are outstanding, and hearty egg dishes like the flavorful truffled egg sandwich with chives, feta, and bacon are served all day. For lunch, I'm a huge fan of the classic reuben sandwich, along with the shrimp po' boy with spicy kimchi slaw. Brunch is worth the wait, especially for the proper beignets blanketed in powdered sugar, but as they have live music, when you're in such a small space, you might be shouting to be heard by the person next to you.

707 Carson Ave. (at 7th Ave.). www.eatdtlv.com. © **702/534-1515.** Main courses $6–$13. Mon–Fri 8am–3pm; Sat–Sun 8am–2pm.

Goodwich ★ SANDWICHES   Originally housed in a weird little kiosk outside of a local dive bar, Dino's, Goodwich quickly made a name for itself with excellent, reasonably priced gourmet sandwiches. Now that it's moved into its own brick-and-mortar space, the prices have slightly gone up, but the sandwiches are just as fantastic. Starting at $6.50, Goodwich offers bites like the thick-cut ham, cheddar, and greens with a tangy mostarda, or an egg salad Sammie with crispy chorizo. A nice innovation: the BTLG (bacon, tomato, lettuce, and pimento cheese grits). The Reuben-ish features house-made corned beef that's stacked with Swiss and fennel sauerkraut, dressed with a luscious thousand island sauce.

1516 Las Vegas Blvd. S. www.the-goodwich.com. © **702/910-8681.** Sandwiches $6.50–$10. Mon–Fri 7am–10pm; Sat–Sun 8am–10pm.

Heart Attack Grill BURGERS   The only reason we can think of including this absolutely ridiculous restaurant in this book is so you can make an educated, conscious decision to *not* go here. Sure, the hospital theme, where the waitresses are dressed as naughty nurses and guests are wearing hospital gowns is "cute." And offering vegans non-filtered cigarettes as an entree is not "PC" but it's darn funny. But when you tout items like butterfat shakes, onion rings and french fries cooked in pure lard, plus an 8,000-calorie Quadruple Bypass burger to which you can add 20 slices of bacon, even in a town known for excess, you might as well promise yourself a seat in Circle 3 along with the other gluttons in *Dante's Inferno*. Promise guests who are over 350 pounds that they can eat for free? Now that's just tempting the same fate that befell their unofficial spokesperson who dropped dead of guess what? A heart attack. Those who don't finish their bypass burgers get spanked by a nurse with a paddle—filmed and placed on the Internet for all to see. We know, we know, 'Merica, freedom of choice, don't tread on me, fine. If you really want to, go, just don't say we didn't warn you.

450 E. Fremont St. © **702/254-0171.** www.heartattackgrill.com. Main courses $8–$15. Cash only. Daily 11am–2am.

Pinches Tacos ★★ MEXICAN   Spanish speakers might be taken aback at the name (*pinches* isn't a nice word) but most see the humor in it. And most enjoy the straightforward, affordable food of this Los Angeles-based chain. It's your standard menu, including tacos, sopes, tortas, burritos, flautas, and enchiladas, with typical fillings of beef, chicken, pork, and shrimp (the addition of cactus for vegetarians is a nice touch). None of it is fancy, but the food does have a nice home-style flavor, which is a welcome reprieve from the many other Mexican restaurants in town that just phone it in. The restaurant is set in Container Park in a small container with minimal seating, so guests mostly eat in the park itself, which is fine as long as it's not the throes of summer.

In the Downtown Container Park, 707 Fremont St. (at 7th St.). www.pinchestacos.com. © **702/910-3100.** Main courses $3–$9. Sun–Thurs 11am–11pm; Fri–Sat 11am–1am.

Viva Las Arepas ★★ VENEZUELAN   Las Vegas strip malls are where you can find some of the best hole-in-the-walls we've got. Take Viva Las Arepas, which began in the kiosk now occupied by Goodwich, and gained such a following it needed a bigger kitchen and an actual dining room. If you've never eaten the Venezuelan street snack, arepas are savory, griddled cornmeal cakes that are stuffed with a wide variety of ingredients. I prefer them chock full, as in the *Reina Pepiada,* which has chicken breast, avocados, mayo, and cilantro. Vegetarians can opt for vegetables, black beans, or cheese, or all three. Other than the arepas, the roasted, marinated chicken is a big seller here, cooked over mesquite wood for nice char and flavor. Add in a few authentic sides, like fried yucca or plantain, for a filling and tasty, but still inexpensive, meal.

1616 Las Vegas Blvd. S. (at Oakey Blvd.). www.vivalasarepas.com. © **702/366-9696.** Main courses $4–$10. Daily 8am–midnight.

JUST OFF THE STRIP

Expensive

Alizé ★★★ FRENCH   As one of the first French chefs to arrive in Las Vegas, Andre Rochat set the tone of fine dining, first in his eponymous cottage restaurant Downtown, and later, here, at the top of the Palms. Whereas the other Andre's at Monte Carlo serves classic French fare, Alizé's mandate is for exciting haute cuisine to match its setting: the corner restaurant has three walls of floor-to-ceiling windows that offer panoramic views of the city. Just as much beauty is on the plate. The seasonal menu can be enjoyed a la carte, but for $155, the seven-course tasting menu isn't outrageous by Vegas standards, and it offers the opportunity to try a little bit of everything that makes this restaurant so special. Diners are offered three options for each course, and at least one is vegetarian (often the most appetizing one). One of the last times we visited, we were treated to elegant presentations of foie gras torchon with just-sweet-enough fruit, and a rack of lamb accented with Moroccan merguez sausage and a galette of summer vegetables. With a menu that changes this frequently, it's hard to say that your dishes will be anything close to ours, but I do know that the experience will likely be just as divine.

In Palms Resort & Casino, 4321 W. Flamingo Rd. www.alizelv.com. ✆ **702/951-7000.** Reservations strongly recommended. Main courses $47–$57, 7-course tasting menu $155. Daily 5:30–10:30pm.

Pamplemousse ★ FRENCH   It doesn't get a lot of play in the press these days, but that doesn't mean that Pamplemousse isn't still very much a part of the Las Vegas landscape. Set in a low-slung building on East Sahara, the restaurant has been around almost 4 decades, and was once the epitome of fine dining in town. Outside, it looks like something you might find in the French countryside. Inside, it's as though time has stood still, and you're transported to Vegas in the late 1970s: low ceilings, round red booths, and a domed Tiffany ceiling above the main dining room. Although the building and interiors have seen better days, the food is still as elegant as ever, starting with a mandatory starter of *crudite* (raw vegetables), with their signature house-made vinaigrette. Most of the menu derives from Provence, like the osso buco with a white wine sauce, mushrooms, olives, and tomatoes, and the rack of spring lamb with crusted pistachios, served with a light rosemary sauce. In an era when many chefs are creating their presentations with tweezers and microgreens, Pamplemousse plates dishes in the continental-style; that is to say,

CHEF ANDRÉ ROCHAT'S TOP 10 THINGS ONE SHOULD NEVER ASK A french chef

French-born chef André Rochat has been delighting Las Vegas audiences with his fine cuisine since 1973. His restaurants Alizé at the Palms and André's at Monte Carlo are among the most popular and best-reviewed French restaurants in the city, so who better to ask what you *shouldn't* ask him?

1. May I have my duck breast well done?
2. May I have A-1 sauce with steak au poivre?
3. I brought this from my garden; can you cook it for me?
4. I want the lobster Thermidor; but can you hold the cream?
5. Can I have the crème brûlée as an appetizer?
6. May I order a soufflé to go?
7. Can we do the seven-course chef's tasting menu in 45 minutes?
8. Can I have mint jelly with the rack of lamb?
9. Will you keep the food under the heat lamps in the kitchen while we go smoke?
10. May I have ketchup with the lobster Thermidor?

And yes . . . Chef André says he's actually been asked these questions. Welcome to Las Vegas!

Restaurants Beyond the Strip

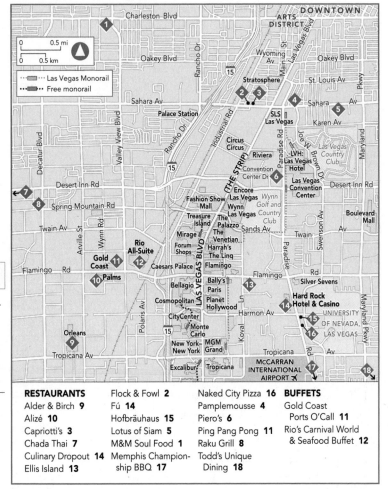

RESTAURANTS

Alder & Birch **9**
Alizé **10**
Capriotti's **3**
Chada Thai **7**
Culinary Dropout **14**
Ellis Island **13**
Flock & Fowl **2**
Fú **14**
Hofbräuhaus **15**
Lotus of Siam **5**
M&M Soul Food **1**
Memphis Championship BBQ **17**
Naked City Pizza **16**
Pamplemousse **4**
Piero's **6**
Ping Pang Pong **11**
Raku Grill **8**
Todd's Unique Dining **18**

BUFFETS

Gold Coast Ports O'Call **11**
Rio's Carnival World & Seafood Buffet **12**

with its sauce and a simple side garnish. The food doesn't need more than that. Plus, it's super dark inside so you can't see much anyway.

400 E. Sahara Ave. (btw. Santa Paula and Santa Rita drives, just east of Paradise Rd.). www.pamplemousserestaurant.com. **©** **702/733-2066.** Main courses $24–$42. Tues–Sun 5–10pm.

Moderate

Alder & Birch ★★ STEAK   As you're navigating your way through the Mardi Gras-themed Orleans casino to find its new steakhouse, it might help to know that Alder & Birch looks completely out of place. In stark contrast to the garish holiday decor, the restaurant has a modern facade and floor-to-ceiling windows separated by tall panels of rich wood. Inside, away from the madness of the casino floor, the surprise continues, with the a downright sleek dining room, its decor a mix of neutral colors and natural and industrial finishes. The menu is classic for a contemporary Vegas steakhouse, with intriguing selections such as watermelon salad with goat cheese and sea salt, and beef carpaccio with arugula, mustard and capers. I was pleased to learn that the raw oysters came direct from New Orleans, as sort of proof that Alder & Birch knew exactly where it was. The dry-aged Wagyu sirloin looks tempting, but for more bang for your buck (which you can get quite a lot of here), the rib eye makes more sense for serious carnivores. The other nice touch is the craft beer selection on tap—several from local brewery Joseph James—plus a thoughtful cocktail list. The Orleans has been in the midst of a $30 million renovation, and we're glad they started with its restaurants.

In the Orleans, 4500 W. Tropicana Ave. (at Arville St.). www.orleanscasino.com. ℭ **702/365-7111.** Reservations recommended. Main courses $24–$49. Sun–Thurs 5–10pm; Fri–Sat 5–11pm.

Culinary Dropout ★★ AMERICAN   As you might be able to tell from the name, this restaurant wants to be the cool kid on the block. And I gotta say: they succeed. The inside is a black box, with open ductwork running across the ceiling, intentionally mismatched furniture, and ornate chandeliers. There's no set uniform for the servers, who wear what they like to work each day, which gets very confusing for patrons trying to get the check. Hipster aesthetic aside, CDO's food is less confusing, even though the menu is diverse. Comfort food reigns supreme, starting with signature soft pretzels, served with a beer cheese dipping sauce, or the fragrant mussels in bath of Stella Artois broth, served with grilled bread. The fried chicken is a specialty, and it's made to order, which means it will come 20 minutes after the other food. It's worth the wait: with a flaky buttermilk biscuit and a drizzle of honey, you'll burn your fingers because you'll want to eat it so fast. The outdoor patio seating is one of my favorite spots when it's nice out, mainly because each section is set up like a living room, great for group lounging.

In the Hard Rock Hotel, 4455 Paradise Rd. (at Harmon Ave.). www.culinarydropout.com. ℭ **702/522-8100.** Main courses $14–$32. Mon–Thurs 11am–11pm; Fri 11am–midnight; Sat 10am–midnight; Sun 10am–11pm.

Fú ★★ ASIAN   From the family who ran the original Mayflower, one of the first upscale Chinese restaurants in town, comes this contemporary Asian eatery at Hard Rock. Fú means "luck," which is what they're hoping to bring you with dishes like their Hong Kong-style wonton noodle soup and a reasonably priced Peking Duck presentation. Fú recognizes the diversity of its clientele, so the food straddles the fine line between authentic and Americanized, offering familiar dishes like General Tso's chicken and Mongolian beef alongside bona fide spicy ma po tofu and fish maw soup with crab. In addition to Chinese offerings, there are a few other pan-Asian options, like the Korean marinated short ribs and the miso cod in lettuce cups.

In the Hard Rock Hotel, 4455 Paradise Rd. (at Harmon Ave.). www.hardrockhotel.com. © **702/522-8188.** Main courses $16–$30. Sun–Thurs 11:30am–10pm; Fri–Sat 11:30am–11pm.

Hofbräuhaus ★ GERMAN   If the name—and the looks—of this restaurant are familiar, that's because it's a Madame Tussaud's-worthy replica of the famed beer hall in Munich (the one that's been around for four centuries). The food is *sehr* German, including schnitzel, strudel, and wurst, but the real treats are from the *schmankerl* (which means "treat") section. Sauerbraten cooked in red wine is the Bavarian equivalent of pot roast, *jägerschnitzel* is a hunter's dish of a pork cutlet topped with mushrooms, bacon, onion, and *spaetzle*. It's all hearty, all meaty, and all meant to be eaten with a cold brew in the other hand, while listening to live polka and oom-pah bands. The beer, it turns out, tastes this authentic because it's brewed at the original site and imported here, so even the Dunkel and Hefeweizen are the real deal. In the event you can't make it to Germany, the Oktoberfest here, like in Munich, starts in September, with parties every week featuring local Vegas celebrities in keg-tapping ceremonies.

4150 Paradise Rd. (at Harmon Ave.). www.hofbrauhauslasvegas.com. © **702/853-2337.** Main courses $10–$25. Sun–Thurs 11am–11pm; Fri–Sat 11am–midnight.

Naked City Pizza ★ PIZZA   It turns out Buffalo isn't just known for its chicken wings. The chef here, who started out at a casino on the Strip before breaking out on his own, was born and raised in upstate New York, and he's introduced Las Vegas to his regional pie, made in rectangular pants like Sicilian-style, but with a thinner crust. Yes, you can order it by the slice (which are pretty sizeable on their own), but a slice of cheese can be had anywhere on the Strip. What you're going for at Naked City are the specialty pizzas, like the Stinger, topped with chicken fingers, steak, mozzarella and cheddar and bleu cheese, plus sweet and hot peppers. Or the Fat Boy, a red sauce meat-lover's dream with salami, pepperoni, ham and Italian sausage. And if you're going big, you should also know they come in three sizes: Wee, Not So Wee, and Frickin' Huge (translated from Buffalo, NY parlance, that's a quarter sheet pan, half a sheet pan, and a full sheet pan, respectively). And yes, they've got chicken wings, too.

4608 Paradise Rd. (at E. Naples Dr.). www.nakedcitylv.com. © **702/722-2241.** Pizzas $8–$38. Mon–Wed 11am–11pm; Thurs–Sat 11am–3am; Sun 11am–1am.

Piero's Italian Cuisine ★★ ITALIAN   A beloved Las Vegas institution, Piero's has been a longtime hangout for Vegas bigwigs from every industry—Rat Packers, hotel bosses, performers, and even folks they refer to as "casino industry businessmen," which is a nice way of not calling them mob guys. On any given night, you can still see local execs and politicians having dinner around the tables with their families. The rule of the house: everybody gets to eat in peace, so even if you see a celebrity, play it cool. If you walk in and think you've been there before, you might recognize the dining room from the film *Casino,* which shot several iconic scenes with Joe Pesci, Robert DeNiro, and Sharon Stone in the low, leather booths here. To encourage a convivial atmosphere, bartenders are heavy-handed with what they call a "stiff pour." The menu has stayed essentially the same since Piero's first opened in 1982, if only because the Glusman family who runs it has a very "if it ain't broke, don't fix it" attitude. Favorites include the chef's special veal scallopine, pounded thin and tender, then battered and covered with prosciutto and cheese, and linguine *alla vongole,* or with clams, a favorite of Sinatra's whenever he came in. If their guests who have been coming in for 30 years don't need a change, neither do we.

355 Convention Center Dr. www.pieroscuisine.com. © **702/369-2305.** Main courses $32–$49. Daily 5:30–10pm.

Ping Pang Pong ★★ CHINESE   When high rollers jet in from Asia, this is usually the first place they head for a meal. In fact, the vast majority of the clientele is from that corner of the globe, because it's near impossible to find Chinese fare this authentic elsewhere in Las Vegas. A lot of the menu is Cantonese fare—noodle soups, barbecue meats, roasted duck, and clay pots stuffed with rice and other meaty bits—but other regions are represented as well. One of our favorite times to go is for dim sum brunch, when the steam carts piled high with bamboo and metal containers are pushed around the room. The caliber of dim sum here is close to what I've eaten in Hong Kong, especially the fresh *har gow,* shrimp dumplings with translucent wrappers, the long rolls of rice noodles, and the dense, steamed meatballs with cilantro. It's also a popular late night dining spot.

In the Gold Coast Hotel & Casino, 4000 W. Flamingo Rd. www.goldcoastcasino.com. © **702/367-7111.** Main courses $10–$25. Daily 10am–3pm and 5pm–3am.

Inexpensive

Capriotti's ★★★ SANDWICHES   Originally from Delaware, this smallish chain (only in about a dozen other states, so it's no Subway, thankfully) has had a hold on Las Vegas ever since it opened its first here 15 years ago. The storefront isn't much to look at, but that's ok when you've got enormous sandwiches to dig into. Most popular is "the Bobbie," with its combination of thick cut turkey, stuffing, and cranberry sauce, reminiscent of your favorite Thanksgiving leftovers, but I'm more partial to the Capistrami, a pseudo-Reuben made with hot pastrami, Swiss cheese, Russian dressing, and coleslaw. If that's too much stuff on a sandwich for you, the submarine options have more classic combinations, like Italian deli meats, or ham and cheese. The turkey and beef are all roasted in-house. The perfect bread—so nice and soft, but with the proper integrity so that it doesn't disintegrate under the weight of multiple toppings—is also made in house. There are several outposts throughout the Valley, but this is the closest to the Strip and freeway.

322 W. Sahara Ave. (at Las Vegas Blvd. S.). www.capriottis.com. © **702/474-0229.** Most regular sandwiches under $10. Mon–Sat 10am–8pm; Sun 11am–7pm.

Chada Thai ★ THAI   It was only a matter of time before a Lotus of Siam (see below) alum left the nest to open his own place. Located in west Chinatown, this small, modern storefront tends to get busy late at night, when chefs and other industry folk get off their shifts. They've got a few Northern specialties here, but leave that to Lotus of Siam. Here, the dishes you're already familiar with are the must-haves. Watch out for spice levels, as they're serious about the term "Thai spicy." Crab lettuce wraps, for example, offer a kick to the throat that will surprise even chili-heads. Classic tom yum soup with shrimp is fragrant, and will clear you right up if you're having sinus issues. Try to get there early enough to sample the *nua dad diew,* a tender beef jerky served with a sweet chili fish sauce that often runs out by the end of the night. After you eat it here, you'll realize you've never known pad thai was supposed to be this nuanced. The owner, Bank Atacharawan was the former general manager and sommelier at Lotus, and he's transferred his knowledge here, with a well-curated list heavy on white, sweeter wines that complement Thai spices, at reasonable price points.

3400 S. Jones Blvd., Suite 11A. www.chadavegas.com. ✆ **702/641-1345.** Reservations recommended. Main courses $8–$23. Daily 5pm–3am.

Ellis Island Cafe ★ DINER   Prime rib, $14.99. That's all you really need to know about this 24-hour coffee shop. Not only is that one of the best prices that we've ever seen for a king cut slab of roast beef plus two sides, but it also happens to be the most expensive thing on the menu. And for that, Ellis Island is a huge hit with both locals and visitors. But in the event that you're not in the mood for prime rib, the kitchen does a good job on the rest of the menu, starting with an even better-priced steak and eggs ($10.99), a solid assortment of sandwiches, and a build-your-own burger. Additionally, the brewery on premises produces seven different types of suds, some of which are seasonal, and a primo pairing for your reasonably priced meal.

In Ellis Island Casino, 4178 Koval Lane (at Flamingo Rd.). www.ellisislandcasino.com. ✆ **702/733-8901.** Main courses $5–$15. Daily 24 hr.

Flock & Fowl ★★ ASIAN   You may be wondering why I'm sending you to a sketchy strip mall on Sahara for something that sounds as mundane as boiled chicken and rice. What if I were to tell you this was the best chicken and rice you'll probably have in the United States? It's not just chicken and rice, of course, but Hainanese chicken and rice, an Asian comfort food that sounds simple, but is far from easy to make and perfect when done correctly. Restaurants in Singapore have cult followings for this dish alone. Chef Sheridan Su, who cut his chops at Strip restaurants such as Joel Robuchon before striking out on his own (he also owns the fun Fat Choy in the Eureka casino), fell in love with the humble dish when he and his wife (who works behind the counter) were traveling in Asia, and decided to open a restaurant serving just that. Organic chicken is poached until cooked to the proper texture and temperature, and the broth is used to cook the fragrant rice. It's served with traditional condiments all made in-house, like garlic, ginger and scallions minced in oil, sweet soy sauce and spicy sambal. Everyone doctors their chicken and rice in their own way, sometimes customizing it with every bite. For now, the restaurant is only open for lunch and seats about 15, but it's not uncommon for them to sell out. It's that good.

380 W. Sahara Ave. (at Las Vegas Blvd. S.). www.flockandfowl.com. © **626/616-6632.** Entrees under $10. Tues–Sat 10:30am–3:30pm.

Lotus of Siam ★★★ THAI   The grand poobah of the city's ethnic restaurants, once named the "Single Best Thai Restaurant in North America" (by the late, great *Gourmet* magazine), and winner of the James Beard "Best Chef in the Southwest" award in 2011, the venerable Lotus of Siam remains one of the city's best-reviewed and best-loved restaurants. It gets all its plaudits without all the extras that tend to dazzle diners at other restaurants. Its location is terrible, in a dingy strip mall; its decor ho-hum, most notable for the dozens of photos of beaming, full-looking celebrities; and if you come late at lunchtime you'll likely be upset that the buffet is one of diminishing returns, as it doesn't get refilled when the food runs out. But this is not a buffet-type place anyway, nor should you just expect upgrades of your same-old, same-old Pad Thai. To really get why foodies drive down from L.A. regularly just to dine here (and I know a couple who do), you have to put yourself in Bill's hands. Bill is the husband of chef Saipin Chutina, and he makes the reverse trip to L.A. once a week to buy fresh ingredients, jetting off to Thailand about once a month to get spices blended to his wife's specifications. Bill will know what's best that day (and if Bill's not there, ask for Tony) and he'll steer you towards the Saipin (Northern) Thai specialties that really make this place unique. As an example: *Nua Dad Deaw,* a dry fried beef, almost like a lime-infused beef jerky, that's so addictive, I save the leftovers to munch in my car the next day. Or the *Nam Kao Tod* ($7.95), a wonderfully tart sausage, dry in texture, nutty, minty, and sided by crispy deep-fried rice. Or the jackfruit curry with smoked fish, or a crispy mussel omelet served with a spicy red sauce that makes this dish so much more special than just eggs. I list all of these just to give you an idea of what your meal could be like, but really, ignore what I'm writing here, and go with what Bill recommends, as he knows best. Just be sure to tell him how much spice you can take, and don't overestimate your tolerance; the kitchen will sear your tongue off if you ask for it hot. Mr. Chutima is also in charge of the stellar wine program, heavy on Rieslings and other vintages that pair well with spicy cuisine.

In the Commercial Center, 953 E. Sahara Ave. www.lotusofsiamlv.com. © **702/735-3033.** Main courses $10–$29. Mon–Fri 11am–2:30pm and 5:30–10pm; Sat–Sun 5:30–10pm.

SOUTH & EAST OF THE STRIP

Expensive

Todd's Unique Dining ★★★ CONTINENTAL   Chef Todd was at the helm of the Sterling Brunch at Bally's for many years before he opened his

sweet SENSATIONS

Plenty of opportunities exist in Vegas for satisfying your sweet tooth, but for the discriminating, here are four spots you may have to make a detour for.

Jean-Philippe Patisserie ★★★ in Bellagio, 3600 Las Vegas Blvd. S. (www. jpchocolates.com; *©* **702/693-8788**), makes me swoon, not just because it has the world's largest chocolate fountain (20 feet high! Though only 11 feet are on view, and they won't let us drink from it. Darn!), but perhaps, more to the point, it's the home of World Pastry champion Jean-Philippe Maury. (Yes, you can win gold medals for pastries.) From perfect gourmet chocolates, to ice cream, to diet-conscious sorbets, to the eponymous pastries, each of which are little works of art, I hit greed overload. For me, this is true Vegas decadence—if only "what happens in Vegas, stays in Vegas" applied to calories. The patisserie also serves some solidly good sandwiches, and some adequate savory crepes. It is open Monday through Thursday from 6am to 11pm and Friday through Sunday from 6am until midnight. There's a second location inside Aria Las Vegas, but they don't have the chocolate fountain.

A local favorite for more than 50 years is **Freed's Bakery**, 9815 S. Eastern Ave., at Silverado Ranch Blvd. (www.freeds bakery.com; *©* **702/456-7762**), open Monday through Thursday from 9am to 8pm, Friday and Saturday from 8am to 8pm, and Sunday from 9am to 6pm. Visiting here is like walking into Grandma's kitchen, provided you had an old-fashioned granny who felt pastries should be gooey, chocolaty, and buttery. Their signature wedding cakes will make you want to rush down the aisle, but

you'll want to bring a basket for the fresh bread, napoleons, strawberry cheese-cake, cream puffs, sweet rolls, danishes, and doughnuts, many of which are made with surprisingly fresh ingredients. Some may find the goodies too heavy and rich, but for those of us with a powerful sweet tooth, this place hits the spot. There is no dining area so everything is to go; do try to at least make it to your car before you start digging in.

Just down the street is the delightful **The Cupcakery ★★★**, 9680 S. Eastern Ave. (www.thecupcakery.com; *©* **702/207-2253**). The delectable goodies here aren't large, but they pack a wallop of moist cake and creamy frosting. Clever combinations include Boston cream pie (filled with custardy cream), but even the basic chocolate-on-chocolate is a butter-cream pleasure. There are even sugar-free cupcakes for those with such dietary needs. The Cupcakery is open Monday through Friday from 8am to 8pm, Saturday from 10am to 8pm, and Sunday from 10am to 6pm.

Hot Vegas days call for cool desserts, and frozen custard (softer than regular ice cream, but harder than soft serve) is a fine way to go. Head for **Luv-It Frozen Custard,** 505 E. Oakey (www.luvitfrozen custard.com; *©* **702/384-6452**), open Sunday through Thursday from 1 to 10pm and Friday and Saturday from 1 to 11pm. Because custard has less fat and sugar than premium ice cream, you can even fool yourself into thinking this is somewhat healthful (ha!). Made every few hours using fresh cream and eggs, the custard is available in basic flavors for cup or cone. More exotic flavors (maple walnut, apple spice, and others) come in tubs.

own spot in Green Valley, wanting to serve the community he'd lived in for so many years, rather than just the tourists. Somehow, visitors got wind of his place too, so they've followed him here. The menu changes daily, which keeps the locals very happy. His signature goat cheese wontons are a staple, served with a drizzle of raspberry basil sauce. Boneless short ribs are another favorite, cooked long and slow until they're falling apart, accompanied by jalapeno mashed potatoes. Most of the main entrees follow this template: protein, starch, and vegetable, and that's the way his guests like it. A full meal at a great price, prepared by a guy they know in the kitchen. If you've got a definite date when you're coming to town, sign up for the restaurant's mailing list on the website and you'll be updated with events and special offers.

4350 E. Sunset Rd., Henderson (just east of Green Valley Pkwy.). www.toddsunique. com. © **702/259-8633.** Main courses $25–$35. Mon–Sat 4:30pm–close.

Moderate

Memphis Championship Barbecue ★★ BARBECUE   Twice a year, two 18-wheelers loaded up with apple wood from Murphysboro, Illinois, head to Vegas to feed the pits here. The wood provides the low and slow heat, and the scented smoke that gives the meat here its distinctive pink hue and full-bodied flavor. All is done to the specifications of co-owner Mike Mills— one of the most-celebrated BBQ chefs ever, and the only man to have won the "Super Bowl of BBQ," the International Memphis in May BBQ cook-off, four times. The barbecue you'll taste here is made from the same recipes that won those awards, using the vinegar-based sauce his maternal grandmother created—the brisket and pork shoulders cooking for 18 hours on average, and the baby backs for five to six. It is, no exaggeration, gut-bustingly delicious. And the meal you'll have here doesn't start and end with the meats or barbecue chicken; the sides and appetizers are fabulous as well, from the deep-fried sour pickles, to red beans and rice as good as you'd get in New Orleans, and candy-like creamed corn. Note that there is another location near the Las Vegas Motor Speedway. The location listed below is closer to the Strip.

2250 E. Warm Springs Rd. (near I-215). www.memphis-bbq.com. © **702/260-6909.** Main courses $8–$23, special barbecue dinner (serves 4) $70. Daily 11am–10pm.

NORTH & WEST OF THE STRIP

Moderate

M&M Soul Food ★★ SOUL FOOD   Despite all the famous chefs who are trying to recreate their versions of comfort food, finding true soul food in Las Vegas isn't easy. Especially when you have to trek off the Strip to get it. Before, you'd have to head to a potentially sketchy neighborhood, but M&M recently added a second location just behind the Stratosphere. Admittedly, this area is only marginally nicer than its original, but at least it's closer. M&M looks like a greasy spoon diner from the outside, but inside there's a menu of no-nonsense, stick-to-your-ribs fare that begins with an order of mini-cornbread pancakes delivered to every table. The smothered chicken will make you rethink your cholesterol levels, but with gravy like that you can't say no. Finding oxtails not in a soup in Las Vegas is hard, here they're also covered with luscious gravy instead of broth. Collard greens, fried okra, and mac and cheese are mandatory as sides if you want the full experience. Dishes like liver and onions and chitterlings are other faves, as well-prepared as they are south of the Mason-Dixon line.

3923 W. Charleston. www.mmsoulfoodcafe.com. ✆ **702/453-7685.** 2211 Las Vegas Blvd. S. ✆ **702/478-5767.** Main courses $9–$19. Daily Sun–Thurs 8am–8pm; Fri–Sat 8am–10pm

Raku Grill ★★★ JAPANESE   If you're one of those travelers who insist on knowing where chefs go to eat in their own towns, look no further than Raku. This tiny restaurant in an unassuming strip mall in Chinatown has earned a reputation for being one of the best restaurants in Las Vegas under the care of chef Mitsuo Endo. He was a semi-finalist in both 2014 and 2015 for the James Beard "Best Chef in the Southwest" award, and has also earned plaudits from *GQ,* the *New York Times,* and a number of other outlets. Because it's so small and popular, reservations (which you can only make by calling) are mandatory, although if you're lucky you can catch a seat at the bar in front of the kitchen. While there are some raw options, this isn't a sushi joint, but rather a *robata* grill, where most items are cooked over clean-burning *bin-chotan* charcoal on skewers. There are conventional bites, like Kobe beef filet and duck glazed with balsamic soy sauce, but more adventurous eaters will love the Kurobuta pork cheek, beef tendon, and foie gras with a soy glaze. One of our favorites is the bacon-wrapped enoki mushrooms, a cluster of crunchy fungi held together by a thin, nicely rendered piece of salty pork belly. A favorite splurge is the cold foie gras custard soup with udon noodles, a slippery, savory dish that is meant to be slurped with abandon. Raku also make its own tofu, best enjoyed cold and dressed at the table with soy sauce also brewed by the restaurant. Individually, the skewers—which come one or two to an order—are inexpensive, but order enough of them and it can add up. There are exceptional desserts, like a green tea crème brûlée and the weird, but tasty, custard-like bubbling brown sugar, but for chef Endo's take on the end to the meal, head across the way to Raku Sweets, which offers a full tasting menu solely of confections.

Want to run into those chefs we were talking about? Make sure you go late night, long after the Strip kitchens have been cleaned and closed, and you'll find a gaggle of them here.

5030 W. Spring Mountain Rd., no. 2 (at Decatur). www.raku-grill.com. ✆ **702/367-3511.** Reservations required. *Robata* grill items $3–$16. Mon–Sat 6pm–3am.

BUFFETS

Like so much else that was Vegas tradition, buffets have evolved. Gone, mostly, are the days of trays and cafeteria-style lines serving heaping mounds of warmed-over blandness at bargain-basement prices. The modern buffet uses come-and-go serving areas, live-action cooking stations, and multiple ethnic and regional cuisines. A general rise in quality puts many on par with traditional restaurants.

Of course, as the quality has gone up, so too have the prices, which now make them less of a bargain. But consider it this way: You would pay much more per person at one of the fancier restaurants in town, where you would order just one, potentially disappointing, item. At a buffet there's more variety and more chance to find something you love. More variety per person means less likelihood for disappointment, so if you hate what you picked you can simply dump your plate and start all over. They are, generally speaking, not nearly as atmospheric as a proper restaurant, but how else can you combine good barbecue with excellent Chinese and a cupcake or 10?

Buffets are extremely popular, and reservations are not taken, so be prepared for a long line at peak times. Eating at offbeat hours (lunch at 2pm, for example) will mean a shorter wait to get in, as will some hotel/casino players' club cards, which can get you line cuts.

Note: At press time, several hotels were offering all-you-can-eat all-day-long packages where you could pay one flat fee and come back to the buffets as many times as you like in a given day. Caesars Entertainment (Harrah's, Flamingo, Rio, and so on) is even offering a full-day pass to most of their buffets for as low as $50 so you can mix and match. Details and pricing on these change often, so visit the hotel's website or call ahead to see if they are offering any special deals when you're in town.

South Strip
EXPENSIVE

The Buffet at Aria ★ BUFFET   Like everything else in Aria, its buffet is very pretty. Many stations are spread throughout the orange-tinted room, accented with brick and chrome. Unusually for Vegas, you can have your buffet food in the sunshine: floor-to-ceiling windows let loads of natural light in. High-quality ingredients and international flavors abound here, including *naan* and roasted meats straight from a tandoor oven, fresh sushi from a sushi chef, and carving stations serving up nice slabs of tri-tip. The American game is strong as well, with a really tasty meatloaf that's almost like mom's. Desserts are fantastic here, mixing such usual items as gelato and cookies with a few new ones, like cream puffs and macarons.

At Aria Las Vegas, 3730 Las Vegas Blvd. S. www.arialasvegas.com. © **702/590-7111.** Breakfast $21, lunch $25, dinner $36–$41, Sat–Sun brunch $32 (not including cocktails). Daily 7am–10pm.

MODERATE

The Buffet at Excalibur ★ BUFFET   We get it: All buffets should keep up with the Joneses, but is there a way to do this without making everything look and sound alike? Sigh. Millions have been spent to rid the Buffet at Excalibur of its former King Arthur-and-his-round-table theme, making way for a bright, open, cheery space with sleek lines, and (sigh again) small plates, global cuisine. Despite my personal aversion to the trend of small-plates dining, the upgrade to the food here is monumental, considering it's still one of the cheapest buffets on the Strip. Best new dishes include interesting bites like vanilla bean adobo tacos, or stuffed tortellini pasta with Tasso ham, and lobster polenta with truffle oil and shiitake mushrooms. Desserts are fun as well, with ice cream bars hand-dipped to order. The beverages are self service, and there's even a self-pay station in the front, in the event you'd like to have an entire meal with no contact with another human being. Want to save a few bucks? Opt for the all day, all-you-can-eat package where you can also visit MORE, The Buffet at Luxor for one low price.

In Excalibur, 3850 Las Vegas Blvd. S. www.excalibur.com. © **702/597-7777**. Breakfast $17, lunch $18, dinner $23–$26, brunch $21. Daily 7am–10pm.

Mandalay Bay's Bayside Buffet ★★ BUFFET   The Asian bites are why I come here. Steamed barbecue pork buns are soft, sweet, and savory; shell-on salt and pepper shrimp are crunchy and eaten whole; and for whatever reason, I can't stop eating the pot stickers. I also like the off-the-beaten path Mexican selections, like the shredded pork carnitas and Laredo beans with rice. Everything else is about average, but the setting is unusually pleasant with a view of the pool (great people watching) and lots of natural light (there's nothing more uncomfortable than dozens of people binge eating in a stuffy space).

In Mandalay Bay, 3950 Las Vegas Blvd. S. www.mandalaybay.com. © **702/632-7402.** Breakfast $18, lunch $22, dinner $33, Sun brunch $26. Reduced prices for children 5–12; free for children 4 and under. Daily 7am–2:30pm, 4:30–9:45pm.

MORE, The Buffet at Luxor ★ BUFFET   The mummies that used to rule this all-you-can-eat at Luxor have fallen victim to rebranding. Which is a shame, because now this buffet is really boring to look at. Fortunately, the food quality has remained as consistent as it was during pharaoh's reign. There's the 30-foot salad bar and international offerings, like Mexican and Chinese, that aren't authentic, but still are tasty. This is all to say that it's not mind-blowing, but your kids will eat it. As noted above, this buffet can be combined with the offer at Excalibur, saving diners a few bucks.

In Luxor, 3900 Las Vegas Blvd. S. www.luxor.com. © **702/262-4000**. Breakfast $17, lunch $18, dinner $23; free for children 4 and under. Daily 7am–10pm.

Mid-Strip
EXPENSIVE
Bellagio Buffet ★★ BUFFET   This is one of the most expensive buffets in town, but it was also the first to elevate the buffet experience when it opened in 1989, focusing on high-quality dishes and ingredients. The raw bar is a great place to start, with oysters, cocktail shrimp, crab legs, and smoked salmon, and while normally we eschew pizzas at buffets (we can get that at home!), their wood-fired oven works magic. Champagne brunch is one of the most popular meals here, but I prefer the Friday and Saturday dinner service, which includes caviar with all the proper accoutrement. High rollers may want to ante up for the so-called Chef's Table, where you and at least eight of your friends bypass the entire line, and have a seat at a dedicated table near the buffet. Chefs come over, greet you, and pass hors d'oeuvres, before wheeling over carts to present

meats like prime rib and chops, as well as desserts. You are, of course, also welcome to eat from the buffet itself. At $20 to $30 higher than the regular dinner prices, you're paying for the privilege, but we think it's almost worth the awkward "who is that?" stares that come from the regular guests.

In Bellagio, 3600 Las Vegas Blvd. S. www.bellagio.com. © **877/234-6358.** Breakfast $20, lunch $24, dinner $35–$40, weekend brunch $30 ($42 with champagne), chef's table experience $60–$65. Daily 7am–10pm.

Caesars Palace Bacchanal Buffet ★★★ BUFFET   The beautiful Bacchanal Buffet is the crown jewel of the Caesars Entertainment empire. It isn't so much an all-you-can-eat buffet as it is nine different restaurants in one massive area. The space is divided into different, and different-looking, sections (one is glass enclosed, the back dining room is based around reclaimed wood, and a gleaming all-metal space finishes the trio.) More than 500 items are offered on any given day between the cold and raw bar, carving, Mexican, Asian, charcuterie, salad, and pizza stations. In addition are off-menu specials based on the chef's whimsy. Each item we've eaten here, whether it was the little basket of fried chicken and waffles, delicate dim sum, red velvet pancakes, or the big hunks of Polish sausage cut just for us, has been prepared extremely well, like it was made just for us. The desserts deserve an entry on their own, but they are some of our favorites in town, including Japanese mochi, macarons, and unusual gelatos (like brown butter gelato).

In Caesars Palace, 3570 Las Vegas Blvd. S. www.caesarspalace.com. © **702/731-7928.** Breakfast $30, lunch $38, dinner $54, weekend brunch $49 (includes champagne). Mon–Fri 7:30am–10pm; Sat–Sun 8am–10pm.

Mirage Cravings Buffet ★★ BUFFET   Mirage is one of those hotels that believes in the concept of under-promise, over-deliver. Visitors come to Las Vegas knowing about the Mirage, but they never have any idea of how good it is inside. The buffet is as underrated. It's a gorgeous, ultra-modern space with familiar, but top-notch fare. Delivered by eleven live action stations, it includes prime rib that's juicy and sliced to order, sushi as good as you'd get in your favorite Japanese restaurant, and Sunday brunch with such hangover-friendly items as pho, and, classic but pretty, eggs Benedict (plus more champagne). Beverages are self-service from one of those new-fangled soda machines, so there's something like 150 different flavors of Coca-Cola to choose from. Unlimited beer and wine for those 21-and-over is a nice touch.

In The Mirage, 3400 Las Vegas Blvd. S. www.mirage.com. © **702/791-7111.** Breakfast $17, lunch $22, dinner $31, Sat–Sun brunch $28. Reduced prices for children 5–10; free for children 4 and under. Daily 7am–9pm.

Paris Las Vegas Le Village Buffet ★★★ BUFFET   The French theme goes into overdrive at this buffet modeled after a countryside village, complete with faux outdoor patio seating and a painted sky on the ceiling above. The food is served at stations hailing the five regions of France, offering recognizable dishes, like charcuterie and pate, a hearty onion soup, and even an ambitious bouillabaisse. As good as you'd find in Provence? Maybe not, but it's still flavorful and often teeming with seafood. Classics like custom-made crepes, are hugely popular, as are desserts, like macarons and crème brûlée, because, hey, if you're faking France, you should at least get the pastries right. There are of course, American options here, like prime rib and snow crab legs, but we like the touches of truffles on the mac and cheese to remind us of why we're really here. Even after all these years, this is still one of the most popular buffets in town, so on weekends long lines are *de rigeur.*

In Paris Las Vegas, 3655 Las Vegas Blvd. S. www.parislasvegas.com. ℰ **702/946-7000.** Mon–Fri breakfast $22–$24, lunch $25, dinner $31–$34; Sat–Sun brunch $31. Reduced prices for children 4–10 and for Total Rewards Players Club members; free for children 3 and under. Daily 7am–10pm.

Wicked Spoon Buffet ★★ BUFFET   When Cosmopolitan opened this buffet, they set into motion a revolution that many other buffets would follow. Modeled after food halls you'd find in Asia, Wicked Spoon began the trend of offering guests individual portions of dishes like eggs Benedict and short rib pasta in ramekins and small pots rather than just placed in a steam tray on the line. It allows for better turnover of the dishes, ensuring that whatever is out there is as fresh as possible. Gathering all these individual dishes on one plate can be challenging, but it also makes you very aware of just how much food you're eating, so they cut down on waste as well. Among the dishes are foodie-oriented finds like roasted bone marrow at dinner, and mac and cheese studded with ham hocks and truffled potato gratin. The selection of desserts has been lauded as some of the best in the city, all in mini sizes so you can get a little bite of everything without going into a coma after. While all the other restaurants in the resort are in the East tower, this (along with Rose.Rabbit. Lie) is tucked into the West tower on the second floor.

In The Cosmopolitan of Las Vegas, 3708 Las Vegas Blvd. S. www.cosmopolitanlasvegas. com. ℰ **877/551-7772.** Weekday brunch $26, weekend brunch $34; dinner $38–$41. Brunch Mon–Fri 8am–2pm, Sat–Sun 8am–3pm; dinner Sun–Thurs 5–9pm, Fri–Sat 5–10pm.

MODERATE

The Buffet at TI ★ BUFFET   The buffet at TI is old-school and not in a good way. Don't get us wrong, the room is attractive, a contemporary space done in dark woods with exposed brick touches on the lines. But the menu sorely needs updating. What they do have, like made-to-order sushi and salads, Vietnamese pho (that you can customize to your own tastes), and a nice selection of meats from the carving station, is done properly. Fresh made doughnuts are a huge hit as well. So maybe in our quest for both novelty and quantity, we were only given the latter, and for some, that's all that counts.

In Treasure Island, 3300 Las Vegas Blvd. S. www.treasureisland.com. ℰ **702/894-7111.** Breakfast $19; lunch $23; dinner Mon–Thurs $29, Fri–Sun $31; Sat–Sun champagne brunch $26. Reduced prices for children 4–10; free for children 3 and under. Daily 7am–10pm.

Flavors at Harrah's ★ BUFFET   The meat section is the most laudable part of this buffet. In addition to an excellent carving station that includes gorgeous specimens of hams, turkey breasts, and prime ribs waiting to be sliced, Flavors also sometimes feature Brazilian barbecue known as *churrasco,* not a typical buffet offering. Since the other stations are average, fill up on meat and head to dessert. The selection of mini-cupcakes and cookies allows guests to sample many at once; kids and grown-ups alike love walking out of Flavors with cotton candy to-go.

In Harrah's, 3475 Las Vegas Blvd. S. www.harrahslv.com. ✆ **702/369-5000.** Breakfast and lunch $23, dinner $28, brunch Sat–Sun $27. Reduced prices for children 4–10; free for children 3 and under. Daily 7am–10pm.

Spice Market Buffet ★★ BUFFET   Out of all the buffets in the city, this is one of our underrated favorites. Planet Hollywood's former life as the Aladdin left the Middle Eastern cuisine of this buffet as its legacy. With well-prepared and flavorful options like a huge mezze spread of hummus, baba ghanoush, and rice-stuffed grape leaves, it's a big hit with our vegetarian friends (who are happy to find more than just salad and pizza to eat). Never fear, carnivores, there's still stuff for you, like lamb skewers and chicken curry, plus a carving station with prime rib, and an impressive seafood selection with fish and chips and sushi.

3667 Las Vegas Blvd. S. www.planethollywoodresort.com. ✆ **702/785-5555.** Breakfast $25, lunch $27, dinner $33–$40, Sat–Sun brunch $32. Daily 7am–11pm.

North Strip
EXPENSIVE

Wynn Las Vegas Buffet ★★★ BUFFET   Bottom line: It's darn nice to stuff your faces in such lovely surroundings. Arched ceilings allow natural light to stream into the atrium, where pots and pots of flowers and plants give vibrant life to the otherwise neutrally colored decor. And for a mass-eating experience, much attention is paid to individual guest's needs. There are 15 live action stations here, some of which allow guests to interact with chefs, like at the carving station, where they slice off your specific choice of prime rib or sausage. Some are self service, but still swanky, like the pre-portioned salad station, where the greens are served in glasses that evoke the mason jar salad-craze that was going around a couple of years ago. Many of the bites feature premium ingredients like Wagyu beef and veal short ribs (does that justify the elevated prices? You'll have to decide). Desserts are a high point here, whether you choose made-to-order crepes, bon bons, excellent gelato . . . or all of the above.

In Wynn Las Vegas, 3131 Las Vegas Blvd. S. www.wynnlasvegas.com. ✆ **702/248-3463.** Breakfast $21, lunch $26, dinner $39–$40, Sat–Sun brunch $33 (not including cocktails). Daily 8am–10pm.

Downtown
INEXPENSIVE

Main Street Station Garden Court Buffet ★★★ BUFFET   The Garden Court Buffet is Downtown's prettiest and most extensive buffet—and a darn good deal at half what the Strip casinos are charging for meals.

Reminiscent of a Victorian train station, its ceilings are grandly arched, covered with white tile and small pinpoint lights, which glow daintily at dinnertime. At lunch, sunshine pours through the lovely stained glass windows, one of the few in-casino eateries that allows sunlight to enter (blame Vegas' large vampire clientele, I guess). It may also be the most spacious buffet in town, with tables that are shouting distance apart and comfortable chairs. The buffet itself is a massive, highly staffed affair with nine live-action stations, each attended by a friendly chef popping pizzas into a brick oven, wokking up Chinese food, or running the Southern soul food station (which sometimes has chicken fried steak with gravy). As a nod to the frequent Hawaiian visitors that come through, there are a lot of island options, like sweet Portuguese sausage for breakfast, sticky rice wrapped in banana leaves, and shredded kalua pork and cabbage.

At Main Street Station, 200 N. Main St. www.mainstreetcasino.com. © **702/387-1896.** Breakfast $8; lunch $9; dinner $12–$23, Sat–Sun champagne brunch $12. Free for children 3 and under. Daily 7–10:30am breakfast; 11am–3pm lunch; Mon–Thurs 4–9pm dinner; Fri–Sun 4–10pm dinner.

Just Off the Strip

EXPENSIVE

Rio's Carnival World & Seafood Buffet ★★ BUFFET Locals love this all-you-can-eat, as it was one of the first to offer a truly global dining experience (that went beyond the standard Italian, Chinese and American at other buffets), plus they loved the Village Seafood Buffet, which offered the best catches from the Pacific Rim, Mediterranean and Baja. Only recently did they consolidate the two into one mega buffet. The food court setting allows diners to navigate between the various cuisines—the meat-laden Brazilian grill, and the Japanese *teppanyaki* station serve up just some of the more than 300 other dishes on offer. On top of those are more than 70 desserts at the finish, with almost a dozen gelato flavors, pies, and cakes, all made on-site just for this restaurant.

In Rio All-Suite Hotel & Casino, 3700 W. Flamingo Rd. www.riolasvegas.com. © **702/252-7777.** Lunch $25, dinner $32–$50, Sat–Sun champagne brunch $32. Reduced prices for children 4–8; free for children 3 and under. Mon–Fri 11am–10pm; Sat–Sun 8am–10pm.

Online Restaurant Inspections

The Southern Nevada Health District is the organization responsible for inspecting restaurants. Each is visited at least twice a year and then graded (A, B, or C), given demerits for infractions (improper food storage and handling, and the like), and in extreme cases, shut down. You can now read the inspections online for every restaurant in town, although you may not want to if you ever feel like eating in Las Vegas again. If you think you and your stomach can handle it, visit www.southernnevada healthdistrict.org.

INEXPENSIVE

Gold Coast's Ports O' Call ★ BUFFET   There's nothing wrong with seeking out a cheaper buffet in the name of sustenance. While you won't have the myriad of choices as other buffets on the Strip, Ports o' Call has a respectable seven live cooking stations, and some genuine hits among its dishes, like the full rotisserie chickens at the carving station, the steak tacos from the Mexican line, and fried oysters from the seafood station. Fridays are seafood night, but I think the prime rib is a better choice. Gold Coast's buffet is clean, the food is decent, and the lines won't be insane, and sometimes that's all you need.

In Gold Coast, 4000 W. Flamingo Rd. www.goldcoastcasino.com. ✆ **702/367-7111.** Breakfast $8, lunch $10, dinner $16–$21, Sun brunch $18. Reduced prices for children 4–9; free for children 3 and under. Mon–Sat 7–10am, 11am–3pm, 4–9pm; Sun 8am–3pm, 4–9pm.

EXPLORING LAS VEGAS

Y ou aren't going to lack for things to do in Las Vegas. More than likely, you've come here for the gambling, which should keep you pretty busy. But you can't sit at a slot machine forever. After all, you're going to have to get up to go to the bathroom at some point! When you do, maybe you should look around at some of the other things here that can keep you entertained.

Just walking on the Strip and gazing at the gaudy, garish, absurd wonder of it all can occupy quite a lot of time. This is the number-one activity we recommend in Vegas; at night, it is a mind-boggling sight. Beyond that there are options galore, from popular bits of Vegas silliness like volcanoes and crooning gondoliers, to museums, thrill rides, spas, recreation, and beyond. And, of course, you can engage in those most iconic Vegas traditions, getting married and gambling. All of that and more is covered in this chapter. Don't forget there are shows and plenty of other nighttime entertainment, which you can read more about in chapter 8. There are also out-of-town sightseeing options, such as **Hoover Dam** (a major tourist destination), **Red Rock Canyon,** and excursions to the **Grand Canyon.** We've listed the best of these in chapter 9.

Las Vegas Iconic Sights

Entertainment Complexes

Exhibits

Museums & Galleries

Theme Parks & Rides

Zoos

Other Attractions

SOUTH STRIP

Big Apple Coaster & Arcade ★★ THRILL RIDE   As if the outside of New York-New York wasn't busy enough, someone decided to knock it up a few notches by having a roller coaster wind around the whole thing. The whimsically designed cars evoke Manhattan taxi cabs and run at speeds up to 67 mph while going through drops of as much as 144 feet, a full loop, and the "heartline" twist, which simulates a jet-fighter barrel roll. Adrenaline junkies may find it too tame, but the average fun-seeker will do a lot of screaming. If that's too much for you, try the tamer amusements in the arcade that features carnival and video games.

In New York–New York, 3790 Las Vegas Blvd. S. www.newyorknewyork.com. ⓒ **702/740-6969.** Single rides $14 adults, all-day pass $25. Must be 54 in. tall to ride. Sun–Thurs 11am–11pm; Fri–Sat 10:30am–midnight. Closed during inclement weather.

Bodies . . . The Exhibition ★★ EXHIBIT

A stunning and controversial exhibit featuring real live dead bodies (over 200 full and partial specimens, some possibly executed Chinese prisoners who may never have given permission for their bodies to be used in this way—hence the controversy). Utilizing a patented freeze-dry operation, full bodies, artfully dissected body parts, and stripped cadavers are on display not for sensationalism—though it is pretty sensational in nearly all senses of the word—but for visitors to fully appreciate the wonder and mechanics that go into our transient flesh. When a body is positioned in an athletic pose, you can see how the muscles work, and when a cross section of a lung afflicted with cancer is right in front of you, you may be glad Vegas has passed stricter smoking laws. It's educational and bizarre and not something you're likely to forget soon. Surprisingly not grotesque, but not for the ultra-squeamish.

In the Luxor, 3900 Las Vegas Blvd. S. www.bodiestheexhibition.com/lasvegas. ☏ **702/ 262-4000.** Admission $32 adults, $30 military, seniors 65 and over, $24 ages 4–12, free 3 and under, $29 Nevada residents. Daily 10am–10pm; last admission 9pm.

CityCenter Fine Art Collection ★★ ART MUSEUM

Art in outdoor public spaces is a relatively new phenomenon to Las Vegas, mostly because the only time people spend outside is by the pool or hustling to get to another casino. But City Center wisely (I think) decided not to confine its works by 15 major artists to a stuffy museum within the resort, opting to make the entire hotel, and its neighbors, the gallery. A free app leads viewers through the casino to such works as the 250-foot LED wall by Jenny Holzer that scrolls "Vegas-isms" hidden at North Valet; or Big Edge, an installation of recycled aluminum canoes. The app will also let you know why you should walk between the Kirins when you enter the casino for energy and good luck. There's also ephemeral art, like Glacia at The Shops at Crystals, which are ice columns that rise and melt each day; or the Lumia fountain which spouts color-infused water in the circle drive. Remember that the resort and its surroundings are huge—wear comfortable shoes to get you through the art hike.

At CityCenter, 3730 Las Vegas Blvd. S. www.aria.com. ☏ **702/590-7111.** Free admission. Most artworks are outdoors or in 24-hr. public spaces.

CSI: The Experience ★★ ENTERTAINMENT COMPLEX

Although spinoffs have moved the sleuthing to Miami and New York, the original *CSI* television show takes place in Las Vegas, so how apropos is this major attraction, which allows visitors to work a crime scene right on the Strip? Three different crimes have occurred—a car has crashed into a house, a woman has been murdered behind a motel, and a skeleton has been found in the desert—and it's up to the participants to examine the crime scene, look for clues, take notes, and then run it all through an interactive lab of sorts with help from videos of various stars of the show (we miss you, Gil Grissom!) and real-life CSI technicians. It's silly, gory fun and highly engrossing if you have an analytical mind (all but the most sullen of teenagers will love this).

In MGM Grand, 3799 Las Vegas Blvd. S. http://lasvegas.csiexhibit.com. ☏ **877/660- 0660** or 702/891-5738. Admission $32 adults, $25 children 4–11. Daily 9am–9pm (last admission 8pm).

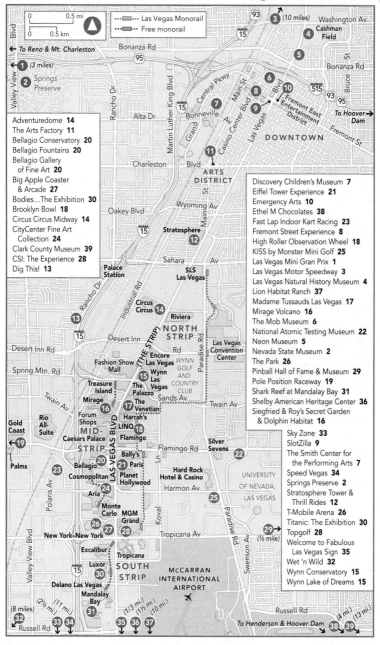

Las Vegas Monorail

Free monorail

← To Reno & Mt. Charleston

Bonanza Rd

0   0.5 mi

0   0.5 km

(3 miles) **1**

Springs Preserve **2**

Washington Av

(10 miles) **3**

Cashman Field **4**

5

Bonanza Rd

6

8   **10**

7

9

Fremont East Entertainment District

To Hoover → Dam

DOWNTOWN

Fremont St

11

ARTS DISTRICT

Charleston Blvd

Oakey Blvd

Wyoming Av

Sahara Av

Adventuredome **14**
The Arts Factory **11**
Bellagio Conservatory **20**
Bellagio Fountains **20**
Bellagio Gallery of Fine Art **20**
Big Apple Coaster & Arcade **27**
Bodies…The Exhibition **30**
Brooklyn Bowl **18**
Circus Circus Midway **14**
CityCenter Fine Art Collection **24**
Clark County Museum **39**
CSI: The Experience **28**
Dig This! **13**

Discovery Children's Museum **7**
Eiffel Tower Experience **21**
Emergency Arts **10**
Ethel M Chocolates **38**
Fast Lap Indoor Kart Racing **23**
Fremont Street Experience **8**
High Roller Observation Wheel **18**
KISS by Monster Mini Golf **25**
Las Vegas Mini Gran Prix **1**
Las Vegas Motor Speedway **3**
Las Vegas Natural History Museum **4**
Lion Habitat Ranch **37**
Madame Tussauds Las Vegas **17**
Mirage Volcano **16**
The Mob Museum **6**
National Atomic Testing Museum **22**
Neon Museum **5**
Nevada State Museum **2**
The Park **26**
Pinball Hall of Fame & Museum **29**
Pole Position Raceway **19**
Shark Reef at Mandalay Bay **31**
Shelby American Heritage Center **36**
Siegfried & Roy's Secret Garden & Dolphin Habitat **16**

Palace Station

SLS Las Vegas

Stratosphere **12**

Circus Circus **14**

13

15

Desert Inn Rd

Riviera

NORTH STRIP

Las Vegas Convention Center

Desert Inn Rd

Spring Mtn. Rd

Fashion Show Mall

Encore Las Vegas

WYNN GOLF AND COUNTRY CLUB

Wynn **15**

Treasure Island

The Palazzo

Mirage

Forum Shops

The Venetian **17**

Sands Av

Twain Av

Gold Coast

Rio All-Suite

19

MID-STRIP

Caesars Palace

Harrah's

LINQ **18**

Flamingo

Palms

Bellagio **20**

Cosmopolitan

Paris **21**

Planet Hollywood

Aria **24**

23

Flamingo Rd

Silver Sevens

22

Hard Rock Hotel & Casino

Harmon Av

UNIVERSITY OF NEVADA, LAS VEGAS

25

Monte Carlo

New York–New York

26   MGM Grand **28**

27

Tropicana Av

Paradise Rd

(½ mile) **29**

Sky Zone **33**
SlotZilla **9**
The Smith Center for the Performing Arts **7**
Speed Vegas **34**
Springs Preserve **2**
Stratosphere Tower & Thrill Rides **12**
T-Mobile Arena **26**
Titanic: The Exhibition **30**
Topgolf **28**
Welcome to Fabulous Las Vegas Sign **35**
Wet 'n Wild **32**
Wynn Conservatory **15**
Wynn Lake of Dreams **15**

Excalibur

Tropicana

Luxor **15**

SOUTH STRIP

McCARRAN INTERNATIONAL AIRPORT

Delano Las Vegas

Mandalay Bay **31**

(2½ mi.) (11 mi.)

(8 miles) **32**

Russell Rd

33   **34**

(1/3 mi.) (1½ mi.) (10 mi.)

35   **36**   **37**

Russell Rd

To Henderson & Hoover Dam

(4 mi.) **38** (13 mi.) **39**

Shark Reef at Mandalay Bay ★ AQUARIUM   Given that watching fish can lower your blood pressure, it's practically a public service for Mandalay Bay to provide this facility in a city where craps tables and other gaming areas can bring excitement levels to dangerous heights. Although I admire the style (it's built to look like a sunken temple), and standing in the all-glass tunnel surrounded by sharks is cool, it's just a giant aquarium, which is disappointing at these prices. *Note:* It is *waaay* off in a remote part of Mandalay Bay, which might be a hassle for those with limited mobility.

In Mandalay Bay, 3950 Las Vegas Blvd. S. www.sharkreef.com. © **702/632-4555.** Admission $20 adults, $18 seniors, $14 children 5–12, free for children 4 and under, $17 Nevada residents. Sun–Thurs 10am–8pm; Fri–Sat 10am–10pm. Last admission 1 hr. before closing; hours vary seasonally.

Titanic: The Exhibition ★ EXHIBIT   It's too easy to say "you've seen the movie, now see the exhibit." But that is sort of the case; if you were captivated by the Oscar-winning epic, you will definitely want to take in this exhibit on the unsinkable luxury liner that sank on its maiden voyage. While it's a can't-miss for buffs, it might still be of some interest for those with only marginal feelings about the massive 1912 disaster. It's a strangely somber subject for Vegas, featuring displays explaining the ship's ill-fated maiden voyage; relics salvaged from the sunken liner; and even re-creations of sample cabins from first, second, and third class, including atmospheric conditions, giving one a sense of how it felt to travel aboard what was an incredible vessel. There is even a large chunk of real ice standing in for the culprit berg.

In the Luxor, 3900 Las Vegas Blvd. S. www.luxor.com. © **702/262-4400.** Admission $32 adults, $30 military, seniors 65 and over, $24 children 4–12, free for children 3 and under, $29 Nevada residents with ID. Daily 10am–10pm. Last admission 9pm.

MID-STRIP

Bellagio Gallery of Fine Art ★★ ART MUSEUM   As if there wasn't enough to look at in the rest of the resort! Should you tire of the thousands of glass flowers on the lobby ceiling or the real ones in the Conservatory, head here for actual art…in Las Vegas. The exhibits are small (alas, the price of admission isn't), but the artists showcased are of the highest caliber, running the gamut over the years, from Monet to Faberge to Georgia O'Keefe.

In Bellagio, 3600 Las Vegas Blvd. S. www.bellagio.com. © **702/693-7871.** Admission $16 adults; $14 seniors and Nevada residents; $12 teachers, students with ID, military. Daily 10am–7pm. Last admission 5:30pm.

Eiffel Tower Experience ★ OBSERVATION TOWER   Whether this is worth the dough depends on how much you like views. The "ride" portion is a glass-enclosed elevator to the top as a guide delivers a few facts ("this is a half-size exact replica, down to the paint color of the original" and more). At the uppermost platform, viewers are welcome to stand around and look out for as long as they want, which probably isn't 2 hours, the length of the average movie, which costs about what this does. If you'd like a view that's just as spectacular but a little lower to the ground, opt instead for a cocktail in the lounge of the

Eiffel Tower Restaurant, located on the 11th floor of the structure. The price of a drink is about the same as the cost of the ride up to the top, but this is a much more relaxed way to enjoy the view. Plus now you have a cocktail.

In Paris Las Vegas, 3655 Las Vegas Blvd. S. www.parislv.com. © **702/946-7000.** Admission $14 adults 9:30am–7:15pm, $19 7:15pm–close; $10 seniors 60 and over and children 12 and under 9:30am–7:15pm, $14 7:15pm–close. Mon–Fri 9:30am–12:30am; Sat–Sun 9:30am–1am; weather permitting.

High Roller Observation Wheel ★★ THRILL RIDE   The *if bigger is better, then biggest is best* ethos that Las Vegas loves so much continues here with the world's tallest observation wheel. Standing at nearly 550 feet high, the massive structure has fundamentally changed the skyline and provides some of the best views of the Strip (and much of southern Nevada). The wheel has 28 fully enclosed, air-conditioned cabs, each capable of holding up to 40 people, although if you get stuck in one that full you will need to fight your way to good snapshot-worthy window space. One full revolution takes about 30 minutes, so it's less of a thrill ride than a leisurely, albeit really high, walk in the park. Even those with height phobias may find this tolerable. Go at night for the best photo opportunities of the city in its fully lit-up glory—it's worth the extra few bucks you have to pay for the privilege. Prices are high for this relatively short experience—a pass to the top of the even-taller Stratosphere Tower (see below) is significantly less expensive. Maybe it's because the tower doesn't go around in a circle? The good news is that they not only allow drinks on board, they practically encourage it, with a bar on your way to the boarding area, or if you're willing to pony up a bit more, a cabin with an open bar. Of course, there are no bathrooms on the ride, so drink at your own peril. Note that lines can be long during peak periods, both to get tickets and to queue up for the cabs, so it's best to buy online beforehand and budget some extra time for standing in line.

3545 Las Vegas Blvd. S. www.thelinq.com. © **800/CAESARS.** High Roller admission $27 day, $37 night, $32–$47 Happy Half Hour cabins. Daily 10am–2am.

Madame Tussauds Las Vegas ★★ MUSEUM   Madame T's has outposts in nearly every major tourist city, and for two centuries it has been the best (borderline creepy) way to get close to celebrities. The figures themselves are quite impressive, both for their meticulous attention to detail and the eerie way they (often) reflect the personalities of their subjects.

rambling THROUGH RESORTS

Las Vegas is unlike most every other place on earth in that you don't necessarily leave your hotel to sightsee—the hotels themselves are attractions. So when planning your daily itinerary, don't skip chapter 4, "Where to Stay." It will introduce you to all of the glorious, and goofy, architectural elements of the Strip resorts (and off-Strip ones, as well), their shopping opportunities and shows, the highlights of their casinos, their over-the-top restaurants, nightlife venues and more. Who knew wandering through hotels could be this fun?

The Vegas-specific exhibits are the star attractions, from the bedazzled, stuck-in-time Liberace to the "Hangover Experience" with Bradley Cooper (that stubble is so perfect) and Zach Galifinakis, complete with his man-satchel. You may have heard of the questionable poses visitors were holding with singer Nicki Minaj, one the most recent additions; not Vegas-specific, but hey, it fits in. Sadly, the tuxedo-clad George Clooney, who visitors used to be able to "marry," has been replaced with a boring, regular, suit-wearing, already-married Clooney. If you're a fan of the Avengers franchise, there's an entire room dedicated to Marvel's superheroes, complete with a 4-D cinema attraction created just for the museum.

In The Venetian, 3355 Las Vegas Blvd. S. www.madametussauds.com/lasvegas. ✆ **702/862-7800.** Admission $30 adults, $20 children 4–12, free for children 3 and under. Discounts for booking online. Sun–Thurs 10am–9pm; Fri–Sat 10am–10pm; hours vary seasonally.

The Park ★★ ENTERTAINMENT COMPLEX The space between Monte Carlo and New York-New York has been developed into the very first outdoor gathering space on the Strip . . . that has nothing to do with a resort pool. There's certainly water though, thanks to two welcoming 100-footlong waterfalls near the Las Vegas Boulevard entrance of this bona fide park, complete with art installations, live entertainment, and restaurants. The Park combines natural and industrial design to create a comfortable oasis in the desert, including 16 75-foot-tall shade "trees" that line the area, blocking sun by day, casting cool shadows, and lighting up the paths by night. The 40-foot-tall Bliss Dance sculpture made her way from Burning Man to shimmy on the Strip, illuminated by 3,000 colored LED lights. Even if you're not headed to a show at the T-Mobile Arena, which sits behind The Park, there's plenty of reasons to take a stroll, including several restaurants which all offer indoor and outdoor space, such as the theatrical sushi spot Sake Rok and the waffle-driven Bruxie, which takes the Belgian specialty and uses it as a vehicle for some great sandwiches.

3784 Las Vegas Blvd. S. www.theparkvegas.com. ✆ **702/693-7275.** Free admission.

Siegfried & Roy's Secret Garden & Dolphin Habitat ★★★ ZOO After more than 20 years, this engaging animal habitat remains one of the best antidotes to Las Vegas stress. Spend an hour watching dolphins and tigers and you won't care how much money you lost on the slots. The bulk of your time will most likely be spent in the well-regarded dolphin habitat, a 2.5-million-gallon home for bottlenose dolphins that were either rescued or born here. This is more than just a SeaWorld–style, sit in bleachers and watch the animals cavort kind of place (although they have that, too). Here you can get up close to the pools and sometimes interact with them (splashing is involved), which is a treat, especially for kids. Pay extra and you can get VIP, behind-the-scenes tours; spend an entire day as a trainer, complete with time in the pool; and even "paint" with them as you hold a canvas and the dolphin holds a special brush in its mouth. The latter is an unmitigated thrill that allows you to connect with these amazing animals, or at least pretend you are.

The Secret Garden part is a small zoo originally designed as an on-site home for the animals used in Siegfried & Roy's magic show, which ended in

2003 after a disagreement between Roy and a tiger. The animals that remain are mostly of the big cat variety, including some of the illusionists' famed white tigers. It's fine, but don't expect a lot of excitement. On hot Vegas days they mostly (and wisely) just lay in the shade or shallow pools, so don't expect them to be hunting elk or playing with big balls of yarn.

While it's easy to have a pang of environmentally conscious guilt over animals in captivity, the entire facility is well run and scrupulously maintained, the trainers are obviously passionate, and the animals seem to thrive here. Several of the dolphins are more than 30 years old, which is more than double their life expectancy in the wild.

In The Mirage, 3400 Las Vegas Blvd. S. www.miragehabitat.com. ✆ **702/791-7188.** Admission $22 adults, $17 children 4–10, free for children 3 and under. Daily 10am–6:30pm; hours vary seasonally.

NORTH STRIP

Adventuredome ★★ AMUSEMENT PARK   This is a more than okay place to spend a hot afternoon, especially since it's one of the few family-friendly attractions in town. Plus, unlike most theme parks, it's indoors! The glass dome that towers overhead lets in natural light so you get the best of both worlds—sunlight and air-conditioning. A double-loop roller coaster careens around the simulated Grand Canyon, and there's a laser-tag area, some bouncy/twirly/stomach-churning rides, and a modest number of other, tamer rides for kids of all ages. Video games and a carnival-style arcade are separate from the attractions, though it all still feels pretty hectic. The log flume ride closed in 2013 to make way for a cutting-edge roller coaster, El Loco, which is one of only six of its kind in the world. Although it's a short ride (a little longer than a minute), it's a scary one, with negative-g drops, reverse barrel rolls, and open cars that seem ready to tip you out.

2880 Las Vegas Blvd. S. (behind Circus Circus). www.adventuredome.com. ✆ **702/794-3939.** Free admission; $5–$12 per ride; daily pass $32 adults, $18 children 33–47 in. tall. Mon–Thurs 11am–6pm; Fri–Sat 10am–midnight; Sun 10am–9pm; hours vary seasonally.

Circus Circus Midway ★ ENTERTAINMENT COMPLEX   First inaugurated in 1968, the big-top action at this family-friendly hotel is billed as the largest permanent circus in the world. High-wire, trapeze, juggling, acrobatics, and more fill the top of the "tent" daily from 11am until late at night, while more than 200 carnival-style midway games get the young ones inured to the joys (and heartache) of risking money for questionable odds of a reward. Note that while the attractions here are definitely kid-friendly, you have to go through the casino to get to them.

In Circus Circus, 2880 Las Vegas Blvd. S. www.circuscircus.com. ✆ **702/734-0410.** Free admission. Daily 11am–midnight.

Stratosphere Tower & Thrill Rides ★★ THRILL RIDE   Whether you come for the views or the scary rides, the Stratosphere Tower is a uniquely Vegas experience. Indoor and outdoor decks provide remarkable views of the

free VEGAS

Vegas used to be the land of freebies—or at least, stuff so cheap it seemed free. Those days are an increasingly dim memory, but some hotels still offer free attractions designed to lure you into their casinos, where you might then drop far more than the cost of a day ticket to Disney World. Here's a handy list of the best of the free bait—er, sights:

Bellagio Conservatory (in Bellagio) ★★★ PARK/GARDEN A totally preposterous idea, a larger-than-life greenhouse atrium, filled with seasonal living foliage in riotous colors and styles, changed with meticulous regularity. From Easter to Chinese New Year, events are celebrated with carefully designed splashes of flowers, plants, and remarkable decorations—it's an incredible amount of labor for absolutely no immediate financial payoff. No wonder it's one of the most popular sights in Vegas. Open 24 hours.

Bellagio Fountains (outside Bellagio) ★★★ ICON Giant spouts of water shoot up and down and sideways, and dance their little aquatic hearts out to music ranging from show tunes to Chopin. When we tell people about this, they roll their eyes when they think we aren't looking, and then they go see it for themselves . . . and end up staying for several numbers. Shows are daily every half-hour, starting early afternoon, then every 15 minutes 7pm to midnight. Closed when it's windy; hours vary seasonally.

Mirage Volcano (outside The Mirage) ★★ ICON When it first opened with the hotel in 1989, this erupting "volcano" literally stopped traffic on the Strip. The fact that it's not quite as spectacular these days—even after a 2008 makeover amped up the fire, lights, sound, and effects to a much more entertaining level—says more about how jaded we've become than how cool it is. Get up close to feel the heat of the "lava" blasts and the rumble of the sound system. Eruptions are daily on the hour after dark until 11pm.

Welcome to Fabulous Las Vegas Sign ★★★ ICON Erected in 1959, this colorfully lit neon sign is probably the most iconic and most photographed attraction in Las Vegas. Located in the median of Las Vegas Boulevard about a mile south of Mandalay Bay, visiting was made easier a few years back with the addition of a parking lot, which means you no longer need to play chicken with oncoming traffic to get to it. It has no formal address, but GPS users should use 5200 Las Vegas Blvd. S. to get in the vicinity. The lot is open 24 hours, but go at night when it's all lit up for the best photo opportunities.

Wynn Conservatory (in Wynn Las Vegas) ★ PARK/GARDEN Although not as jaw-dropping as its spiritual cousin, the Bellagio Conservatory (see above), this indoor atrium of floral displays is still worth a gander, if for no other reason than it's on your way from the front door to the casino. The arrangements change regularly, though they may reflect the striking floral mosaics on the floor below. It's open 24 hours.

Wynn Lake of Dreams (in Wynn Las Vegas) ★ ICON Masked as it is from the street by a 150-foot-tall "mountain," this light, laser, fog, and special-effect show can only be seen from select areas inside the hotel, mostly in bars requiring you to buy expensive drinks. Should you bother? Maybe. Basically, twice an hour, a lake lights up with pretty colors, cued to tunes ranging from classical to Louis Armstrong for "interludes." At the top of the hour are bigger extravaganzas of weird hologram erotic-psychedelic images projected on the wall waterfall, while shapes and puppets pop out for even more weird action, with some rather adult imagery at times. Shows are every 30 minutes, from 6pm to midnight.

city, southern Nevada, and perhaps even California on a clear day, from this, the tallest observation tower west of the Mississippi (more than 1,100 ft.). Obviously, acrophobics should avoid the tower at all costs.

Atop the tower are four marvelous thrill rides that will test your mettle and perhaps how strong your stomach is. The **Big Shot** is a breathtaking free-fall ride that thrusts you 160 feet in the air along a 228-foot spire at the top of the tower, and then plummets back down again. Sitting in an open car, you seem to be dangling in space over Las Vegas. Amping up the terror factor is **X-Scream,** a giant teeter-totter-style device that propels you in an open car off the side of the 100-story tower and lets you dangle there weightlessly before returning you to relative safety. Then there's the aptly named **Insanity,** a spinning whirligig of a contraption that straps you into a seat and twirls you around 1,000 feet or so above terra firma. Insanity is right.

Finally, if whirling and twirling and spinning around at the top of the tower is just not rad enough for you, there's **SkyJump,** in which you get to leap off the top of the thing. We wish we were kidding. Jumpers are put into flight suits and harnesses, then taken up to the 108th floor where they get connected to a big cable/winch contraption. Then, they jump. It's a "controlled" descent, meaning that you don't just drop the roughly 830 feet to the landing pad, but you are flying down at speeds of up to 40 mph with nothing but a couple of metal wires keeping you in place. There are lots of safety features that they tout and the three other SkyJumps around the world (in New Zealand, China, and South Korea) have sterling safety records. Nevertheless, though they call the other ride Insanity, I think this one is the truly insane option. *Note:* The rides are shut down in inclement weather and high winds.

Atop Stratosphere Las Vegas, 2000 Las Vegas Blvd. S. www.stratospherehotel.com. © **702/380-7777.** Tower: Admission $20 adults and hotel guests; $14 seniors, Nevada residents; $12 children 4–12; free for children 3 and under. Rides: Big Shot $25, X-Scream $25, Insanity $25, SkyJump $120. Tower admission waived with ride purchase. Multi-ride and all-day packages available. Sun–Thurs 10am–1am; Fri–Sat 10am–2am; hours vary seasonally. Minimum height 48 in. for Big Shot, 52 in. for X-Scream and Insanity. Maximum weight 275 lb. for SkyJump.

DOWNTOWN

The Arts Factory ★ COMMERCIAL ART GALLERY Believe it or not, Las Vegas has a pretty decent art scene (what some would consider soul-crushing is what others consider inspirational), and this complex, located in the 18b Arts District, is the place to find proof. It features several galleries, boutiques, and a number of workspaces for local artists, plus a bistro and bar.

107 E. Charleston Blvd. www.theartsfactory.com. © **702/383-3133.** Free admission. Hours vary by gallery.

Discovery Children's Museum ★★★ MUSEUM Bringing your little ones to Vegas isn't as taboo as it used to be, but it can be a drag for them to be dragged around to a bunch of over-stimulating places where they can't do a thing. Thankfully, there's this lifesaver, located near the Smith Center of the

Performing Arts. Its filled with interactive exhibits, meaning the wee ones can touch and play, all the while learning about science, nutrition, and the environment (even if they might not realize it). There are three floors of hands-on fun where the kids storm a fantasy castle (Excalibur!), discover an ancient city (Luxor!) and scramble around on a 70-foot-tall science-filled jungle gym. You, and they, will definitely be tuckered out afterwards.

360 Promenade Place (at The Smith Center for the Performing Arts). www.discoverykids lv.com. ☏ **702/382-5437.** Admission $15 ages 1–99. Tue–Fri 9am–4pm; Sat 10am–5pm; Sun noon–5pm.

Emergency Arts ★★ COMMERCIAL ART GALLERY   The artists in residence here rescued a derelict Downtown building that was once a medical clinic and turned it into a funky, fun, bohemian space dedicated to the creation and conservation of all things art. The first floor has a small cafe (perfect for having a coffee while discussing Sartre), a used record store, and the temporary home of the Burlesque Hall of Fame and Museum. The latter is a small couple of rooms with what is said to be a tiny fraction of photos and memorabilia honoring the peek-a-boo art form. The rest of the first floor and all of the second floor is taken up by small boutiques where local artists show and sell their wares. These include paintings, sculpture, jewelry, clothing, and much more. While the quality obviously varies from artist to artist, it's all unique, and a much better way to spend your souvenir dollars than on a Las Vegas snow globe.

520 E. Fremont St. www.emergencyartslv.com. ☏ **702/686-3164.** Free admission. Hours vary by gallery.

Fremont Street Experience ★★★ ICON   The Fremont Street Experience is a five-block, open-air, landscaped strip of outdoor snack shops, vendor carts, and colorful kiosks purveying food and merchandise. Overhead is a 90-foot-high steel-mesh "celestial vault" that at night becomes **Viva Vision,** a high-tech video-and-sound show (the canopy is equipped with more than 12.5 million lights), enhanced by a concert hall–quality sound system. There are a number of different shows, and there's music between the light performances as well. It's really cool, in that Vegas over-the-top way that we love so much. The addition of several hotel bars open to the pedestrian street has upped the "party" quotient, and frequent concerts and events have made it even more popular than ever. Oh, and look up to see people zooming by on a zip line! It's a great place where you can stroll, eat, or even dance to the music under the lights.

Fremont St. (btw. Main St. and Las Vegas Blvd.), Downtown. www.vegasexperience. com. Free admission. Shows nightly on the hour.

Las Vegas Natural History Museum ★ MUSEUM   Like most natural history museums, this one has its share of stuffed-and-posed animals. It's an often dusty, mangy collection of taxidermy, so I suggest breezing past it quickly to get to the museum's star attraction: its dinosaur exhibit. It showcases 35-foot long *Jurassic World*–quality monsters that are able to growl and move (when you push the appropriate buttons). Deductive text next to the exhibits teaches children (and adults) about their habits and the theories surrounding their extinction. Along with the dinos are rooms with live lizards, sharks and stingrays that guests can feed at certain days and times; and inter-active displays that allow kids to dig for fossils as paleontologists, or pretend they're marine biologists in a submarine. Old fashioned? Maybe. An interest-ing, educational way to spend an afternoon? Absolutely.

900 Las Vegas Blvd. N. (at Washington Ave.). www.lvnhm.org. © **702/384-3466.** Admission $10 adults; $8 seniors, students, and military; $5 children 3–11; free for chil-dren 2 and under. Daily 9am–4pm. Closed Thanksgiving and Dec 25.

The Mob Museum ★★★ MUSEUM This three-story former court-house contains the actual courtroom where Senator Estes Kefauver held his famous syndicated crime hearings in 1950 and 1951. Watched by 30 million people, the most for any televised event of the time, the trials made it incon-trovertibly clear that organized crime *did* exist in the U.S. This famed, and beautifully restored, courtroom is the centerpiece of the museum and gives heft to the idea that a new museum should open here, in a city where the majority of museums last no longer than mob stooges.

To avoid that fate, the designers and founders have added a healthy dose of razzmatazz to the proceedings: a fascinating 10-minute film on mob movies narrated by Nicholas Pileggi, slot machine-like displays of video testimonials, the opportunity to take part in a line up, and fake machine guns to fire.

The museum also makes a gripping case for the idea that mob history may actually be the truest history of the United States. "If you go deep enough, you can see the mob's fingerprints on everything," one bit of wall text grimly asserts, followed by exhibits on fixed elections, presidential assassinations, and labor disputes. It's a dark vision, enhanced by the unrelenting gore that assaults the visitor (this is NOT a museum for kids), with pictures of blood splattered crime scenes adorning at least half the walls in the place. (They start to look like grisly Rorschach Tests after a while.) Though, to its credit, the museum does not glorify crime. You'll learn not only about the battle for the soul of Las Vegas (and the country) from the mob side, but also from that of law enforcement.

In a town where it's easy to get caught up in the fantasy that's spoon-fed to visitors, this is a welcome, must-see attraction that will help you understand exactly what sins this city was built on.

300 Stewart Ave. www.themobmuseum.org. © **702/229-2734.** Admission $20–$24 adults; $14 children 5–17 and students with ID; $18 seniors, military, law enforcement, and teachers; $14 NV residents with ID. Sun–Thurs 10am–7pm; Fri–Sat 10am–8pm.

The Neon Museum ★★★ MUSEUM This is where old Las Vegas signs go to retire. Enter through the former La Concha Motel lobby, which was transplanted, then transformed, into a visitor's center, then follow your guide out to the yard which is crammed full of fabulous old neon signs. But this experience isn't just about eye candy: the tour guides are freakishly knowl-edgeable about Las Vegas design history, with lots of great anecdotes to share about not just the neon signs, but also their creators and the city. Some of the 150 signs are familiar from iconic photos of Las Vegas, like those from the Stardust and Algiers casinos, while others are completely new to most visitors, like the splendidly curvaceous Silver Slipper sign and the funky Queen of Hearts. The Neon Museum has restored quite a few back to full function, so try to visit at night to get the full dazzle. Capitalizing on its unique collection, the Boneyard (as it's affectionately called by locals) lets individuals and professionals book time for private shoots, so the iconic signs have become the backdrop for many a wedding and engagement photo. Tour groups are kept small and intimate, so you must book early, preferably online.

770 Las Vegas Blvd. N. (at McWilliams Ave.). www.neonmuseum.org. © **702/387-6366.** Admission $18 daytime tours adults; $12 seniors, students, military, NV residents; $25 nighttime tours adults; $22 seniors, students, military, NV residents; children 6 and under free. No kids under 13 allowed on nighttime tours. Daily 9am–9pm; hours vary seasonally.

SlotZilla ★★ THRILL RIDE   Here it is, the newest Vegas attraction that deserves to take a place in the Pantheon of iconic Sin City silliness alongside the Bellagio Fountains and the Welcome to Fabulous Las Vegas sign. Billed as, and shaped like, the world's tallest slot machine, it's really a launching platform for two sets of zip lines that run down Fremont Street. The lower four are traditional, seated lines running from about 6 stories up by Neonopolis about three blocks to Binion's. The top "zoom" lines feature an opportunity to fly superhero-style, face down, from 12 stories up all the way to a platform next to Main Street some five blocks away. Compared to some zip lines in more adventurous settings, this one is pretty tame, but it's still not for the faint of heart, especially as you step out over the edge and then come in for the unexpectedly jerky landing. Go at night for the full effect of all the Glitter Gulch neon lights. This thing started out popular and there is no reason to believe it will be anything but that in the future, so rides may be sold out and/or wait times could be epic.

425 Fremont St. www.vegasexperience.com. © **702/ZIPVEGAS.** Admission $25–$45. Must be over 60 lb. and under 300 lb. to ride. Sun–Thurs noon–midnight; Fri–Sat noon–2am.

The Smith Center for the Performing Arts ★★★ PERFORMING ARTS VENUE   Although Las Vegas has been synonymous with entertainment for decades, filled with showrooms and theaters galore, the one thing the city never had was a true performing arts venue—the kind of place where symphonies and true Broadway shows (not the cut-down versions that happen on the Strip) could spread their wings. The Smith Center changes all that, and should firmly establish Sin City as a cultural center to be reckoned with.

The buildings are stunning, designed with a timeless Art Deco style inspired by the Hoover Dam—notice the chandeliers, which look like an inverted version of the water intake towers. The whole thing is bright, modern, and dramatic, yet comfortable, familiar, and built to last. While many Vegas buildings attempt scope and grandeur, they feel impermanent somehow—as if they are just waiting to be imploded so the next big thing can be built. The Smith Center feels like the kind of place that will be here for centuries.

The main space, Reynolds Hall, is a finely tuned, Carnegie Hall–worthy, 2,050-seat concert venue that hosts philharmonics, headliners, and touring versions of Broadway shows like *Hamilton* and *The Book of Mormon.* The 240-seat Cabaret Theater is a classic nightclub-style space with big windows, giving it a sense of airiness missing in most theaters. It features a jazz series, and more intimate concerts from acts that run from swing to doo wop to funk. A third, 200-seat "black box"-style theater holds smaller theater and dance productions. Outside is a beautiful park that can also be used for performances, or just a place to sit and enjoy the view.

361 Symphony Park Ave. (at Grand Central Pkwy.). www.thesmithcenter.com. ℂ **702/ 749-2000.** Prices and times vary by show.

JUST OFF THE STRIP

Dig This! ★★ ENTERTAINMENT COMPLEX   Did you have a sandbox that you used to play in when you were a kid? Well, then you're going to love this: a big kid's sandbox where you get to play with real bulldozers and excavators. The program starts with classroom instruction where you get the overview on how to operate the big machines. It's a lot more complicated than you'd think, requiring a level of hand-eye coordination far beyond that of piloting an SUV. Next, you get to climb into the machine out in a big dirt lot and get used to the controls. Then the real fun starts, with a series of games and challenges that include digging holes, moving rocks, and even playing a version of excavator basketball. It isn't cheap, but fantasy fulfillment rarely is.

3012 Rancho Dr. (btw. Meade and Sirius aves.). www.digthisvegas.com. ℂ **888/344- 8447** or 702/222-4344. Admission $169 and up. Open daily; hours vary seasonally.

Fast Lap Indoor Kart Racing ★★ ENTERTAINMENT COMPLEX When NASCAR pro Kurt Busch is in Las Vegas, this is the place he comes to play. Tucked away on a dead-end street in a mostly industrial part of town near the Strip, this is a no-frills go-kart experience, with a short track filling a former warehouse space that still looks like a warehouse. The gasoline-powered karts are equipped with 200cc Honda motors, allowing you to push the little monsters up to 50 mph (if you dare) as you battle in 10-minute-long races (as many laps as you can get) against other drivers. While bumping and other unsportsman-like contact is officially frowned upon, in reality this is a grown-up (mostly testosterone-driven) sport. So put your foot on the gas and see if you can be first to the checkered flag! *Note:* You must be at least 5 feet tall to participate, and children 17 and under must be accompanied by a guardian.

4288 Polaris Ave. www.fastlaplv.com. ℂ **702/736-8113.** $26 per race or $65 for 3 races. Mon–Sat 10am–11pm; Sun 10am–10pm.

KISS by Monster Mini Golf ★★ ENTERTAINMENT COMPLEX   If they had stopped at the indoor, glow-in-the-dark, 18-hole miniature golf course themed to the classic rock band KISS, it probably would've been just mildly amusing. But then they went and added a gift shop, a cafe, a wedding chapel (where KISS impersonators will marry you), arcade games, a DJ playing nonstop KISS tunes, and more KISS memorabilia than the members of the band probably have in their garages. The entire package reaches an almost

THE resurgence OF DOWNTOWN LAS VEGAS

For decades, the bulk of the attention, and development dollars, in Las Vegas has gone to the Strip, while the original part of Sin City, the Downtown area, languished and seemed on the verge of extinction.

Credit, at least in part, online retailer Zappos.com for changing all that. Its plan to move its headquarters and a couple of thousand employees into the former city hall building spurred a resurgence in Downtown Las Vegas, with major revamps to old hotels, new restaurants, fun and funky bars, attractions, street festivals, and more, all lending a new sense of life to the area.

The bulk of the action happens on the **Fremont Street Experience,** the pedestrian-only mall on Fremont Street between Main Street and Las Vegas Boulevard. That's where you'll find most of the casinos, shopping, and restaurants.

The **Fremont East Entertainment District** takes up several blocks of Fremont Street just east of Las Vegas Boulevard, and has several bars, lounges, and clubs all within a few feet of each other, so no matter how much you may be stumbling, you can probably still make it to the next one in your all-night pub crawl.

This is the area where you'll find the **Downtown Container Park** (p. 198), a shopping and dining complex made out of recycled shipping containers and pre-fabricated metal cubes. In addition to the retail and food options, there's a giant treehouse-style jungle gym inside for the kids, and a fire-breathing praying mantis sculpture out front for kids of all ages.

The **18b Arts District** is a few blocks south of Fremont Street, bounded, more or less, by Las Vegas Boulevard to the east, Commerce Street to the west, Hoover Avenue on the north, and Colorado Avenue on the south. Art galleries, antique and collectible stores, and more than a few pawn shops and bail bonds offices (to give it color, we suppose) are scattered about the neighborhood, giving it a refreshingly bohemian feeling as it sits in the shadow of the overprocessed Strip.

The monthly **First Friday Las Vegas** street festival happens in the heart of the 18b Arts District on the blocks surrounding the intersection of Casino Center Drive and Colorado Avenue. Local artists hawk their wares while live bands and DJs keep the crowds moving, play areas (complete with a video game truck) keep the kids entertained, and a sea of food vendors and food trucks keep everyone fat and happy. It's one of the few places where there is a true sense of community in Vegas. It happens, appropriately enough, on the first Friday of every month from 5pm until 11pm. For more information, visit www.firstfridaylasvegas.com.

The area has even qualified for its own big-time music, arts, and food event with the **Life is Beautiful Festival,** held in the fall. The inaugural event in 2013 drew more than 65,000 people and featured stages with Beck, the Killers, Kings of Leon, Imagine Dragons, and more, while food tents had eats from Cat Cora, Hubert Keller, Todd English, and Paul Bartolotta, among others. For more information, visit www.lifeisbeautifulfestival.com.

epic level of giddy, grin-worthy silliness. And yes, there is a hole where you have to putt the ball up a giant replica of Gene Simmons's tongue.

Rio Hotel and Casino, 3700 Flamingo Rd. www.monsterminigolf.com/kiss. © **702/558-6256.** Free admission; 18 holes of mini-golf $12 ages 7 and up; free for children 6 and under. Daily 10am–midnight.

National Atomic Testing Museum ★★★ MUSEUM No thrill ride on the Strip will scare the wits out of you as effectively as the Atomic Testing

Museum. That's not its purpose, of course. This is a science and history museum (an affiliate museum of the mighty Smithsonian Institution) covering the 50 years of atomic testing, from 1951 to 1992 (928 nuclear tests in all), that occurred in the desert outside Vegas. But there comes a moment in the exhibit when your heart will race, your stomach will drop down to your knees, and all at once the reality of the power of the nuclear bomb will hit you with the force of a nightmare. The moment comes early in the exhibit. After an effective and dramatic retelling of the history that led up to the invention of the bomb, you'll be ushered into a small room resembling a concrete bunker for a video about the testing, with shots of actual explosions. As the mushroom cloud rises in front of you, the lights flash a blinding white, subwoofers send vibrations to the center of your sternum, your bench shakes, and air cannons blast you with wind. It's intense.

After that wrenching start the rest of the exhibit helps visitors put into context what they've seen. You'll learn about the physics behind the bomb; the myriad of innovations, from high-speed photography to bigger drills, that emerged from the scientific work going on at the testing site; and the cultural "fallout," if you will, of the Cold War, from advertisements glamorizing the bomb to panic-provoking bomb shelters. Iconic items from the test site—a decoupler, a massive drill bit, a farm silo—are interspersed with news clips and state-of-the-art, truly whiz-bang, interactive exhibits. Pull your attention from these, however, if a docent happens by. Many of these volunteers are former employees of the Testing Site; no they don't glow, but get one talking and they'll regale you with insider's tales of what it was like to wrestle with the bomb, live in its shadow, and work for the government.

755 E. Flamingo Rd. www.nationalatomictestingmuseum.org. ✆ **702/794-5151.** Admission $22 adults; $16 kids 7–14, $18 seniors, military, students with ID, and Nevada residents; free for children 6 and under. Mon–Sat 10am–5pm; Sun noon–5pm.

SpeedVegas ★★★ RACECOURSE   Those who feel the need for speed don't necessarily need to haul themselves all the way out to the Las Vegas Motor Speedway anymore. The latest fast and furious addition to the Strip is located 10 minutes from the Welcome to Las Vegas sign, with a full arsenal of exotic muscle and supercars ready to be taken around the track. After a quick peek around the 100-acre complex, which includes a 2-story welcome center, peel around the 1.5 mile Formula One-inspired racetrack (the longest in Las Vegas); it features 12 20-degree banked turns and a half-mile straightaway. The only thing more fun than driving the track is choosing which car you'll take for a spin: feel flashy with the Lamborghini? Experience the German precision of the Porsche? Or ride the horsepower of American muscle with the Mustang? You're paying per lap, so why not all three?

14200 Las Vegas Blvd. S. www.speedvegas.com. ✆ **702/874-8888.** $49–$89 per lap. Daily 10am–6pm.

Topgolf ★★★ ENTERTAINMENT COMPLEX   Some days you just want to hit a few balls, but a trip to Topgolf is a far cry from a day at the driving range. Opened in May 2016, the four-level, 105,000-square-foot venue not only holds 102 hitting bays, but also a live performance stage, multiple kitchens and bars and VIP areas with water features and cabanas. Even if you consider yourself a "non-golfer," you'll find a way to work on your swing. Rent out a hitting bay with some friends and take your best shot, scoring points by hitting at targets located across the 215-yard outfield. Microchip technology in the balls and the targets lets you know how accurate and far (or not) you've launched that projectile with your club. Various games coded into the experience will help you with your competitive spirit.

4627 Koval Ln. www.topgolf.com/us/lasvegas. ⓒ **702/963-0000.** Admission $5 one-time fee for membership card, $25–$45/hr. per bay, up to 6 players. Sun–Thurs 8am–2am; Fri–Sat 8am–4am.

SOUTH & EAST OF THE STRIP

Clark County Museum ★★ MUSEUM   It's telling, I think, that the history of a doomed ocean liner is center stage on the Strip, but a history museum that actually details the story of Sin City itself is relegated to the side of the highway, about 10 miles southeast of the center. (This is a city after all with a penchant for bulldozing over its history and for imploding anything that gets in the way of bigger profits.) Which is a shame because the Clark County Heritage Museum is a real gem, chockablock with richly evocative artifacts and interactive exhibits detailing the story of the area, from Native Americans through gangsters through the pack of corporate thieves who control the Strip today. And for a museum set this far off the Strip, and so cheap to visit, it's startlingly high tech: Sensors turn on narration, sound effects, and even visual effects whenever a visitor enters a gallery, and many of the exhibits are interactive. Highlights are half a dozen actual houses that you wander through, hearing about the lives of the real people who lived in them at different times in the area's history, from a Paiute twig hut village to a house lived in by men involved in the construction of the Hoover dam, to a gold miner's house and a 1960s abode from the Atomic Testing Site. Back outside is a garden with native plants, all well marked along winding trails. The downside: Because it is a good, long drive from the Strip, you'll need a rental car to get here. A taxi really isn't practical.

1830 S. Boulder Hwy., Henderson. www.clarkcountynv.gov. ⓒ **702/455-7955.** Admission $2 adults, $1 seniors and children 3–15, free for children 2 and under. Daily 9am–4:30pm. Closed Thanksgiving, Dec 25, and Jan 1.

Ethel M Chocolates ★ FACTORY TOUR   Ethel Mars began making fine chocolates in a little candy kitchen in the early 20th century. Her small enterprise evolved to produce not only dozens of varieties of superb boxed chocolates, but also some of the world's most famous candies: M&Ms, Milky Way, 3 Musketeers, Snickers, and Mars bars. Alas, the tour lasts only about 10 minutes and consists entirely of viewing stations with an audiotape explaining the chocolate-baking process. Even more sadly, you get only one small chocolate as a sample—delicious, but hardly satisfying. Of course, there is a fully stocked gift shop if you want to buy more. *Note:* Come before 2:30pm, which is when the workers start to pack up and go home.

What's really worth seeing is outside: a lovely and extensive **4-acre garden ★** displaying over 300 species of rare and exotic cacti with signs provided for self-guided tours. It's best appreciated in spring when the cacti are in full bloom, or in December when the garden is bedecked with holiday lights.

2 Cactus Garden Dr. (just off Mountain Vista and Sunset Way, in the Green Valley Business Park). www.ethelschocolate.com. © **702/435-2655** or 702/435-2608. Free admission. Daily 8:30am–6pm. Self-guided chocolate factory tours Mon–Thurs 8:30am–4:30pm. Holiday hours may vary.

Lion Habitat Ranch ★★★ ZOO

Longtime Vegas visitors roared with displeasure when the MGM Grand closed their signature lion habitat after nearly 20 years of amusing tourists. The big secret, however, was that populating those casino-facing digs was merely the lions' day job, and their "main office" is now open for tours that are significantly more satisfying. More than two dozen lions, from infant to ancient, are in residence at the facility run by Keith and Bev Evans for more than 20 years. All of the animals are either rescues or born here, and while it always gives one pause to see these kinds of majestic creatures in captivity instead of running wild, the digs are plush and the animals are obviously well taken care of. Visitation programs vary from simple do-it-yourself tours to "Trainer for a Day" options that will put you in direct contact with the lions. *Note:* Finding the place can be challenging; it's in the middle of a scrub brush desert, close to the M Resort on the southernmost edge of Las Vegas. Consult a map or GPS before you go.

382 Bruner Ave. (near St. Rose Pkwy.). www.lionhabitatranch.com. © **702/595-6666.** Admission $25 and up adults; 1 child per adult free, $10 extra child. Fri–Mon 11am–3pm; hours vary seasonally.

Pinball Hall of Fame & Museum ★★★ MUSEUM

And you thought only children's museums could be interactive. Arguably the most fun museum in Las Vegas, this is 10,000 square feet of hands-on entertainment and history for a bargain. A nice departure from the slot machines in casinos, there are more than 150 pinball machines lined up wall-to-wall for visitors to play. Some of them go as far back as the 1940s and are still fully operational (though with the older ones you may need a lighter touch) and are maintained on a daily basis. The games are actual works of art in themselves. Consider Elton John's costumes on the 1975 *Captain Fantastic* machine, or the campy cartoons of the *Star Trek* machine from 1979. You can even nerd-out on the non-pinball games, like when you sit in the cabin for the *Star Trek* arcade game direct from the '80s. You still have to pop in a quarter to play (two if the game is from 1990 or after), but it's money well spent, as proceeds go towards maintenance of the machines and to charity. In a modern twist, scan the QR bar code found on many of the machines with your smartphone to learn more about these old school relics.

1610 E. Tropicana Ave. www.pinballmuseum.org. © **702/597-2627.** Free admission; game costs vary. Sun–Thurs 11am–11pm; Fri–Sat 11am–midnight.

Shelby American Heritage Center ★ MUSEUM

That's Shelby as in Carroll Shelby, who in the 1960s helped shape the American muscle car as we know it. Now that the museum has moved from its original location near the Las Vegas Motor Speedway to across from Town Square on Las Vegas Boulevard, gear heads don't have to go as far to get their Shelby fix. On display is the first Cobra roadster CSX2000 that Shelby ever built, along with cherry Mustangs and the Shelby Series 1 prototype, and about 20 more rides, all with spiffy racing stripes. The space also features the modification shop where fast cars become even faster, but you can't get near those. The guided tour takes about 90 minutes and is comprehensive, complete with anecdotes and a complete history of Shelby and his craft. Admission and tours are free, but consider donating to the Carroll Shelby Foundation, dedicated to organ transplant education, as Shelby was a heart transplant recipient in 1990. The museum offers a round trip from select resorts for only $7.

6405 Ensworth St. (at Sunset Rd.) www.shelbyamerican.com. © **702/942-7325.** Free admission. Mon–Sat 9:30am–6pm, Sun 10am–4pm; guided tours Mon–Fri 10:30am and 1:30pm, and Sat 10:30am.

SkyZone ★ ENTERTAINMENT COMPLEX   So you brought the kids to Vegas and they're bouncing off the walls with boredom. How about giving them a chance to bounce off the walls with glee instead? This indoor facility features several trampoline arenas; some are used for organized games and activities such as dodgeball, and others are open for random bouncing about. There are other amusements here as well, including a foam-block pit that kids can jump into, games, and a small snack shop, plus a much-needed quiet area for parents. Adults are allowed, but this is mainly a place for children, so if you're hoping to practice your Cirque du Soleil skills you may want to find someplace else to do it.

7440 Dean Martin Dr. (at Warm Springs Rd.) www.skyzone.com/lasvegas. © **702/560-5900.** Admission $13–$26. Mon–Thurs 3pm–8pm; Fri 3pm–10pm; Sat 11am–11pm; Sun 11am–8pm.

NORTH & WEST OF THE STRIP

Las Vegas Mini Gran Prix ★★ ENTERTAINMENT COMPLEX   Finally, after all our yammering about how Vegas isn't for families and how most of the kid-friendly options are really overpriced tourist traps, we can wholeheartedly recommend an actual family-appropriate entertainment option. Part arcade, part go-kart racetrack, this is exactly what you want to help your kids (and maybe yourselves) work their ya-yas out. The arcade is well stocked, with a better quality of prizes than one often finds, but we suggest not spending too much time in there and instead hustling outside to the slide, the little roller coaster, and best of all, the four go-kart tracks. Each offers a different thrill, from the longest track in Vegas, full of twists and turns as you try to outrace other drivers (be a sport, let the little kids win occasionally), to a high-banked oval built just so you can try to make other drivers take spills onto the grass, to, best of all, a timed course. The last requires a driver's license, so it's for you rather than your kids (but the wee ones will find the fourth course is just for them), and here you can live out your Le Mans or police-chase fantasies as you blast through twisting runs one kart at a time, trying to beat your personal best. The staff is friendly, and the pizzas at the food court are triple the size and half the price of those found in your hotel. The one drawback: It's far from the Strip, so you'll need a rental car. *Note:* Kids have to be at least 36 inches tall to ride any of the attractions.

1401 N. Rainbow Rd. (just off U.S. 95 N.). www.lvmgp.com. ℭ **702/259-7000.** Ride tickets $8 each, $7.50 each for 5 or more; ride wristbands $23 per hr. Sun–Fri 10am–10pm; Sat 10am–11pm; hours vary seasonally.

Las Vegas Motor Speedway ★★RACECOURSE   This impressive facility is widely considered to be the premiere racing venue in the Southwest United States, and rivals fabled speedways in Talladega, Charlotte, and Daytona for its scope and the deep catalogue of year-round events. The main oval hosts a major NASCAR race weekend in March, packing pretty much every one of the 135,000 seats, but there are happenings on it and the other tracks more than 260 days a year. There is an NHRA-sanctioned drag strip that runs high-octane funny cars and motorcycles, two road courses, a dirt track, a short oval "bullring," and more.

Of the many unique features (how many raceways have a view of the Strip?), one of the most interesting for race fans is the Neon Garage, an infield facility where the drivers and their teams set up camp for the major races. Big windows and overhead galleries allow people to watch the cars being worked on and give up-close access to the men and women behind the wheel. You pay a premium, obviously, but true speed freaks should get their tickets early.

If watching the action is not enough for you, there are several programs available to put you behind the wheel for some adrenaline junkie action. **The Richard Petty Driving Experience** (www.drivepetty.com; ℭ **800/237-3889)** offers both NASCAR-style vehicles and new American muscle cars (Camaro, Mustang, Challenger, and the like) that are raced on the superspeedway; **Dream Racing** (www.dreamracing.com; ℭ **702/605-3000)** has specially modified Ferrari race cars running the inside road track; and **Exotics Racing** (www.exoticsracing.com; ℭ **702/405-7223)** has a full fleet of Ferraris, Porsches, Lamborghinis, McLarens, and more that run on their proprietary 1.2-mile course. All give you classroom instruction and time behind the wheel, and while they are not cheap, there are few things more thrilling than going down the back straightaway in a race car doing 140 miles per hour, or trying to find the perfect path out of tight curve you are taking in a 430 Scuderia at stupid grin-worthy speeds.

7000 Las Vegas Blvd. N. (directly across from Nellis Air Force Base). www.lvms.com. ℭ**702/644-4443.** Tickets $10–$75 (higher for major events). Race days vary. Take I-15 north to exit 54.

Nevada State Museum ★ MUSEUM   Part nature museum, part Native American museum, part Las Vegas museum, there's certainly a lot of history jam packed into 13,000 square feet; too bad none of it is particularly in-depth. But it's worth a stop if you want to learn about the entire Silver State from soup to nuts, without committing much time to the endeavor. Sundays offer a few interactive activities geared towards kids. If your time is limited, skip this place in favor of the far more interesting **Springs Preserve** (p. 170).

309 S. Valley View Blvd. (at Meadows Lane). museums.nevadaculture.org. ℭ **702/486-5205.** Tickets $20 adults, $10 for NV residents, free for children 17 and under. Admission includes neighboring Springs Preserve. Thurs–Mon 10am–6pm.

Pole Position Raceway ★ ENTERTAINMENT COMPLEX   Similar in concept to the **Fast Lap** facility (p. 163), Pole Position is a more polished go-kart racing venue owing to its sleek, modern facility, and electric-powered racers. The indoor course is short but satisfying, and the lack of gas-powered engines doesn't mean you sacrifice any of the speed. You may retain your hearing for longer, which is definitely a good thing. It's worth noting that the karts are small and the mandatory helmets are tight, so claustrophobics may want to seek alternative fun. The facility also has a small video and virtual-reality game arcade, and a gift shop.

4175 S. Arville Rd. www.polepositionraceway.com. ✆ **702/227-7223.** Adults 56 in. or taller $26, kids 17 and under or 48 in. and taller $22; multi-race packages available. Sun–Thurs 11am–11pm; Fri–Sat 11am–midnight.

Springs Preserve ★★★ NATURAL RESERVE   By now, perhaps you've learned that *Las Vegas* is Spanish for "the meadows." This facility is set on the 180-acre site of the original springs that fed Las Vegas until it dried in the 1960s (told you that Hoover Dam comes in handy). These days, Las Vegas is an environmental nightmare, along with much of the rest of this planet, and this remarkable attraction educates visitors about the possibilities of reversing some of the damage.

Set amid nature and hiking trails, plus man-made wetlands (which is an interesting concept), the focal point is a large interpretive center that gives the history of Las Vegas from a land- and water-use perspective. The displays are creative and interactive, including a room with a reproduction flash flood that uses 5,000 gallons of water; and one with a simulation of the experience of working on Hoover Dam. The other buildings are all built according to standards that have the least environmental impact, using modern construction versions of adobe and other green concepts. Each building tackles an aspect of desert living and the environment, including one that instructs kids on the glories of recycling, complete with a compost tunnel to crawl through! Other displays focus on environmentally friendly kitchens and bathrooms, while the gardens demonstrate "green" gardening.

The outdoor kids' play area is made from recycled materials, and has big fake animals to climb on and real live ones to look at, in case the kiddies have grown tired of learning responsible stuff. Given the care, knowledge, and urgency of the issues addressed, this is an extraordinary facility for any town, but particularly for this one.

Note: Admission includes entrance to the adjacent Nevada State Museum reviewed above.

333 S. Valley View Blvd. www.springspreserve.org. ✆ **702/822-8344.** Admission $19 adults, $17 seniors and students with ID, $11 children 5–17, free for children 4 and under, $10 Nevada residents. Free admission to trails and gardens. Daily 10am–6pm.

Wet 'n Wild ★ AMUSEMENT PARK   This is the city's only (for now) water amusement park. A descendant of the Wet 'n Wild that was on the Strip for 2 decades, this state-of-the-art facility is located on the far west side of town at the foothills of the famous Red Rock National Conservancy Area. It has more than 20 slides, rides, and attractions, from scary dropping, looping things to lazy, play-around-in-the-water–type features. Adrenaline junkies should try the Constrictor, featuring what are billed as the tightest, highest banked curves in the world; and the Tornado, a multi-person raft ride that shoots you 36 feet in the air before blasting you through a tunnel and into a whirlpool funnel. Shade is at a premium and the crowds make the lines long, but if you want something fun to do with your kids, this is one of your few good Vegas options.

7055 S. Fort Apache Rd. (at Arby Ave.). www.wetnwildlasvegas.com. © **702/800-7474.** Admission $40 adults, $30 kids under 42 in. tall. Discounts available online. Season passes available. Sun–Thurs 10am–6pm; Fri–Sat 10am–10pm.

CASINO GAMBLING

Las Vegas is no longer the gambling capital of the world. That title belongs to Macau, China, where casinos with familiar names like MGM Grand, the Venetian, and Wynn pull in more money in 2 months than the casinos on the Strip generate all year. Even in the United States, the proliferation of legal gambling in other areas is eclipsing Las Vegas in terms of revenue and scope. As of this writing, there are more than two dozen states that have Indian or riverboat casinos, and nearly that many that have commercial casinos, with more on the way. And in Las Vegas, gambling is no longer the biggest revenue generator, earning less than half of most resorts' revenue (the rest comes from hotel rates, dining, nightclubs, and the like).

But strip away all the facts and figures, and what you are left with is the undeniable lure of Las Vegas as a gambling mecca. It is, in no small part, what built this city and what continues to drive it, as evidenced by the fact that you can find gaming almost everywhere. There are slot machines at the airport, waiting for you to get off the plane or giving you something to do while you wait for your baggage. Convenience stores and gas stations have video poker so you can play a few hands while filling up. And the average Strip casino has literally dozens of blackjack, craps, roulette, and other gaming tables.

People come here to play, and although they may lose more often than they win, it doesn't stop anyone from trying to win the Big One. You know, like that woman in 2010 who won $2.9 million on a "Wizard of Oz" penny slot (whose name was Dorothy, by the way). That only a few ever do win big doesn't stop people from trying again and again and again. That's how the casinos make their money.

As you walk through the labyrinthine twists and turns of a casino floor, your attention will likely be dragged to the various games and, your interest piqued, your fingers may begin to twitch in anticipation of hitting it big. Before you put your money on the line, it's imperative to know the rules of the game you want to play. Most casinos offer **free gambling lessons** at scheduled times on weekdays and occasionally on weekends. This provides a risk-free environment for you to learn the games that tickle your fancy. Some casinos follow their lessons with low-stakes game play, enabling you to put your newfound knowledge to the test at small risk. During those instructional sessions, and even when playing on your own, dealers in most casinos will be more than happy to answer any questions you might have. Remember, the casino doesn't need to trick you into losing your money . . . the odds are already in their favor across the board; that's why it's called gambling. Another rule of thumb: Take a few minutes to watch a game being played in order to familiarize yourself with the motions and lingo.

And of course, the Internet has revolutionized gambling in more ways than one, not the least of which is that you can find a free, online version of just about every casino game imaginable. Spend a few hours online betting virtual bucks before you haul out your wallet to try the real deal.

If you are planning on gambling at all, it pays to join a **players' club.** These so-called clubs are designed to attract and keep customers in a given casino by providing incentives: meals, shows, discounts on rooms, gifts, tournament invitations, discounts at hotel shops, VIP treatment, and (more and more) cash rebates. Join a players' club (it doesn't cost a cent to sign up), and soon you too will be getting those great hotel-rate offers—$20-a-night rooms, affordable rooms at the luxury resorts, and even free rooms.

These days, players' clubs go beyond the casino as well. Many of them track your overall spending at participating casinos, including what you pay for meals, shopping, rooms, spa treatments, and more. This means you can earn points toward rewards pretty much anytime you pull out your wallet.

Baccarat

The ancient game of baccarat, or *chemin de fer,* is played with eight decks of cards. Firm rules apply, and there is no skill involved other than deciding whether to bet on the bank or the player. No, really—that's all you have to do. The dealer does all the other work. You can essentially stop reading here. Oh, all right, carry on.

Any beginner can play, but check the betting minimum before you sit down, as baccarat tends to be a high-stakes game. The cards are shuffled by the croupier and then placed in a box called the "shoe." Players may wager on "bank" or "player" at any time. Two cards are dealt from the shoe and given to the player who has the largest wager against the bank, and two cards are dealt to the croupier, acting as banker. If the rules call for a third card, the player or banker, or both, must take the third card. In the event of a tie, the hand is dealt over. *Note:* The guidelines that determine whether a third card must be drawn (by the player or banker) are provided at the baccarat table upon request.

The object of the game is to come as close as possible to the number 9. To score the hands, the cards of each hand are totaled and the *last digit* is used. All cards have face value. For example: 10 plus 5 equals 15 (score is 5); 10 plus 4 plus 9 equals 23 (score is 3); 4 plus 3 plus 3 equals 10 (score is 0); and 4 plus 3 plus 2 equals 9 (score is 9). The closest hand to 9 wins.

Each player has a chance to deal the cards. The shoe passes to the player on the right each time the bank loses. If the player wishes, he may pass the shoe at any time.

Note: When you bet on the bank and the bank wins, you're charged a 5% commission. This must be paid at the start of a new game or when you leave the table.

Blackjack

In this, the most popular casino card game, the dealer starts by dealing each player two cards. In some casinos, they're dealt to the player face up, in others face down, but the dealer always gets one card up and one card down. Everybody plays against the dealer. The object is to get a total that is higher than that of the dealer without exceeding 21. All face cards count as 10; all other number cards, except aces, are counted at their face value. An ace may be counted as 1 or 11, whichever you choose it to be.

Starting at her left, the dealer gives additional cards to the players who wish to draw (be "hit") or none to a player who wishes to "stand" or "hold." If your count is nearer to 21 than the dealer's, you win. If it's under the dealer's, you lose. Ties are a "push" (standoff) and nobody wins. After all the players are satisfied with their counts, the dealer exposes her face-down card. If her two cards total 16 or less, the dealer must hit until reaching 17 or over. If the dealer's total exceeds 21, she must pay all the players whose hands have not gone "bust." It is important to note here that the blackjack dealer has no choice as to whether she should stay or draw. A dealer's decisions are predetermined and known to all the players at the table.

If you're a novice or just rusty, do yourself a favor and buy one of the small laminated cards available in shops all over town that illustrate proper play for every possible hand in blackjack. Even longtime players have been known to pull them out, and they can save you from making costly errors.

Craps

The most exciting casino action is usually found at the craps tables. Betting is frenetic, play is fast-paced, and groups quickly bond while yelling and screaming in response to the action.

While it can be intimidating, it's very easy to play a basic game of craps, but figuring out the various bets and the odds associated with the advanced bets is sort of like learning rocket science, only with dice. Entire books are written about the game and so it would be impossible to explain it all in a couple of paragraphs, but here is enough to at least get you started.

The table is divided into marked areas (Pass, Come, Field, Big Six, Big Eight, and so on), where you place your chips to bet. Novices should stick with the "Pass Line" or "Come" bets until they get used to the rhythm of the game.

PASS LINE   A "Pass Line" bet pays even money. If the first roll of the dice adds up to 7 or 11, you win your bet; if the first roll adds up to 2, 3, or 12, you lose your bet. If any other number comes up, it becomes your "point." If you roll your point again, you win, but if a 7 comes up again before your point is rolled, you lose.

DON'T PASS LINE   Betting on the "Don't Pass Line" is the opposite of betting on the Pass Line. This time, you lose if a 7 or an 11 is thrown on the first roll, and you win if a 2 or a 3 is thrown on the first roll.

If the first roll is 12, however, it's a "push" (standoff), and nobody wins. If none of these numbers is thrown and you have a point instead, in order to win, a 7 will have to be thrown before the point comes up again. A Don't Pass bet also pays even money.

COME Betting on "Come" is the same as betting on the Pass Line, but you must bet after the first roll or on any following roll. Again, you'll win on 7 or 11 and lose on 2, 3, or 12. Any other number is your point, and you win if your point comes up again before a 7.

DON'T COME This is the opposite of a Come bet. Again, you wait until after the first roll to bet. A 7 or an 11 means you lose; a 2 or a 3 means you win; 12 is a push, and nobody wins. You win if 7 comes up before the point. (The point, you'll recall, was the first number rolled if it was none of the above.)

Poker

For most of the new millennium, poker was just about the biggest thing going, thanks to the popularity of celebrity poker TV shows, poker tours, books, and magazines. Just about every casino had a poker room and those that didn't wanted one.

That popularity has waned a bit in the last few years with several of the poker rooms getting smaller, offering fewer games, or closing altogether. What's behind the trend? Nothing more than the cooling of a hot fad, really. The game is still played by lots of people and you can easily find a table, but these days you probably won't have to wait as long to get a seat.

There are lots of variations on the basic game, but one of the most popular is **Texas Hold 'Em.** Two cards are dealt, face down, to the players. After a betting round, five community cards (everyone can use them) are dealt face up on the table. Players make the best five-card hand, using their own cards and the "board" (the community cards), and the best hand wins. The house dealer takes care of the shuffling and the dealing, and moves a marker around the table to alternate the start of the deal. The house usually rakes around 10% (it depends on the casino) from each pot. Most casinos also provide tables for playing Seven-Card Stud, Omaha High, and Omaha Hi-Lo. A few even have Seven-Card Stud Hi-Lo split. To learn how these variations are played, either read a book or take lessons.

PAI GOW

Pai Gow is a variation on poker that has become popular. The game is played with a traditional deck plus one joker. The joker is a wild card that can be used as an ace or to complete a straight, a flush, a straight flush, or a royal flush. Each player is dealt seven cards to arrange into two hands: a two-card hand and a five-card hand. As in standard poker, the highest two-card hand is two aces, and the highest five-card hand is a royal flush. The five-card hand *must* be higher than the two-card hand (if the two-card hand is a pair of 6s, for example, the five-card hand must be a pair of 7s or better). Any player's hand that is set incorrectly is an automatic loser. The object of the game is for both of the players' hands to rank higher than both of the banker's hands. Should one hand rank exactly the same as the banker's hand, this is a tie (called a "copy"), *and the banker wins all tie hands.* If the player wins one hand but loses the other, this is a "push," and no money changes hands. The house dealer or any player may be the banker. The bank is offered to each player, and each player may accept or pass. Winning hands are paid even money, less a 5% commission.

LET IT RIDE

Let It Ride is another popular game that involves poker hands. You place three bets at the outset and are dealt three cards. The dealer is dealt two cards that act as community cards (you're not playing against the dealer). Once you've seen your cards, you can choose to pull the first of your three bets back or "let it ride." The object of this game is to get a pair of 10s or better by combining your cards with the community cards. If you're holding a pair of 10s or better in your first three cards (called a "no-brainer"), you want to let your bets ride the entire way through. Once you've decided whether or not to let your first bet ride, the dealer exposes one of his two cards. Once again, you must make a decision to take back your middle bet or keep on going. Then the dealer exposes the last of his cards; your third bet must stay. The dealer then turns over the hands of the players and determines whether you've won. Winning bets are paid on a scale, ranging from even money for a single pair up to 1,000 to 1 for a royal flush. These payouts are for each bet you have in play. Similar to Caribbean Stud, Let It Ride has a bonus that you can win for high hands if you cough up an additional $1 per hand, but be advised that the house advantage on that $1 is obscene. But hey, that's why it's called gambling.

THREE-CARD POKER

Three-Card Poker has become one of the most popular table games in Las Vegas, with gamblers appreciating the relatively low mental input requirements and relatively high payout possibilities. It's actually more difficult to explain than to play. For this reason, we recommend watching a table for a while. You should grasp it pretty quickly.

Basically, players are dealt three cards with no draw and have to make the best poker hand out of those three cards. Possible combinations include a straight flush (three sequential cards of the same suit), three of a kind (three queens, for example), a straight (three sequential cards of any suit), a flush (three cards of the same suit), and a pair (two queens, for example). Even if you don't have one of the favored combinations, you can still win if you have cards higher than the dealer's.

On the table are three betting areas—Ante, Play, and Pair Plus. There are actually two games in one on a Three-Card Poker table—"Pair Plus" and "Ante and Play." You can play only Pair Plus or only Ante, or both. You place your chips in the areas in which you want to bet.

In Pair Plus, you are betting only on your hand, not competing against anyone else at the table or the dealer. If you get a pair or better, depending on your hand, the payoff can be pretty fab—straight flush: 40 to 1; three of a kind: 30 to 1; straight: 6 to 1; flush: 3 to 1; and pair: 1 to 1.

In Ante and Play, you are betting that your hand will be better than the dealer's, but you're not competing against anyone else at the table. You place an Ante bet, view your cards, and then, if you decide you like your hand, you place a bet in the Play area equal to your Ante bet. If you get lousy cards and don't want to go forward, you can fold, losing only your Ante bet and your Pair Plus bet, if you made one. Once all bets are made, the dealer's hand is revealed—he must have at least a single queen for the bet to count; if not, your Ante and Play bets are returned. If you beat the dealer's hand, you get a 1 to 1 payoff, but there is a bonus for a particularly good winning hand: straight flush, 5 to 1; three of a kind, 4 to 1; straight, 1 to 1.

Your three cards are dealt. If you play only Pair Plus, it doesn't matter what the dealer has—you get paid if you have a pair or better. If you don't, you lose your bet. If you play the Ante bet, you must then either fold and lose the Ante bet or match the Ante bet by placing the same amount on the Play area. The dealer's hand is revealed, and payouts happen accordingly. Each hand consists of one fresh 52-card deck.

There are several variants to this game, including a bonus bet that can win a progressive jackpot (usually $1) and a six-card version where your cards are combined with the dealer's cards to come up with the best five- or six-card hand. Caesars Entertainment casinos are even offering a million-dollar top prize in their six-card games if, between you and the dealer, you come up with the 9-10-J-Q-K-A of diamonds. Don't scoff—several people have actually won it already!

OTHER POKER VARIANTS

Meanwhile, as if all this weren't enough, new variations on poker games keep popping up. There's Crazy 4 Poker, similar to Three-Card Poker, only with five cards dealt, no draw, and make your best four-card poker hand out of it; a version of Texas Hold 'Em, where you are not competing against other players; several riffs on Three-Card poker that include secondary bonus bets, progressive jackpots, and multiple betting strategies; and more. All of them follow the basic tenets of poker (highest hand wins), but each has its own set of rules, betting strategies, and payouts; if you see one of these games, look for an instructional pamphlet at the table or ask the dealer for a quick lesson.

Roulette

Roulette is an easy game to play, and it's really quite colorful and exciting to watch. The wheel spins and the little ball bounces around, finally dropping into one of the slots, numbered 1 to 36, plus 0 and 00. You can place bets "Inside" the table and "Outside" the table. Inside bets are bets placed on a particular number or a set of numbers. Outside bets are those placed in the boxes surrounding the number table. If you bet on a specific number and it comes up, you are paid 35 to 1 on your bet. Bear in mind, however, that the odds of a particular number coming up are actually 38 to 1 (don't forget the 0 and 00!), so the house has an advantage the moment you place an inside bet. The methods of placing single-number bets, column bets, and others are fairly obvious. The dealer will be happy to show you how to make many interesting betting combinations, such as betting on six numbers at once. Each player is given different-colored chips so that it's easy to follow the numbers you've bet on.

Slots

You put the coin in the slot and pull the handle. What, you thought there was a trick to this?

Actually, there is a bit more to it. But first, some background. Old-timers will tell you slots were invented to give wives something to do while their husbands gambled. Slots used to be stuck at the edges of the casino and could be counted on one hand, maybe two. But now they *are* the casino. The casinos make more from slots than from craps, blackjack, and roulette combined. There are more than 150,000 slot machines (not including video poker) in the county. Some of these are at the airport, steps away from you as you deplane. It's just a matter of time before the planes flying into Vegas feature slots that pop up as soon as you cross the state line.

But to keep up with the increasing competition, the plain old machine, where reels just spin, has become nearly obsolete. Now they are all computerized and have buttons to push so you can avoid getting carpal tunnel syndrome from yanking the handle all night (though the handles are still there on some of them). Many don't even have reels anymore but are entirely video screens, which offer a number of little extras that have nothing to do with actual play. The idea is still simple: Get 3 (or 4, or 10) cherries (clowns, sevens, dinosaurs, whatever) in a row, and you win something. Each machine has its own combination. Some will pay you something with just one symbol showing; on most, the more combinations there are, the more opportunities for loot. Some will even pay if you get three blanks. Study each machine to learn what it does. *Note:* The **payback** goes up considerably if you bet the limit (from 2 to hundreds of coins on penny slots, for instance).

Progressive slots are groups of linked machines (sometimes spread over several casinos) where the jackpot gets bigger every few moments (just as lottery jackpots build up). Some machines have their own progressive jackpot, which can be slightly less stressful because you're not competing with other players to win the top prize.

Themes and interactivity are the watchwords these days. Pick a pop culture reference and there's probably a slot machine dedicated to it. *Wizard of Oz, The Walking Dead, Airplane!* ("Don't call me Shirley!"), *Sex and the City,* **Michael Jackson,** and *The Hangover* are just a few of the familiar titles you'll see on casino floors. Each of them features bonus rounds and side games that have animations, video clips, music, competitions between other players, and, in some cases, even motion-activated seats.

Penny and nickel slots, which for a long time had been overlooked, relegated to a lonely spot somewhere by a back wall because they were not as profitable for the casinos as quarter and dollar slots, have made a comeback. You can bet just a penny or nickel, but maximum bets for the bigger jackpots are usually in the $2 to $3 range, sometimes even more. As a result, more cash is pocketed by the casino (which keeps a higher percentage of cash off of

CASINO royale

When it comes right down to it, all casinos are basically the same—they all have slot machines, table games, too many people (often), lots of cigarette smoke (usually), and a general sense of hullaballoo that is completely unlike anyplace else on Earth.

But not all casinos are created equally. Some are big and feel like it, some are big and don't feel like it, some are loud, some are bright, some are light, some are cheap, some are overwhelming, and on and on it goes. Where you decide to gamble away little Billy's college fund really is a matter of taste, budget, and timing, but here are a few of our favorites, and not just because we have won money in them. Well, not *entirely* because we have won money in them.

If you are looking for a classic Las Vegas casino, go no further than **Caesars Palace**, 3570 Las Vegas Blvd. S. (www.caesarspalace.com; ℭ **702/731-7110**). The domed ceiling over the main pit just off the lobby dates all the way back to 1966, but has been kept up-to-date and sparkling. Plus, you might still see a toga-clad wench or an armor-plated gladiator wandering around posing for pictures.

If you prefer modern, try either **Aria Las Vegas**, 3730 Las Vegas Blvd. S. (www.arialasvegas.com; ℭ **702/590-7111**) or the **Cosmopolitan of Las Vegas**, 3708 Las Vegas Blvd. S. (www.cosmopolitanlasvegas.com; ℭ **702/698-7000**). Both offer dramatic, art-inspired rooms bursting with eye-candy, with Aria's dramatic sculptures and natural lighting and the Cosmo's three-story chandelier and evocative decor.

The themed madness has been toned down at most casinos, but you can still

get a geo-location giggle with the Big Apple silliness at New York-New York, 3790 Las Vegas Blvd. S. (www.newyorknewyork.com; ℭ **702/740-6969**), complete with the facades of famous Gotham landmarks looming around you; the walk-like-an-Egyptian madness of Luxor Las Vegas, 3900 Las Vegas Blvd. S. (www.luxor.com; ℭ **702/262-4444**), which is still there if you look hard enough for it; or the Gallic-inspired romance of Paris Las Vegas, 3655 Las Vegas Blvd. S. (www.parislasvegas.com; ℭ **702/946-7000**), including legs of the Eiffel Tower replica sticking down into the casino.

If luxury and high limits are your thing, go to the fraternal twin casinos at **Wynn Las Vegas/Encore Las Vegas**, 3131 Las Vegas Blvd. S. (www.wynnlasvegas.com; ℭ **800/320-7125**). The former is a large garden-inspired space with luxurious seating and fabrics, while the latter is a more intimate, European-gambling-parlor–style room infused with natural light.

If you prefer your gambling more down-to-earth and affordable, check out one of the Downtown or locals' casinos. Our personal favorites are the lovely earth-toned space at **The Golden Nugget**, 129 Fremont St. (www.goldennugget.com; ℭ **702/385-7111**); the retro-modern industrial chic at **The Downtown Grand**, 206 N. 3rd St. (www.downtowngrand.com; ℭ **702/719-5100**); the richly textured stunner at **Red Rock Resort**, 10973 W. Charleston Ave. (www.redrocklasvegas.com; ℭ **702/767-7773**); and the warm Mediterranean-inspired space at **Green Valley Ranch**, 2300 Paseo Verde Dr., Henderson (www.greenvalleyranchresort.com; ℭ **702/617-7777**).

lower-denomination slots than it does off of higher ones), which is happy to accommodate this trend by offering up more and more cheaper slots. See how this all works? Are you paying attention?

Cashless machines are the standard these days. Now when gambling, players insert their money, they play, and when they cash out, they get—instead of the clanging sound of coins cascading out into the tray—a little paper ticket with their total winnings on it. Hand in your ticket at a cashier's window (or use the omnipresent ATM-style redemption machines), and you get your winnings. Purists howl, bemoaning the loss of the auditory and tactile thrill of dealing with coins, but most of them are the type of people who would put $5 in a machine, lose it, and then be done with gambling for the rest of the trip. Those who are more than just casual players love the convenience and simplicity of the tickets and wouldn't go back to the days of having to lug big buckets of change around if you promised them better payoff odds.

Are there surefire ways to win on a slot machine? No. But you can lose more slowly. The slot machines use minicomputers known as random number generators (RNGs) to determine the winning combinations on a machine, and though each spin may indeed be random, individual machines are programmed to pay back different percentages over the long haul. As a result, a machine programmed to return a higher percentage might be "looser" than others. A bank of empty slots probably (but not certainly) means the machines are tight. Go find a line where lots of people are sitting around with lots of credits on their meters. A good rule of thumb is that if your slot doesn't hit something in four or five pulls, leave it and go find another. Also, each casino has a bank of slots that they advertise as more loose or with a bigger payback. Try these. It's what they want you to do, but what the heck.

Sports Books

Most of the larger hotels in Las Vegas have sports-book operations, which look a lot like commodities-futures trading boards. In some, almost as large as theaters, you can sit comfortably, occasionally in recliners, and sometimes with your own video screen, and watch ball games, fights, and, at some casinos, horse races on huge TV screens. To add to your enjoyment, there's usually a deli/bar nearby that serves sandwiches, hot dogs, soft drinks, and beer. As a matter of fact, some of the best sandwiches in Las Vegas are served next to the sports books. Sports books take bets on virtually every sport (and not just who'll win, but what the final score will be, who'll be first to hit a home run, who'll be MVP, who'll wear red shoes, you name it). They are best during important playoff games or big horse races, when everyone in the place is watching the same event—shrieking, shouting, and moaning, sometimes in unison. Joining in with a cheap bet (so you feel like you, too, have a personal stake in the matter) makes for bargain entertainment.

Speaking of the future, in early 2010, the Nevada Gaming Commission approved rules that would allow casino sports books to take wagers on the outcomes of nonsporting events such as the Academy Awards, *American Idol,* and even presidential elections. In the past, you couldn't bet on these types of events because in many of them the outcome is known by someone before the results are announced (those Oscar accountants get all the luck!) or there was too high a risk that the outcomes could be influenced. At press time, no major casino in Vegas was offering these types of wagers because of all of the restrictions the commission put on them to guard against the concerns that made them illegal before, but it is only a matter of time—the casinos smell big money here and they'll figure out a way to make it work. So who do you think is going to win *Dancing With the Stars?* Wanna bet?

Video Poker

Video poker works the same way as regular poker, except you play against the machine. You are dealt a hand, you pick which cards to keep and which to discard, and then you get your new hand. And, it is hoped, you collect your winnings. This is somewhat more of a challenge than slots because you have some control (or at least the illusion of control) over your fate, and it's easier than playing actual poker with a table full of serious poker players.

There are a number of varieties of video poker machines, including **Jacks or Better, Deuces Wild,** and so forth. Be sure to study your machine before you play. (The best returns are offered on the **Bonus Poker** machines; the payback for a pair of jacks or better is two times your bet, and three times for three of a kind.) The Holy Grail of video-poker machines is the 9/6 (it pays nine coins for a full house, six coins for a flush), but you'll need to pray a lot before you find one in town. Some machines offer **double down:** After you have won, you get a chance to draw cards against the machine, with the higher card the winner. If you win, your money is doubled, and you are offered a chance to go again. Your money can increase nicely during this time, and you can also lose it all very quickly, which is most annoying.

Other options include multi-hand video poker, where you play anywhere from 3 to 100 hands at the same time; bonus spin poker, allowing you to spin a wheel for extra credits when you get certain hands; and progressive jackpots for things like royal flushes or four aces.

GETTING MARRIED

Getting hitched is one of the most popular things to do in Las Vegas. Just ask Britney Spears—as she rather infamously revealed, it's all too easy to get married here. See that total stranger/childhood friend standing next to you? Grab him or her and head down to the **Clark County Marriage License Bureau,** 201 Clark Ave. (© **702/761-0600;** daily, including holidays, 8am–midnight), to get your license. Find a wedding chapel (not hard, as there are about 50 of them; they line the north end of the Strip, and most hotels have them) and tie the knot. Just like that. No blood test, no waiting period—heck, not even an awkward dating period . . . though you may have a potentially very awkward time explaining it afterward to your mother, your manager, and the press.

Even if you have actually known your intended for some time, Las Vegas is a great place to get married. The ease is the primary attraction, but there are a number of other appealing reasons. You can have any kind of wedding you want, from a big, traditional production number to a small, intimate affair; from a spur-of-the-moment "just-the-happy-couple-in-blue-jeans" kind of thing to an "Elvis-in-a-pink-Cadillac-at-a-drive-thru-window" kind of thing (see the box "Vows with a Wow," on p. 185). The wedding chapels take care of everything; usually they'll even provide a limo to take you to the license bureau and back. Most offer all the accessories, from rings to flowers to a videotaped record of the event.

More than 100,000 couples who yearly take advantage of all this can't be wrong. If you want to follow in the footsteps of Elvis and Priscilla (at the first incarnation of the Aladdin Hotel); Michael Jordan; Jon Bon Jovi; Richard Gere and Cindy Crawford; Pamela Anderson and ill-fated husband no. 3; Angelina Jolie and Billy Bob; and, of course, Britney and What's-His-Name; you'll want to peruse the following list of the most notable wedding chapels on or near the Strip.

You can also call **Las Vegas Weddings** (www.lasvegasweddings.com; ✆ **800/322-8697**), which offers one-stop shopping for wedding services.

Weddings can be very inexpensive in Vegas: A license is $77 and a basic service not much more. Even a full-blown shebang package—photos, music, flowers, video, cake, and other doodads—will run only about $500 total. We haven't quoted any prices here because the ultimate cost depends entirely on how much you want to spend. Go cheap, and the whole thing will set you back maybe $150, including the license; go elaborate, and the price is still reasonable by today's wedding-price standards. Be sure to remember that there are often hidden charges, such as expected gratuities for the minister (about $25 should do; no real need to tip anyone else), and so forth. If you're penny-pinching, you'll want to keep those in mind.

Same-sex marriage is legal across the United States.

Be aware that Valentine's Day is a very popular day to get married in Vegas. Some of the chapels perform as many as 80 services on February 14. But remember, you also don't have to plan ahead. Just show up, get your paperwork, close your eyes, and pick a chapel. And above all, have fun. Good luck and best wishes to you both.

Chapel of the Bells ★   Sporting the largest and gaudiest wedding chapel sign on the Strip, this is one of the longest-running chapels, operating since 1957. This combination of classic Vegas "style" and "tradition" is most of what this place has going for it. The chapel is pretty, garnished with swaths of white material and light green accents, seating 25 to 35, but nothing dazzling. It's not particularly distinctive, but Kelly Ripa got married here, so there is that. The chapel prefers advance booking but can do same-day ceremonies.

2233 Las Vegas Blvd. S. (at Sahara Ave.). www.chapelofthebellslasvegas.com. ✆ **800/ 233-2391** or 702/735-6803. Sun–Thurs 9am–9pm; Fri–Sat 9am–midnight.

Chapel of the Flowers ★★   This chapel's claim to fame is that Dennis Rodman and Carmen Electra exchanged their deathless vows here—but don't hold it against the place. They offer full services from photos to flowers, and more, with three chapels to choose from. The La Capella Chapel fits 50 and has a rustic Tuscan feel, with wood pews and frosted-glass sconces. The Victorian chapel, which holds only 30, has white walls and dark-wood pews and doesn't look very Victorian at all—but as the plainest, it's also the nicest. The smallest is the Magnolia Chapel, done in simple white marble with a

AN ELVIS IMPERSONATOR'S TOP 10 REASONS TO get married IN LAS VEGAS

Jesse Garon has appeared in numerous Las Vegas productions as "Young Elvis." He arrives at any special event in a 1955 pink, neon-lit Cadillac, and does weddings, receptions, birthdays, conventions, grand openings, and so on. For all your Elvis impersonator needs, call ✆ **702/588-8188,** or visit his website at www.vegaselvis.com.

1. It's the only place in the world where Elvis will marry you, at a drive-up window, in a pink Cadillac—24 hours a day.
2. Chances are, you'll never forget your anniversary.
3. Where else can you treat all your guests to a wedding buffet for only 99¢ a head?
4. Four words: One helluva bachelor party.
5. On your wedding night, show your spouse that new "watch me disappear" act you learned from Siegfried & Roy.
6. Show your parents who's boss—have your wedding your way.
7. Wedding bells ring for you everywhere you go. They just sound like slot machines.
8. You can throw dice instead of rice.
9. It's easy to lie about your age on the marriage certificate—just like Joan Collins did!
10. With all the money you save, it's dice clocks for everyone!

free-standing arch. If you want an outdoor vow exchange, you might choose the gazebo by a running stream and waterfall that nearly drowns out the Strip noise. There's also a medium-size reception room and live organ music upon request, plus Internet streaming of services is available for those of you who have second thoughts about not inviting the family to your vows. It's a pretty, friendly place, owned by the same family for more than 50 years. It does not allow rice or confetti throwing.

1717 Las Vegas Blvd. S. (at E. Oakey Blvd.). www.littlechapel.com. ✆ **800/843-2410** or 702/735-4331. Mon–Thurs 7am–8pm; Fri–Sat 7am–9pm.

Graceland Wedding Chapel ★ Housed in a landmark building that's one of the oldest wedding chapels in Vegas, the Graceland bills itself as "the proverbial mom and pop outfit." No, Elvis never slept here, but one of the owners was friends with Elvis and asked his permission to use the name. This is a tiny New England church building with a small bridge and white picket fence out front. Inside is a 30-seat chapel; the walls are off-white, with a large, modern, stained-glass window of doves and roses behind the pulpit. It's not the nicest of the chapels, but Jon Bon Jovi and Billy Ray Cyrus got married here (though not to each other). Naturally, an Elvis package is available.

619 Las Vegas Blvd. S. (at E. Bonneville Ave.). www.gracelandchapel.com. ✆ **800/824-5732** or 702/382-0091. Daily 9am–11pm.

Little Church of the West ★★ Built in 1942 on the grounds of the Frontier, this gorgeous traditional chapel has been moved three times in its history and has hosted weddings for everyone from Judy Garland to Angelina Jolie. Elvis even got married here, at least on film—the building played the backdrop for his nuptials to Ann-Margret in *Viva Las Vegas*. There are rich wood walls, ceiling, and pews; stained-glass windows; and a traditional steeple amongst the well-landscaped grounds, making it a really lovely option for those looking to walk down the aisle.

4617 Las Vegas Blvd. S. (at Russell Rd.). www.littlechurchlv.com. © **800/821-2452** or 702/739-7971. Daily 8am–11pm.

Little White Wedding Chapel ★   This is arguably the most famous of the chapels on the Strip, maybe because there is a big sign saying Michael Jordan and Joan Collins were married here (again, not to each other), maybe because they were the first to do the drive-up window, or maybe because this is where Britney and what's-his-name began their 51 hours of wedded bliss (no, we will never, ever get tired of mocking that bit of bad decision making). There are four separate chapels plus a drive-thru (allegedly the first of its kind), and an outdoor gazebo. It's all fine, but it has a factory-line atmosphere, processing wedding after wedding all day. Move 'em in and move 'em out. If you want something special, there are probably better choices.

1301 Las Vegas Blvd. S. (btw. E. Oakey and Charleston blvds). www.alittlewhitechapel. com. © **800/545-8111** or 702/382-5943. Daily 8am–midnight.

A Special Memory Wedding Chapel ★   This is absolutely the place to go if you want a traditional, big-production wedding; you won't feel it the least bit tacky. It's a New England church–style building, complete with steeple. The interior looks like a proper church (well, a plain one—don't think ornate Gothic cathedral), with a peaked roof, pews with padded red seats, modern stained-glass windows of doves and flowers, and lots of dark wood. It's all very clean and new and seats about 87 comfortably. There is a short staircase leading to an actual bride's room; she can make an entrance coming down it or through the double doors at the back. The area outside the chapel is like a mini-mall of bridal paraphernalia stores. Should all this just be too darned nice and proper for you, they also offer a drive-up window. They have a photo studio on-site and will do receptions featuring a small cake, cold cuts, and champagne. There's a gazebo for outside weddings, and they sell T-shirts!

800 S. 4th St. (at Gass Ave.). www.aspecialmemory.com. © **800/962-7798** or 702/384-2211. Sun–Thurs 8am–10pm; Fri–Sat 8am–midnight.

Viva Las Vegas Weddings ★★★   Yes, you could come to Las Vegas and have a traditional wedding in a tasteful chapel where you walk down the aisle to a kindly minister. But wouldn't you rather literally ride into the chapel in the back of a pink Cadillac and get married by Elvis? Or wade in through dry ice fog while Dracula performs your ceremony? Or float in from the ceiling a la *Cirque du Soleil?* This is the mecca of the wacky-themed Vegas wedding, complete with indoor and outdoor spaces, tux and costume rentals, florists, theme rooms for receptions, and a staff of former stage performers who love to put on a show. *This* is what a Vegas wedding should be like.

1205 Las Vegas Blvd. S. (btw. Charleston and Oakey blvds.). www.vivalasvegasweddings. com. © **800/574-4450** or 702/384-0771. Sun–Thurs 9am–9pm; Fri–Sat 8am–10pm.

Wee Kirk O' the Heather ★★   The oldest wedding chapel in Las Vegas (it's been here since 1940; ah, Vegas, and its mixed-up view of age) it's the one at the very end of the Strip, right before Downtown (and thus close to the license bureau). It was originally built as a house in 1925 for a local minister, but marriage bureau officials kept sending couples there to get married, and they eventually just gave up and turned it into a chapel. The decor is entirely fresh, and while that means gold-satin-patterned wallpaper in the chapel, we like it a great deal. Just the right balance between kitsch and classic, and that's what you want in a Vegas wedding chapel. Plus, if there were a competition for the friendliest chapel in town, this one would win hands down.

231 Las Vegas Blvd. S. (btw. Bridger and Carson aves.). www.weekirk.com. © **800/843-5266** or 702/382-9830. Daily 10am–8pm.

OUTDOOR ACTIVITIES

Biking

Bicycle rentals can be arranged through the concierge at most of the major hotels in town. If you'd prefer to do it on your own, check out **Las Vegas Cyclery** (www.lasvegascyclery.com; © **702/596-2953**), a rental and tour operator offering everything from street to mountain to tandem bikes and the necessary safety equipment and accessories. Guided tours of Red Rock Canyon, Mount Charleston, and more are also offered. Prices for mountain bike rentals start at around $40 for a half-day and guided tours at around $130.

Boating & Fishing

The bulk of the water-based activities in the area take place at the **Lake Mead National Recreation Area,** located about 20 miles east of Las Vegas. Several harbors offer rentals of power, fishing, and houseboats and personal watercraft. They can also help you with fishing licenses and equipment. For more information, see chapter 9.

Golf

See "Fore! Great Desert Golf" on p. 187.

Gyms

All of the major hotels (and many of the minor ones) have fully stocked gyms on the premises. The size and quality varies, of course, but the bigger resorts have facilities that would make most commercial fitness centers green with envy. Entrance to most is covered by the nightly resort fee, but if the hotel you are staying in doesn't have one, expect a charge of anywhere from $15 to $35 per day. Several national chains, including **24 Hour Fitness,** have outlets in Las Vegas, and your membership may allow you to use the local branch.

VOWS WITH A WOW

Simply getting married is not a big enough deal for some people. No, they can't trust that the exchange of vows with the person they love will create memories that will last forever, they have to make sure it is truly memorable by throwing in a volcano, a giant fountain, or maybe even a roller coaster. If you are such a person, Las Vegas has plenty of places to put a little wow into your vows.

If you want to have the iconic dancing waters as a backdrop, you can get married on a balcony overlooking the Bellagio Fountains at **Bellagio,** 3600 Las Vegas Blvd. S. (www.bellagio.com/weddings; 𝄐 **702/693-7700**). As you might expect, it ain't cheap, but you can time your "I do" to the fountains' big climax.

An almost aerial view of the fountains is available across the street from the Eiffel Tower at **Paris Las Vegas,** 3655 Las Vegas Blvd. S. (www.parislv.com; 𝄐 **877/650-5021**). You can get married on the observation deck at the top of the tower replica. Similar wow-worthy vistas are available at the world's tallest observation wheel, **High Roller,** 3545 Las Vegas Blvd. S. (𝄐 **800/CAESARS**).

An even higher view is available at the top of the **Stratosphere Las Vegas,** 2000 Las Vegas Blvd. S. (www.chapelin theclouds.com; 𝄐 **800/789-9436**). Their chapels overlook the city from more than 100 stories up, or you can get married on the indoor or outdoor observation decks. They even have packages that will include the thrill rides, so you can take the plunge both metaphorically and literally.

Adrenaline junkies can also join in holy matrimony while zooming along at nearly 70 mph on the roller coaster at **New York–New York,** 3790 Las Vegas Blvd. S. (www.newyorknewyork.com; 𝄐 **702/740-6616**).

If you want to add a little fire to the festivities, try getting married in front of the volcano at **The Mirage,** 3400 Las Vegas Blvd. S. (www.mirage.com; 𝄐 **702/791-7155**). You can have the ceremony during the day, or at night when the thing is all lava-riffic.

Finally, several of the city's most popular museums offer themed wedding packages with very interesting backdrops, including **The Mob Museum** (p. 161) and **The Neon Museum** (p. 161).

Hiking

We consider the length you have to walk between hotels on the Strip, or from your room to the front door enough of a hike, but if you are looking for something more traditional, the **Red Rock Canyon** and **Mount Charleston** areas have numerous hiking trails. For more information, see chapter 9.

Horseback Riding

Looking to indulge your inner cowboy/girl? There are several stables and horseback-tour companies in town, most of which are located near **Red Rock Canyon** and **Mount Charleston.** For more information, see chapter 9.

Ice Skating

The **SoBe Ice Arena** at the Fiesta Rancho, 2400 N. Rancho Rd. (http://fiesta rancho.sclv.com; 𝄐 **702/631-7000**), features an NHL regulation–size rink and offers daily open skating hours, lessons, and equipment rental. Public skating times vary from week to week based on the schedules of the various hockey leagues that use the facility; usually the rink is open for at least a couple of hours every afternoon and after 8pm on Friday and Saturday nights, which is when a DJ and nightclub-worthy lighting may help mask the sound and sight of you falling down a lot.

During the holiday season, the **Cosmopolitan** transforms its pool into an outdoor skating rink, complete with faux snow, hot cocoa vendors (with an option to add a little booze for extra warmth) and occasional Olympic skaters, like U.S. Gold Medalist Scott Hamilton.

Skiing & Snowboarding

See information about the **Las Vegas Ski and Snowboard Resort** in the Mt. Charleston section of chapter 9.

Swimming

Part of the delight of the Vegas resort complexes is the gorgeous pools—what could be better for beating the summer heat? But there are pools and there are pools, so you'll need to keep several things in mind when searching for the right one for you.

During the winter, it's often too cold or windy to do much lounging, and even if the weather is amenable, the hotels often close part of their pool areas during winter and early spring. Also, the pools are not heated, for the most part—but in fairness, they largely don't need to be.

Most hotel pools are shallow, chest-high at best, only about 3 feet deep in many spots (the hotels want you gambling, not swimming). Diving is impossible—not that a single pool allows it anyway.

And finally, during those hot days, be warned that sitting by pools next to heavily windowed buildings such as the Mirage and Treasure Island allows you to experience the same thing a bug does under a magnifying glass with a sun ray directed on it. Regardless of time of year, be sure to slather on the sunscreen; there's a reason you see so many unhappy lobster-red people roaming the streets. Many pool areas don't offer much in the way of shade.

At any of the pools, you can rent a cabana (which often includes a TV, special lounge chairs, and even better—poolside service), but these should be reserved as far in advance as possible, and, with the exception of the Four Seasons' complimentary shaded lounging area, most cost a hefty fee. If you are staying at a chain hotel, you will most likely find an average pool, but if you want to spend some time at a better one, be aware that most of the casino-hotel pool attendants will ask to see your room key. If they are busy, you might be able to sneak in, or at least blend in with a group ahead of you.

Tennis

Tennis used to be a popular pastime in Vegas, but these days, buffs only have a couple of choices at hotels in town that have courts. **Bally's** (© **702/967-4598**) has eight night-lit hard courts. Fees start at $20 per hour per court for guests of Bally's or Paris Las Vegas and $25 per hour for nonguests, with rackets available for rental. Facilities include a pro shop. Hours vary seasonally.

Reservations are advised. The **Westgate Las Vegas** (© **702/732-5009**) has six outdoor hard courts (four night-lit) and a pro shop. It's open to the public but hours vary seasonally. Rates are $20 per hour for guests and $25 per hour for nonguests. Lessons are available. Reservations required.

FORE! GREAT DESERT GOLF

In addition to the listings below, there are dozens of local courses, including some very challenging ones that have hosted PGA tournaments. *Note:* Greens fees vary radically depending on time of day and year. Also, call for opening and closing times, because these change frequently. Because of the heat, you will want to take advantage of the cart that in most cases is included in the greens fee.

Angel Park Golf Club ★★ This 36-hole, par-70/71 public course is a local favorite. Arnold Palmer originally designed the Mountain and Palm courses. (The Palm Course was redesigned several years later by Bob Cupp.) Players call this a great escape from the casinos, claiming that no matter how many times they play it, they never get tired of it. The Palm Course has gently rolling fairways that offer golfers of all abilities a challenging yet forgiving layout. The Mountain Course has rolling natural terrain and gorgeous panoramic views. Facilities include a pro shop, night-lit driving range, 18-hole putting course, restaurant, cocktail bar, snack bar, and more.

100 S. Rampart Blvd. (btw. Summerlin Pkwy. and Alta St., 20 min. NW of the Strip). www.angelpark.com. © **888/446-5358** or 702/254-4653. Greens fees $65–$125. Internet specials available.

Arroyo Golf Club ★ Also designed by Arnold Palmer, this 18-hole, par-72 course is one of the more scenic in town owing to its location nestled along Red Rock Canyon. Stunning mountains on one side and Las Vegas in the distance on the other side; what more could you want? Well, you get a challenging (but not insanity-inducing) course that will keep all but the most competitive of golfers entertained. Facilities include a pro shop, night-lit driving range, 18-hole putting course, restaurant, cocktail bar, snack bar, and more.

2250 C Red Springs Dr. (just west of the 215, 25 min. NW of the Strip). www.thearroyo golfclub.com. © **866/934-4653** or 702/258-3200. Greens fees $77–$189.

Bali Hai Golf Club ★★★ One of the most exclusive golf addresses belongs to this multimillion-dollar course on the Strip, just south of Mandalay Bay. Done in a wild South Seas theme, the par-72 course has over 7 acres of water features, including an island green, palm trees, and tropical foliage everywhere you look. Not impressed yet? How about the fact that all their golf carts are equipped with GPS? Okay, if that doesn't convince you of the upscale nature of the joint, check out the greens fees. Even at those prices, premium tee times are often booked months in advance. Among the many facilities are a pro shop, putting green, gourmet restaurant, grill, and lounge.

5150 Las Vegas Blvd. S. www.balihaigolfclub.com. © **888/427-6678.** Greens fees $99–$395.

ORGANIZED tours

Just about every hotel in town has a tour desk offering a seemingly infinite number of sightseeing opportunities in and around Las Vegas. You're sure to find a tour company that will take you where you want to go. For example, **Gray Line** (www.grayline.com; ☏ **800/634-6579**) offers a rather comprehensive roster, including the following:

o A pair of 5- to 6-hour **city tours** (day or night) with various itineraries, including visits to **Ethel M**

Chocolates and the **Fremont Street Experience**

o Half-day excursions to **Hoover Dam** and **Red Rock Canyon**

o A half-day tour to **Lake Mead** and **Hoover Dam**

o Several full-day **Grand Canyon** excursions

Call for details or inquire at your hotel's tour desk, where you'll also find free magazines with coupons for discounts on these tours.

Bear's Best Las Vegas ★★★   Golf legend Jack Nicklaus has designed hundreds of courses around the world, but here he has taken 18 of his favorite holes and put them all together in one delightfully challenging package. From courses in Mexico to Montana and back again, the bunkers, water features, and traps have all been faithfully re-created, giving you an opportunity to try the best of "The Bear." Facilities include a pro shop, putting green, restaurant (with Nicklaus memorabilia), and clubhouse.

11111 W. Flamingo Rd. www.clubcorp.com. ☏ **702/804-8500.** Greens fees $79–$259.

Las Vegas National Golf Club ★   This 18-hole, par-71 public course is one of the most historic in town. Built in 1961, it was at various times associated with, or run by, the Stardust, Sahara, and the Las Vegas Hilton. Yes, the Rat Pack played here, and you can, too. The course itself is classically designed (not the desert layout that most in Vegas have), and although it's not the most challenging in town, it will keep you entertained. Facilities include a pro shop, driving range, restaurant, cocktail lounge, and golf school.

1911 Desert Inn Rd. (btw. Maryland Pkwy. and Eastern Ave.). www.lasvegasnational. com. ☏ **866/695-1961.** Greens fees $39–$129.

Rio Secco Golf Club ★★   You don't have to be staying at the Rio Suites (or another Caesars Entertainment property) to play this gorgeous 18-hole course, but you get preferred tee times and discounts if you do. Set in the foothills of the mountains overlooking Las Vegas, the views are incredible and the course, designed by Rees Jones, is one of the most in demand in town. Facilities include a pro shop, driving range, restaurant, and bar.

2851 Grand Hills Dr., Henderson. www.riosecco.net. ☏ **702/777-2400.** Greens fees $79–$219.

TPC Las Vegas ★★   Justin Timberlake has held his charity golf tournament at this course, so if it's good enough for him, it should be good enough for you, right? Luckily the sexy-back guy has good taste, as this scenic course, which follows the arroyos and plateaus of the terrain, is also a favorite of the PGA. That should tell you there are no windmills or clown's mouths here. It's a very challenging course, so bring your A game. Facilities include a pro shop, driving range, restaurant, clubhouse, and golf school.

9851 Canyon Run Dr. www.tpc.com. ℂ **702/256-2500.** Greens fees $69–$249.

Wynn Las Vegas Golf Club ★★　Before Mr. Wynn came along and bulldozed the legendary Desert Inn Golf Club, he rescued a bunch of the landscaping and then reinstalled it here on his elegant 18-hole, par-70 course behind Wynn Las Vegas. The facility is as gorgeous as you would expect it to be, with waterfalls, lush foliage, and stunning greens designed by the acclaimed Thomas Fazio. It ain't cheap, but many golfers say it is totally worth it. Note that it is only open to guests of Wynn or Encore. Facilities include a pro shop, driving range, putting green, and food service.

At Wynn Las Vegas, 3131 Las Vegas Blvd. S. www.wynnlasvegas.com. ℂ **888/320-7122.** Greens fees $300 and up.

SPAS

Most of the major resorts in Las Vegas have spa facilities that range from pretty basic (sauna, Jacuzzi, some treatment rooms for massages) to extravagant (is that a rock climbing wall?), but many are only available to guests of the hotels in which they are located.

The spas that follow all have hours during which they are open to the general public. Those hours change seasonally and sometimes even weekly based on hotel guest demand, so call ahead or visit the websites.

Aquae Sulis Spa ★★　The centerpiece here is the "Ritual," a series of dunks and soaks in cold, warm, hydrotherapy, and floating pools, some of which are outside in a gorgeously landscaped grotto. It's totally unique and worth the 20-minute drive from the Strip.

At the JW Marriott, 221 N. Rampart Blvd. (at Summerlin Pkwy.). www.jwlasvegasresort.com. ℂ **877/869-8777.** Massage and treatments $70–$215.

Canyon Ranch SpaClub ★　The largest spa in Las Vegas has more than 130,000-square-feet worth of treatment rooms, workout facilities, and even a rock climbing wall. Although they do a good job of keeping things relatively peaceful, the sheer size of the place and the number of people who visit may inhibit your relaxation efforts. Note that prices are more expensive on the weekends, so go on a weekday if you can.

At The Venetian, 3355 Las Vegas Blvd. S. www.canyonranch.com/lasvegas. ℂ **877/220-2688.** Massage and treatments $50–$355.

Qua Baths & Spa ★★　Check out the Environment rooms at this lavishly designed spa, which include the Arctic Ice room complete with snow showers

striking OUT

Las Vegas is one of the favorite cities in the world for bowlers of all levels, with several huge alleys offering everything from regular bowling to rock-'n'-roll-style action.

- The Strip got its first serious bowling alley in 2014 at **Brooklyn Bowl,** 3545 Las Vegas Blvd. S. (at the LINQ; ℂ **702/862-2695**). The 32-lane facility has two floors of state-of-the-art scoring from Brunswick, swank couches at the lanes instead of hard plastic seats, and high-definition projection screens over the alleys. Be warned that the nice surroundings come with a high price ($25 and up per lane per hour). It's open Sunday through Thursday from 11am until 2am and Friday and Saturday until 4am.

- **Gold Coast Bowling Center,** 4000 W. Flamingo Rd. (at Valley View; ℂ **702/367-7111**), has a 70-lane bowling center; open daily 24 hours.

- The **Orleans Bowling Center,** 4500 W. Tropicana Ave. (ℂ **702/365-7400**), has 70 lanes, a pro shop, lockers, meeting rooms, and more; open daily 24 hours.

- **Red Rock Lanes,** 11011 W. Charleston Ave. (ℂ **702/797-7467**), is a luxury bowling center with 72 lanes, plasma TVs, and VIP suites where you can pick your own music and get bottle service. It's open Monday through Thursday from 8am until 2am, and 24 hours on Fridays and Saturdays.

- **Santa Fe Station Bowling Center,** 4949 N. Rancho Rd. (ℂ **702/658-4995**), has a 60-lane alley with the most modern scoring equipment, new furnishings, a fun and funky bar, a small cafe, and much more. Open Sunday through Thursday 7am until midnight, and Friday and Saturday 7am until 1am.

- **Sam's Town Bowling Center,** 5111 Boulder Hwy. (ℂ **702/456-7777**), offers 56 lanes plus a snack shop, cocktail lounge, video arcade, day-care center, pro shop, and more. It's open daily 24 hours.

- **South Point Bowling Center,** 9777 Las Vegas Blvd. (ℂ **702/797-8080**), has a 64-lane facility with a similar divided layout to its sister at Suncoast (see below). It has all the latest gee-whiz scoring and automation, plus the usual facilities, and is open 24 hours. A separate $30-million, 60-lane facility designed to host pro-bowling tournaments should be open by the time you read this.

- **Strike Zone** at Sunset Station, 1301 W. Sunset Rd., in Henderson (ℂ **702/547-7467**), has a high-tech, 72-lane facility with all the latest automated scoring gizmos, giant video screens, a full bar, a snack shop, a pro shop, a video arcade, and more. It's open daily 24 hours.

- **Suncoast Bowling Center,** 9090 Alta Dr., in Summerlin (ℂ **702/636-7111**), offers 64 lanes divided by a center aisle. The high-tech center with touchscreen scoring has become a regular stop on the Pro Bowlers tours. It's open daily 24 hours.

- **Texas Star Lanes,** 2101 Texas Star Lane (ℂ **702/631-8128**), offers a 60-lane alley, video arcade, billiards, a snack bar and lounge, and more. It's open daily 24 hours.

and a Roman Baths section that would make Caesar proud. Treatments and massages are not cheap, but the spa faithful say this is one of the best in town.

At Caesars Palace, 3570 Las Vegas Blvd. S. www.caesarspalace.com. ℂ **866/782-0655.** Massage and treatments $185–$650.

Red Rock Resort Adventure Spa ★★★

The facility has the requisite spa accoutrement—a Zen-like space, massages, facials, sauna, and so on—but it's the "Adventure" part of the program that makes it truly unique. Capitalizing on the hotel's location on the edge of the Red Rock Canyon National Conservancy Area, the spa offers horseback riding, river rafting, kayaking, hiking, rock climbing, biking, and more. Go get a great outdoors workout and then come back for a massage to soothe your aches and pains.

At Red Rock Resort, 11011 W. Charleston Ave. (at I-215). www.redrocklasvegas.com. ℂ **866/328-9270.** Massage and treatments $90–$285.

Spa at Bellagio ★★

The surroundings are luxe and the staff is so soothingly attentive that you just know it's going to cost you a fortune to get worked on here—but it's totally worth it. Few other spas in town will make you feel so richly pampered.

At Bellagio, 3600 Las Vegas Blvd. S. www.bellagio.com. ℂ **702/693-7472.** Massage and treatments $95–$350.

Spa at Encore ★★★

By far the most beautifully designed spa in Las Vegas, the Moroccan garden decor is at once breathtaking and calming. Your bill can get shocking really fast, but one walk down the lantern-lit treatment room hallway will make all your cares melt away.

At Encore Las Vegas, 3121 Las Vegas Blvd. S. www.encorelasvegas.com. ℂ **702/770-4772.** Massage and treatments $85–$750.

SHOPPING

Las Vegas is one of the top shopping destinations in the world, and many visitors list the malls, stores, outlets, and boutiques as one of their primary reasons for coming to the city. Several top-grossing retail outlets are in Las Vegas, including the Forum Shops at Caesars Palace, which makes more money per square foot than any other mall in the United States. But in between the big malls and high-end luxury stores are lots of fun and offbeat boutiques that help to make Vegas a shopper's paradise, no matter your taste or budget.

Because they are as much tourist attractions as shopping destinations, the malls, stores, and boutiques on the Strip are open longer than you may expect, generally from 10am until 11pm on weekdays, and until midnight on weekends. Once you get off the Strip, things become more normal, with typical operating hours between 9am and 6 or 7pm. Some of the smaller independent stores are closed on Sundays.

Generally speaking, the further away you get from the Strip, the cheaper the prices. This applies to just about all categories of merchandise, even at name-brand chain stores where they will bump up prices by a few bucks just because they can. So if you're planning on getting a pair of shoes or jeans at a familiar chain store, check to see if they have an outlet elsewhere in the city and you can often save yourself some dough.

This also holds true for sundry items like toothpaste, shampoo, and deodorant. If you buy these at the hotel gift shops, expect to pay significantly more than you would if you go off the Strip to a regular retailer like Target or Wal-Mart.

SOUTH STRIP

Crystals ★ The jagged, sparkly facade that is front and center on Las Vegas boulevard is a dramatic come hither for the high end shops within: Fendi, Gucci, and Tiffany & Co. The Shops at Crystals has often been called the jewel (see what they did there?) of Las Vegas retail for the one percent. There's not only the largest Louis Vuitton in North America and the biggest Prada in the United States, but also the 10,000-square-foot Tiffany & Co. All that ultra-modern design of the exterior is offset by high ceilings and plenty of white space inside. If there weren't stores lining the walls, you might think this was an art gallery, with plenty of art installations inside the

Las Vegas Shopping

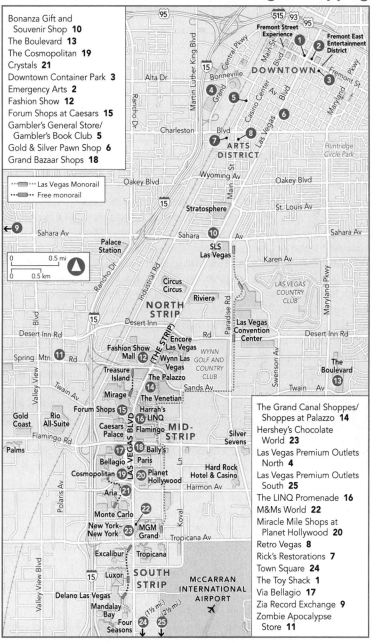

Bonanza Gift and
  Souvenir Shop **10**
The Boulevard **13**
The Cosmopolitan **19**
Crystals **21**
Downtown Container Park **3**
Emergency Arts **2**
Fashion Show **12**
Forum Shops at Caesars **15**
Gambler's General Store/
  Gambler's Book Club **5**
Gold & Silver Pawn Shop **6**
Grand Bazaar Shops **18**

···▭··· Las Vegas Monorail
···▭··· Free monorail

The Grand Canal Shoppes/
  Shoppes at Palazzo **14**
Hershey's Chocolate
  World **23**
Las Vegas Premium Outlets
  North **4**
Las Vegas Premium Outlets
  South **25**
The LINQ Promenade **16**
M&Ms World **22**
Miracle Mile Shops at
  Planet Hollywood **20**
Retro Vegas **8**
Rick's Restorations **7**
Town Square **24**
The Toy Shack **1**
Via Bellagio **17**
Zia Record Exchange **9**
Zombie Apocalypse
  Store **11**

shops themselves as well. Louis Vuitton has a permanent installation by light and space artist James Turrell, which you can see by appointment only, while a 7,000 Swarovski-crystal horse chandelier dazzles inside Stella McCartney. Have a nosh at Wolfgang Puck's pizzeria, or relax with one of many craft beers at **Todd English P.U.B.** (p. 104). The two-story wooden structure that stands in the middle is called The Treehouse and houses tony seafood restaurant **Mastro's Ocean Club** on the second floor, as well as concierge shopping services on the first. And yes, it does look like a bong. The mall is open Sunday through Thursday 10am until 11pm, and Friday and Saturday 10am to midnight, but individual store and restaurant hours may vary. 3720 Las Vegas Blvd. S. (at CityCenter). www.simon.com/mall/the-shops-at-crystals. © **702/590-9299.**

Hershey's Chocolate World ★★ Heaven forbid that when the apocalypse happens, this and M&M's World across the street lose power at the same time, resulting in Wonka-proportion rivers of chocolate spilling onto Las Vegas Boulevard. A fantasy, for sure, but one that's welcome at the new flagship at New York–New York. A scaled down, no-ride version of the original theme park in Hershey, Pennsylvania, inside the lures include an 800-pound chocolate Statue of Liberty, the ability to customize your own candy bar wrapper, and a bakery serving cookies, cupcakes, and plenty of other chocolate-infused goodies. Unlike its neighbor, this store is dedicated to more than just the iconic Hershey's chocolate, including interactive displays about Reese's Peanut Butter Cups and Jolly Ranchers. It's open Sunday through Thursday 9am to 11pm, and Friday and Saturday 9am to midnight. In New York–New York, 3790 Las Vegas Blvd. S. www.hersheyschocolateworldlasvegas.com. © **702/437-7439.**

M&M's World ★★ The four stories dedicated solely to the chocolate that melts in your mouth, but not in your hand, is a great place to get the kids all hepped up on sugar before passing out from the crash. Part of a bright, frenetic facade for the Showcase Mall (that includes a giant Coca-Cola bottle and a frenetic Gameworks sign), this shop draws kids like flies to honey. But where else would you go to pay for overpriced M&Ms in a rainbow of colors you've never seen before? There's a 3-D movie that tracks the famed Red and Yellow M&Ms as they search for the monogram they apparently lost in Vegas. It's cute, and the good teen employees who introduce the film are seemingly more excited about their jobs than one would expect. If you've ever wanted your M&Ms to read something other than their original imprint, you can print a personal message—it'll be short and sweet because of the surface area, but that's kind of the point of M&Ms. M&M's World is open daily from 9am until midnight. In the Showcase Mall, 3785 Las Vegas Blvd. S. (just north of the MGM Grand Hotel). www.mmsworld.com. © **702/740-2504.**

MID-STRIP

The Cosmopolitan ★★★ There are few real boutique shopping options on the Strip, but most of them can be found on the second floor of the Cosmopolitan. Local kicks shop CRSVR is a destination for sneaker-heads, and you can complete your hipster look with threads from AllSaints. The art-driven resort also features re-purposed cigarette machines that dispense tiny works by local artists for about $5 a pop. Finally, you don't necessarily have to buy goods here to be on the cutting edge of fashion while in town. Rent the Runway lets you don a designer dress just for a night, while sartorial-minded gents can dress up their suits from Stitched. The majority of the shops are open daily from 10am to 11pm. 3708 Las Vegas Blvd. S. www.cosmopolitanlasvegas.com. ℂ **702/698-7000.**

The Forum Shops at Caesars Palace ★★★ A shopping spree at the Forum Shops is one of those events you'd see in the movies, after the hero has beat the house and wants to spend his casino winnings. He steps off the carpeted casino floor through the 48-foot Roman archway and onto the bright, cold, marble floor, surrounded by enormous columns and stone carvings, a painted blue sky on the domed ceiling. A statue of the goddess Fortuna smiles down at our hero, welcoming him and his money. Cue the montage of luxury brand storefronts: John Varvatos, Gucci, Louboutin, Fendi, Henri Bendel, Ferragamo.

For those of us who haven't hit the Megamillions progressive, it's still easy to appreciate the glory of the Forum Shops, the 675,000 square feet of retail space that set the tone for the Vegas shopping experience when it opened in 1992. It's not just high-end stores, but also an elaborate maze with fantastic details. Many just walk through to see the sights.

And those sights are pretty swell. The three-story annex with an entrance directly on Las Vegas Boulevard features arched, cathedral ceilings with frescos painted on them, acres of marble columns, and one of the few spiral escalators in the world. Look for the silly but fun "Fall of Atlantis," a fountain display in the Roman Great Hall with animatronic statues of gods that spring to life for 11 minutes every hour, on the hour. The show got an upgrade in 2013, so gone are Bacchus, Apollo and Venus, replaced with more lifelike (sort of) statues than the previous ones and an updated story that pits the children of Atlas, Gadrius and Alia, against each other. The multi-sensory experience is completed with 14 LED screens playing video elements relevant to the story, pyrotechnics, and 40 speakers in a surround sound system so powerful it reverberates in your chest as you feel the gods' wrath.

Even if you don't have Ferragamo money, there are still plenty of middle-of-the road retail options to enact your own shopping spree, like the largest H&M in the United States, Banana Republic, All Saints, and Diesel.

If all this window-shopping makes you peckish, you have the choice of Vegas-classic **Spago,** old-school steak house **The Palm,** or modern sushi from **Sushi Roku.**

The majority of the shops are open Sunday through Thursday from 10am to 11pm, and Friday and Saturday from 10am to midnight. In Caesars Palace, 3500 Las Vegas Blvd. S. www.forumshops.com. ℂ **702/893-4800.**

Grand Bazaar Shops ★★ Flamingo and Las Vegas Boulevard is one of the busiest intersections on the Las Vegas Strip, with millions of pedestrians strolling past it on a daily basis. The Grand Bazaar Shops seeks to corral these people, hoping they'll spend their casino winnings (cough!) at this Moroccan-inspired shopping mecca. The Grand Bazaar Shops are, most definitely, a colorful place to shop: a flagship Swarovski outlet anchors the a colorful place to shop, anchored by a Swarovski outlet that has a 14-foot sphere composed of 911 custom-cut Swarovski crystals and more than 1,800 points of light. Nightly, from 9pm to midnight, the Swarovski Starburst coordinates its lights with music and those multi-colored mosaic panels on the roofs of the shops for a dazzling show. Under the canopies, you'll find mainstream, but eclectic stores such as Superdry and Swatch, plus essentials like Lush, Havaianas and Hammitt. Snack-wise, the Grand Bazaar Shops houses one of the largest Star-bucks stores in the country, complete with grandstand seating. Wahlburgers—the burger joint from the reality show of the same name, has been "coming soon" for quite some time, but we're not holding our breath while there are plenty of other spots to eat close by. The shops are open Sunday through Thursday from 10am to 10pm and Friday and Saturday from 10am to 11pm. 3635 Las Vegas Blvd. S. (in front of Bally's). www.grandbazaarshops.com. ✆ **702/736-4988.**

The Grand Canal Shoppes ★★   The 160 shops and restaurants of this meandering mall are divided between the Venetian and Palazzo, though one side is definitely more ornate than the other. Wander through the Venetian part and you'll see that the meticulous attention to detail given to the hotel's rec-reation of an Italian village is carried through here, including a ceiling that's cunningly painted like a cloud-dappled sky. Canals flow through the mall, complete with gondoliers who will take you (for a fee, of course) on a slow float on the water. An extra tip will ensure that your captain serenades you as well, from classic opera arias to vintage Rat Pack tunes. Pick up the gondolas near St. Mark's Square, entertainment central with wandering minstrels, liv-ing statues, and more opera singers. The Venetian stores include such afford-able choices as Kenneth Cole, Ann Taylor, and Victoria's Secret. For food, we recommend Mario Batali's pizza and wine bar, Otto. There's "outdoor" seat-ing on the faux patio, so order some antipasti and a glass of wine and watch the world go by, like you'd do in Italy.

The Shoppes at Palazzo aren't as exciting, partially because their setting is elegant but bland, and partially because the Palazzo houses crazy-expensive retailers like Barney's New York, Jimmy Choo, and Cartier, along with Bau-man Rare Books (possibly the only bookstore on the Strip). Navigating from one mall to the other isn't exactly intuitive, so you may have to ask for direc-tions if you have a specific destination in mind. The shops are open Sunday through Thursday from 10am to 11pm and Friday and Saturday from 10am to midnight. In The Venetian/Palazzo, 3327-3377 Las Vegas Blvd. S. www.grandcanal shoppes.com. ✆ **702/414-4500.**

The LINQ Promenade ★★   The ongoing trend in Las Vegas has been to capture the visitors while they're walking elsewhere. You turn into this unexpected gap between the Flamingo and the LINQ and boom, you're no longer *on* the Strip. Suddenly, you're on a long, narrow urban thoroughfare, complete with palm trees lining either side of the street, along with stores and restaurants. The latest addition to the Las Vegas skyline, the High Roller, is the anchor of this block. You'll pass **Brooklyn Bowl** (p. 113), a spot with great fried chicken that also happens to be a concert venue featuring indie acts), a Goorin Brothers hat shop, and sneaker spot 12amrun (where you can buy limited-edition kicks). Need a cupcake to go? You can purchase one, 24 hours, at the cupcake ATM on the side of Sprinkles, a Los Angeles-based bakery, now on this block. This little stretch has a Miami-vibe to it, which all dissipates once you board one of the pods of the world's tallest observation wheel to see what surrounds you. That's okay, you didn't come to Vegas for that SoFlo feel anyway. Hours vary by store. 3454 Las Vegas Blvd. S. (btw The LINQ and The Flamingo). www.thelinq.com. © **800/CAESARS.**

Miracle Mile Shops at Planet Hollywood ★ The retail outlets here are just prettier, Vegas-ier versions of the stores at the nice mall in your hometown, like White House Black Market, Lucky Brand, Guess, H&M, and a giant Urban Outfitters that looms over the Strip. But there are some one-off boutiques, as well, such as Fredrick's of Hollywood, an Original Penguin, and an importer of products made with alpaca wool, one of the last holdouts from when this shopping mall was known as Desert Passage (when the attached hotel was Aladdin). The AXIS Theatre has become the home for major pop residencies, where Britney Spears showcases her *Piece of Me,* Jennifer Lopez wants to give you *All I Have* and Lionel Richie plays *All The Hits.* One thing to note about this mall: it's not the easiest to navigate. It's essentially one big circle, so if the shop you want is on one side and you don't realize you've gone the wrong way from the entrance, you might end up taking an entire lap of the mall to get to your destination. The shops are open Sunday through Thursday from 10am to 11pm and Friday and Saturday from 10am to midnight. In Planet Hollywood Resort & Casino, 3663 Las Vegas Blvd. S. www.miraclemileshopslv.com. © **702/866-0704.**

Via Bellagio ★★ There are only about a dozen boutiques in this well-lit corridor of the Bellagio, and like most everything else at this hotel, they'll cost you a pretty penny. On the clothing side, that means Prada, Chanel, Gucci, Louis Vuitton, Dior, and Armani; sparkly, pretty things are on sale from Tiffany & Co. and a timeless timepiece from 18th century watchmaker Breguet is also available here. It's worth a stroll, even if you're there just to window shop. That's still free. Hours vary by store. In Bellagio, 3600 Las Vegas Blvd. S. www.bellagio.com. © **702/693-7111.**

NORTH STRIP

Bonanza Gift and Souvenir Shop ★★ Even though it says it's the "World's Largest Gift Shop" outside, it isn't, and we don't care! It's 40,000 square feet of pure Vegas-oriented kitsch, from T-shirts to tchotchkes, Native American crafts and jewelry, casino accoutrement like retired dice and decks of playing cards, Elvis stuff, Rat Pack stuff, atomic age stuff—the Vegas things that run from tacky to tasteful—all for really good prices. Besides, no one really wants that plastic yard you drank warm daiquiri from all day when you stumbled down the Strip. It's open daily from 8am until midnight. 2440 Las Vegas Blvd. S. (at Sahara Ave.). www.worldslargestgiftshop.com. © **702/385-7359.**

Fashion Show ★★   That saucer-looking thing hovering over the exterior may make you wonder when it will return to the mothership, but it's actually the front for probably the best mall on the Strip. The 250 stores here are comprehensive, covering the basics of a mall you're already familiar with (Gap, Banana Republic, The Limited), some higher-end, cooler options (Superdry, Diesel), all anchored by department stores like Dillard's, Neiman Marcus, and the Silver State's only Nordstrom. On select weekends, the place lives up to its name and has actual fashion shows within the mall itself. A hydraulic runway lifts out of the floor, sometimes with fog, and models march down. It's all very dramatic, which is what you'd expect from a mall front and center on the Strip. Fashion Show is open Monday through Saturday from 10am to 9pm, and Sunday from 11am to 7pm. 3200 Las Vegas Blvd. S. (at the corner of Spring Mountain Rd.). www.thefashionshow.com. © **702/369-8382.**

DOWNTOWN

Downtown Container Park ★★★   In an attempt to revitalize Downtown Las Vegas into an urban counterpart to the Strip, it wasn't enough to add loft apartments, trendy restaurants and mixology bars. The area needed a playground; a communal space for locals and visitors to gather, and Downtown Container Park has filled that role. You're greeted by the 40-foot Praying Mantis, straight from Burning Man, which breathes fire at night. No matter how many times I've passed it, I'm always startled when it happens. The retail side of the venture is housed in an assortment of stacked shipping containers and pre-fabricated cubes that contain independent fashion and art boutiques, jewelers, confectioners, bars, and restaurants. The 20,000-square-foot structure features a courtyard in the middle with a treehouse, complete with a 33-foot slide. Kids are welcome during the day, but after 9pm the whole complex is 21 and over. Live entertainment and outdoor movie nights (when it's not blazing hot) make this a nice neighborhood oasis for getting away from the real Vegas. The center is open Sunday through Thursday from 11am to 11pm, and Friday and Saturday from 11am to 1am, although store hours vary. 707 Fremont St. (at 7th St.). www.downtowncontainerpark.com. © **702/637-4244.**

Emergency Arts ★★   Right at the heart of the Fremont East Entertainment District, this repurposed medical clinic has been given new life as a multipurpose gallery, studio, boutique, and cafe space. It's a collective of local artists and artisans who produce cool, funky, one-of-a-kind pieces, so the odds of finding something very Vegas, yet completely unique, are good. The Beat Coffeehouse on the first floor is a popular meeting and brainstorming spot for locals, while the Burlesque Hall of Fame is a cute, fun look at the history of showgirls

from Vegas and beyond. Gallery and boutique hours vary, but are generally 10am until 6pm. 520 E. Fremont St. www.emergencyartslv.com. ℰ **702/409-5663.**

Gamblers General Store/Gambler's Book Club ★ If you can't bear to leave the gambling in Las Vegas, this is your ultimate resource. Everything you need to furnish your own casino at home is here, and not just dice and decks of cards. We're talking full-size blackjack and craps tables, slot machines, and roulette wheels too. Need an extra edge on your game? More than 3,000 titles are available with tips and tricks of the trade. As the house is almost always guaranteed to win, we question the veracity of the tips in some of these books, but they're not bad guides to learning every game inside and out. Want to have casino chips or cards customized for your own habits? They'll do that, too. The only thing that would make this place better is if there was a Gamblers Anonymous meeting being held in the basement. Just kidding; Las Vegas doesn't have basements. The store is open Monday through Saturday from 9am to 6pm and Sunday from 9am to 5pm. 800 S. Main St. (Downtown). www.gamblersgeneralstore.com. ℰ **800/522-1777** or 702/382-9903.

Las Vegas Premium Outlets North ★ The good news: this shopping emporium is situated between the Strip and Downtown Las Vegas, so it's more convenient to get to than its counterpart, **Outlets South** (see below). The bad news: it's outdoors. So on summer days, despite the water misters and misguided attempts at shade, shopping here is unbearable. But if the weather is ok, you'll get to navigate some decent outlet shopping which includes brands like Diesel, AllSaints, Diane von Furstenberg, Dolce & Gabbana, True Religion and Calvin Klein. The mall is open Monday through Saturday from 9am to 9pm, and Sunday from 9am to 8pm. 875 S. Grand Central Pkwy. (at I-15). www.premiumoutlets.com. ℰ **702/474-7500.**

Retro Vegas ★★ Though it's got Vegas in its name, this little boutique has so much more than vintage Vegas design in its selection. There's a good chunk of beautiful Danish and midcentury modern furniture that many collectors would love to get their hands on. And for those who want to take home a bit of Sin City history, there's all kinds of items that evoke the best of Vegas vices, including old school, sturdy, colored glass ashtrays from casinos of Vegas past, and delicate, ornate cocktail glasses from the *Mad Men* era. It's open Monday through Saturday from 11am to 6pm, and Sunday from noon to 5pm. 1131 S. Main St. (at Charleston Ave.). www.retro-vegas.com. ℰ **702/384-2700.**

The Toy Shack ★★★ Probably the only reason to visit Neonopolis (besides parking), The Toy Shack is where Jimmy Jiminez, a toy expert who makes frequent appearance on the History Channel's *Pawn Stars,* actually works. The story carries everything from pristine collectibles to new-fangled toys, dolls, and action figures. Comic book nerds (and the people who love them) use the goods here for superhero cosplay parties; the country's biggest collection of Hot Wheels is a big draw for those sorts of aficionados. Who says you can't play with toys when you're an adult? The Toy Shack is open Mondays

SHOPPING gets real

The proliferation of reality TV shows has turned an island's worth of Average Joes, from ice road truck drivers and overly tanned Jersey boys, into pop-culture stars. Although you can't go trawling on a fishing boat with your favorite demi-celebrities, in Las Vegas you can visit the shopkeepers-turned-stars who appear on some of the most popular History Channel show.

Pawn Stars is set at the **Gold & Silver Pawn Shop,** 713 Las Vegas Blvd. S. (www.gspawn.com; ℭ 702/385-7912). Operated by the colorful Harrison family, the store is heavy on hocked jewelry—but there are lots of other odds and ends worth a quick browse. The bad news is that the Harrisons themselves are rarely on-site anymore, which can be a disappointment to the hordes of people waiting in line (seriously!) at all times of the day to get inside. But there is a life-sized cut-out of Chumlee, Rick, Corey, and Richard to pose in front of (because if you don't get a selfie, well, the visit

never really happened, right?). The store is open daily from 9am until 9pm.

You'll have a much better chance of seeing people you've seen on TV at **Rick's Restorations,** 1112 S. Commerce St. (www.ricksrestorations.com; ℭ 702/366-7030), where *American Restoration* is filmed. Owner Rick Dale, his wife Kelly, and a crew of lovable oddballs restore classic Americana (soda machines, gas pumps, bicycles, slot machines, and more) in a rambling facility that offers tours, a showroom, a gift shop, and more. Big windows in the public areas give visitors a glimpse into the working facility, and people from the show, including Rick, will often pop out to say hi and sign autographs. The restorations themselves are stunning accomplishments, but you're going to need a high credit limit to afford any of it. Recently offered gas pumps, for instance, started at around $7,000 and went up from there. The store is open Monday through Friday from 9am until 5pm.

through Saturdays from 11am until 10pm. In Neonopolis, 450 E. Fremont St. www.worldfamoustoyshack.com. ℭ 702/538-8600.

JUST OFF THE STRIP

The Boulevard ★ Las Vegans off the Strip; they're just like you! They need large appliances and new backpacks for the kids for school and sensible shoes, and they get them at malls just like this one, like you would at home. The selection of stores here are of the everyday kind: Foot Locker, Lane Bryant, JCPenney. They come in handy when you need to a pair of shoes that aren't wrecking your feet, or if you forgot to pack khakis for your conference, at prices that are probably a little more reasonable than at boutiques on the Strip. It's close enough that it won't cost you too much in cab fare, and it's a nice little taste to see what real life is like in Sin City. The mall is open Monday through Saturday from 10am to 9pm, and Sunday from 11am to 7pm. 3528 S. Maryland Pkwy. (btw. Twain Ave. and Desert Inn Rd.). www.boulevardmall.com. ℭ 702/735-8268.

Zia Record Exchange ★★ Record stores? They still have these? Yes, and this is actually a very good one. Okay, so there are more CDs than vinyl on the shelves (but still way more vinyl than we've seen in quite some time), and the selection is vast. Hunting through the crates you might find anything from Mumford and Sons and Tech N9ne to Rolling Stones' classic *Sticky Fingers* and Willie Nelson and Merle Haggard's *Django and Jimmie*—it's an eclectic collection. Vegas bands, obviously, get a lot of love, with a bin dedicated exclusively to local up-and-comers, who sometimes even do in-store performances and signings. Both locations are open daily from 10am to midnight. 4503 W. Sahara Ave. www.ziarecords.com. ✆ **702/233-4942.** 4225 S. Eastern Ave., Ste. 17. ✆ **702/735-4942.**

Zombie Apocalypse Store ★★   There's been some speculation that should the zombie apocalypse (or insert your favorite doomsday scenario) happen, Las Vegas would hold on for quite awhile before the complete collapse of civilization. Electricity is harnessed from Hoover Dam rather than fossil fuels, the city is surrounded by mountains (and zombies aren't the greatest climbers), and Sin City is already excellent at water conservation, not to mention the Southern Nevada Health District's website has a handy primer on zombie prevention (it's really about the flu). All of that, plus this store, which embraces both the zombie fantasy as well as real doomsday preparation (a big deal in Las Vegas). Aside from zombie survival guides, medical quarantine signs and souvenir T-shirts that say "This is my zombie killing T-shirt," the store offers survival gear like bug out bags, stun guns, knives, and military-style meals-ready-to-eat. There are worse places to be when the world ends. The store is usually open every day 10am to 7pm (though hours vary seasonally). 3420 Spring Mountain Rd. (at Polaris Ave.). www.zombieapocalypsestore. com. ✆ **702/320-0703.**

SOUTH & EAST OF THE STRIP

Las Vegas Premium Outlets South ★   The sister location at the north end of the Strip might have fancier brands, but this one has the real bargains. There are a few shared names between the two outposts, like the BCBG-MaxAzria, DKNY and Calvin Klein. For the most part the rest on the south side are old familiar faces like Dressbarn, Levi's, and Tommy Hilfiger, and it seems like these stores often have better deals than the ones up north. It's also a straight shot down Las Vegas Boulevard to get here, in the event you're driving. But the real reason this one wins out? The added bonus of being indoors and air-conditioned. The mall is open Monday through Saturday from 9am to 9pm and Sunday from 9am to 8pm. 7400 Las Vegas Blvd. S. (at Warm Springs Rd.). www.premiumoutlets.com. ✆ **702/896-5599.**

Town Square ★   This is the closest shopping center to the Strip where you'll see actual Las Vegans spending time, thanks to its town-like design. The 150-or-so stores and restaurants are along tree-lined streets that are set up in a grid like city blocks. You can even park in front of the stores themselves if there's a spot open; if not, there's also a couple of massive parking lots and covered garages. Stroll past quaint storefronts of an Apple store, Armani Exchange, Paper Source, and Tommy Bahama. Catch a blockbuster at the 18-screen movie theater, chill out with a pint or three at Yardhouse, or grab a bite at one of the dozen (mostly chain) restaurants, like **Brio Tuscan Grille** or **Bonefish Grill.** For kids, there's even a park in the center to play in, and a giant Gameworks, complete with a bowling alley, arcade, and laser tag. Baobab Stage is a live theater venue where performers from Strip productions spend their night off doing cabaret shows. It's pretty much all the stuff you'd do at this type of mall in your hometown, this one just happens to have a Las Vegas Boulevard address. Hours vary by store. 6605 Las Vegas Blvd. S. (at I-215). www.mytownsquarelasvegas.com. © **702/269-5000.**

ENTERTAINMENT & NIGHTLIFE

According to an advertising slogan, Hollywood is the "Entertainment Capital of the World." But consider for a moment the sheer number of shows, headliners, bars, nightclubs, lounges, and other forms of entertainment and nightlife in Las Vegas. Your options are almost limitless: Cirque du Soleil has more than a half-dozen permanent shows here; virtually every hotel has at least one showroom, if not four; Mariah Carey, Elton John, and Britney Spears are among the big names who perform regularly, and sometimes exclusively, in Vegas; most bars are open 24 hours a day; 7 of the top 10 grossing nightclubs in the U.S. are in Vegas, accounting for over half a billion dollars in revenue in 2015; and yes, there are even a few showgirls left. Hollywood may have the slogan, but Las Vegas is the real capital.

You certainly won't be lacking in things to do; in fact, the opposite may be true in that there are simply not enough hours in your vacation to do all the things you may want to do. The key is to cover the basics—a Cirque show if you've never seen one; a headliner, if one is in town; a fun bar; a high-energy nightclub—and then start layering in the off-the-beaten-track, the one-of-a-kind, and the less-high-profile shows, clubs, and entertainment offerings that will make your trip more memorable.

What follows are the things you should not miss—and some that are not worth your time no matter what you may have heard—in the category of performing arts, which includes shows both big, small, and in between; the bar scene, including lounges, piano bars, and pubs; the club and music scene, which covers the big dance clubs, ultralounges, comedy clubs, and more; and, of course, the strip clubs, which are big business in Vegas. There's also a section for gay and lesbian visitors showcasing the best and brightest bars and clubs around town.

THE PERFORMING ARTS

This category covers all the major Las Vegas production shows, and a few of the minor ones as well. Note that shows can close without warning, even ones that have been running just shy of forever, so

Las Vegas Shows

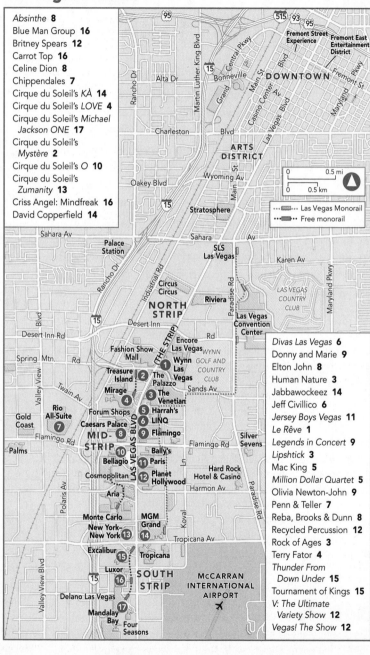

Absinthe **8**
Blue Man Group **16**
Britney Spears **12**
Carrot Top **16**
Celine Dion **8**
Chippendales **7**
Cirque du Soleil's *KÀ* **14**
Cirque du Soleil's *LOVE* **4**
Cirque du Soleil's *Michael Jackson ONE* **17**
Cirque du Soleil's *Mystère* **2**
Cirque du Soleil's *O* **10**
Cirque du Soleil's *Zumanity* **13**
Criss Angel: Mindfreak **16**
David Copperfield **14**

Divas Las Vegas **6**
Donny and Marie **9**
Elton John **8**
Human Nature **3**
Jabbawockeez **14**
Jeff Civillico **6**
Jersey Boys Vegas **11**
Le Rêve **1**
Legends in Concert **9**
Lipshtick **3**
Mac King **5**
Million Dollar Quartet **5**
Olivia Newton-John **9**
Penn & Teller **7**
Reba, Brooks & Dunn **8**
Recycled Percussion **12**
Rock of Ages **3**
Terry Fator **4**
Thunder From Down Under **15**
Tournament of Kings **15**
V: The Ultimate Variety Show **12**
Vegas! The Show **12**

····▬▬▬···· Las Vegas Monorail
···▬▬▬··· Free monorail

please call first. You might also want to double-check on days and times of performances; schedules can change without notice. *Note:* Most ticket prices do not include taxes, fees, or drinks, so you might also check for those potential hidden costs.

Absinthe ★★★   Like the supposedly hallucinatory drink it is named after, this Cirque du Soleil–style revue may leave you reeling. But, boy, will that hangover be worth it. The show is performed in the round in a small tent-like structure in front of Caesars Palace, with a tiny circular stage and only a few rows of seating. That means all of the "death-defying stunts"—acrobats, trapeze artists, high-wire walkers, and even high-speed roller skaters will be just feet—and in some cases, inches—from your face. Adding to the thrills are the raunchy host, The Gazillionaire, and his faithfully dimwitted sidekick assistant, who introduce the acts with a dirty glee and X-rated humor that will leave you laughing so hard you'll forget to be offended or shocked. Sidekick Joy Jenkins' hilarious, jaw-dropping potty-mouthed rant is worth the price of admission alone. The cast rotates so the show differs from performance to performance. Definitely not for kids or prudes! Shows are Wednesday through Sunday at 8 and 10pm only. In Caesars Palace, 3570 Las Vegas Blvd. S. www.absinthe vegas.com. ✆ **800/745-3000.** Tickets $99–$139.

Blue Man Group ★   Are they blue? Indeed they are—three bald, non-speaking men dipped in azure paint, doing decidedly odd stunts with marshmallows, art supplies, smoke-ring blowing cannons, giant inflatable balls, commenting on the use of technology and social media without saying a word, and an amazing array of percussion instruments fashioned fancifully from PVC piping. Blue Man has moved back to its original Las Vegas home, Luxor, with an updated and re-imagined show to fit into the new, smaller space. Moments of silly genius are a staple—those oddly compelling, giant smoke rings, for example, and a routine with a Twinkie and a hapless audience member are classics—but the new, cozier theater allows the troupe to create a more intimate, immersive experience and a few new surprises. In the end, the show that used to be unique in Vegas is now uniquely Vegas, as much a part of the entertainment landscape as Cirque du Soleil, and for that alone it is worth a visit. Shows are nightly at 7 and 9:30pm. At Luxor, 3900 Las Vegas Blvd. S. www.blueman.com. ✆ **702/262-4400.** Tickets $64–$125; VIP and backstage tour packages available.

Cirque du Soleil's KÀ ★★★ KÀ overturns expectations by largely ignoring the usual Cirque format—acrobatic-style acts and ethereal performance art trappings with a tenuous-at-best connective tissue—in favor of an actual plot, as a sister and brother from some mythical Asian kingdom are separated by enemy raiders and have to endure various trials and tribulations before being reunited. Gleefully borrowing imagery from magical realist martial-arts movies such as *Crouching Tiger, Hidden Dragon,* the production makes use of a technically extraordinary set that shifts the stage not just horizontally but vertically, as the action moves from under the sea to the side of a steep cliff and beyond. The circus elements—clowns and acrobats—are incorporated into the show in a way that makes loose narrative sense.

The story is by turns funny, whimsical, and pulse-pounding, with moments of exquisitely perfect bits of theater. It might be too long and intense for younger children, but older ones will be enthralled—and so will you.

The tragic death of one of the show's performers during a show in 2013 has had only a minor impact on the fundamentals of this production but should have profound impact on the audience's interpretation of what Cirque does, reminding us that these are real human beings performing dangerous stunts for our amusement. Stand up at the end of the show and applaud that.

Performances are held Saturday through Wednesday at 7 and 9:30pm. In the MGM Grand, 3799 Las Vegas Blvd. S. www.cirquedusoleil.com/ka. ✆ **866/740-7711.** Tickets $88–$196.

Cirque du Soleil's LOVE ★ A collaboration between the Beatles (by way of Sir George Martin's son, who re-configured and remixed the music with a free hand that may distress purists) and Cirque du Soleil, this is the usual Cirque triumph of imaginative design, but it also feels surprisingly hollow. Yes, there's inspiration in the idea of pairing Beatles' music with Cirque's joyous spectacle. But while Cirque shows have never been big on plot, the intense aimlessness of this production means that the show too quickly dissolves into simply the introduction of one novel staging element after another. In other words, its visual fabulousness ends up repetitious rather than thrilling. Still, the familiar music provides an aura of accessibility to the sometimes-dense world of Cirque du Soleil that other Vegas productions don't, so it could be good for Cirque newbies. Shows are held Thursday through Monday at 7 and 9:30pm. At The Mirage, 3400 Las Vegas Blvd. S. www.cirquedusoleil.com/love. ✆ **800/963-9634** or 702/792-7777. Tickets $88–$209.

Cirque du Soleil's *Michael Jackson ONE* ★★★ Unlike *LOVE,* Cirque's Beatle-themed show, *Michael Jackson ONE* works like gangbusters. Its blend of the brilliantly conceived pop music (and pop culture touchstones)

BIG NAMES, bigger shows

During its fallow days in the 1970s and '80s, Las Vegas was the place where an entertainer's act went to die. The headliner showrooms were the refuge for singers whose careers' best days were years, and sometimes decades, behind them.

That all changed when Céline Dion came to town in 2003. Her 5-year engagement at Caesars Palace shattered box office records and made it safe for big-name headliners to call Vegas their home. In the last decade we have seen marquee-topping extended runs from Elton John, Cher, Bette Midler, Prince, Garth Brooks, Tim McGraw & Faith Hill, Shania Twain, Rod Stewart, and more.

Tickets are expensive, with the best seats going for upward of $300, and the concerts are not performed every week, so if you want to see one you have to plan your vacation around their schedule rather than yours. But many of the shows are exclusive engagements, meaning if you want to see the stars, you have to come to Vegas.

Céline Dion is deep into her second headlining run at Caesars Palace, 3570 Las Vegas Blvd. S. (www.celinedion.com; ℂ **877/423-5463;** show times vary; tickets $55–$250). Backed by a 31-piece orchestra, this is a more dignified affair than her dance-heavy 2003–2008 show. It showcases her voice in a way that proves she is probably one of the most naturally gifted singers in the world. On signature ballads like "Because You Loved Me" and the inevitable "My Heart Will Go On," it's easy to understand how she can sell out a 4,000-seat theater on a regular basis. We would've liked to have heard more of her hits rather than her covers of other's music that take up big chunks of the show, and we longed for more up-tempo moments, but fans will likely be rapt.

Sharing the same stage (but not at the same time, sadly), **Elton John,** at Caesars Palace, 3570 Las Vegas Blvd. S.

(www.eltonjohn.com; ℂ **888/435-8665;** show times vary; tickets $55–$500), is also back for a second run of shows entitled *The Million Dollar Piano.* Sir Elton's canon of work is irreproachable: "Benny and the Jets," "Rocket Man," "Don't Let the Sun Go Down on Me." We could be here all day just listing his 5 decades' worth of hits. He's also a master showman; king of the bling and the tricked-out pianos like the one used in this production, complete with LED video panels built into it. Downsides (depending on your viewpoint) include a ballad-heavy playlist and some deep album cuts that only the most rabid of fans will recognize, along with less-energetic staging than we've seen in the past, but musically speaking, Elton John is a genius and this production proves why.

Country icons unite in **Reba, Brooks & Dunn: Together in Vegas** at Caesars Palace, 3570 Las Vegas Blvd. S. (www.thecolosseum.com; ℂ **800/745-3000;** show times vary; tickets $60–$205), a show exclusively created for Las Vegas. Reba McEntire collaborated with country duo Kix Brooks and Ronnie Dunn for this fun, 90-minute honky-tonk, packed with plenty of number one songs from both their extensive catalogs.

Finally, pop princess **Britney Spears** has taken up residency at Planet Hollywood, 3667 Las Vegas Blvd. S. (www.britneyspears.com; ℂ **866/919-7472;** show times vary; tickets $65–$255), making the revamped Theater for the Performing Arts, now the Axis Theater, her home until at least the end of 2017. The show is heavy on the type of special-effects staging and energetic choreography that Brit's concerts have been famous for, and leans, heavily on her roster of hits like "Oops, I Did it Again," "Toxic," and "Scream and Shout." That she lip-syncs her way through most of the show (sorry, "sings to track") should not be a surprise to anyone who has been paying attention.

created by Michael Jackson and the pop-art interpretive lens of Cirque du Soleil is a perfect union. Massive walls of video seem to envelop the audience while speakers, built into the seats, pump the timeless soundtrack of Jackson classics, remixed and remastered, directly into your brain. Each is presented with a set piece that ranges from evocative to stunning to giddy glee-inducing. "Bad" features a gang zooming in on zip lines and bouncing around on what amounts to a giant rubber band stretched across the stage; "Wanna Be Starting Something" showcases an acrobatic troupe using Jackson's iconic fedoras as twirling and twisting props; a mashup of "Human Nature" and "Never Can Say Goodbye" has a solo dancer doing expert human animation; "Billie Jean" evokes the lighted sidewalk in the music video with lighted suits on dancers performing in an otherwise darkened theater. By the time they get to the part where it "snows" on the audience, or the "Thriller" homage with zombies on trampolines, you'll want to stand up and cheer. And when the company dances with a so-realistic-it-hurts hologram of Jackson during "Man in the Mirror," you may have a lump in your throat. It's okay if you do. You need to be at least an appreciator of the music and also willing to overlook the subtle hagiography of the guy who created it to properly enjoy the show. But anyone who ever danced to a track of "Thriller"—which is pretty much everybody—will be, in a word, thrilled. Shows are held Friday through Tuesday at 7 and 9:30pm. At Mandalay Bay, 3950 Las Vegas Blvd. S. www.cirquedusoleil.com/one. © **877/632-7400** or 800/745-3000. Tickets $69–$180.

Cirque du Soleil's _Mystère_ ★★★   2013 marked the 20th anniversary of the first (and many say the best) of Cirque du Soleil's multiple Las Vegas productions. Although there have been some tweaks here and there and a few new acts were added in 2012, the show is pretty much the same as it always has been, which, in a word, is _stunning_. It's the closest to the original ethos of the Montréal-based company's unique circus experience, which focuses on feats of human strength and agility all wrapped up in performance art elements both absurd and surreal. The show features one unbelievable act after another (breathtakingly beautiful aerial maneuvers, seemingly boneless contortionists and acrobats), interspersed with Dadaist/_Commedia dell'arte_ clowns. All this and a giant snail! The thesaurus runs dry trying to describe it: dreamlike, suspenseful, erotic, funny, mesmerizing, and just lovely. At times, you might even find yourself moved to tears. I'm not ashamed to admit I was. Catch it Saturday through Wednesday at 7 and 9:30pm, or pop in for free dress rehearsals on Saturdays from 3 to 3:30pm or Sunday from 4:30 to 5pm. In Treasure Island, 3300 Las Vegas Blvd. S. www.cirquedusoleil.com/mystere. © **800/392-1999** or 702/894-7722. Tickets $69–$119, discounts for children under 12 based on availability.

Cirque du Soleil's _O_ ★★★   Franco Dragone, the director, gave Cirque's next smash hit its one-letter-name because it's a symbol for infinity; moreover, "O" is the phonetic pronunciation of "eau," the French word for water. Go to see O, and turn your attention from the stage for a moment and you'll find another reason for this odd-title: the saucer eyes and open mouths of the audience. This is simply the most astounding, profound, exhilarating, eye-poppingly

family-friendly SHOWS

Appropriate shows for kids, all described in this chapter, include:

- **Cirque du Soleil's KÀ,** at the MGM Grand (p. 206)
- **Cirque du Soleil's LOVE,** at The Mirage (p. 206)
- **Cirque du Soleil's Mystère,** at Treasure Island (p. 208)
- **David Copperfield,** at MGM Grand (p. 210)
- **Jeff Civillico: Comedy in Action,** at Flamingo (p. 212)
- **Mac King,** at Harrah's (p. 214)
- **Tournament of Kings,** at Excalibur (p. 218)

beautiful show in Vegas. I know that's a long chain of superlatives but if I had more space, I'd probably add a couple more. The show is centered around a 1.5-million-gallon pool, an engineering marvel: In seconds flat it transforms from pool to a shallow African watering hole, to a dry platform filled with dancers and acrobats, to a plateau with dancing fountains, or to a shimmering lake studded with islands and clown-steered houseboats. Synchronized swimmers plunge into its depths, staying submerged for what seems like ten minutes while above-the-water divers twist and knife in, as brilliantly costumed parades traverse the edges of the water. It's a spectacle like no other and does the impossible: It tops all of the other brilliant Cirque shows. Performances are held Wednesday through Sunday at 7:30 and 9:30pm. In Bellagio, 3600 Las Vegas Blvd. S. www.cirquedusoleil.com/o. (℃) **888/488-7111** or 702/796-9999. Tickets $132–$210.

Cirque du Soleil's Zumanity ★ Most controversial among Cirque's offerings, Zumanity is an erotic circus that celebrates sexuality in all its myriad incarnations: men with women, women with women, men with men, senior citizens with other seniors or with young folks, little people with Amazon-sized women, group sex, masturbation, you name it. Which means that when the two strong men are lifting one another in the classic "watch our veins pop out as we imitate Atlas" act, it's clear that there's a lot more than just lifting going on between these two. And when the aerialist hanging from the long silk ribbon is flinging herself around the stage, it's all about S&M and autoerotic asphyxiation. Those who are open-minded will find the Cirque magic here, as much of it is visually arresting. When I was last there, however, a number of people did walk out, so think honestly about what makes you squeamish before you book. Shows are held Friday through Tuesday at 7 and 9:30pm (show times vary seasonally). In New York–New York, 3790 Las Vegas Blvd. S. www.zumanity.com. (℃) **866/606-7111** or 702/740-6815. Tickets $88–$127. Only ages 18 and over admitted.

Criss Angel: Mindfreak Live! ★★ And for his next trick, rockstar illusionist Criss Angel transforms his original collaboration with Cirque du Soleil into a brand new show. Seven years into his contract with the human circus, Angel said goodbye to BeLIEve to return to the TV show that put him

bachelorette party SHOWS

Las Vegas gained its Sin City reputation for gambling, free-flowing alcohol, and entertainment that often involved big, feathered headdresses and bare breasts. But women also get their titillation in Sin City. Of the several beefcake revues in town, **Chippendales ★** at The Rio, 3700 W. Flamingo (www.chippendales.com; © **855/234-7469;** nightly 8:30pm with an additional 10:30pm show Thurs–Sat; tickets $50–$73) gets the most attention simply because of its well-known brand name. The show ticks all of the boxes: inhumanly handsome and fit men; fantasy fulfillment sketches featuring the guys as cowboys and firemen and the like; and an audience of (mostly) women who go quite, quite crazy. Bring earplugs because the screaming is non-stop.

Check the website for frequent guest appearances by "famous" hunks like Tyson Beckford, Ian Ziering or Antonio Sabato, Jr. (it's okay if you don't know who they are).

If we were the ones screaming for more skin, we'd probably do so for the hunks of **Thunder from Down Under ★★** at Excalibur, 3850 Las Vegas Blvd. S. Flamingo (www.thunderfromdownunder. com; © **702/597-7600;** Mon–Wed at 9pm; Thurs and Sun at 9 and 11pm; and Fri and Sat at 7, 9, and 11pm; tickets $51–$71). It's not that the guys are any hotter or the dancing any better, but this production has an edgier, anything-could-happen vibe that amps up the energy and the fun. Plus, the guys here are all Australian. Oh, those accents.

on the map, *Mindfreak.* As of press time, the show had yet to open officially, but sources told us that this version will be based on Angel's popular touring show, with those only-in-Vegas touches: fancy animated LED lighting, laser explosions, 3-D immersive effects that put audiences in virtual worlds and pyrotechnic landscapes, plus original illusions. While his first show opened with many hiccups, Angel has finally figured out how to be a presence on stage, so hopefully he won't have to go through those growing pains again. Although this is technically still a Cirque du Soleil–related production, there are very little (if any) Cirque-style theatrics, which is ultimately a good thing, considering they were the weakest part when the show first debuted. Shows are held Wednesday through Sunday at 7 and 9:30pm. In the Luxor, 3900 Las Vegas Blvd. S. www.cirquedusoleil.com. © **877/826-0255.** Tickets start at $59.

David Copperfield ★   Illusionists don't come any more illustrious than David Copperfield, who has been in the business for decades and has done everything from making the Statue of Liberty disappear to walking through the Great Wall of China. He has played semi-regular sets at the MGM Grand for years, but now is making the hotel his home with his name on the showroom. He mixes small, up-close magic like popping balloons "with his mind" and making a small piece of tissue dance up someone's arm, with larger stunts like making a car appear out of nowhere and causing an entire group from the audience to disappear (from the stage, not their seats). His laconic, "I'm so good at this I don't need to make a big deal about it" stage presence is a welcome relief from the hyper-dramatic theatrics that other magicians of his caliber often embrace, and Copperfield's ever-evolving act means that even if you have seen one of his TV specials, you'll witness new tricks here. Shows are held nightly at 7 and 9:30pm with an additional 4pm show on Saturday. In the MGM Grand, 3555 Las Vegas Blvd. S. www.davidcopperfield.com. ✆ **877/880-0880.** Tickets $83–$240.

Divas Las Vegas ★   Star impersonator Frank Marino hosted the similar *La Cage* for more than 2 decades up the street at the Riviera. This show at The LINQ isn't really all that different, in that it still features Marino as Joan Rivers in a series of Bob Mackie–esque gowns telling groan-worthy jokes and introducing a lineup of female impersonators. The "ladies" vary in quality and illusion: "Beyoncé" is done more for laughs and "Madonna" and "Dolly" are good, but "Céline Dion" is dead-on and "Lady Gaga" is frighteningly accurate (but hey, she kind of looks like a drag queen anyway). They lip-sync their way through hits, often accompanied by scantily clad male dancers, which gives you something to look at if the impersonator isn't up to snuff. Interesting side note: Marino's partner proposed on stage in 2013 on the couple's 20th anniversary. Shows are held nightly at 9:30pm. In The LINQ, 3535 Las Vegas Blvd. S. www.thelinq.com. ✆ **888/777-7664.** Tickets $27–$101.

Donny and Marie ★   Proving that a good fainting spell on *Dancing with the Stars* is worth a lot more than you'd expect, the wholesome brother-sister duo of Donny and Marie has made a comeback on the stages of Las Vegas, performing their personal blend of music, comedy, and variety at the Flamingo. The show is a lot more fun than it has any right to be as long as you go in with your tongue placed firmly in cheek and aren't flabbergasted by the $260 top-end ticket price. The duo is doing fewer shows each year here to give them room to perform elsewhere, but this is still their home base. Shows are

BROADWAY & beyond

The opening of the **Smith Center for the Performing Arts** (p. 162) in 2012 changed the scope of entertainment for Las Vegas in dramatic ways. Despite the numerous showrooms, arenas, and theaters in this town, the closest thing to a performing arts stage was a 40-year-old concert hall in the middle of a shopping mall, adjacent to a casino that occasionally hosted a third-string Broadway touring show.

Now that the Smith Center has arrived, there is a legitimate home for cultural pursuits of all types, including the Las Vegas Philharmonic; in-demand Broadway touring companies like *Book of Mormon* and *A Gentleman's Guide to Love and Murder*—they're even getting

Hamilton in 2017; a New York Stage series with concerts from Broadway luminaries like Patty Lupone and Audra McDonald; a monthly jazz-tinged set from longtime Vegas showman Clint Holmes (which is one of the best shows and best values in town); a speaker series that has hosted legends like Carol Burnett to Alan Alda; and a host of other concerts from classical to contemporary to choral and more. This is all in a multi-venue facility that has become the envy of cities around the globe.

Visit the Smith Center website at www.thesmithcenter.com or call ✆ **702/749-2000** for information on shows that will be playing when you are in town.

held Tuesday through Saturday at 7:30pm. In the Flamingo, 3555 Las Vegas Blvd. S. www.flamingolasvegas.com. ✆ **855/234-7469.** Tickets $95–$260.

Human Nature: *Jukebox* ★★   It might have been crooning Motown hits that put Australian quartet Human Nature on the map, but after a long run on the Strip, the other guys from Down Under have expanded their repertoire with Jukebox (which also happens to be the name of their platinum-selling album). Their tight harmonies are delightful throwbacks to the era when the Miracles, the Supremes, the Four Tops, and the Jackson 5 ruled the charts, but they whip audiences into the 21st century with just as exciting pop covers of Taylor Swift, Bruno Mars and The Beatles. Make no mistake, Human Nature started as a boy band (though at this age they really are a man band), so you'll also be delighted by renditions of other all-male groups like The Beach Boys, Boyz II Men and Backstreet Boys. Save your quarters. This is a jukebox where you won't want to skip any songs. Shows are Tuesday through Saturday at 7pm. At The Venetian/Palazzo, 3355 Las Vegas Blvd. S. www.humannaturelive.com. ✆ **866/641-7469** or 702/414-9000. Tickets $49–$118.

Jabbawockeez: *JREAMZ* ★★   The shtick here is that each of the crew of hip-hop dancers is totally covered with clothes and serene blank masks, so issues of race, gender, and physical perfection are left at the door. It's interesting and sporadically amusing as they use their bodies to communicate everything from lust to disgust, but the real benefit is that it allows the group to function as a single unit; almost like a multicell organism, only one that pops and locks. Their show's latest incarnation, in a new home at MGM Grand, is set on a smaller stage, which may seem confining for their acrobatic dance style, but the addition of video mapping and intricate lighting effects makes the stage as big a part of the show as the dancers. Shows are Thursday through Monday, 7 and 9:30pm. In the MGM Grand, 3799 Las Vegas Blvd. S. www.jbwkz.com. ✆ **702/891-3577.** Tickets $55–$120.

Jeff Civillico: *Comedy in Action* ★★   Family-friendly shows are few and far between in Vegas, especially ones that can be as entertaining for adults as they are for children. This one hits both of those targets with kids wowed by the manic-energy juggling of everything from bowling balls to chainsaws, and grown-ups appreciating that it is all presented with Civillico's lightning-quick wit and sardonic patter. Some of the stunts are wow-worthy—he was a world-champion juggler by the time he was 15, after all—and some of his jokes are so sly that it'll take you a moment to fully appreciate how funny they are. Lots of audience participation gives the show an off-the-cuff vibe and will keep it fresh for repeat viewings. With tickets starting at just over $40, this is a great entertainment value even before you add in all the discounts and bonus offers on other show tickets and meals that come with admission. Shows are daily Saturdays through Wednesdays at 5:30pm. In Flamingo, 3555 Las Vegas Blvd. S. www.flamingolasvegas.com. ✆ **702/794-3296.** Tickets $40–$104.

Jersey Boys Vegas ★★   Between 1962 and 1975, Frankie Valli and the Four Seasons racked up an astonishingly long string of catchy, well-crafted pop hits that are as beloved as any in pop music. These time-tested songs are the central draw of the massively popular, Tony Award–winning (for Best Musical) *Jersey Boys.* But this is far more than a rote musical revue, or just another re-creation of a popular oldies act, as anyone who saw the film now knows. It's a real musical play, with a compelling street-to-suite storyline, a fair share of drama, and enough humor and uplift to satisfy both the theater veteran and the vacationing family (with a mild warning for some salty, Jersey-esque language). A dazzlingly visual production that crackles with energy and shines with precision stagecraft, *Jersey Boys* has already had an enthusiastic post-Broadway life, including here with its second incarnation in Vegas at Paris Las Vegas after several years of sold-out performances at the Palazzo up the street. Performances are Tuesday through Sunday at 7pm. In Paris Las Vegas, 3655 Las Vegas Blvd. S. www.jerseyboysinfo.com/vegas. ℂ **702/777-7776.** Tickets $59–$200.

Legends in Concert ★   After more than 25 years as a nighttime show at hotels like the Imperial Palace and Harrah's, this parade of faux celebrities made the move to afternoons at the Flamingo in 2013. The only real difference is that it is daylight when you walk out of the showroom. Performers vary depending on when you see the show; you may catch "Janet Jackson" and "Diana Ross," or you could get "Lady Gaga" and "Prince," but you will almost always get "Elvis." Unlike other impersonator shows, the singing is live (no lip-syncing, even when "Britney" is performing), which can enhance the illusion or destroy it. Some performers succeed more in appearance and others do better with vocal mimicry, and while most are at least passable, there are a few that will leave you wondering if he or she is the real thing playing a joke on the audience. Don't scoff; Ellen DeGeneres did that very thing during a 2008 show and captured the audience reactions ("didn't look anything like her") for her daytime talkfest. Shows are daily 9:30pm, with additional shows on Tuesday, Thursday and Friday at 4pm, and Sunday and Monday at 7:30pm. In the Flamingo Las Vegas, 3555 Las Vegas Blvd. S. www.flamingolasvegas.com. ℂ **855/234-7469.** Tickets $53–$82.

Le Rêve ★★   Challenged from the get-go, thanks to a decision to base this Cirque-like show around a stage of water, thus prompting inevitable comparisons with _O_ down the street, this production has received major revamps, both in staging and choreography. By and large, the choices—particularly to get revered avant-garde choreographer and MOMIX-genius Moses Pendleton to take over the choreography (thus increasing the presence of dance)—have been good ones, and this production is a worthy competitor to its rival. Set in a dramatic theater in the round, the "stage" at the center of the bowl-shaped room can be solid, a shallow pool, or deep enough to dive into from what seem like insane heights—proven in a gasp-inducing moment. Certainly the acrobatic, diving, aerial work, and ballroom dance is as good as what you'll see in any Cirque show, but it is the moody atmospherics and visually arresting staging that really set the show apart. The wordless storyline concerns a woman considering love but needing to face her own demons and past as she wanders through a dreamscape of betrayal, passion, fear, and ultimately salvation. Provocative moments include a sultry tango performed in ankle deep water and a set piece involving performers descending from the rafters, limp and motionless until they hit the water and spring to life. The latter ends with some of them being jerked back up into the smoky ceiling, screaming as they go. It, like much of the rest of the show, is dark and a bit disconcerting at times, but in a good way, staying with you long after you leave the showroom. Glimpse behind-the-scenes action without ever leaving the theater with a VIP package that gives you your own theater box, bottle of Champagne and video screens of the underwater action as the show happens. Avid divers can opt for a package that includes the VIP experience, plus a backstage tour that takes you not only from the deep pools to the towering dive platform, but also into the water itself for a SCUBA training session guided by the Le Rêve diving team. Shows are held Friday through Tuesday at 7 and 9:30pm. In Wynn Las Vegas, 3131 Las Vegas Blvd. S. www.wynnlas vegas.com. ✆ **888/320-7110.** Tickets $105–$205. Only ages 13 and over admitted.

Mac King ★★★   The best daytime show, in fact one of the most exceptional shows in Vegas period, the Mac King Show is that rare breed of entertainment that's not only appropriate for all ages, it's actually a show that junior, grandma, and the hot date you met in Vegas will enjoy. A comedian with a big talent for magic—King is the only magician who was asked to appear on all five of NBC's "World's Greatest Magic Show" specials—King looks like a refugee from _The Music Man,_ wearing an old-fashioned plaid suit and a goofy aw-shucks expression. His tricks are oddball illusions (featuring fellows in bear suits, a "cloak of invisibility," and disappearing heads), which he performs with a generous dose of whimsy and intelligence. If there's any justice in the world, he'll soon be headlining his own evening show. He's that good. Shows are held Tuesday through Saturday at 1 and 3pm. In Harrah's, 3475 Las Vegas Blvd. S. www.mackingshow.com. ✆ **800/427-7247** or 702/369-5222. Tickets $32–$43.

Million Dollar Quartet ★★   Musical history was made on a chilly night in 1956 in Nashville when Elvis Presley, Johnny Cash, Jerry Lee Lewis, and Carl Perkins wandered into a studio at the famed Sun Records and had an

PENN & TELLER'S TOP 10 THINGS ONE SHOULD NEVER DO IN A VEGAS magic show

Penn & Teller have been exercising their acerbic wit and magical talents in numerous forums together for more than 25 years, and their show at the Rio is one of Vegas's best and most intelligent. We must confess that we couldn't get the quieter half of the duo, Teller, to cough up a few words, but the more verbose Penn Jillette was happy to share.

1. Costume yourself in a gray business suit totally lacking in rhinestones, animal patterns, Mylar, capes, bell-bottoms, shoulder pads, and top hats.
2. Wear your hair in any style that could *not* be described as "feathered" or "spiked."
3. Use really good live jazz music instead of canned, sound-alike, cheesy, rip-off, fake pop "music."
4. Cruelly (but truthfully) make fun of your siblings in the magic brotherhood.
5. Do the dangerous tricks on each other instead of anonymous show women with aftermarket breasts and/or endangered species.
6. Toss a cute little magic bunny into a cute little chipper-shredder.
7. Open your show by explaining *and* demonstrating how other magicians on the Strip do their most amazing tricks, and then do that venerable classic of magic, "the Cups and Balls," with transparent plastic cups.
8. Treat the audience as if they have a brain in their collective head.
9. Allow audience members to sign real bullets, load them into real guns, and fire those bullets into your face.
10. Bleed.

(You will find many of these "don'ts" in the Penn & Teller show at the Rio All-Suite Hotel & Casino.)

impromptu jam session. This pared-down version of the hit Broadway musical imagines what that night might have been like with rock-'n'-roll classics like "Hound Dog," "Whole Lotta Shakin' Goin' On," and "I Walk the Line" driving the barely there storyline. The actors are excellent stewards of both the sounds and affectations of the legends they are embodying and bring down the house with their top-quality musicianship. Shows are held Wednesday through Friday at 8pm, and Sunday and Monday at 5:30pm. At Harrah's Las Vegas, 3475 Las Vegas Blvd. S. www.mdqvegas.com. © **888/746-7784** or 702/369-5111. Tickets $57–$79.

Olivia Newton-John ★★   From her "I Honestly Love You" beginnings through her "You're the One That I Want" and "Physical" superstardom and beyond, pop singer Olivia Newton-John puts on a terrific show that is more than just a retrospective of her career, it's a soundtrack to a lot of people's lives. She still sounds and looks great and could teach some of today's pop stars a thing or two about showmanship. She's made her latest go-round "Summer Nights," so she's only in the showroom from July through August, with show times (usually) Tuesday through Saturday at 7:30pm. In the Flamingo, 3555 Las Vegas Blvd. S. www.flamingolasvegas.com. © **855/234-7469.** Tickets $75–$350.

Penn & Teller ★★★   The most intelligent show in Vegas, as these two— magicians? illusionists? truth-tellers? BS artists? geniuses?—put on 90

headliner VENUES

Pretty much every singer worth their Twitter followings makes a stop in Vegas on their national tour. While the big acts usually play the big arenas, some go for the more intimate rooms so you may get a chance to see your favorites up close and in person. Major headliner showrooms in Vegas include the following:

o The Cosmopolitan of Las Vegas, 3708 Las Vegas Blvd. S. (www.cosmopolitanlasvegas.com; ✆ **877/551-7778**) has two venues, the laid-back, open-air **Boulevard Pool** overlooking the Las Vegas Strip, and the **Chelsea,** which is a surprisingly intimate venue considering the fact that it can accommodate more than 3,000 people. This converted ballroom feels less like that and more like an industrial-chic play space complete with reclaimed wood accents, subway tile, and a cheeky attitude perfect for the hotel in which it is located. Both draw big names including Lorde, Adele, and Bruno Mars.

o The 4,000-seat **Colosseum,** in Caesars Palace, 3570 Las Vegas Blvd. S. (www.caesarspalace.com;

✆ **866/227-5938**) has been home to extended runs for big-name artists like Céline Dion, Elton John, Shania Twain, Rod Stewart, and more, with shorter stands by big-name singing and comedy acts like Janet Jackson and Jerry Seinfeld.

o Hard Rock Hotel's **The Joint,** 4455 Paradise Rd. (www.hardrockhotel. com; ✆ **800/693-7625** or 702/693-5000) was rebuilt in 2009 and now holds 4,000 people for rock concerts and special events. The smaller **Vinyl** club is like a rock-'n'-roll haven on the Sunset Strip.

o The **House of Blues** can hold several hundred people for smaller rock and blues concerts and their weekly gospel brunch (in Mandalay Bay, 3950 Las Vegas Blvd. S.; www.hob.com; ✆ **877/632-7400** or 702/632-7600).

o **Brooklyn Bowl** opened in 2014 and has cornered the market on the indy-rock market for Vegas. The concert venue is intimate and relaxed; a perfect place to catch the general-admission shows from artists both

minutes of, yes, magic and juggling, but also acerbic comedy, mean stunts, and quiet beauty. Looking like two characters out of Dr. Seuss, big, loud Penn and smaller, silent Teller (to reduce them to their basic characteristics) perform magic, reveal the secrets behind a few major magic tricks, discuss why magic is nothing but a bunch of lies, and then turn around and show why magic is as lovely an art form as any other. We won't tell you much about the various tricks and acts for fear of ruining the illusions, but watching Teller fish money out of an empty glass aquarium or play with shadows is to belie Penn's earlier caveats about learning how tricks are done—it doesn't ruin the wonder of it, not at all, nor the serenity that settles in your Vegas-sensory-overloaded brain. Hang around the lobby after the show for a free meet-and-greet, something other Vegas headliners charge a hefty fee for. Shows are held Saturday through Wednesday at 9pm. In the Rio All-Suite Hotel & Casino, 3700 W. Flamingo Rd. www.riolasvegas.com. ✆ **888/746-7784.** Tickets $87–$97. Only ages 5 and over admitted.

Recycled Percussion ★ If, for whatever reason, you are averse to loud noises and you think going to a show with the word "percussion" in the title edgy (Jane's Addiction, Fishbone, and so on) and safe—hey, where have you been, Steve Winwood? (at the LINQ, 3545 Las Vegas Blvd. S., Suite 22; www.brooklynbowl.com; ✆ 702/862-2695).

o **Mandalay Bay Events Center** seats 12,000 people for arena-style concert tours and indoor sporting events (in Mandalay Bay, 3950 Las Vegas Blvd. S.; www.mandalaybay.com; ✆ 877/632-7400 or 702/632-7580).

o **MGM Grand Garden Events Arena** can hold over 17,000 people and is home to big-name concert tours and events (in the MGM Grand, 3799 Las Vegas Blvd. S.; www.mgmgrand.com; ✆ 800/929-1111 or 702/891-7777).

o **The Orleans Showroom** seats 9,500 people and often has concerts, ice hockey, traveling circuses, and other events (in the Orleans, 4500 W. Tropicana Ave.; www.orleanscasino.com; ✆ 800/675-3267).

o **The Pearl Theater** is a three-level venue that seats up to 2,500

people for pop, rock, R&B, and comedy concerts (in the Palms, 4321 W. Flamingo Rd.; www.palms.com; ✆ 866/942-7770).

o **Sam Boyd Stadium** is a 36,800-seat stadium that features big concerts and sporting events (7000 E. Russell Rd.; www.ticketmaster.com; ✆ 800/745-3000).

o **The Smith Center for the Performing Arts** has a 2,000-seat concert hall for big stage shows (including a Broadway series), a 300-seat Cabaret Jazz theater, and a 200-seat theater for smaller productions. See p. 162 for more details (361 Symphony Park Ave.; ✆ 702/614-0109).

o **The Thomas and Mack Center** is a 19,522-seat arena that hosts concerts and sporting events (UNLV Campus; www.ticketmaster.com; ✆ 800/745-3000).

o **The Fremont Country Club** is Downtown Las Vegas' only real concert venue, hosting rock shows and other special events. (601 E. Fremont St.; ✆ 702/382-6601).

is not a good idea, we are here to counsel you otherwise. This quartet of cacophony-makers will bust out a beat on anything they can get their hands on, from real drum sets to improvised ones made from plastic buckets or, in one stunning set-piece, their own bodies. As if that's not enough, they also pass out metal pots and drumsticks to the audience before the show and encourage sonic mayhem throughout. It's a bit loud, is what we're saying. But the four lads are insanely talented, and their cheeky, oddball sense of humor plays well. Be on the lookout for a "totally random cookie break," which lives up to the random part of its name in a delightful way. Shows are held Tuesday, Wednesday, Friday and Saturday at 5:30pm. In Planet Hollywood, 3667 Las Vegas Blvd. S. www.planethollywoodresort.com. ✆ 866/919-7472. Tickets $60–$70.

Rock of Ages ★ If you ever wondered what you'd get if you crossed a corny, over-the-top movie musical from the '40s with a heavy metal music video from the '80s, it would look a lot like this silly confection of a jukebox revue. The plot, about the lives and loves of a group of people affiliated with an imperiled Sunset Strip rock club, is kind of stupid (and knows it) and the music, from Journey, Bon Jovi, Pat Benatar, and other hair band icons, is often bastardized to the point where it is unrecognizable as the "classic rock" it occasionally is. But there is something undeniably infectious about its throw-everything-at-the-wall energy and gamely talented cast. The move to the Rio took the show out of a stuffy theater and into a showroom, so it feels more like seeing a rock show in a club. Shows are nightly at 7:30pm. In the Rio All-Suite Hotel & Casino, 3700 W. Flamingo Rd. www.riolasvegas.com. ✆ **888/746-7784.** Tickets $59–$149.

Terry Fator ★ *America's Got Talent* winner Fator is no Susan Boyle, that's for sure, but his shtick—ventriloquism meets impersonation—is entertaining. The format of the 80-minute show is fairly standard: A series of puppets joins Fator on stage, and they proceed to do a song or three impersonating a famous voice. Winston the Turtle does a serviceable Justin Bieber and a very good Kermit the Frog (which is weird if you think too long about it—turtle, frog, felt), while Walter the Cowboy kills on a Brooks & Dunn song—or rather Fator does, of course. Even the less-than-perfect impressions are still impressive considering the fact that he's doing it all with his mouth closed. Fator's overall demeanor is a little too laconic, especially when he doesn't have a piece of felt on his hand, but the show mostly hits its middle-of-the-road target on the bull's-eye, offering up some decent chuckles and a nice night of music. Try to get a seat in the center section, otherwise you'll spend most of your time watching the giant TV screens instead of the guy (and his friends) on stage. Shows are Monday through Thursday at 7:30pm. At The Mirage, 3400 Las Vegas Blvd. S. www.mirage.com. ✆ **800/963-9634** or 702/792-7777. Tickets $65–$163.

Tournament of Kings ★ "Lords and Ladies, Wizards and Wenches, hasten thee to thy throne, for the battle is about to commence." Yes, that's how they talk at this dinner show—like a Renaissance fair, only with better production values. There's nothing different here than you'll find at one of those Medieval Times chain restaurants, with a decent dinner and lots of knights-in-shining-armor–style theatrics. It's not *Game of Thrones* (now THAT would be an interesting Vegas show), so it's one of the few family-friendly options in town; younger kids will like it, teenagers will be too jaded, and adults will probably be bored. Shows are Monday and Friday at 6pm and Wednesday, Thursday, Saturday, and Sunday at 6 and 8:30pm. In Excalibur, 3850 Las Vegas Blvd. S. www.excalibur.com. ✆ **800/933-1334** or 702/597-7600. Tickets $44–$58.

V: The Ultimate Variety Show ★ Although not as big-budget as the Cirque productions, V can still offer some big thrills if you happen to see it on the right night. It's a collection of variety acts that could include acrobats, magicians, musicians, dancers, and more, but since the acts vary, so does the quality. Check to see if the thrilling roller-skating couple Vittorio and Jenny Aratas are on the roster. They only do 5 minutes of a 70-minute show, but their hold-your-breath stunts performed mere inches from the audience will make whatever you have to watch in the other 65 minutes totally worth it. Shows are nightly at 7 and 8:30pm. In the Miracle Mile Shops at Planet Hollywood Resort, 3667 Las Vegas Blvd. S. www.vtheshow.com. ✆ **866/932-1818** or 702/260-7200. Tickets $70–$90.

Vegas! The Show ★★★   What would happen if you took the best bits of classic Las Vegas entertainment from the last 70 years or so and put it in one package? That's the basic question behind this loving look back at the ghosts of the Sin City stages, and the answer is this: It would be a heck of a lot of fun. A gateway to the days of Vegas past, with beautiful showgirls in skimpy costumes and big headdresses; headliners like the Rat Pack and Elvis; variety acts (tap dancing! magic!); dancing; singing; even Elton John and implosions. The show plays like a history channel special done by Busby Berkeley. The singing and dancing are among the best you'll find in Vegas, which may very well make you long for the days before those French Canadian acrobats took over the showrooms. Shows are nightly at 7 and 9pm. In the Miracle Mile Shops at Planet Hollywood Resort, 3667 Las Vegas Blvd. S. www.vegas theshow.com. ✆ **866/932-1818** or 702/260-7200. Tickets $80–$100.

THE BAR SCENE

In addition to the venues listed below, you might check out the incredible nighttime view at the bars and lounges atop the **Stratosphere Casino Hotel & Tower** (p. 70) or midway up on the **Eiffel Tower Ride** (p. 154)—nothing beats them, except for maybe the more up-close view of the bar adjacent to the 23rd-floor lobby at the **Mandarin Oriental** (p. 49). The floor-to-ceiling windows make you feel like you're floating in the middle of the Strip, especially at night.

Bars & Cocktail Lounges

Atomic Liquors ★   Las Vegas history is on glorious display in this reinvention of a classic watering hole. The building dates back to 1945 and is the oldest freestanding bar in the city. It got its name in 1952 when people used to go up on the roof to watch the aboveground nuclear blasts from the Atomic Test Site north of Las Vegas and became a go-to spot for everyone from the Rat Pack to Barbra Streisand, who has her own memorial stool at the bar. Now fully restored after years of decline, there's a classic neon sign out front and a big bar and plenty of comfy seating inside, plus nearly two dozen microbrews, a craft cocktail menu (featuring some classic "Atomic" concoctions), and a variety of events to keep things interesting. *One note:* This is one Vegas bar that is *not* open 24 hours. Atomic Liquors is open Monday through Wednesday from 4pm until 2am; Thursday from 2pm until 3am, Friday from 2pm until 4am; Saturday from noon until 4am; and Sunday from noon until 2am. 917 Fremont St. (at 9th St.) www.atomic.vegas. ✆ **702/349-2283.** No cover except for special events.

Backstage Bar & Billiards ★   Intended to be the actual backstage area for Fremont Country Club, local producers and musicians transformed it into an intimate, cool hang out space, complete with rock paraphernalia, band equipment crates from Anvil Cases as furnishings, and 8 decades worth of DJ and turntable history as decor. It's basically where you want to be for an afterparty with the band. Live performances by mostly punk rock bands are a big draw for the tatted-and-pierced set, as are cheap beers and lack of pretentious

Las Vegas Nightlife

Martin Luther King Blvd
95
515 93 95
↑ (1½ miles)
1
2
3
Fremont East Entertainment District
4
Fremont Street Experience
5
Fremont St
Maryland Pkwy
DOWNTOWN
Av
Grand Central Pkwy
Bonneville
Main St
Casino Ctr Blvd
Las Vegas Blvd
Alta Dr
Rancho Dr
Charleston
Blvd
6
7
ARTS DISTRICT
Las
Main St
Las Vegas Monorail
Free monorail
Oakey Blvd
Wyoming Av
8
Oakey Blvd
Drai's **24**
Stratosphere
9
Sahara Av
SLS Las Vegas
10
Karen Av
Palace Station
11
Circus Circus
Riviera
NORTH STRIP
12
Desert Inn Rd
Industrial Rd
Paradise Rd
Las Vegas Convention Center
Desert Inn Rd
13
Fashion Show Mall
Encore Las Vegas
14
WYNN GOLF AND COUNTRY CLUB
Wynn Las Vegas
Spring Mtn. Rd
Twain Av
Treasure Island
15
16
The Palazzo
17
The Venetian
Sands Av
Mirage
18
Twain Av
19
Rio All-Suite
21
Forum Shops
20 Harrah's
Caesars Palace
23 LINQ
22
MID-STRIP
24
Flamingo
Gold Coast
Flamingo Rd
Silver Sevens
Palms
25
Bally's
26
27 Paris
Bellagio
Hard Rock Hotel & Casino
Cosmopolitan
28
Planet Hollywood
Harmon Av
29
Aria
Monte Carlo
MGM Grand
30 31
32
33
34
New York–New York
Koval
Paradise Rd
Tropicana Av
Excalibur
35
Tropicana
Luxor
SOUTH STRIP
36
McCARRAN INTERNATIONAL AIRPORT
✈
Delano Las Vegas
37
(½ mile) Mandalay Bay
Four Seasons
38
↓

0   0.5 mi
0   0.5 km

attitude. A little rough around the edges compared to the other wannabe posh bars in the area, but it wouldn't be punk rock any other way. It's open nightly from 7pm until late. 601 E. Fremont St. (at 6th St.) www.backstagebarandbilliards. com. ✆ **702/382-2227.** No cover except for special events.

Beauty Bar ★   Take a vintage beauty parlor and add cocktails: that's the formula that's been so popular it's turned into a hipster chain with outlets in New York City, Chicago, and Los Angeles. At Las Vegas' Downtown version, you get a lot of diversity thanks to its location near Fremont Street Experience. During the day, it's a more chill experience where you can get a decent manicure and pedicure whilst sipping on fruity cocktails, but the evening features live bands and DJs on both its indoor and outdoor stages. It's open nightly from 9pm until 4am. 517 E. Fremont St. www.thebeautybar.com. ✆ **702/598-1965.** No cover except for special events.

Beerhaus ★   The stretch of real estate between the new T-Mobile Arena and Las Vegas Boulevard is intended to coax pedestrians to pause from traipsing up and down the Strip. And there's no better way to keep tourists in one spot than giving them somewhere to drink, preferably outdoors and with games. Billing itself as a "modern American beer hall" Beerhaus is where you might fondly relive your college days, complete with live cover bands, foosball, ping pong, cornhole and shuffleboard. But at two beers averaging around $22, these are definitely not college bar prices. The patio seating allows guests to soak up the sun while people watching. Large garage doors open between the main dining room and the elements, in the event you'd rather soak up the air conditioning while still eyeing the crowds. One more detail isn't exactly obvious: servers only serve drinks, so if you want to order food—nothing fancy, bar bites like pretzels with cheese, cheese-filled brats, etc—it's served fast casual style. Order from the bar and they'll give you a buzzer to pick up your snacks when it's ready. It's open Sunday through Thursday from 11am until 1am and Friday and Saturday until 2am. In The Park, 3784 Las Vegas Blvd. S. www.theparkvegas.com. ✆ **702/693-7275.** No cover.

Beer Park ★   Based on the name, you'd think that this second beer garden to open on the Strip this year would be at The Park, but surprise! This one is on the rooftop of the Paris hotel, and produced by the king of beers itself, Budweiser. There's way more than just the classic red label beer being served from the more than 36 taps and additional 60 or so bottle and can selections. Not surprisingly, most are Budweiser products, even those you that give the appearance of being craft beer labels (or once were craft beers only to be bought up by the likes of Anheuser Busch), like Goose Island, Shock Top and Firestone Walker. Nevada local Joseph James brewery does make an appearance, though. As far as outdoor beer drinking vibes go, compared to the one across the street, the Beer Park is less yuppie and more sports-oriented, while giant Jenga and burgers from the grill make it feel more like an evening in your own backyard. It's open daily from 11am until late. In Paris Las Vegas, 3655 Las Vegas Blvd. S. www.beerpark.com. ✆ **702/444-4500.** No cover.

The Commonwealth ★★   Part speakeasy, part neighborhood bar, Commonwealth has earned itself a reputation as one of the true hot spots to come out of the revitalization of this stretch of Fremont Street. The 6,000-square-foot, swanky, multi-level space has a pre-Prohibition era vibe, with a mix of vintage and modern artwork (peacocks are a big deal here) and stiff cocktails. The main floor is a bustling mix of folks from the neighborhood and tourists who found their way here from the Fremont Street Experience, while the rooftop patio is one of the few outdoor spaces comfortable to hang out above the hubbub of the main drag. Cocktail aficionados should secure themselves an invite into the Laundry Room, the true speakeasy located in back of the main floor (just ask and they'll walk you back there). This intimate room allows for a one-on-one session with one of Commonwealth's expert mixologists who are at the ready to dazzle you with custom concoctions based on your tastes. Open Tuesday through Saturday 7pm until late. 525 E. Fremont St. (at 6th St.) www.commonwealthlv.com. ✆ **702/798-7000.** No cover except for special events.

Dino's Lounge ★★   This dive bar on Las Vegas Boulevard marks the divide between the glitzy part of the Strip and grittier Downtown, and chances are you've breezed right past it. Which, if you ask the locals perched on stools at the bar, is just fine with them. The family-run watering hole has been an unofficial landmark since 1962, as the city has grown around it. If you've ever wondered what a bona fide locals bar looks like in Las Vegas, this is it, complete with smoky atmosphere, video poker nestled into counters, cheap, no-frills drinks, cold beer, and not a lick of sunlight, even in the daylight hours. Come in often enough and you've got a shot to be nominated to by bartenders to be Drunk of the Month. On weekends you'll find some of the best karaoke in town, hosted by a guy named Danny whose pipes are so good, you'll wonder why he doesn't just sing the whole show himself. The kiosk in the parking lot is a recent addition, having served as an incubator for several dining concepts that have gone on to become brick-and-mortar restaurants. Whoever's cooking in the kiosk when you're there is bound to be putting out great food, which you can eat inside the bar. Dino's is open daily 24 hours. 1516 Las Vegas Blvd. S. (at Wyoming Ave.) www.dinoslv.com. ✆ **702/382-3894.** No cover.

Double Down Saloon ★★   Leave the multiple-ingredient cocktails to the Strip. Here you're going to be listening to live punk, rock, or blues bands while pounding PBR and shots of Ass Juice, a fruity, if not unappealing-looking mystery concoction that the bar has been selling for 2 decades. If the idea of Ass Juice isn't your idea of a good time at a place whose motto is "You puke, you clean," then try their other house specialty, the bacon martini, which Double Down claims to have invented. It's like every other punk bar you've been to in other cities, with psychedelic murals, second hand furniture, weird videos playing on the TVs, and a very punk rock jukebox, but this one just happens to be the antithesis of the city surrounding it. The Double Down is open daily 24 hours. 4640 Paradise Rd. (at Naples Dr.). www.doubledownsaloon.com. ✆ **702/791-5775.** No cover except for special events.

Fizz ★★★   The schtick here is that you're being invited into one of the city's biggest power couple's circles: Elton John and David Furnish (he's the creative director here, and John is often performing his show at the Colosseum next door). So this narrow, elegant champagne bar is decorated with photographs by international artists such as Guy Bourdin, Denise De La Rue, and Guido Mocafico. Never heard of them? That's ok, Furnish and John have, and they've shared their excellent taste with you. Bubbles are a must, of course, with vintages and prices that range from the accessible to the gasp-inducing (the Fizz Deluxe cocktail, a twist on the classic French 75 is $2,500 a flute. And for that price, yes, there is gold in it). You can even snack as Elton and David do, with a menu prepared by the couple's private chef. Upstairs, when you're hunting for the bathroom, if there's a chance to glimpse into Elton's private VIP booth, do so. The bar is open nightly from 5pm until 2am. At Caesars Palace, 3570 Las Vegas Blvd. S. www.fizzlv.com. ✆ **702/776-3200.** No cover.

The Griffin ★★   This is one of the few bars you can walk into in Las Vegas that doesn't feel like Las Vegas at all. The strong brickwork and arched ceiling inside offer that post-industrial feel you'd get in old-school-turned-hipster bars in Chicago or New York, while two fire pits give it an almost Aspen-vibe (the lack of video poker machines inset into the bar also help). There are better mixology programs in the surrounding bars, but this is where you'd come to relax, maybe have a real conversation with real people, and get out of that Vegas mindset, if only for a little while. Live bands and DJs play on weekends. It's open Monday through Friday from 5pm until 3am; Saturday from 7pm until 3am; and Sunday from 8pm until 3am. 511 E. Fremont St. ✆ **702/382-0577.** No cover except for special events.

Hogs & Heifers Saloon ★   Hot, midriff-revealing chicks dancing on the bars, screaming at you with bullhorns, cold cans of PBR, all with a collection of bras hanging above your head: that's the scene at Hogs & Heifers and it's not my idea of a good time, but I may be in the minority. This outlet is part of a chain started in New York City, where the original outpost of Hogs (as in motorcycles) & Heifers was born and inspired a movie and a competing outfit called Coyote Ugly. It's open daily, usually 1pm to 6am (call to check, as hours vary by month). 201 N. 3rd St. (btw. Ogden and Stewart aves., 1 block from the Fremont Street Experience). www.hogsandheifers.com. ✆ **702/676-1457.** No cover.

O'Sheas ★   With its beer pong and omnipresent host Mr. Lucky (see below), O'Sheas is like a fraternity bar that celebrates St. Patrick's Day year-round. When its home, the stretch between the former Imperial Palace and Flamingo, was imploded to make way for The LINQ promenade, many wondered if that was the end of the rowdy casino/bar. Fortunately, Mr. Lucky (a little person dressed as a leprechaun) and O'Sheas have been reinstated to their rightful spot on the Strip. The current O'Sheas is smaller and slightly less seedy than the original, but the now 5,000 square feet is still the place for cheap beer (they've got more than 50 brews), some gaming, and those always-popular daily beer pong tournaments. Plus its access to The LINQ and High Roller make it a great place to pre-game before taking a ride on the observation wheel. The bar is open 24 hours a day. In The LINQ, 3535 Las Vegas Blvd. S., www.thelinq.com. © **702/697-2711.** No cover.

Park on Fremont ★   While Commonwealth (p. 222), Vanguard (below), and Downtown Cocktail Room (p. 233) are more sophisticated drinking establishments, Griffin and this spot are casual watering holes, which is perfect considering its proximity to the Fremont Street Experience. Rest assured, there are fine cocktails on the menu at Park, along with a decent bar food menu (Sunday brunch, complete with stacked Bloody Marys is a busy time), but Park is a much more relaxed, come-as-you-are spot to throw back some brewskies. The front patio offers great people watching on Fremont Street, while behind the bar is another, walled-in backyard that you'd kill to find at your own neighborhood bar, complete with a fireplace, murals, and artwork from local artisans. And tucked behind that is another secret alcove with a seesaw. It is called a "park," after all. Open Monday through Wednesday from 4pm to midnight, and Thursday and Sunday from 11am until midnight and Friday and Saturday from 11am until 3am. 506 Fremont St. (at Las Vegas Blvd.). www.parkonfremont.com. © **702/834-3160.** No cover.

Peppermill Fireside Lounge ★★   Austin Powers would be in his element at the Peppermill Fireside Lounge. With its bubbling fire pool, mirrored walls, circular booths, neon tubes of blue and pink, and cocktail servers dressed in elegant black gowns, it harkens back to a groovier era, baby. Voted one of "America's 10 Best Make-Out Bars" by *Nerve Magazine,* this is not the bar to bring someone who wants to be "just friends." It is, however, the bar to bring someone who appreciates old fashioned cocktails (Harvey Wallbanger, anyone?) and who can hold their liquor—the signature Scorpion is an alky's dream come true, with six different kinds of liquor and ice cream. It's served in what looks like a fishbowl and it tastes great going down, but by the time you get to the bottom of the 64-ouncer, the flavor will be the least of your concerns. The Peppermill is open daily 24 hours. 2985 Las Vegas Blvd. S. www.peppermilllasvegas.com. © **702/735-4177.** No cover.

Vanguard Lounge ★★   The long, narrow bar is the most minimally appointed one that you'll find on this stretch of Fremont Street, but that is by design. Cocktails take center stage here, made by a team of talented mixologists who use seasonal, artisanal, and house-made ingredients for well-executed tipples that focus on balance and flavor. Be prepared for the usage of lots of bitters and stuff like Falernum and amaro in some pretty mind-blowing drinks. These folks can do more than just sling a gin and tonic or pour you a beer (though they do have an excellent craft selection, too). On weekends, house and techno DJs liven things up. Vanguard is open Monday through Friday from 4pm until 2am, and Saturday from 6pm until 2am. 516 E. Fremont St. www.vanguardlv.com. © **702/868-7800.** No cover.

Velveteen Rabbit ★★   Located in the ever up-and-coming Arts District near Downtown, this is probably the most hipster of the hipster bars in Las Vegas, complete with funky, boho-chic, vintage furniture decor, and tatted-up, mustachioed mixologists furiously shaking their metal Boston shakers. While each drink might take about 10 minutes to make, they're worth the wait, running on the herbal, floral, and savory side of the palate, presented in beautiful vintage crystal tumblers and coupes. If you can't wait that long, they have a selection of interesting craft beers. And at $8 a pop, you can't beat these prices, considering you'd be paying twice as much for the same caliber of cocktail on the Strip. It's open Monday through Saturday 5pm until 2am and Sunday 5pm to midnight. 1218 Main St. (near Colorado Ave.). www.velveteen rabbitlv.com. © **702/685-9645.** No cover.

Hotel Bars

Alibi ★★   Set right in the center of Aria's casino floor, this opulent, back-lit gem of a bar has a lovely, vintage vibe. I especially like the crystal decanters on display and the ornate wooden and faux mother-of-pearl accents (though don't mistake the large, round *objet d'art* above the bar for a clock, this is on a casino floor, after all). More often than not, you'll find tourists stopping in to re-up their Bud Light, but you're missing out if you don't put the bartenders through their paces. They're expert at giving classic cocktails modern twists, and have a really fun "craft ice" program (you'll see what I mean). At night, the curtains around the round space are drawn, creating a nice barrier between the bar and the buzz of the casino. It's open 24 hours. In Aria, 3730 Las Vegas Blvd. S. www.alibiloungelv.com. © **702/693-8300.** No cover.

Bond ★★   It's hard to know just where to look first at Bond, the glam lounge that combines video poker screens with chandeliers of downy feathers. Those who aren't gazing down at the Strip below through the floor-to-ceiling windows, are staring up at the go-go dancers, shimmying in boxes above the main floor (tastefully attired, these gals can actually dance, which is a nice change). Take the time to also take a gander down at your cocktail, which will be expertly mixed, many of its ingredients pureed, distilled, and infused in-house. Bond is open Monday through Friday from 11am until 5am, and Saturday and Sunday from 10am until 5am. In The Cosmopolitan of Las Vegas, 3708 Las Vegas Blvd. S. www.cosmopolitanlasvegas.com. © **702/698-7929.** No cover.

Bound ★★   Just one vowel away from Bond, this lobby bar at The Cromwell features a drink list created by famed mixologist Salvatore Calabrese. Located near registration, it's a sophisticated oasis before you enter into the madness of the casino floor, done up in lots of gold, with plush seating and a cabinet full of rare spirits. Calabrese, who once set the Guinness World Record for creating the World's Most Expensive Cocktail, left that one off this list, but does serve up his Breakfast Martini here. Legend has it that he created it after his wife implored him to eat breakfast (as opposed to drinking it, we're assuming), so he made this with the orange marmalade he puts on his toast. To go along with this theme, Bound also has a selection of nice, strong coffee cocktails, to give you a nice jolt as well as a buzz. Bound is open Monday through Thursday from noon to 3am and Friday through Sunday from 10am to 3am. In The Cromwell of Las Vegas, 3595 Las Vegas Blvd. S. www.thecromwell.com. © **702/777-3777.** No cover.

The Chandelier ★★★   The Cosmopolitan of Las Vegas really does love its chandeliers. So much so, that it's got a three-story one in the middle of its casino, made of millions of crystals strung together in one towering, shimmering masterpiece. The crystal curtains envelop the top two floors of this elaborate space, while one stunning centerpiece chandelier hangs above the ground level bar. The main floor on the casino floor features plush seating and a raised platform where live trios sometimes play; the mezzanine is more secluded, featuring a mixology-driven menu; the top level is a stark white lounge, where you can often find folks who are waiting to get into the adjacent Marquee nightclub hanging out with a drink. No matter what level you choose, this is one of the most unique places to sip a cocktail on the Strip. The Chandelier is open 24 hours. In The Cosmopolitan of Las Vegas, 3708 Las Vegas Blvd. S. www.cosmopolitanlasvegas.com. ℂ **702/698-7979.** No cover.

Franklin ★★   Just like the hotel, this bar is named for the 32nd president of the United States, and it's a welcome watering hole in this casino-free venue. (Having it here means you don't have to walk all the way over and through the casino of adjoining Mandalay Bay to get a drink.) It has a sleek, contemporary look, all browns and blues, though the twinkling lights above the bar make us think of fireflies (or maybe we had one too many on the last visit). Classic cocktails are the focus, prepared with high end spirits, like the Delano Daiquri with Bacardi 1909 Heritage Rum, or the barrel-aged drinks, made with the resort's own exclusive reserve of bourbon. Open daily from 10am to 2am. In Delano, 3940 Las Vegas Blvd. S. www.delanolasvegas.com. ℂ **877/632-5400.** No cover.

Petrossian Bar ★★★   Vodka? Caviar? Live piano? Afternoon tea? This one spot serves many needs. Under the garden of Dale Chihuly flowers on the lobby ceiling, Petrossian is one of the most beautiful, if underrated, places to have a drink on the Strip. The bartenders here are seasoned professionals who not only know how to make a proper martini, but can give you a solid education on their selection of vodka, not to mention which caviar you should pair with each tipple. The pianists who tickle the ivories night after night are amazing entertainers in their own right; come in earlier for an elegant spread of afternoon tea. It's open daily 24 hours. In Bellagio, 3600 Las Vegas Blvd. S. www.bellagio.com. ℂ **702/693-7111.** No cover.

Vesper ★★   The most low key of the three main bars of Cosmopolitan, Vesper is relatively small, and that's how we like it. While tourists might be cramming themselves into the Bond and Chandelier bars, this is where you'll find savvy locals and hotel executives unwinding after their days (we wonder if it's because of its close proximity to the parking garage elevators). Named for an obscure cocktail created by James Bond in *Casino Royale,* the focus here is on other cocktails of the same ilk: classic and with a twist. The music can get a little loud on weekend nights, but the steady stream of stumbling club-goers through the lobby make the people watching pretty hilarious. Vesper is open daily 24 hours. In The Cosmopolitan of Las Vegas, 3708 Las Vegas Blvd. S. www.cosmopolitanlasvegas.com. ℂ **702/698-7000.** No cover.

Piano Bars

The Bar at Times Square ★ Much like the actual Times Square, this bar is usually jam-packed full of tourists looking for a night of revelry. Dueling pianos are the draw, and create the perfect soundtrack for a booze-driven night of camaraderie with your fellow Vegas visitors. Lord help you when they start playing Billy Joel's *Piano Man.* The bar is open Monday through Thursday from 1pm until 2:30am, and Friday and Sunday from 11am through the wee hours. Shows are from 8pm to 2am, but if you want to be able to have a conversation without shouting over the music, stop in for happy hour, weekdays from 3pm to 7pm. In New York–New York, 3790 Las Vegas Blvd. S. www.new yorknewyork.com. ✆ **702/740-6969.** No cover.

Don't Tell Mama ★ This piano bar, named again for a New York City classic, is less group sing-along (like the Bar at Times Square, above), and more live karaoke. Audience members get up to sing standards with the crack pianists (they can play anything) and, though in other towns this would lead to hours of painful howling, there's so much talent in Vegas that the impromptu show is often darn good. In fact, many of the performers who appear in visiting Broadway musicals and other Strip shows, often head here to belt out a tune or two after they've finished up their paid performance, just for fun. Not that that should intimidate you from getting up there and singing a heartfelt version of *Me and Mr. Jones* with a live pianist backing you. Don't Tell Mama is ready for you Tuesday through Sunday 8pm until late. 517 E. Fremont St. www. donttellmama.com. ✆ **702/207-0788.** No cover; one drink minimum.

THE CLUB & MUSIC SCENE

Most of the clubs in town have DJs, often famous ones, and on those rare occasions when you do have live entertainment, it's usually a pop or cover band. If you prefer alternative or real rock music, your choices used to be limited, but that's all changed. Most touring rock bands make at least one stop in the city. But otherwise, the alternative club scene in town is no great shakes. If you want to know what's playing during your stay, consult the local free alternative papers: the *Las Vegas Weekly* (with great club and bar descriptions in its listings; www.lasvegasweekly.com), and *Vegas Seven* (weekly, with a funnily curated list of the must-sees each week; www.vegasseven.com). Both can be picked up at restaurants, bars, record and music stores, and hip retail stores. If you're looking for good alt-culture tips, try asking the cool staff at **Zia Records** (✆ **702/735-4942**); not only does it have bins dedicated to local artists, but local acts also play live in stores on the weekend.

Dance Clubs

In many ways, especially monetarily, the nightclub scene in Vegas has eclipsed famous party spots like Ibiza, New York, and Los Angeles. Almost every hotel has at least one club and almost all of them are packed whenever their doors are open.

Many of the following have insanely high cover charges ($30 and up), outrageously priced drinks ($10 for a domestic beer), and seating that is reserved for patrons willing to pay hundreds or even thousands of dollars to get bottle service. For the uninitiated it sounds crazy, and is, but the hordes of people willing to pay those kinds of costs seem to be having a good time, so maybe they know something we don't.

One bright note: Women are usually charged less for admission than men (sometimes even allowed in free), and any guest can get a comped ticket to even the hottest clubs, if you play it right. If you are gambling for any length of time, ask the pit boss for comps.

1 OAK ★   In a town where celebrities are often paid to make appearances (read: they get paid stupid money to hang out in a private booth and drink free booze), this is one of the few clubs where the celebrities actually go of their own free will. The New York transplant opened with a bang: performances by Fergie and a legendary 3-hour DJ set by none other than Kanye West, setting the tone for the star-studded years to come. The 16,000-square-foot space is actually visually interesting, with cool modern artwork, dark woods, track lighting, and elevated poles ready to be danced around. Low ceilings, and clusters of booths ready for bottle service, make this a tight space to walk through if you're not seated at a table, but mostly you're just there to see and, hopefully, be seen by any number of A-listers that stop in, like Katy Perry, Joseph Gordon-Leavitt, and Adam Levine, who all just want to have a good time like everyone else. Though 1 OAK stands for One Of A Kind, we question the veracity of this acronym considering that there are also 1 OAKs in New York and Los Angeles. It's open Friday and Saturday from 10:30pm until 4am. In The Mirage, 3400 Las Vegas Blvd. S. www.1oaklasvegas.com. ✆ **702/588-5656.** Cover $30 and up.

Artifice ★   While not a nightclub per se, this multi-purpose space is one of the few places in town where you'll hear decent local DJs who aren't bumping only mainstream electronic pop music. Fitting in with its Arts District locale, Artifice also features a gallery space with work from up-and-coming artists, and an eclectic assortment of events, from singles mixers to neo-burlesque shows to open mic nights. Open Monday through Friday from 5pm until 2am, Saturday from 6pm until 2am, and Sunday from 8pm until 1am. 1025 First St. #3 (at Charleston Blvd.). www.artificebar.com. ✆ **702/489-6339.** No cover except for special events.

Chateau ★   This is definitely not a Paris, France nightclub. Chateau may sport some lovely French touches in the decor, but the club is all high-energy, high-rent Las Vegas. Three distinct spaces offer three different nightlife experiences. Head up the spiral staircase from the casino floor to enter the nightclub, a long, narrow room flanked by bottle service tables. The sultry red lightings complement the modern French-inspired furnishings, complete with crystal chandeliers hanging from the high ceilings, along with classy touches like the DJ booth planted atop a 10-foot-tall marble fireplace mantel. When it gets too crammed inside, head out to one of two outdoor sections. The first is a VIP deck two stories above the Strip, with unobstructed views of the Fountains of

crowd CONTROL

Huge lines outside are a point of pride for Vegas clubs. So if you're into dancing, you may spend a good chunk of the night single-file, double-file, or in an enormous, unwieldy cluster out in front of a club—particularly on Friday or Saturday. We're not kidding: Lines can be hours long (see below), and once you get to the front, you'll find that there's no actual order. You're at the mercy of a power-wielding, eye-contact-avoiding "executive doorman"—bouncer—who gives attractive women priority. To minimize your time in line, try the following strategies:

Arrive before 11pm. You'll have a harder time getting in if you show up between 12:30 and 1am, the busiest period at clubs.

Group yourself smartly. The larger the group, the longer the wait—especially a large group of mostly (or all) guys. Split up if you have to, but always keep some women with each part of your group (it's much harder for unaccompanied men to get into the clubs).

If you're trying to tip your way in, don't make it obvious. It's a negotiation. Don't wave cash above your head (the IRS has recently been clamping down on unreported tip income, so that tactic will make you *very* unpopular). Discreetly and respectfully hand the doorman $20 and ask if he can take care of you.

***Don't* buy a VIP Pass.** Can you say "scam"? Many passes require you get there before midnight (a time when there'd normally be no line), and with others you're paying big bucks just to have someone make the call ahead that you could have made yourself. Again: *Don't* fall for this scam.

Do check the websites. Many clubs will offer front-of-line passes, cover discounts, and drink specials via text alerts and/or if you check-in via a social networking site like Facebook or Twitter. Details change often, so check the club's website for the latest offer.

Dress to impress. For women: Antediluvian but true—showing more cleavage is a line-skipping tactic. If that's not an option, stick with a little black dress or nice jeans and a sexy or club-wear–style top. For men: Look good. Avoid baggy jeans, shorts, tennis shoes, or work boots. Nice jeans or pants and a collared shirt work well.

Look confident. While cockiness never helps, assertiveness never hurts.

Bellagio; it's the perfect spot to have a more intimate conversation with that stranger you just met on the dance floor. There's also the 22,000-square-foot rooftop garden, set at the base of the Eiffel Tower, that is essentially a whole other club with its own dance floor and bars. You won't convince yourself that you're in Paris proper, but as far as romantic locations, this is just as effective. Chateau is open Wednesday, Friday, and Saturday from 10:30pm until close. In Paris Las Vegas, 3655 Las Vegas Blvd. S. www.chateaunights.com. © **702/776-7770.** Cover varies, usually $20 and up.

Drai's ★   Nightlife impresario Victor Drai ruled the underground—literally—in Las Vegas. His after-hours club (which still exists in the underbelly of The Cromwell) was around for nearly 2 decades as one of the only house-music-fueled after-parties, with attendees who often spilled back on to the Strip when the sun was already well up in the sky. Now the sunlight shines on Drai's all day long at his 65,000-square-foot rooftop club atop The Cromwell, which hosts the beach club around the hotel pool until the sun goes down, when it transitions into a dance club. A roster of well-known resident DJs provide the EDM-heavy soundtrack, but hip hop acts such as Nas, Chris Brown and Fat Joe have been making their way into the residential rotation as well. The dress code still applies here—even if you've been hanging out at the pool party all day, you still have to put on more clothes to attend the club at night. The nightclub is open Thursday through Sunday from 10:30pm until 4am. In The Cromwell, 3595 Las Vegas Blvd. S. www.draislv.com. ℂ **702/777-3800.** Hotel guests are free, non-guests are $20 and up.

Foxtail ★ Foxtail serves double duty as both nightlife hot spot and day club for SLS Las Vegas. The 43,000-square-foot complex splits up as the 8,000-square-foot nightclub, which features state-of-the-art technology like an LED light fixture directly above the dance floor, plus a Funktion One sound system over which DJs pump their beats. Elaborate graffiti by French-Moroccan artist Tarek Benaoum flows along the walls, which draws your eye to the outdoor Foxtail Pool club that pops off on weekends (during the week, it's simply one of two pools for the hotel). At night, the pool stays open (though most go back and change out of their bathing suits) and the party moves between both spaces, for performances by more DJs or live concerts. Foxtail Pool Clubs is open Friday, Saturday, and Sunday from 9 a.m. to 7 p.m., then transitions into the nightclub, which is open usually Friday through Sunday, from 10pm until close. In SLS Las Vegas, 2535 Las Vegas Blvd. S. www.slslasvegas. com. ℂ **702/761-7621.** Cover varies, usually $20 and up.

Hakkasan Las Vegas ★★ At the biggest nightclub in the world, you'll have to navigate through five levels in the course of an evening. These include an elegant modern Chinese restaurant, an ultralounge, tables with exorbitantly-priced bottle service and a booth where a roster of world-famous EDM DJs spin their magic. Kudos to whatever lighting designer strung the LED lighting along the ceiling of the club and behind the DJ booth—the effect is mesmerizing. Lines to get in are long and filled with young and excited partiers who don't mind being crammed onto a dance floor, so long as they can get a glimpse of the world's highest-paid DJ Calvin Harris or watch Steve Aoki take a ride on the crowd in an inflatable boat. Open Wednesday through Sunday from 10pm until close. In the MGM Grand, 3799 Las Vegas Blvd. S. www.hakkasanlv. com. ℂ **702/212-8804.** Cover varies, usually $40 and up.

Intrigue ★★ Occupying the space formerly known as Tryst, Intrigue opened to much fanfare, but mixed reviews. Tryst was a groundbreaking club for its time (that time being the mid '00s), one of the first to fully capitalize on the growing EDM scene, and creating what we know as bottle service today (and along with the latter that odious distinction between being VIP and a mere mortal). Tryst was starting to feel a little dated, but it knew exactly what it was. To take its place, Intrigue wanted to break its own ground, promising to move away from overpaid DJs and focus more on the guest experience for ALL the guests, not just the ones who paid for table service. Yet opening night featured a big-name DJ. Even more telling that we've got the same old same old going on here: one of the most noted feature of Intrigue is a club-within-a-club that only the true elite will ever see. The social media-free zone is hidden behind a secret door, and admittance can only be gained through approval by some cabal of executives. So much for breaking ground. So what *is* new? Well they've added a "selfie wall," choreographed pole dancers and cocktail waitresses who wear different uniforms every night. More than that, the club itself is slated to change in mood and theme every month, promising a new experience every time you visit. For the part us mere mortals can see, I do appreciate that the rest of club was lightened up all around, and that the 94-foot man-made waterfall that was the centerpiece to Tryst's outdoor section remains, though I imagine that wasn't easy to demolish it just for a new club. Intrigue is open Thursday through Saturday from 10pm until late. In Wynn Las Vegas, 3131 Las Vegas Blvd. S. www.trystlasvegas.com. © **702/770-7070.** Cover varies, usually $30 and up.

LAX ★   The club that was once RA Nightclub can't seem to fill the shoes of its predecessor, and has changed owners more than once in the past few years. But Luxor needed a club, apparently, so LAX is it. To be fair, the club itself is beautifully appointed. Semi-private booths on the mezzanine level are separated by red curtains and feature their own ornate chandeliers (though they're not always lit enough for you to see them). While you won't hear any world-famous DJs behind the decks, LAX has been making a niche for itself on Throwback Thursdays with a solid lineup of '90s favorites, including Kid 'n' Play, Naughty By Nature, Young M.C. and yes, even Vanilla Ice. Half the time you're wondering, "These people still perform?" While the other half you're too busy enjoying the blast from the past. LAX is open Thursday through Saturday 10:30pm until 4am. In Luxor Las Vegas, 3900 Las Vegas Blvd. S. www.laxthenightclub.com. © **702/242-4529.** Cover varies, usually $30 and up.

Light ★★★   While once upon a time Cirque du Soleil "powered" this nightclub at Mandalay Bay, that is no longer the case; Cirque pulled out of the venture in late 2015. So while periodic performances by acrobats, dancers, and other artists have gone away, the light show is still spectacular. It's a lot of fun, as is the massive video wall that projects ambient visuals while illuminating the room, and the killer, well-balanced sound system (your entire sternum will quiver from the reverberation of the bass used by acts like Disclosure and Baauer). It's the only major club on the Strip to host any semblance of non-mainstream electronic acts, though bottle service—and the crowds that love bottle service—still reigns supreme. Its sun-up component, Daylight, is one of the cooler pool parties on the weekend, if only because the music is slightly better than the other options. Open Wednesday from 10:30pm until 4am and Friday and Saturday from 10pm until 4am. In Mandalay Bay, 3950 Las Vegas Blvd. S. www.thelightvegas.com. © **702/632-7777.** Cover varies, usually $30 and up.

Marquee ★★★   At more than 60,000 square feet and containing three different party atmospheres within, the mega club at Cosmopolitan is here to say: size matters. It's exactly what you'd expect from a Vegas club: massive main floor, huge LED wall behind the DJ booth that projects an amazing laser show while internationally renowned house DJs play, and lots of low booths to be sold to the highest bidder for bottle service. The main room can be over-whelming, especially when people are wall-to-wall and it's six deep even to get a drink. Hole up in the Library, the more exclusive lounge, where the music is more chill, there are pool tables, and you can actually pull a seat up to the bar. Need a break from all the EDM? The hip-hop and pop-driven soundtrack in the intimate Boombox will clear your head from all those synths. There's also an outdoor patio with cabana seating (where tables will run cheaper than inside the main club) and gaming if you can't stay away from the slots too long. The line to enter will snake across the second floor of the Cosmopolitan, so unless you've got a table, be prepared to wait for a long time. Marquee is open Monday, Friday, and Saturday from 10pm until 5am. The pool club is open seasonally on weekend afternoons. In The Cosmopolitan of Las Vegas, 3708 Las Vegas Blvd. S. www.marqueelasvegas.com. ✆ **702/333-9000.** Cover varies, usually $30 and up.

Omnia ★ Now occupying the space of former mega club Pure, the new mega club Omnia was created by the same people who did Hakkasan at MGM Grand. The 75,000-square-foot space underwent a $100-million renovation, which ditched the white, airy, 1990s vibe of Pure, replacing it with a dark, ultra-modern vibe, accented by the multi-million dollar, spaceship-looking chandelier above the middle of the dance floor. Why does a chandelier cost so much money? When it's really a high-tech installation of eight concentric rings that slowly drop from the ceiling while projecting lights and lasers, and move and shift along with the music played by star DJs (like Afrojack and Calvin Harris). It's breathtaking to watch, actually, and everyone will stop in their tracks when it comes to life. Get a better view of it from the second level, where you won't be nearly as jam-packed as on the main floor. Omnia also inherited Pure's prime terrace, which overlooks the Strip, and offers an exclusive VIP lounge, the Heart of Omnia. As it's the newest kid on the block, everyone is clamoring to get in here, so dress to impress and employ some pre-game as needed. Patience will be key as you're simmering in between the stanchions. It's open Tuesday and Thursday through Saturday from 10pm until close. In Caesars Palace, 3570 Las Vegas Blvd. S. www.omnianightclub.com. ✆ **702/785-6200.** Cover varies, usually $30 and up.

Tao Nightclub ★ Once the palace where the Hiltons, Kardashians, and other reality TV celebrities partied the night away, the Asian-themed club at the Venetian has lost a bit of the limelight to bigger, newer Strip clubs. Ah well, it's still fun. Enter into the Buddhist temple—if Buddhist temples were opulent palaces that offered high-end bottle service—under the arched hall-way, flanked by bathtubs, which appear again on raised platforms on the dance floor. Where you'd usually find go-go dancers inciting the crowd, bath-ing beauties are trying to not splash water everywhere to the beat of the pounding bass. The footprint of the main floor of the club is small compared to current standards, which ensures that everyone dancing gets to know each other really well. The bathrooms on the second level are, er, interesting; they overlook the main floor, but once you enter them and lock the door behind you, the frosted glass door goes opaque, so you will have privacy while you do your business. Bottle service tables line up against a long banquette, so unless you pony up for a truly private table, your party will have to mingle with the one next to you. But that's ok, you came to make new friends, didn't you? It's open Thursday through Saturday from 10pm until 5am. In The Venetian, 3355 Las Vegas Blvd. S. www.taolasvegas.com. ✆ **702/388-8588.** Cover varies.

XS ★★★ As the abbreviated name suggests, this gold-plated crown jewel of Wynn nightlife is excessive. A recent $10-million redesign upgraded the entire space (both the inside area and its outdoor pool deck) to include a pyrotechnic system that shoots flames above the pool, and added a DJ booth with 14,000 LED lights, moveable video screens, and more lasers. An update like this costs a pretty penny, but as the highest grossing nightclub in the country (thanks to the contributions of appreciated visitors like yourself), XS can afford lots of lasers. XS is open Friday through Monday from 10pm to 4am. In Encore Las Vegas, 3121 Las Vegas Blvd. S. www.xslasvegas.com. ✆ **702/770-0097.** Cover varies, usually $30 and up.

Ultralounges

What, you may be asking, is an ultralounge? That's an excellent question, since it is loosely defined at best. Generally speaking, ultralounges are smaller than traditional nightclubs, offering a more intimate vibe. Some have dance floors and some don't, although even the ones that don't usually have DJs and people will dance wherever they can find the room to do so. You'll also usually find a lot more seating at an ultralounge, but most of it will probably be reserved for people willing to pay for bottle service. Drink and cover prices may be a bit less than the big nightclubs. The type of crowd they draw depends on the location and theme, with the most popular bringing in the same young and pretty crowd that goes to the hot dance clubs. (They'll often come to an ultralounge first, and then head to the dance floor elsewhere.)

Downtown Cocktail Room ★★ This intimate mixology bar is a go-to joint for those who want a chill evening without all the craziness that comes with other bars, both on and off-Strip. Its entrance on Las Vegas Boulevard, across from the Fremont Street Experience, hides in plain sight; a big metal sheet that looks like it shouldn't move opens when you pull it. Sheer drapes and low banquettes offer private seating when you maneuver them to your liking. Low ceilings, large Picasso-esque paintings, and deep red tones make things cozy and calm, while talented mixologists behind the bar whip up avant garde cocktails. The punch bowls, delicious and dangerous, are meant to be shared. It's open Monday through Friday from 4pm until 2am and Saturday from 7pm until 2am. 111 Las Vegas Blvd. www.downtowncocktailroom.com. ✆ **702/880-3696.** No cover.

ghostbar ★ The club on the 55th floor of the Palms has been an old standby for Vegas nightlife, reinventing itself as recently as 2013. It's gorgeous, if not small for a modern club, with crystal chandeliers dangling from the ceiling in the white space, accented with black and pink. Step out onto the outdoor patio for one of the best views of the Strip; if you're not afraid of heights, head to the edge to look down through a Plexiglass window to see how far up you are from the ground. During the non-pool season, ghostbar hosts Saturday afternoon excuses to drink called ghostbar Day Club (GBDC for short) that are themed parties from week to week. This club is open daily from 8pm until late. In the Palms, 4321 W. Flamingo Rd. www.palms.com. ✆ **702/942-6832.** Cover varies, usually $20 and up.

Hyde Bellagio ★★ Get there early enough, and Hyde Bellagio is the perfect perch from which to watch a couple of rounds of the Fountains of Bellagio show while sipping on well-executed cocktails. Head over later, and that's when the party gets started (and you may forget all about the fountains). Though it looks like an Italian villa on the inside, the lounge transforms into a serious nightlife destination, complete with ridiculous bottle service presentations (at one point you could pay tens of thousands of dollars to press the "button" that starts one of the Fountains' performances). The lounge opens nightly at 5pm until late, while the club opens at 10:30pm on Tuesday, Friday, and Saturday. In Bellagio, 3600 Las Vegas Blvd. S. www.hydebellagio.com. ✆ **702/693-8700.** Cover varies, usually $20 and up.

Surrender ★★ Another feather in the cap of the Wynn and Encore resorts, the intimate Surrender is a stunning space. A giant, golden snake poses on the wall above the bar, while white, plush leather curved couches dot the room, enticing partiers to take a seat and pay through the nose for it (with outrageously costly bottle service). The real party happens outside, however, when the wall of windows open up to **Encore Beach Club** (p. 237), and big name DJs like David Guetta, Diplo and Martin Solveig set the soundtrack for the biggest day party in town. Surrender is open Wednesday, Friday, and Saturday from 10pm until dawn. In Encore Las Vegas, 3121 Las Vegas Blvd. S. www.surrender nightclub.com. ✆ **702/770-7300.** Cover varies, usually $30 and up.

VooDoo Rooftop Nightclub ★ The two-floor behemoth, on the 50 and 51st floors of the Rio, was one of the original mega clubs before nightclubs became the huge deal that they are today. The steakhouse component occupies the first level. After a dinner there, head up to the club to continue your night. There are two sections in which you can spend your time: the lounge with voodoo-themed decor and furniture (yeah, it feels a bit dated), or the more contemporary dance floor area. The two-story rooftop terrace is the winning feature here affording some of the best views of the city, not to mention a breath of fresh air when you need it; you can head even higher up if you take the spiral staircase. Beware the blacklit hallway into the club; it's meant to highlight the neon voodoo paintings on the wall, but also succeeds in pointing out any lint you have on your clothes. The lounge portion is open nightly 5pm to 3am and the nightclub operates Sunday through Thursday from 8pm until 2am, and Friday and Saturday until 3am. In the Rio All-Suite Hotel & Casino, 3700 Las Vegas Blvd. S. www.riolasvegas.com. ✆ **702/777-6875.** Cover varies, usually $20 and up.

Hotel Lounges

Most of the nightclubs in town are ruled by the young and pretty—you know who we mean: the 23-year-olds in impossibly short dresses, with tiny waists, and an attitude that can be seen from space. Not that there's anything wrong with that. If I were thin and pretty, I'd want to hang out at these nightclubs, too.

But what about the rest of us? What about older people who may no longer be a size 0 but still want to go out, dance, and have a good time?

For them we offer what some consider to be a dinosaur of a bygone age: the hotel lounge. Don't roll your eyes! Many hotel lounges offer entertainment, dance floors, low or no cover charge, cheaper drink prices, and an almost total absence of the kind of "hey, look at me" posing that's *de rigeur* at the trendy nightclubs. These are great places to go to simply have a night out of fun that doesn't involve a slot machine or blackjack table. All of the major hotels have at least one, so you can just wander by to see if it strikes your fancy, but here are a couple that might be worth the extra effort to visit.

Carnaval Court ★   If partying front and center right on the Las Vegas Strip is on your bucket list, you can cross it off here. This open-air party blares music day and night, luring in passers-by, and the party just gets bigger and bigger as the night goes on. Lounge bands channeling the '70s and '80s get a ton of play here, so you're guaranteed to know just about every song . . . if you're of a certain age. If the faux "hair bands" aren't entertaining enough, the bartenders' flair will get your attention, flipping bottles and shakers around before mixing a cocktail. All in all, when all you want to do is dance like no one's watching, to music that you actually recognize, it's a nice alternative to the casino nightclubs. Carnaval Court is open daily from 11am until 3am. At Harrah's Las Vegas, 3475 Las Vegas Blvd. S. www.harrahslv.com. ☎ **702/731-7778.** Cover varies.

Gilley's ★★   One of the few Country & Western spots on the Strip, Treasure Island inherited Gilley's from the Frontier after it closed. The mechanical bull gets a workout all night (as do those trying to test their ability to hang on for 8 seconds), while live honky-tonk bands and country rock bands perform several nights a week. Think you sound like Reba or Garth? There's Cowboy Karaoke on Tuesdays and Wednesdays. Line dancing is, of course, a must, with lessons offered Monday through Friday at 7pm. The BBQ is worth a taste, as well. The saloon opens at 11am daily, while the nightclub portion of the facility gets going around 7 or 8pm and stays open until 2am weeknights and later on weekends. In Treasure Island, 3300 Las Vegas Blvd. S. www.gilleyslasvegas.com ☎ **702/894-7111.** Cover varies.

Mizuya Lounge ★★   This Japanese-themed lounge serves sushi, but also happens to be an incredibly chill place to take a break from the casino floor. Nightly entertainment is, usually, provided by local cover bands, who play classic rock and some pop. While there's no cover, there is a two-drink minimum when the band is playing, but they're usually decent enough that you don't mind

The Club & Music Scene

paying to stick around. It's open Monday through Thursday from 11am until 3am, Friday from 11am until 4am, Saturday from 9am until 4am, and Sunday from 9am until 3am, but the party part doesn't usually start until evening. In Mandalay Bay, 3950 Las Vegas Blvd. S. www.mandalaybay.com. ✆ **702/632-4760.**

Comedy Clubs

Brad Garrett's Comedy Club ★   Set off a walkway between the MGM Grand parking garage and the casino, this comedy club isn't the easiest to find. But for *Everybody Loves Raymond's* Brad Garrett's self-deprecating-style of stand-up, this underground lair, with its cabaret-style stage and intimate seating, has just the right, pretention-free ambiance. The star appears here regularly, along with an ever-revolving roster of talented comedians. The humor tends to run on the raunchy side; if you're easily offended, remember you're in Vegas. Lighten up. Photos of comedy legends hang on the walls; reserve a booth to feel like a VIP. If by chance Mike Tyson is performing his one-man-show, Undisputed Truth, while you're there, I highly recommend it. He's a surprisingly good storyteller. There's no food, but there are three different types of flavored popcorn to snack on; specialty cocktails are a must, but be aware that there will be a pre-added gratuity to your bill. Shows are nightly at 8pm. In MGM Grand, 3799 Las Vegas Blvd. S. www.bradgarrettcomedy.com. ✆ **866/740-7711.** Tickets $47–$90.

The Improv ★   The brick wall of the Improv is an iconic sight for those who know of the comedy club's storied past. Started by Budd Friedman in New York City in the '60s, The Improv has become an institution, with alums like Jay Mohr, Margaret Cho, and Chris Rock. The intimate, 400-seat Vegas showroom features three new comedians each week, and while they might not be household names yet, it's a great spot to catch some up-and-coming talent or obscure acts. Shows are nightly at 8:30 and 10pm, and only 10pm on Friday and Saturday. In Harrah's Las Vegas, 3475 Las Vegas Blvd. S. www.harrahslv.com. ✆ **800/392-9002** or 702/369-5000. Tickets $30–$65.

The Laugh Factory ★   Another comedy institution, this one was born in Hollywood with names like George Carlin and Ellen DeGeneres on its roster. Much like the Improv, three new comedians put their comedic skills to the test each week. It's not really fair to compare the two clubs; both are showcasing the best talent out there right now. Shows are nightly at 8:30 and 10:30pm. In The Tropicana Las Vegas, 3801 Las Vegas Blvd. S. www.troplv.com. ✆ **800/462-8767.** Tickets $35–$55.

THE GAY & LESBIAN SCENE

Hip and happening Vegas locals know that some of the best scenes and dance action can be found in the city's gay bars. And no, they don't ask for sexuality ID at the door. All are welcome at any of the following establishments—as long as you don't have a problem with the people inside, they aren't going to have a problem with you. For women, this can be a fun way to dance and not get hassled by overeager Lotharios.

cool BY THE POOL

A critical part of the nightclub scene is that it takes place at night. Maybe that's why they call them "night" clubs. But you don't have to wait until the sun goes down to start partying, especially in Vegas, where a host of daytime pool clubs give vacationers an opportunity to boogie down while working on your tan.

Most of the major hotels have some form of a poolside day club that usually operates on weekends and only in season (Mar–Oct mostly). They all feature DJs or live music, bars, private cabanas, and lots of opportunity to splash around in pools that are separated from the main recreational facilities, for people over 21 years of age only. All charge a cover (although they vary as much as nightclub covers do) and some offer table games (like blackjack) and topless sunbathing. All are open to the general public (you don't have to be staying at the host hotel).

It should go without saying that these usually draw a younger, fit crowd who aren't embarrassed about how they look in a bikini or board shorts. If that isn't you, you may want to consider alternate afternoon entertainment.

Here are the most noteworthy of the current pool clubs:

- **Bare** At the Mirage, 3400 Las Vegas Blvd. S. (✆ **702/696-8300;** www.barepool.com). Small pool, cabanas, DJ, and bar. Topless sunbathing allowed. Open daily 11am to 6pm. Cover $20 and up.

- **Daylight** At Mandalay Bay, 3950 Las Vegas Blvd. S. (✆ **702/693-8300**). 50,000-square-foot beach area with pool, three wet decks, private cabanas, DJ, bars, and food service. No topless sunbathing. Open Wednesday 11am to 3am and Friday to Sunday 11am to 6pm. Cover $25 and up.

- **Encore Beach Club** At Encore Las Vegas, 3121 Las Vegas Blvd. S. (www.encorebeachclub.com; ✆ **702/770-7300**). 60,000-square-foot facility, three pools, cabanas, DJ, gaming, bar, grill. No topless sunbathing. Open Friday 12 to 6pm and Saturday to Sunday from 11am to 6pm. Cover $25 and up.

- **Liquid** At Aria Las Vegas, 3730 Las Vegas Blvd. S. (www.arialasvegas.com; ✆ **702/693-8300**). Three pools, cabanas, DJ, bar, restaurant. No topless sunbathing. Open daily 11am to 6pm. Cover $20 and up.

- **Marquee Dayclub** At the Cosmopolitan of Las Vegas, 3801 Las Vegas Blvd. S. (www.marqueelasvegas.com; ✆ **702/333-9000**). Two pools, cabanas with private pools, DJ, gaming, bar, food service. No topless sunbathing. Open daily 10am to sunset. Cover $25 and up.

- **Rehab** At the Hard Rock Hotel, 4455 Paradise Rd. (www.rehablv.com; ✆ **800/473-7625**). Several pools, sandy beaches, cabanas, DJ, gaming, bar, food service. No topless sunbathing. Open daily 10am to sunset. Cover $25 and up.

- **Tao Beach** At the Venetian, 3355 Las Vegas Blvd. S. (www.taobeach.com; ✆ **702/388-8588**). One pool, cabanas, DJ, bar, food service. Topless sunbathing allowed. Open daily 10am to sunset. Cover $20 and up.

- **Wet Republic** At MGM Grand, 3799 Las Vegas Blvd. S. (www.wetrepublic.com; ✆ **800/851-1703**). Two pools, cabanas, DJ, bar, food service. No topless sunbathing. Open Thursday to Monday 11am to 6pm. Cover $20 and up.

If you want to know what's going on in gay Las Vegas during your visit, pick up a copy of *Q Vegas,* which is also available at any of the places described below. You can also call ✆ **702/650-0636** or check out the online edition at www.qvegas.com.

Funhog Ranch ★　Forget lines, high cover charges, and overpriced drinks, this is not the place for those things. Funhog Ranch is the dive bar of Vegas' gay bars, which isn't a bad thing; it's tiresome to be surrounded by so much manufactured opulence all the time. This is a relaxed, casual environment where partiers have no expectations beyond having a good time. The atmosphere is rustic, with wooden booths, a jukebox, video poker, and cheap drinks. Fetish and leather gear is encouraged, though you're not required to be a bear to have fun. Funhog is open daily 24 hours. 495 E. Twain Ave. (just east of Paradise Rd.). www.funhogranchlv.com. ✆ **702/791-7001.** No cover.

Piranha Las Vegas ★★　The jewel of the Fruit Loop—the small "boystown" of Las Vegas—is this see-and-be-seen club for the city's gay elite. The brick facade makes the building look unassuming from the outside, but once you enter, it's a whole new world. The small, but banging, blue-lit nightclub is constantly teeming with bodies. For a better view, and some air, head to the lounge on the second floor. Even more air (and a break from the loud music) is available on the outdoor patio, a popular spot where partiers warm up by the fireplace. Now that it's open 24 hours it's not unusual for the party to go from a Saturday night into a Sunday mid-morning. A professional drag show takes the stage nightly, and if you need more drag in your life, Drag Queen Bingo takes place on Thursdays. Open 24 hours. 4633 Paradise Rd. (at Naples Dr.). www.piranhavegas.com. ✆ **702/791-0100.** No cover.

STRIP CLUBS

No, we don't mean entertainment establishments on Las Vegas Boulevard South. We mean the other kind of "strip." Yes, people come to town for the gambling and the wedding chapels, but the lure of Vegas doesn't stop there. Though prostitution is not legal within the city, the sex industry is an active and obvious force in town. Every other cab carries a placard for a strip club, and a walk down the Strip at night will have dozens of men thrusting fliers at you for clubs, escort services, phone-sex lines, and more. And some of you are going to want to check it out.

And why not? An essential part of the Vegas allure is decadence, and naked flesh would certainly qualify, as does the thrill of trying something new and daring. Of course, by and large, the nicer bars aren't particularly daring, and if

For Men Only?

Many of the strip clubs will not allow women in unless they're escorted by a man—presumably to protect ogling husbands from suspicious wives. If you're looking for a ladies' night out and want to check out the topless action, be sure and call ahead to find out what each individual club allows.

you go to more than one in an evening, the thrill wears off, and the breasts don't look quite so bare.

In the finest of Vegas traditions, the "something for everyone" mentality extends to strip clubs. Here is a guide to the most prominent and heavily advertised; there are plenty more, of increasing seediness, out there. You don't have to look too hard. The most crowded and zoo-like times are after midnight, especially on Friday and Saturday nights. Should you want a "meaningful" experience, you might wish to avoid the rush and choose an off-hour for a visit.

Cheetah's ★   The club that was featured in *Showgirls* employs 500 women in a 24-hour period on the weekends, quite possibly outnumbering the number of men who are there at the same time. This is a good thing, as variety is the spice of life in a lively club like this. Mirrored walls around the booths give you a good look at all the flesh around you, and yes, there are lots of fake cheetahs prowling around the main and five smaller stages. Lap dances are $20. Cheetah's is open daily 24 hours. 2112 Western Ave. www.cheetahslasvegas. com. © **702/384-0074.** Topless. Cover $30.

Larry Flynt's Hustler Club ★   Comparable in size to the "World's Largest Strip Club" Sapphire, the interior of porn king Larry Flynt's joint is just as gaudy as its "you can't miss it from the highway" exterior, with three floors of entertainment, featuring spaces with names like the "Beaver Stage" and "Honey Suites." It's a maze to navigate, and easy to get separated from your group. In the event one of you gets a private dance make sure you can locate him, lest you lose him and he loses too much money. There's also a 25,000-square-foot adult superstore. Lap dances are $30. The Hustler Club is open daily 4pm until 9am. 6007 Dean Martin Dr. www.hustlerclubs.com. © **702/795-3131.** Topless. Cover $30 (includes first lap dance).

Question Your Cabbie

If there's a particular strip club you want to visit, don't let your cabdriver talk you out of it. Clubs give cabdrivers kickbacks for delivering customers. So be leery of drivers who suggest one club over another. They may be making $20 for delivering you there. And don't accept a higher cover charge than we've listed here; the clubs are trying to get you to cover the kickback they just gave the cabbie.

The Palomino ★   What the Palomino lacks in convenient location or gorgeous decor, it makes up for in nudity. Yes, this is the only strip club in Vegas where all the bits are revealed, thanks to the club's license being grandfathered in before selling alcohol and being totally nekkid were banned from happening in the same place. In addition to women, there are male dancers as well, and they're just as attractive as the ladies. But with great power comes great responsibility: you don't have to sit on your hands during private dances (as is required in other similar establishments), but keep your phones in your pockets. Photos are strictly *verboten*. Topless lap dances are $20; totally nude dances are $40. The Palomino is open Sunday through Thursday from 4pm to 5am and Friday and Saturday from 4pm to 7am. 1848 Las Vegas Blvd. N. www. palominolv.com. ☏ **702/642-2984.** Totally nude. Cover $30.

Sapphire Gentleman's Club ★★★ Charlie Sheen publicly endorsed Sapphire, so yes, things do get crazy here. It's the largest strip club in the world at 70,000 square feet, and features three stages joined together as a bridge across the room, and one big room where multiple dancers vie for your attention from their respective poles. But what might be the most unusual part of the experience is that the women look just like women you'd find on the street: more natural-looking than at other strip clubs and of all shapes and sizes. Sheen isn't the only celebrity to make it rain here, others who choose to remain anonymous take to the private and expensive rooms upstairs for VIP action. During the day, you can spend the day getting hotter under the sun with the girls at the Sapphire Pool. Lap dances start at $20. Sapphire is open daily 24 hours. 3025 S. Industrial. www.sapphirelasvegas.com. ☏ **702/796-6000.** Topless. Cover $30 6pm–6am.

Spearmint Rhino ★★ Ask any man that's never been to Vegas before if he knows of a strip club here, and he'll mention the Spearmint Rhino. If anything, the Rhino, as it's affectionately called, is one of the best looking clubs in town. It's 18,000 square feet of opulence, divided into three main viewing areas done in black and gold notes, along with plenty of tables and VIP rooms for those private encounters with the girl of your dreams. The dancers are as comely as the club; in fact, many would say that the Rhino gets the hottest performers in town. Lap dances are $20 and up. Spearmint Rhino is open 24 hours. 3340 S. Highland Dr. ☏ **702/796-3600.** Topless. Cover $30.

Treasures ★★★ The most Vegas-y of the Vegas strip clubs, Treasures is a favorite of both locals and visitors alike. The outside looks like it was lifted right from Caesars Palace, while the interior is as ornate, modeled after a Victorian brothel. The main stage is a spectacle with two staircases descending down to a platform, where a neon-lit pole is used by dancers who actually take pride in their work. There's no disaffected shimmying here; these dancers put on a show, complete with special effects, props and feats of athleticism. And while we'd normally shy away from eating at a strip club, the steak house is actually quite good. Lap dances are $20 and up. Treasures is open daily from 4pm to 6am. 2801 Westwood Dr. www.treasureslasvegas.com. ☏ **702/257-3030.** Topless. Cover $40.

DAY TRIPS FROM LAS VEGAS

Though Vegas is designed to make you forget that there is an outside world, it might do you and your wallet some good to reacquaint yourself with the non-Vegas realm. The good news is that as the most geographically isolated major city in America, there's nothing but nature in every direction outside its neon-lit borders.

It's a startling contrast between the artificial wonders of Sin City and the natural wonders that, in some cases, lie just a few miles away. Few places are as developed and modern as Vegas; few places are as untouched as some of the canyons, desert, and mountains that surround it. The electrical and design marvel that is the Strip couldn't exist without the extraordinary structural feat that is Hoover Dam. Need some fresh air? There are plenty of opportunities for outdoor recreation, all in landscapes that are completely un-Vegas, in the best ways.

HOOVER DAM, LAKE MEAD & LAKE LAS VEGAS

30 miles SE of Las Vegas

This is one of the most popular excursions from Las Vegas, visited by upward of 7 million people annually. Why should you join them? Because Hoover Dam is an engineering and architectural marvel, and it changed the Southwest forever. Without it, you wouldn't even be going to Vegas. Kids may be bored, unless they like machinery or just plain big things, but expose them to it anyway, for their own good. Buy them ice cream and a Hoover Dam snow globe as a bribe. If you are visiting Lake Mead, it's a must.

Getting There

Drive east on Flamingo Road or Tropicana Avenue to U.S. 515 S, which automatically turns into I-93 S and takes you right to the dam. This involves a dramatic drive as you go through Boulder City and come over a rise, and Lake Mead suddenly appears spread out before you. It's a beautiful sight. After the 2010 opening of a bypass bridge (dramatic on its own for its soaring height over the canyon), vehicles no longer pass directly over the bridge to get from Nevada

Side Trips from Las Vegas

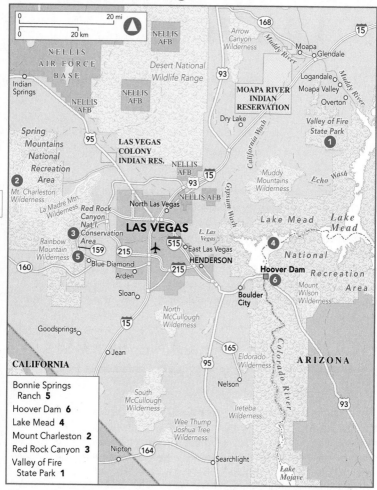

Bonnie Springs
  Ranch **5**
Hoover Dam **6**
Lake Mead **4**
Mount Charleston **2**
Red Rock Canyon **3**
Valley of Fire
  State Park **1**

to Arizona, but despite hopes that the bypass would make the commute better, it hasn't helped much. On a normal day, getting to the dam will take about an hour.

Go past the turnoff to Lake Mead to Nevada State Route 172, the well-marked Hoover Dam Access Road. As you near the dam, you'll see a five-story parking structure tucked into the canyon wall on your left. Park here ($10 charge) and take the elevators or stairs to the walkway leading to the visitor center.

If you would rather go on an **organized tour,** check out **Gray Line** (www. grayline.com; ✆ **800/634-6579**), which offers a half-day tour of the dam from

$47 or a daylong tour that includes a visit to the Welcome to Fabulous Las Vegas sign and a tour of the Ethel M Chocolate factory from $57.

Hoover Dam ★★★

There would be no Las Vegas as we know it without Hoover Dam. Certainly, the neon and glitz that we know and love would not exist. In fact, the growth of the entire Southwest can be tied directly to the electricity created by the dam.

Construction on the dam began in 1931. An army of more than 5,200 laborers was assembled, and work proceeded 24 hours a day. Though 96 workers were killed during construction, contrary to popular myth, none were accidentally buried as the concrete was poured (it was poured only at a level of 8 inches at a time). Look for a monument outside dedicated to the workers who were killed—"they died to make the desert bloom"—along with a tombstone for their doggy mascot who was also killed, albeit after the dam was completed. Compare their wages of 50¢ an hour to those of their Depression-era peers, who made 5¢ to 30¢.

Completed in 1936, 2 years ahead of schedule and $15 million under budget (it is, no doubt, a Wonder of the Modern Fiscal World), the dam stopped the annual floods and conserved water for irrigation, industry, and domestic uses. Equally important, it became one of the world's major electrical-generating plants, providing low-cost, pollution-free hydroelectric power to a score of surrounding communities. Hoover Dam's $165-million cost has been repaid with interest by the sale of inexpensive power to a number of California cities and the states of Arizona and Nevada. The dam is a government project that paid for itself—a feat almost as awe inspiring as its engineering.

The dam itself is a massive curved wall, 660 feet thick at the bottom, tapering to 45 feet where a road crosses it at the top. It towers 726 feet above bedrock (about the height of a 60-story skyscraper) and acts as a plug between the canyon walls to hold back up to trillions of gallons of water in Lake Mead, the reservoir created by its construction. Four concrete intake towers on the lake side drop the water down about 600 feet to drive turbines and create power, after which the water spills out into the river and continues south.

All the architecture is on a grand scale, and the design has beautiful Art Deco elements, unusual in an engineering project. Note, for instance, the monumental 30-foot bronze sculpture, *Winged Figures of the Republic,* flanking a 142-foot flagpole at the Nevada entrance. According to its creator, Oskar Hansen, the sculpture symbolizes "the immutable calm of intellectual resolution, and the enormous power of trained physical strength, equally enthroned in placid triumph of scientific achievement."

TOURING THE DAM

The **Hoover Dam Visitor Center** is a vast three-level circular concrete structure with a rooftop overlook. This facility is where you can buy tour tickets; peruse informational exhibits, photographs, and memorabilia; and view videos about the dam and its construction. The Overlook Level additionally provides an unobstructed view of Lake Mead, the dam, the power plant, the Colorado River, and Black Canyon. Have your camera ready.

It costs $10 to visit just this portion, but for an extra $5 you can get the Powerplant Tour as well (see below). Open every day except for Thanksgiving and Christmas, the center closes at 5pm (4:15pm is the last admission time), though hours vary seasonally.

There are two tours available, the Powerplant Tour and the Hoover Dam Tour. The cost of the former is $15 for adults; $12 for seniors, children 4 to 16, and military personnel and their dependents; and free for children 3 and under and military in uniform. It is self-guided and takes about 2 hours if you really stop to look at and read everything (less if you're a skimmer). The more extensive Hoover Dam Tour includes the self-guided portion but adds an hour-long guided tour into the deeper recesses of the facility. It is $30 per person; no children age 7 and under are allowed. Tickets for the Hoover Dam Tour must be purchased at the Visitor Center, while admission to the Visitor Center and tickets for the Powerplant Tour are available online. Parking is $10 no matter which tour you take, and the lot takes cash only. There is no need to call ahead to reserve a place, but for more information, call © 866/730-9097 or 702/494-2517.

On the Powerplant Tour, visitors go to the center, see a movie, and walk on top of the dam. While both tours include a 530-foot descent via elevator into the dam to view the massive generators, the Powerplant Tour is a self-guided tour aided by the occasional information kiosk or guide/docent stationed at intervals along the way; the pricier Hoover Dam Tour offers the same attractions and viewing opportunities, but it is guided, lasts an hour, and is limited to 20 people. If you plan on taking that tour, be aware that it covers over a mile and a half of walking on concrete and gravel, with no handicapped access. The Hoover Dam Tour is offered every half-hour, with the last tour at 3:30pm, while the final Powerplant Tour admission is at 4:15pm.

For more information on the dam, visit www.usbr.gov/lc/hooverdam.

Lake Mead National Recreation Area ★★

Under the auspices of the National Park Service, 1.5-million-acre Lake Mead National Recreation Area was created in 1936 around Lake Mead (the reservoir lake that is the result of the construction of Hoover Dam) and later Lake Mohave to the south (formed by the construction of Davis Dam). Before the lakes emerged, this desert region was brutally hot, dry, and rugged—unfit for human habitation. Today, it's one of the nation's most popular playgrounds, attracting millions of visitors annually. The two lakes comprise 247 square miles. At an elevation of just over 1,000 feet, Lake Mead itself extends some 110 miles upstream toward the Grand Canyon. Its 700-mile shoreline, backed by spectacular cliff and canyon scenery, forms a perfect setting for a wide variety of watersports and desert hiking.

Having said all that, Lake Mead is in the beginning stages of a crisis so large that if unchecked, it would spell the end for Vegas entirely. The nation's largest reservoir has experienced a severe drop-off in levels since 2000, a combination of drought, global warming, and increased use. Whole portions of the lake's edges are now dry, in the process exposing the remains of some of the small towns that were flooded to build the thing in the first place. These have become tourist spots themselves. In 2010, the lake was at 39% of its capacity and hit a record low height of 1,083 feet above sea level. Things got a little better in recent years with increased water flow into the lake, but it is still a fraction of its former self and the long-term risk is still present. According to a research study published in 2008, there is a 50% chance the lake will go dry by 2021, and because it supplies water to Las Vegas (not to mention hydroelectric power), that has grave implications for that city. Let's encourage those fancy new hotels to put in drought-tolerant plants instead of more grass. And don't ask for your towels to be changed every day.

Keep in mind that if the lake water shortage continues, many of the following outdoor activities will probably be affected, if they aren't already.

The **Lake Mead Visitor Center,** renovated and upgraded in 2013, is 4 miles northeast of Boulder City on U.S. 93, at NV 166 (© **702/293-8990**). Here, you can get information on all area activities and services, pick up trail maps and brochures, view informative films, and find out about scenic drives, accommodations, ranger-guided hikes, naturalist programs and lectures, bird-watching, canoeing, camping, lakeside RV parks, and picnic facilities. The center has some informative exhibits about the area and is staffed by friendly folks full of local pride. It's open daily from 9:00am to 4:30pm except Thanksgiving, Christmas, and New Year's Day.

For information on camping, boat rentals, fishing, tours, and more, visit the National Parks Service website at www.nps.gov/lake.

The **entry fee** for the area is $20 per vehicle, which covers all passengers, $15 if you're motorcycling, or $10 per person if you're walking or biking in. Entry fees cover 1 to 7 days and yearly passes are available for $40 per vehicle or individual.

Outdoor Activities

This is a lovely area for scenic drives amid the dramatic desert landscape. One popular route follows the Lakeshore and Northshore scenic drives along the edge of Lake Mead. From these roads, there are panoramic views of the blue lake, set against a backdrop of the browns, blacks, reds, and grays of the desert mountains. Northshore Scenic Drive also leads through areas of brilliant red boulders and rock formations, and you'll find a picnic area along the way.

BOATING & FISHING The **Las Vegas Boat Harbor** (www.boatinglake mead.com; © **702/293-1191**) rents powerboats, pontoon boats, personal watercraft, and watersports equipment. It also carries groceries, clothing, marine supplies, sporting goods, water-skiing gear, fishing equipment, and bait and tackle. Similar services are offered at the **Callville Bay Resort & Marina** (www.callvillebay.com; © **800/255-5561** or 702/565-8958), which is usually less crowded. Nonresidents can get a fishing license here ($69 for a year or $18 for 1 day plus $7 for each additional day; discounts for children

15 and under are available; additional fees apply for special fishing classifications, including trout, which require a $10 stamp for taking or possessing that fish). Largemouth bass, striped bass, channel catfish, crappie, and bluegill are found in Lake Mead; rainbow trout, largemouth bass, and striped bass are in Lake Mohave. You can also arrange here to rent a fully equipped houseboat at **Echo Bay,** 40 miles north.

CAMPING   Lake Mead's shoreline is dotted with campsites, all of them equipped with running water, picnic tables, and grills. Available on a first-come, first-served basis, they are administered by the **National Park Service** (www.nps.gov/lake; ✆ **702/293-8990**). There's a charge of $20 per night at each tent campsite, and up to $35 for RVs.

CANOEING   The **Lake Mead Visitor Center** (see above) can provide a list of outfitters that rent canoes for trips on the Colorado River. A canoeing permit ($22 per person) is required in advance and is available from livery services licensed by the Bureau of Reclamation. Questions about launch permits should be directed to Willow Beach/Black Canyon River Adventures (www. willowbeachharbor.com; ✆ **928/767-4747**). You can apply for and receive the permit on the same day that you plan to canoe.

HIKING   The best season for hiking is November through March (it's too hot the rest of the year). Three trails, ranging in length from .75 mile to 6 miles, originate at the **Lake Mead Visitor Center** (see above), which stocks detailed trail maps. The 6-mile trail goes past remains of the railroad built for the dam project. Be sure to take all necessary desert-hiking precautions. (See "Desert Hiking Advice," below.)

LAKE CRUISES   A delightful way to enjoy Lake Mead is on a cruise aboard the **Lake Mead Cruises** boat *Desert Princess* ★ (www.lakemead cruises.com; ✆ **866/292-9191**), a Mississippi-style paddle-wheeler. It's a relaxing, scenic trip (enjoyed from an open promenade deck or one of two fully enclosed, climate-controlled decks) through Black Canyon and past colorful rock formations known as the Arizona Paint Pots en route to Hoover Dam, which is lit at night. Options include narrated midday cruises ($26 adults, $13 children), Sunday Champagne brunch cruises ($45 adults, $19.50 children), and dinner cruises ($61.50 adults, $25 children). Dinner is served in a pleasant, windowed, air-conditioned dining room. There's a full onboard bar. Brunch and dinner cruises run April through October, and the midday cruises run February through November. Call for departure times.

VALLEY OF FIRE STATE PARK ★★

60 miles NE of Las Vegas

The 36,000-acre Valley of Fire State Park typifies the mountainous, red Mojave Desert that surrounds Las Vegas. It derives its name from the brilliant sandstone formations that were created 150 million years ago by a great shifting of sand, and that continue to be shaped by the geologic processes of wind and water erosion. These are rock formations like you'll never see anywhere

DESERT hiking ADVICE

Except in summer, when temperatures can reach 120°F (49°C) in the shade, the Las Vegas area is great for hiking. The best hiking season is November through March. Great locales include the incredibly scenic Red Rock Canyon (p. 250) and Valley of Fire State Park (p. 246).

Hiking in the desert is exceptionally rewarding, but it can be dangerous. Here are some safety tips:

1. Don't hike alone.
2. Carry plenty of water and drink it often. Don't assume that spring water is safe to drink. A gallon of water per person per day is recommended for hikers.
3. Be alert for signs of heat exhaustion (headache, nausea, dizziness, fatigue, and cool, damp, pale, or red skin).
4. Gauge your fitness accurately. Desert hiking may involve rough or steep terrain. Don't take on more than you can handle.
5. Check weather forecasts before starting out. Thunderstorms can turn into raging flash floods, which are extremely hazardous to hikers.
6. Dress properly. Wear sturdy walking shoes for rock scrambling, long pants (to protect yourself from rocks and cacti), a hat, and sunglasses.
7. Wear sunscreen and carry a small first-aid kit.
8. Be careful when climbing on sandstone, which can be surprisingly soft and crumbly.
9. Don't feed or play with animals, such as the wild burros in Red Rock Canyon. (It's actually illegal to approach them.)
10. Be alert for snakes and insects. Though they're rarely encountered, you'll want to look into a crevice before putting your hand into it.
11. Visit park or other information offices before you start out and acquaint yourself with rules and regulations and any possible hazards. It's also a good idea to tell the staff where you're going, when you'll return, how many are in your party, and so on. Some park offices offer hiker-registration programs.
12. Follow the hiker's creed: Take only photographs and leave only footprints.

else. There is nothing green, just fiery red rocks swirling unrelieved as far as the eye can see. No wonder various sci-fi movies have used this place as a stand-in for another planet. The entire place is very mysterious, loaded with petroglyphs, and totally inhospitable. It's not hard to believe that for the Indians it was a sacred place where men came as a test of their manhood. It is a natural wonder that must be seen to be appreciated.

Although it's hard to imagine in the sweltering Nevada heat, for billions of years these rocks were under hundreds of feet of ocean. This ocean floor began to rise some 200 million years ago, and the waters became more and more shallow. Eventually the sea made a complete retreat, leaving a muddy terrain traversed by ever-diminishing streams. A great sandy desert covered much of the southwestern part of the American continent until about 140 million years ago. Over eons, winds, massive fault action, and water erosion sculpted fantastic formations of sand and limestone. Oxidation of iron in the sands and mud—and the effect of groundwater leaching the oxidized iron—turned the rocks the many hues of red, pink, russet, lavender, and white that

LEAVING (lake) LAS VEGAS

Originally created as a playground for the rich and famous (Céline Dion had a house here), Lake Las Vegas is a man-made reservoir created in a formerly dry, dusty valley about 20 miles east of the city on the way to Lake Mead. Surrounded by multimillion-dollar houses and rambling upscale condominium complexes, the bulk of the area is privately owned; but curving gracefully around the western lip of the lake is Monte Lago Village, an homage to an Italian seaside community that features accommodations, dining, shopping, entertainment, and recreation options for those with a taste (and a budget) for the finer things in life.

The area was hit hard by the global economic recession, and many of the reasons to visit vanished. The fantastic Ritz-Carlton hotel, the casino, and two of the three golf courses closed. Many of the stores and restaurants went out of business, and most of the development sank into bankruptcy.

Things are improving, with the Ritz reborn as a fancy Hilton, but it's still a far cry from what its developers hoped it would be.

There are several shops and restaurants at **Aston MonteLago Village,** Lake Las Vegas Parkway at Strada di Villagio, Henderson (www.montelagovillage.com;

© 877/997-6667). Done as an Italianate village with cobblestone streets and candy-colored buildings, it's a nice place to stroll on spring days.

The former Ritz-Carlton is now operating as the **Hilton Lake Las Vegas Resort & Spa,** 1610 Lake Las Vegas Pkwy. (www.hilton.com; © 702/567-4700). Though not much has changed in the room and amenities department, a focus on the business traveler has diminished some of the personal touches that made it special. Still the immaculate gardens are serene, the pool is a blissful retreat, and rooms are gorgeous, especially those located on the re-creation of the Ponte Vecchio bridge over the lake.

On the other side of the lake, the **Westin Lake Las Vegas,** 101 MonteLago Blvd. (www.westinlakelasvegas.com; © 702/567-6000), is new but in name only, having formerly been a Loews, and before that a Hyatt. Not much has changed with the new ownership except the addition of their trademark "Heavenly" beds and some toning down of the Moroccan-themed decor. There are more than 500 rooms, a spa, several pools, restaurants, recreation programs, kids programs, and more, so you won't be lacking in things to do here or in ways to be pampered.

---

can be seen today. Logs of ancient forests washed down from faraway highlands and became petrified fossils, which can be seen along two interpretive trails.

Getting There

From Las Vegas, take I-15 N to exit 75 (Valley of Fire turnoff). However, the more scenic route is I-15 N to Lake Mead Boulevard east to Northshore Road (NV 167) and then proceed north to the Valley of Fire exit. The first route takes about an hour, the second, 1½ hours.

There is a $10-per-vehicle admission charge to the park ($8 for Nevada residents), regardless of how many people you cram inside.

Plan on spending a minimum of an hour in the park, though you can spend a great deal more time. It can get very hot in there (there is nothing to relieve the sun beating down and reflecting off of all that red), and there is no water, so be certain to bring a liter, maybe two, per person in the summer. Without a guide you must stay on paved roads, but don't worry if they end; you can always turn around and go back to the main road. You can see a great deal from the car, and there are also hiking trails.

Numerous **sightseeing tours** go to the Valley of Fire; inquire at your hotel.

What to See & Do

There are no food concessions or gas stations in the park; however, you can obtain meals or gas on NV 167 or in nearby **Overton** (15 miles northwest on NV 169).

At the southern edge of town is the **Lost City Museum ★**, 721 S. Moapa Valley Blvd. (✆ **702/397-2193**), a sweet little museum, very nicely done, commemorating an ancient ancestral Puebloan village that was discovered in the region in 1924. Artifacts dating back 12,000 years are on display, as are clay jars, dried corn and beans, arrowheads, seashell necklaces, and willow baskets from the ancient Pueblo culture that inhabited this region between A.D. 300 and 1150. Other exhibits document the Mormon farmers who settled the valley in the 1860s. A large collection of local rocks—petrified wood, fern fossils, iron pyrite, green copper, and red iron oxide, along with manganese blown bottles turned purple by the ultraviolet rays of the sun—are also displayed here. The museum is surrounded by reconstructed wattle-and-daub pueblos. Admission is $5 for adults, free for children 17 and under. It's open daily from 8:30am to 4:30pm, but closed Thanksgiving, December 25, and January 1.

Information headquarters for Valley of Fire is the **Visitor Center** on NV 169, 6 miles west of Northshore Road (✆ **702/397-2088**). It's open daily 8:30am to 4:30pm and is worth a quick stop for information and a glance at some of the informational exhibits before entering the park. Postcards, books, slides, and films are for sale here, and you can pick up hiking maps and brochures. Rangers can answer your park-related questions. For online information about the park, which is open sunrise to sunset, go to www.parks.nv.gov/parks/valley-of-fire-state-park/.

There are **hiking trails, shaded picnic sites,** and **two campgrounds** in the park. Most sites are equipped with tables, grills, water, and restrooms. A $20-per-vehicle, per-night camping fee is charged for use of the campground (plus $10 for utility hookups); if you're not camping, it costs $10 per vehicle to enter the park.

Some of the notable formations in the park have been named for the shapes they vaguely resemble—a duck, an elephant, seven sisters, domes, beehives, and so on. Mouse's Tank is a natural basin that collects rainwater, so named for a fugitive Paiute called Mouse, who hid there in the late 1890s. **Native American petroglyphs** etched into the rock walls and boulders—some dating from 3,000 years ago—can be observed on self-guided trails. Petroglyphs at Atlatl Rock and Petroglyph Canyon are both easily accessible. In summer,

9

DAY TRIPS FROM LAS VEGAS

Valley of Fire State Park

when temperatures are usually over 100°F (38°C), you may have to settle for driving through the park in an air-conditioned car.

RED ROCK CANYON ★★★

19 miles W of Las Vegas

If you need a break from the casinos of Vegas, Red Rock Canyon is a balm for your overstimulated soul. Less than 20 miles away—but a world apart—this is a magnificent, unspoiled vista that should cleanse and refresh you (and if you must, a morning visit should leave you enough time for an afternoon's gambling). You can drive the panoramic 13-mile **Scenic Drive** (daily 6am–dusk, $7 per vehicle) or explore more in depth on foot, making it perfect for athletes and armchair types alike. There are many interesting sights and trail heads along the drive itself. The **National Conservation Area** (www.nv.blm.gov/redrockcanyon) offers hiking trails and internationally acclaimed rock-climbing opportunities. Especially notable is 7,068-foot Mount Wilson, the highest sandstone peak among the bluffs; for information on climbing, contact the **Red Rock Canyon Visitor Center** at ✆ 702/515-5350.

There are picnic areas along the drive and in nearby **Spring Mountain Ranch State Park** (www.parks.nv.gov/smr.htm; ✆ **702/594-7529**), 5 miles south, which also offers plays in an outdoor theater during the summer. The entrance fee is $10 per vehicle.

Getting There

Just drive west on Charleston Boulevard, which becomes NV 159. As soon as you leave the city, the red rocks will begin to loom around you. The visitor center will be on your right.

You can also go on an **organized tour. Gray Line** (www.grayline.com; ✆ **800/634-6579**), among other companies, runs bus tours to Red Rock Canyon. Inquire at your hotel tour desk.

Finally, you can go **by bike.** Not very far out of town (at Rainbow Boulevard), Charleston Boulevard is flanked by a bike path that continues for about 11 miles to the visitor center/scenic drive. The path is hilly but not difficult, if you're in reasonable shape. However, exploring Red Rock Canyon by bike should be attempted only by exceptionally fit and experienced bikers.

Just off NV 159, you'll see the turnoff for the **Red Rock Canyon Visitor Center** (www.nv.blm.gov/redrockcanyon; ✆ 702/515-5350), which marks the entrance to the park. It features outdoor exhibits on the flora and fauna found in the canyon and you can also pick up info on trails and the driving route. The center is open daily from 8am to 4:30pm.

About Red Rock Canyon

The geological history of these ancient stones goes back some 600 million years. Over eons, the forces of nature have formed Red Rock's sandstone monoliths into arches, natural bridges, and massive sculptures painted in a stunning palette of gray-white limestone and dolomite, black mineral deposits, and oxidized minerals in earth-toned sienna hues ranging from pink to crimson and burgundy. Orange and green lichens add further contrast, as do spring-fed areas of lush foliage. And formations, such as **Calico Hill,** are brilliantly white where groundwater has leached out oxidized iron. Cliffs cut by deep canyons tower 2,000 feet above the valley floor.

During most of its history, Red Rock Canyon was below a warm, shallow sea. Massive fault action and volcanic eruptions caused this seabed to begin rising some 225 million years ago. As the waters receded, sea creatures died, and the calcium in their bodies combined with sea minerals to form limestone cliffs studded with ancient fossils. Some 45 million years later, the region was buried beneath thousands of feet of windblown sand. As time progressed, iron oxide and calcium carbonate infiltrated the sand, consolidating it into cross-bedded rock.

About 100 million years ago, massive fault action began dramatically shifting the rock landscape here, forming spectacular limestone and sandstone cliffs and rugged canyons punctuated by waterfalls, shallow streams, and serene oasis pools.

Red Rock's valley is home to more than 45 species of mammals, about 100 species of birds, 30 reptiles and amphibians, and an abundance of plant life. Ascending the slopes from the valley, you'll see cactus and creosote bushes, aromatic purple sage, yellow-flowering blackbrush, yucca and Joshua trees, and, at higher elevations, clusters of forest-green pinyon, juniper, and ponderosa pines. In spring, the desert blooms with extraordinary wildflowers.

In the latter part of the 19th century, Red Rock was a mining site, and later a sandstone quarry that provided materials for many buildings in Los Angeles, San Francisco, and early Las Vegas. In 1990, Red Rock Canyon became a National Conservation Area that comprises approximately 197,000 acres.

What to See & Do

Begin with a stop at the **Visitor Center;** while there is a $7-per-vehicle fee for entering the park, you also can pick up guides, hiking trail maps, and lists of local flora and fauna. You can also view exhibits that tell the history of the canyon and depict its plant and animal life, including the thousands of wild horses and burros, protected by an act of Congress since 1971. Call ahead to find out about ranger-guided tours as well as informative guided hikes offered by such groups as the Sierra Club and the Audubon Society.

The easiest thing to do is to **drive the 13-mile scenic loop ★★★** (or give it a go on your bike for a moderately difficult ride). It really is a loop, and it only goes one way, so once you start, you are committed to driving the entire thing. You can stop the car to admire a number of fabulous views and sights along the way, have a picnic, or hike. As you drive, observe how dramatically the milky-white limestone alternates with iron-rich red rocks. Farther along, the mountains become solid limestone with canyons running between them, which lead to an evergreen forest—a surprising sight in the desert.

If you're up to it, however, we can't stress enough that the way to really see the canyon is by **hiking.** Every trail is incredible—glance over your options and decide what you might be looking for. You can begin from the Visitor Center or drive into the loop, park your car, and start from points therein. Hiking trails range from a .7-mile-loop stroll to a waterfall (its flow varying seasonally) at Lost Creek to much longer and more strenuous treks. Actually, all the hikes involve a certain amount of effort, as you have to scramble over rocks on even the shortest hikes. Unfit or undexterous people should beware. Be sure to wear good shoes, as the rocks can be slippery. You must have a map; you won't get lost forever (there usually are other hikers around to help you out, eventually), but you can still lose your way. Once deep into the rocks, everything looks the same, even with the map, so give yourself extra time for each hike (at least an additional hour), regardless of its billed length.

A popular 2-mile round-trip hike leads to **Pine Creek Canyon** and the creek-side ruins of a historic home site surrounded by ponderosa pine trees. Our hiking trail of choice is the **Calico Basin,** which is accessed along the loop. After an hour walk up the rocks (which is not that well marked), you end up at an oasis surrounded by sheer walls of limestone (which makes the oasis itself inaccessible, alas). In the summer, flowers and deciduous trees grow out of the walls.

As you hike, keep your eyes peeled for lizards, the occasional desert tortoise, herds of bighorn sheep, birds, and other critters. But the rocks themselves are the most fun, with small caves to explore and rock formations to climb on. On trails along Calico Hills and the escarpment, look for "Indian marbles," a local name for small, rounded sandstone rocks that have eroded off larger sandstone formations. Petroglyphs are also tucked away in various locales.

Biking is a tremendous way to travel the loop. There are also terrific off-road mountain-biking trails, with levels from amateur to expert. No need to haul your bike with you on, rent one from one of the recommended shops linked on Friends of Red Rock, (www.friendsofredrockcanyon.org).

The gleaming, luxurious **Red Rock Resort** (p. 90) gives day-trippers a highly desirable refueling point on a trip to the canyon. Stop by the food court Capriotti's, the economical submarine sandwich shop. The subs are ideal for takeout for picnics in the park (buy a cheap Styrofoam ice chest at a convenience store) or for in-room dining as you rest up in your hotel post-hike.

Nearby **Bonnie Springs Ranch** (www.bonniesprings.com; ℂ **702/875-4191**) has a cute Wild West old town, horseback riding, a petting zoo, and more. Horseback riding $60 for 1 hour, pony rides $7.50 per child, zoo admission Monday and Tuesday $7, Wednesday through Sunday $10 adults, $7 children.

MOUNT CHARLESTON ★★

About 35 miles NW of Las Vegas

Although officially known as the Springs Mountains National Recreation Area, this region is more popularly referred to by the name of its most prominent landmark, the 11,918-foot-high Mount Charleston. Visible from Las

Vegas proper, the mountain and its surrounding recreation areas have been a popular getaway for locals and vacationers alike for decades.

Comprising more than 316,000 acres of the Humboldt-Toiyabe National Forest (the largest in the lower 48), the area is practically an earth science class covering geography of such variety that it almost causes whiplash. As you start up the road toward the peak, you are surrounded by the kind of desert sage brush and Joshua trees that are most predominant at the lower levels. Suddenly the road takes a curve and a dip, and the desert gives way to a pinyon-juniper-based ecosystem, full of craggy canyons and trees. Finally, you dive into the full-on forests of ponderosa and bristlecone pines, which create a lush oasis powered by more than 100 natural springs formed by water and snow runoff that soaks through the porous limestone rock and eventually bubbles to the surface.

Outdoor activities are the predominant lure and include hiking, camping, rock climbing, and, during the winter months, skiing and snowboarding.

Getting There

Head north on I-15 away from the Strip and then transition to U.S. 95 N. About 18 miles of freeway-style driving will bring you to the first of two roads in the Mount Charleston area. Kyle Canyon Road/NV 157 will take you about 17 miles up toward the summit and is where you'll find the **Spring Mountain Visitor Center,** open 9am to 4pm daily (© **702/872-5486**), many of the campgrounds and hiking trails, the Mount Charleston Resort, and the Mount Charleston Lodge. A few miles farther is NV 156, which runs about 18 miles up to the Lee Canyon (see "Snow Sports," below). It's only about 35 miles or so from Downtown Las Vegas, but traffic on the freeways in town is often difficult (to say the least) so plan an hour of travel time to be safe. *Note:* Chains are often required during or after snowfalls, which can be epic in the area. A December 2010 storm dumped a record 90 inches here over the course of several days.

Also note that there are no gas stations, convenience stores, or other services (and that often includes cellphone service) in the area, so be sure to fill up the tank and bring whatever supplies you may need with you.

Outdoor Activities

You might well be satisfied with driving up to the region and, if it's wintertime, gazing at the snow from the warmth of your vehicle. We know that many of you come to Las Vegas in the winter to get away from the snow, but for those who don't get to see it very often, snow-covered peaks could very well be an entertaining sight. But if you want to actually get out of the car, there are a number of recreational activities available.

CAMPING There are seven campgrounds in the Mount Charleston area, although only the McWilliams, Fletcher View, and Kyle Canyon sites are open year-round. Some have hookups if you are bringing your camper with you, while others are good for just tents and your sleeping bag; most have toilets,

THE grand canyon

The geographically challenged among us believe that the Grand Canyon is just a hop, skip, and a jump from Las Vegas and therefore a great idea for a side trip while visiting Sin City. While this may be true from a strictly comparative basis— the canyon is closer than say, London— it's not exactly what you'd call "close."

While the West Rim is closer to Las Vegas at 180 miles and about 2 hours away, the more popular side for visitors is the South Rim at 270 miles and another 2 hours farther, as there's more to see and do.

The quickest and easiest way to get to the West Rim is via helicopter. **Papillon** (www.papillon.com; ✆ **888/635-7272**), a popular charter service, offers several packages to the west side, including a bird's eye view of Hoover Dam, Lake Mead, and possibly the Grapevine Mesa. The shorter, 4-hour tour ($129–$219) is just a quick fly-by over the canyon, but the narrated guide, available in multiple languages, is thorough, informative, and excellent. A more expensive package (that extends the tour by an hour for about $100 more) allows for a landing at the bottom of the canyon, 4,000 feet below the rim, where you're treated to a champagne picnic in one of the most gorgeous settings you'll ever dine. If you want a full-day excursion, there's an option to combine the flight to canyon, a boat trip on the Colorado River, and VIP passes on the Sky-Walk bridge ($449–$539).

For the most serene experience, the North Rim is the unsung hero of the Grand Canyon, where visitors can be closer to nature without all the tour bus crowds. But that solitude comes at a price, as the North Rim is the most difficult to get to. Despite it being the same distance as the South rim, this side is more wild and secluded, so a day trip by car isn't advised. Fortunately between April and November, Papillon heads there for a daylong tour ($319–$369) that packs in as much nature as you can muster. The 8-hour day starts with a prop plane ride with stunning views of Hoover Dam, Lake Mead and the Colorado River before dropping you off at an isolated landing strip at Bar 10 Ranch, a bona fide ranch where they sometimes have to shoo the cattle from the runway. Your guide will take you via ATV on a 2-hour round trip tour down to the North Rim, 3,000 feet above the Colorado River, where you can appreciate the majesty of the canyon and not fight tourists to

fire pits, and other outdoorsy conveniences. Fees range from around $10 to $50, depending on the number of people, type of vehicle, and facilities or hookups. A full listing of the campgrounds is available at the USDA Forest Service website at www.fs.fed.us (then search for the Spring Mountains National Recreation Area). To make reservations for any of the sites, use the National Recreation Reservation Service at ✆ **877/444-6777** or head online to www.recreation.gov.

HIKING   Whether you are an expert hiker or a casual walker, there is probably a trail here for you—more than two dozen total. The Echo/Little Falls trail is a relatively easy mile or so through forests that lead to a small waterfall. On the other end of the scale is the South Loop, an 8-mile trek that leads you almost all the way to the summit of Mount Charleston more than 11,000 feet up. You can pick up a trail guide at the Spring Mountain Visitor Center.

breathe in the landscape. The tour includes a cowboy's lunch back at the lodge, and try to stay awake on the flight back home.

Whenever you bring up the West Rim, folks always mention the SkyWalk, and it's usually not in a favorable manner. More than 1 million pounds of steel went into the construction of this U-shaped footbridge that extends 70 feet from the rim over the canyon. The transparent glass base is supposed to allow visitors to look down and absorb the awesomeness of the Grand Canyon. However, exorbitant fees (about $44, which go to the Hualapai tribe whose reservation the bridge is on) and relatively unreasonable demands—no cameras, no backpacks—keep a lot of visitors away. Before you decide to pay the price of admission, consider that just a few yards from the bridge, Eagle's Point offers similar, if not better, views absolutely free.

To visit the South Rim, there are more helicopter tours available, but we suggest if you've got a whole day to kill, get up early and catch the Papillon Bus Tour ($89–$150). The coach is air-conditioned and comfortable, and makes frequent rest stops. You'll get off the bus for photo opps at Hoover Dam, drive through the

900-year-old Joshua tree forest, and also receive a voucher for lunch at the National Geographic food court. Like a trip in school, this will be a learning experience, thanks to a knowledgeable driver well-versed in the history and geology of the American Southwest.

Or be the captain of your ship! Renting a car and driving is an excellent and affordable option, especially if you've got a group. Four to five hours over the two-lane highway (three to the West Rim) is doable, but not unheard of. Plus you'll have the luxury of staying as long as you like and exploring on your own terms. We find that many visitors decide to stay overnight, just for the pleasure of seeing the canyon at dusk and dawn. The shifts in light are a remarkable sight here.

If you're taking your own car, head east on Flamingo Road or Tropicana Boulevard to I-515 S. This becomes NV 93, which crosses over Hoover Dam into Arizona and leads to I-40 at Kingman. Take the interstate east to NV 64 at Williams, Arizona, and follow the signs north. Drivers should be advised that much of the route to the Grand Canyon from Las Vegas is along narrow, twisty roads that can be a challenge and are often jammed with traffic.

There is no fee to use the trails, and follow all of the admonitions about bringing plenty of water and not drinking from the natural springs (they may contain parasites that can make you sick).

ROCK CLIMBING   There are several rock-climbing opportunities available in the Mount Charleston area, but all of them are do-it-yourself—no cushy controlled environments here. The most popular sites are the Hood along the unfortunately named Trail Canyon Trail, or Robber's Roost, accessed from the trail head along Highway 158. For more information, pick up a guide at the Spring Mountain Visitor Center.

SNOW SPORTS   **Lee Canyon** (formerly Las Vegas Ski and Snowboard Resort), Highway 156, Mount Charleston (www.leecanyonlv.com; ☏ **702/385-2754**), offers three chairlifts and more than 30 trails ranging from beginner to advanced, plus terrain parks for snowboarders and a tubing area. Lift tickets are $40 to $60 for adults, and $30 to $45 for children 12 and under and seniors 60 and over. The facility offers a full array of equipment and clothing rentals; there's also a small snack bar and sundry shop if you forgot to bring a camera with which to record yourself in full downhill glory (or falling repeatedly, if you are like us). It is usually open late November through early April from 9am until 4pm, but that may vary based on conditions.

Where to Stay & Dine

In addition to the aforementioned snack shop at the Lee Canyon, there is only one other dining option outside of the Mount Charleston Resort (see below). The **Mount Charleston Lodge,** 5375 Kyle Canyon Rd. (www.mtcharleston lodge.com; ✆ **702/872-5408**), has a rustic dining room with 20-foot ceilings in an A-frame, ski-lodge type building; a big bar; an open fireplace in the center of the room; big windows; and an outdoor patio from which you can enjoy the scenic views from its 7,717-foot elevation. They serve a wide range of American comfort food, and are open from 8am to 8pm Sunday through Thursday and from 8am to 9pm on Friday and Saturday. The lounge is open daily until midnight.

The Resort on Mount Charleston ★   This woodsy retreat has undergone some serious improvements over the last few years that have kept the charm of the place, but modernized it and moved it upscale a notch or two. The ski chalet-style buildings (log and stone exteriors) are tucked into a canyon, providing a gorgeous backdrop for a peaceful respite. The lobby has a big fireplace perfect for warming up after a winter hike, along with a small menagerie of stuffed animals that seem *de rigueur* in a place like this.

The rooms range from standard motel size to presidential suites, all with comfortably modern furnishings, flatscreen TVs, faux fireplaces, iPod radios, DVD players, and more.

On site there is a small spa and fitness center; a full-service restaurant (classic American fare); a sundry store/bistro with quick bites; and a bar complete with billiards and even a few video poker machines if you're going into gambling withdrawal.

2 Kyle Canyon Rd. www.mtcharlestonresort.com. ✆ **888/559-1888** or 702/872-5500. 61 units. $40 and up double. Resort fee $12 tax included. Free self-parking. Extra person $15. Children 17 and under stay free in parent's room. Pets under 25 pounds permitted, $25 per animal up to 2. **Amenities:** 2 restaurants; bar/lounge; spa; free property-wide Wi-Fi.

PLANNING YOUR TRIP TO LAS VEGAS

Whether you are visiting Las Vegas for the first time or the 50th, planning a trip here can be an overwhelming experience—as overwhelming as the city itself. With more than 150,000 hotel rooms, nearly as many slot machines, thousands of restaurants, and dozens of shows and attractions, there are seemingly endless ways to lose or waste your money. This chapter is designed to help you navigate the practical details of designing a Vegas experience that is tailored to your needs, from getting to and around the city to advice on the best times to visit and more.

Lots of people, both from the U.S. and abroad, believe that Las Vegas is the way it is portrayed in movies and television. For the most part, it isn't. Well, okay, you are more likely to run into a random showgirl or Elvis impersonator here than you are in say, Wichita, but they aren't in the background of every photo opportunity. International visitors, especially, should pay close attention to the material that follows in order to prepare for the most common non-showgirl issues you may encounter in Las Vegas or on your way here.

GETTING THERE
By Plane

Las Vegas is served by **McCarran International Airport,** 5757 Wayne Newton Blvd. (www.mccarran.com; ℂ **702/261-5211,** TDD 702/261-3111), just a few minutes' drive from the southern end of the Strip, where the bulk of casinos and hotels are concentrated. The airport is known by the code **LAS.**

Most major domestic and many international airlines fly into Las Vegas, and the city acts as a major routing point for low-cost Southwest Airlines.

The airport has two terminals. Terminal 1 serves mostly domestic carriers with four sets of gates. A and B gates are accessible to the main ticketing area and baggage claim by (very long) hallways, while most of the C and all of the D gates are reached by tram. The ultramodern Terminal 3 primarily services international and some domestic carriers like United with its 14 gates.

In case you're wondering what happened to Terminal 2, it closed when Terminal 3 opened. Why they didn't re-number things is a mystery.

Each terminal has its own baggage-claim facility and services such as dining, shopping, and traveler assistance, along with ground transportation areas for taxis, buses, and shuttles to the rental-car facility.

And yes, all of the terminals and baggage claims have slot machines just in case you want to lose a few bucks while you're waiting for your luggage.

By Car

The main highway connecting Las Vegas with the rest of the country is **I-15**; it links Montana, Idaho, and Utah with Southern California. The drive from Los Angeles is quite popular and can get very crowded on weekends as revelers make their way to and from Las Vegas.

From the east, take **I-70** or **I-80** west to Kingman, Arizona, and then **U.S. 93** north to Downtown Las Vegas (Fremont St.). From the south, take **I-10** west to Phoenix, and then U.S. 93 north to Las Vegas. From San Francisco, take I-80 east to Reno, and then **U.S. 95** south to Las Vegas.

Vegas is 286 miles from Phoenix, 759 miles from Denver, 421 miles from Salt Lake City, 269 miles from Los Angeles, and 586 miles from San Francisco.

International visitors should note that insurance and taxes are almost never included in quoted rental-car rates in the U.S. Be sure to ask your rental agency about these. They can add a significant cost to your car rental.

For information on car rentals and gasoline (petrol) in Las Vegas, see "Getting Around: By Car," below.

By Bus

Bus travel is often the most economical form of public transit for short hops between U.S. cities, but it's certainly not an option for everyone. Though getting to Vegas this way is cheaper, especially if you book in advance, it's also time consuming (a 1-hr. flight from L.A. becomes a 5- to 8-hr. trek by bus) and usually not as comfortable. So you need to figure out how much time and comfort mean to you. **Greyhound** (www.greyhound.com; ℂ **800/231-2222** in the U.S.; ℂ **001/214/849-8100** outside the U.S. without toll-free access) is the sole nationwide bus line.

The main Greyhound terminal in Las Vegas is located Downtown next to the Plaza hotel, 200 S. Main St. (ℂ **702/383-9792**), and is open 24 hours. Although the neighborhood around it has improved dramatically, it is still a busy bus station and so normal safety precautions should be taken in and around it.

Megabus (℡ 877/462-6342; www.megabus.com) operates coaches from Los Angeles to the Regional Transportation Commission's South Strip Transfer Terminal at 6675 Gillespie St. near McCarran International Airport. From there you can easily transfer (hence the name) to many of the city's bus routes, including those that travel to the Strip (see "Getting Around: By Bus," below).

By Train

Amtrak (℡ 800/872-7245; www.amtrak.com) does not currently offer direct rail service, although plans have been in the works for years to restore the rails between Los Angeles and Las Vegas. We've been hearing these reports for so long now, they just make us roll our eyes.

In the meantime, you can take the train to Los Angeles or Barstow, and Amtrak will get you to Las Vegas by bus, which takes 5 to 6 hours depending on traffic.

GETTING AROUND

It isn't too hard to navigate your way around Vegas. But do remember: Thanks to huge hotel acreage, often very slow traffic, and lots and lots of people—like you—trying to explore, getting around takes a lot longer than you might think. Heck, it can take 15 to 20 minutes to get from your room to another part of your hotel! Always allow for plenty of time to get from point A to point B.

Getting into Town from the Airport

Getting to your hotel from the airport is a cinch. You can grab one of the roughly nine gajillion cabs that are lined up waiting for you (see "By Taxi," p. 264), summon your favorite ride share service such as Lyft or Uber (designated pick up areas are in the parking garages of each terminal), or you can grab a shuttle bus. **Bell Transportation** (www.bell-trans.com; ℡ 800/274-7433 or 702/739-7990) runs 20-passenger minibuses daily (3:30am–1am) between the airport and all major Las Vegas hotels and motels. The cost is $7 per person each way to hotels on the Strip or around the Convention Center, and $8.50 to Downtown and other off-Strip properties (north of Sahara Ave. and west of I-15). Several other companies run similar ventures—just look for the signs for the shuttle bus queues, located just outside of the baggage-claim area. Buses from the airport leave every few minutes. When you want to check out of your hotel and head back to the airport, call at least 2 hours in advance to be safe (though often you can just flag down one of the buses outside any major hotel).

Even less expensive are **Citizens Area Transit (CAT)** buses (www.rtcsnv.com/transit; ℡ 702/228-7433). The no. 109 bus goes from the airport to the South Strip Transfer Terminal at Gillespie St. and Sunset Rd., where you can transfer to the Strip and Downtown Express (SDX) or Deuce line that runs along the Strip into Downtown. Alternately, the no. 108 bus departs from the airport and takes you Downtown. The fares for buses on Strip routes are $6 for adults for 2 hours or $8 for 24 hours. Other routes are $2 for a single ride. *Note:* You might have a long walk from the bus stop to the hotel entrance, even if the bus stop is right in front of your hotel. Shuttles and taxis are able to get right up to the entrance, so choose one of those if you're lugging lots of baggage.

If you have a large group with you, you might also try one of the limos that wait curbside at the airport and charge $45 to $65 for a trip to the Strip. The price may go up with additional passengers, so ask about the fee very carefully. The aforementioned Bell Transportation is one reputable company that operates limousines in addition to their fleet of shuttle buses (call in advance).

By Car

If you plan to confine yourself to one part of the Strip (or one cruise down to it) or to Downtown, your feet will suffice. Otherwise, we highly recommend that visitors rent a car. The Strip is too spread out for walking (and Las Vegas is often too hot or too cold to make strolls pleasant); Downtown is too far away for a cheap cab ride, and public transportation is often ineffective in getting you where you want to go. Plus, return visits call for exploration in more remote parts of the city, and a car brings freedom, especially if you want to do any side trips at your own pace.

You should note that places with addresses some 60 blocks east or west of the Strip are actually less than a 10-minute drive—provided there is no traffic.

Having advocated renting a car, we should warn you that traffic is pretty terrible, especially on and around the busy tourist areas. A general rule of thumb is to avoid driving on the Strip whenever you can and give yourself plenty of extra time during rush hour to get where you want to go (see p. 265 for some helpful tips on how to get around the worst of the traffic).

When it comes to parking, it used to be that Las Vegas was where you could park on the most expensive real estate in the country for free. And that's still true—depending on where you want to park. In June 2016, MGM Resorts properties (Mandalay Bay, Delano, Luxor, Excalibur, MGM Grand, Aria, New York–New York, Bellagio, Vdara, The Mirage, and Monte Carlo) instituted parking fees for both valet and self-parking. You'll get 1 hour free at all of the above. For Circus-Circus, Excalibur, Luxor, and Monte Carlo, self-parking is $5 to $8 (except for Circus-Circus, which remains free) and valet is $8 to $13. At Aria/Vdara, Bellagio, Mandalay Bay/Delano, MGM Grand, The Mirage, and New York–New York, self-parking is $7 to $10 and valet is $13 to $18. During events at T-Mobile Arena, all that might go out the window, with possible surge pricing going into effect as well as refusal of entry, even if you're trying to park at your home hotel. Your best bet to avoid a parking headache is to leave your car where it is.

Parking at the rest of the Strip properties, for now, remain free. When it comes to valet, for mere $2 to $5 tip, you can park right at the door, though the valet usually fills up on busy nights and is restricted at some hotels to elite players' club members. In those cases, you can use the gigantic self-parking lots that all hotels have. Mandarin Oriental and Four Seasons are the exceptions to this rule, as both only offer valet parking at $30 and $22, respectively.

If you're visiting from abroad note that insurance and taxes are almost never included in quoted rental-car rates in the U.S. Be sure to ask your rental agency about these. They can add a significant cost to your car rental.

At press time, in Nevada, the cost of gasoline (also known as gas, but never petrol) is around $2.88 per gallon and tends to vary unpredictably. Taxes are already included in the printed price. One U.S. gallon equals 3.8 liters or .85 imperial gallons. Fill-up locations are known as gas or service stations. Las Vegas prices typically fall near the nationwide average. You can also check **www.vegasgasprices.com** for recent costs.

RENTING A CAR

All of the major car rental companies have outlets in Las Vegas, as do **E-Z Rent-A-Car** (www.e-zrentacar.com) and **Payless** (www.paylesscarrental.com).

Rental policies vary from company to company, but generally speaking you must be at least 25 years of age with a major credit or debit card to rent a vehicle in Las Vegas. Some companies will rent to those between 21 and 24, but will usually charge extra ($20–$30 per day) and will require proof of insurance and a major credit card; also, they may restrict the type of vehicle you are allowed to rent (forget those zippy convertibles).

All of the major car rental companies are located at a consolidated facility at 7135 Gilespie St., just a block off Las Vegas Blvd. near Warm Springs Rd. and about 2½ miles from the airport. When you arrive, look for the signs for BUSES AND SHUTTLES in the baggage-claim area and follow them outside, where you'll find blue-and-white buses marked MCCARRAN RENT-A-CAR CENTER. It takes about 10 minutes to make the trip, although it's worth noting that the lines for buses and at the car-rental counters can be long—budget some extra time if you have somewhere to be right after you get to town.

The rental-car facility is modern and easily navigable, and just in case you resisted while at the airport, there are slot machines next to the rental counters as well. Welcome to Vegas!

When exiting the facility, take three right turns and you are on the Strip, about 2 miles south of Mandalay Bay.

Car-rental rates vary even more than airline fares. The price you pay depends on the size of the car, where and when you pick it up and drop it off, the length of the rental period, where and how far you drive it, whether you purchase insurance, and a host of other factors. Finding the answers, online or at the counter, to a few key questions could save you hundreds of dollars:

o Are weekend rates lower than weekday rates? In Vegas this is usually true, although holiday or special events weekends can be more costly. Ask if the rate is the same for pickup Friday morning, for instance, as it is for Thursday night.

- Is a weekly rate cheaper than the daily rate? Even if you need the car for only 4 days, it may be cheaper to keep it for 5.
- Does the agency assess a drop-off charge if you don't return the car to the same location where you picked it up? Is it cheaper to pick up the car at the airport than at a Downtown location?
- Are special promotional rates available? Terms change constantly, and reservations agents are notorious for not mentioning available discounts unless you ask.
- Are discounts available for members of AARP, AAA, frequent-flier programs, or trade unions? If you belong to any of these organizations, you may be eligible for discounts of up to 30%.
- Are there additional fees? In Las Vegas, expect to add about 35% to 40% on top of the rental fee, including a $1.60-per-day vehicle license fee, a $3.75-per-day facility fee, a 10% concession fee, and about 20% in taxes and state government surcharges. Ouch.
- What is the cost of adding an additional driver's name to the contract?
- How many free miles are included in the price? Free mileage is often negotiable, depending on the length of the rental.

Some companies offer "refueling packages," in which you pay for an entire tank of gas up front. The price is usually fairly competitive with local gas prices, but you don't get credit for any gas remaining in the tank; and because it is virtually impossible to use up every last bit of fuel before you return it, you will usually wind up paying more overall than you would if you just filled it up yourself. There are several gas stations within a few blocks of the car-rental center, including three at the intersection of Las Vegas Blvd. and Warm Springs Rd. You may pay a few extra pennies at them than you would at stations elsewhere in town, but in the long run it's still a better deal.

Many available packages include airfare, accommodations, and a rental car with unlimited mileage. Compare these prices with the cost of booking airline tickets and renting a car separately to see if such offers are good deals. Internet resources can make comparison-shopping easier.

SURFING FOR RENTAL CARS

For booking rental cars online, the best deals are usually found at rental-car company websites, although all the major online travel agencies also offer rental-car reservation services. **Priceline** (www.priceline.com) and **Hotwire** (www.hotwire.com) work well for rental cars; the only "mystery" is which major rental company you get, and for most travelers, the difference between Hertz, Avis, and Budget is negligible.

DEMYSTIFYING RENTAL-CAR INSURANCE

Before you drive off in a rental car, be sure you're insured. Hasty assumptions about your personal auto insurance or a rental agency's additional coverage could end up costing you tens of thousands of dollars—even if you are involved in an accident that was clearly the fault of another driver.

DRIVE IN style

If the idea of tooling around Las Vegas in a pedestrian rent-a-box just doesn't sound appealing, you can always indulge your fantasies by going with something more exotic.

Las Vegas Exotic Car Rentals (www. vegasexoticrentals.com; ℭ **866/871-1893** or 702/736-2592) has a fleet from makers such as Lamborghini, Bentley, Ferrari, and Lotus, plus a stable of classic American muscle cars like the Chevrolet Corvette. They even feature an Aston Martin, if you want to work out your inner James Bond while buzzing between casinos. Rates start at about $300 per day and go up from there—sometimes, way up. At press time, the Lamborghini Murcielago roadster was $1,895 per day, or roughly what you'll pay for a week in a suite at a nice Vegas hotel.

If you already hold a **private auto insurance** policy in the United States, you are most likely covered for loss of, or damage to, a rental car, and liability in case of injury to any other party involved in an accident. Be sure to find out whether you are covered in Vegas, whether your policy extends to all persons who will be driving the rental car, how much liability is covered in case an outside party is injured in an accident, and whether the type of vehicle you are renting is included under your contract. (Rental trucks, sport utility vehicles, and luxury vehicles may not be covered.)

Most **major credit cards** provide some degree of coverage as well—provided they were used to pay for the rental. Terms vary widely, however, so be sure to call your credit card company directly before you rent. If you don't have a private auto insurance policy, the credit card you use to rent a car may provide primary coverage if you decline the rental agency's insurance. This means that the credit card company will cover damage or theft of a rental car for the full cost of the vehicle. If you do have a private auto insurance policy, your credit card may provide secondary coverage—which basically covers your deductible. *Credit cards do not cover liability* or the cost of injury to an outside party and/or damage to an outside party's vehicle. If you do not hold an insurance policy, you may want to seriously consider purchasing additional liability insurance from your rental company. Be sure to check the terms, however: Some rental agencies cover liability only if the renter is not at fault; even then, the rental company's obligation varies from state to state. Bear in mind that each credit card company has its own peculiarities; call your own credit card company for details before relying on a card for coverage. Speaking of cards, members of AAA should be sure to carry their membership ID card with them, which provides some of the benefits touted by the rental-car agencies at no additional cost.

The basic insurance coverage offered by most rental-car companies, known as the **Loss/Damage Waiver (LDW)** or **Collision Damage Waiver (CDW),** can cost $20 per day or more. The former should cover everything, including the loss of income to the rental agency, should you get in an accident (normally not covered by your own insurance policy). It usually covers the full value of the vehicle, with no deductible, if an outside party causes an accident or other damage to the rental car. You will probably be covered in case of theft as well. Liability coverage varies, but the minimum is usually at least $15,000. If you are at fault in an accident, you will be covered for the full replacement value of the car—but not for liability. In Nevada, you can buy additional liability coverage for such cases. Most rental companies require a police report in order to process any claims you file, but your private insurer will not be notified of the accident. Check your own policies and credit cards before you shell out money on this extra insurance because you may already be covered.

It's worth noting that rental-car companies seem to be pushing the extra coverage especially hard these days. Doing your research on what types of coverage you do and do not need will allow you to smile politely and decline if it is appropriate. Don't let them pressure or scare you into spending extra money for items you don't need.

By Taxi

Because cabs line up in front of all major hotels, an easy way to get around town is by taxi. Cabs charge $3.30 at the meter drop and $2.60 per mile after that, plus an additional $2.00 fee for being picked up at the airport and time-based penalties if you get stuck in traffic. A taxi from the airport to the Strip will run you $15 to $23, from the airport to Downtown $18 to $25, and between the Strip and Downtown about $12 to $18. You can often save money by sharing a cab with someone going to the same destination (up to five people can ride for the same fare).

All this implies that you have gotten a driver who is honest. Long-hauling—the practice of taking fares on a longer route to the destination to increase fares—is rampant in Las Vegas these days. A 2013 audit by the state found an estimated $15 million in overcharges and nearly 25% of all fares from the airport were charged too much.

The simplest way to avoid this is to always know where you are going and roughly how much it should cost to get there. Use the maps on your phone or online to gauge the distance and calculate the approximate fare or let a website like **taxifarefinder.com** do the math for you. When you get into the cab and state your destination, don't be afraid to add something like "that will cost about $20, right?" It puts the cabbie on notice that you are not a hapless tourist ready to be taken for a metaphorical ride.

If you suspect that you have been long-hauled, call the taxi company to complain and be sure to file a report with the Nevada Taxicab Authority at **taxi.nv.gov**.

If you just can't find a taxi to hail and want to call one, try the following companies: **Desert Cab Company** (© 702/386-9102), **Whittlesea Blue Cab** (© 702/384-6111), or **Yellow/Checker Cab/Star Company** (© 702/873-2000).

TRAFFIC tips

Traffic in Las Vegas can be frustrating at times, especially near the Strip on evenings and weekends. Here are a few tips to help you get around the worst of it:

○ **Spaghetti Bowl:** The "Spaghetti Bowl" is what locals call the mess where I-15 intersects U.S. 95. The latest billion-dollar construction overhaul, called Project Neon, has added to the ongoing traffic congestion and is supposed to be completed in November 2018. Avoid it if you can.

○ **Do D.I. Direct:** Most visitors seem to get a lot of mileage out of the Strip and I-15. But if you're checking out the local scene, you can bypass both of those, using Desert Inn Road, which is now one of the longest streets running from one side of the valley to the other. Plus, the 2-mile "Superarterial" section between Valley View and Paradise zips you nonstop over the interstate and under the Strip.

○ **Grin and Bear It:** Yes, there are ways to avoid traffic jams on the Strip. But at least these traffic jams are entertaining! If you have the time and patience, go ahead and take a ride along the Strip from Mandalay Bay to the Stratosphere. The 4-mile drive might take an hour, but while you're grinding along, you'll see a sphinx, an active volcano, a water ballet, and some uniquely Vegas architecture.

○ **Rat Pack Back Doors:** Frank Sinatra Drive is a bypass road that runs parallel to the Strip from Russell Road north to Industrial. It's a great way to avoid the traffic jams and sneak in the back of hotels such as Mandalay Bay, Luxor, and Monte Carlo. On the other side of I-15, a bunch of high-end condo developers talked the city into re-christening a big portion of Industrial Road as Dean Martin Drive. From near Downtown to Twain, Industrial is now called Sammy Davis Jr., Drive, and it lets you in the back entrances to Circus Circus, Treasure Island, and others. It's a terrific bypass to the Strip and I-15 congestion.

○ **Beltway Bypass:** The 53-mile 215 Beltway wraps three-quarters of the way around the valley, allowing easy access to the outskirts while bypassing the Resort Corridor.

By Uber or Lyft

On-demand car service companies Uber and Lyft finally won their long battles to operate in Las Vegas. As in other cities, you can order either service via mobile app to come collect you and take you wherever you need. Rides are slightly cheaper than taxis, though price surging still happens on busy nights and will wipe out any savings. An Uber or Lyft from the airport to the Strip will run you $11 to $19, from the airport to Downtown $21 to $38, and between the Strip and Downtown about $12 to $21. Hotels now have designated ride share pick-up areas near valet.

By Monorail

The 4-mile monorail route runs from the MGM Grand, at the southern end of the Strip, to the SLS Las Vegas (formerly the Sahara), at the northern end, with stops at Paris/Bally's, the Flamingo, Harrah's, the Las Vegas Convention Center, and Westgate along the way. Note that some of the actual physical stops are not particularly close to their namesakes, so there can be an unexpected—and sometimes time-consuming—additional walk from the monorail stop to wherever you intended to go. Factor in this time accordingly.

These trains can accommodate more than 200 passengers (standing and sitting) and make the end-to-end run in about 15 minutes. They operate Monday from 7am until midnight, Tuesday through Thursday from 7am until 2am, and Friday through Sunday from 7am until 3am. Fares are $5 for a one-way ride (whether you ride from one end to the other or just to the next station); discounts are available for round-trips and multiride/multiday passes.

For more information visit the Las Vegas Monorail website at **www. lvmonorail.com**.

By Bus

The Deuce and SDX (Strip to Downtown Express) buses operated by the **Regional Transportation Commission** (**RTC**; www.rtcsnv.com/transit; *©* **702/228-7433**) are the primary public transportation on the Strip. The double-decker Deuce and double-carriage SDX run a route between the Downtown Transportation Center (at Casino Center Blvd. and Stewart Ave.) and a few miles beyond the southern end of the Strip. The fare is $6 for adults for 2 hours; an all-day pass is $8 and a 3-day pass is $20. There are no discounts for children or seniors. CAT buses run 24 hours a day and are wheelchair accessible. Exact change is required.

Although they are certainly economical transportation choices, they are not the most efficient as it relates to time or convenience. They run often but are usually very crowded and are not immune to the mind-numbing traffic that clogs the Strip at peak times. Patience is required.

There are also a number of **free transportation services,** courtesy of the casinos. A free monorail connects Mandalay Bay with Luxor and Excalibur; another connects Monte Carlo, Bellagio, and CityCenter; and a free tram shuttles between the Mirage and Treasure Island. Given how far apart even neighboring hotels can be, thanks to their size, and how they seem even farther apart on really hot (and cold and windy) days, these are blessed additions.

[Fast FACTS] LAS VEGAS

Area Codes The local area codes in Las Vegas are 702, 775 and 725. The full 10-digit phone number with area code must be dialed to complete the call.

Business Hours Casinos and most bars are open 24 hours a day; nightclubs are usually open only late at night into the early morning hours; and restaurant and attraction hours vary.

Customs Every visitor 21 years of age or older may bring in, free of duty, the following: (1) 1 liter of alcohol as a gift for personal use; (2) 200 cigarettes, 100 cigars (but not from Cuba), or 3 pounds of smoking tobacco; and (3) $100 worth of gifts. These exemptions are offered to travelers who spend at least 72 hours in the United States and who have not claimed them within the preceding 6 months. It is forbidden to bring into the country almost any meat products (including canned, fresh, and dried-meat products such as bouillon, soup mixes, and so forth). Generally, condiments, including vinegars, oils, pickled goods, spices, coffee, tea, and some cheeses and baked goods are permitted. Avoid rice products, as rice can often harbor insects. Bringing fruits and vegetables is prohibited since they may harbor pests or disease. International visitors may carry in or out up to $10,000 in U.S. or foreign currency with no formalities; larger sums must be declared to U.S. Customs on entering or leaving, which includes filing form CM 4790. For details regarding U.S. Customs and Border Protection, consult your nearest U.S. embassy or consulate, or **U.S. Customs** (www.cbp.gov).

For information on what you're allowed to take home, contact your home country's Customs agency.

Disabled Travelers On the one hand, Las Vegas is fairly well equipped for travelers with disabilities, with virtually every hotel having wheelchair-accessible rooms and ramps and other requirements. On the other hand, the distance between hotels (particularly on the Strip) makes a vehicle of some sort virtually mandatory for most people with disabilities, and it may be extremely strenuous and time consuming to get from place to place (even within a single hotel) because of the crowds. Even if you don't intend to gamble, you still may have to go through the casino, and casinos can be quite difficult to maneuver in, particularly for a guest in a wheelchair. Casinos are usually crowded, and the machines and tables are often arranged close together, with chairs, people, and such blocking easy access. You should also consider that it is often a long trek through larger hotels between the entrance and the room elevators (or, for that matter, anywhere in the hotel), and then add a crowded casino to the equation.

For more on organizations that offer resources to travelers with limited mobility, go to **www.frommers.com**.

Doctors Hotels usually have lists of doctors, should you need one, or you can use the physician referral service at **Desert Springs Hospital** (www.desertsprings hospital.com; ✆ **702/388-4888**). Hours are Monday to Friday from 8am to 8pm and Saturday from 9am to 3pm except holidays. Also see "Hospitals," below.

Drinking Laws The legal age for purchase and consumption of alcoholic beverages is 21; proof of age is required and often requested at bars, nightclubs, and restaurants, so it's always a good idea to bring ID when you go out.

Beer, wine, and liquor are sold in all kinds of stores pretty much around the clock in Vegas; trust us, you won't have a hard time finding a drink in this town.

Do not carry open containers of alcohol in your car or any public area that isn't zoned for alcohol consumption, which includes the Strip and the Fremont Street Experience downtown. The police can fine you on the spot. And nothing will ruin your trip faster than getting a citation for DUI (driving under the influence), so don't even think about driving while intoxicated.

While walking around on the Strip with an alcoholic beverage is generally safe (provided you're of age, of course), don't tempt fate by walking around with glass bottles. You'll see plenty of folks stumbling around with large, novelty-size yards and boots, but that doesn't give you an excuse to act like a total fool when out in public. If the drink you ordered in the hotel came in a glass, you can ask the bartender to transfer it to a plastic cup so you can take your roadie to go.

Electricity Like Canada, the United States uses 110–120 volts AC (60 cycles), compared to 220–240 volts AC (50 cycles) in most of Europe, Australia, and New Zealand. Downward converters that change 220–240 volts to 110–120 volts are difficult to find in the United States, so bring one with you.

Emergencies Dial ⓒ **911** to contact the police or fire department, or to call for an ambulance.

Family Travel Family travel can be immensely rewarding, giving you new ways of seeing the world through smaller pairs of eyes. That said, Vegas is hardly an ideal place to bring the kids. For one thing, they're not allowed in casinos at all. Because most hotels are laid out so that you frequently have to walk through their casinos to get to where you are going, you can see how this becomes a headache.

Note also that the Strip is often peppered with people distributing fliers and other information about decidedly adult entertainment options in the city. Sex is everywhere. Just walking down the Strip might give your kids an eyeful of items that you might prefer they avoid. (They don't call it "Sin City" for nothing!)

On top of everything else, there is a curfew law in Vegas: Kids younger than 18 are not permitted on the Strip without a parent after 9pm on weekends and holidays. In the rest of the county, minors can't be out without parents after 10pm on school nights and midnight on the weekends.

Although still an option at most smaller chain hotels and motels, the major casino-hotels on the Strip offer no discount for children staying in your room, so you may have to pay an additional fee ($10–$40 per person per night) to have them bunk with you. You'll definitely want to book a place with a pool. Some hotels also have enormous video arcades and other diversions.

Health By and large, Las Vegas is like most other major American cities in that the water is relatively clean, the air is relatively clear, and illness-bearing insects and animals are rare. However, in a city with this many people coming and going from all over the world, there are a couple of specific concerns worth noting:

o **Food Poisoning** Food preparation guidelines in Las Vegas are among the strictest in the world, but when you're dealing with the sheer volume that this city is, you're bound to run into trouble every now and then. All restaurants are required by law to display a health certificate and letter grade (A, B, or C) that indicate how well they did on their last Health Department inspection. An A grade doesn't mean you won't get food poisoning, but it does mean the staff does a better-than-average job in the kitchen.

o **Norovirus** Over the past few years, there have been a few outbreaks of norovirus at Las Vegas hotels. This virus, most commonly associated with cruise ships, is rarely serious but can turn your vacation into a very unpleasant experience of intestinal illness. Because it is spread by contact, you can protect yourself by washing your hands often, especially after touching all of those slot machines.

o **Sun Exposure** In case you weren't paying attention in geography, Las Vegas is located in the middle of a desert, and so it should come as no surprise that the sun shines particularly bright here. Heat and sunstroke are dangers that all visitors should be concerned about, especially if you are considering spending any amount of time outdoors. Sunscreen (stick to a minimum SPF 30) is a must even if you are just traveling from one hotel to another, and you should always carry a bottle of water with you to stay hydrated even when temperatures are moderate. The low desert humidity means that your body has to work harder to replenish moisture, so help it along with something other than a free cocktail in the casino. The good news: Low humidity means it's hard to have a bad hair day.

Hospitals The closest full-service hospital to the Strip is **Sunrise Hospital,** 3186 Maryland Pkwy. (www.sunrisehospital.com; ℭ **702/731-8000**), but for lesser emergencies, **Harmon Medical Urgent Care,** 150 E. Harmon (www.harmonmedicalcenter.com; ℭ **702/796-1116**), offers treatment from 8am until 5pm Monday through Friday. Additionally, most major hotels in Las Vegas can provide assistance in finding physicians and/or pharmacies that are well suited to your needs.

Insurance Traveler's insurance is not required for visiting Las Vegas, and whether or not it's right for you depends on your circumstances. For example, most Las Vegas travel arrangements that include hotels are refundable or cancelable up to the last moment, so insurance is probably not necessary. If, however, you have prepaid a nonrefundable package, then it could be worth considering insurance.

For information on traveler's insurance, trip cancellation insurance, and medical insurance while traveling, please visit **www.frommers.com/planning**.

Internet & Wi-Fi Most major hotels in Vegas offer wireless access as a part of their nightly resort fee, although some still require an additional fee that can run upward of $20 per day. Some hotels offer free, advertiser-supported Wi-Fi in public areas, meaning you won't have to pay to surf the Web when you're hanging out at the pool, but you'll have to put up with banner ads on your browser. In Las Vegas, you can find free Wi-Fi at most stand-alone McDonald's, Starbucks, and in the Fashion Show mall.

Most major airports have Internet kiosks that provide basic Web access for a per-minute fee that's usually higher than hotel prices. Check out copy shops, such as FedEx Office, which offer computer stations with fully loaded software (as well as Wi-Fi).

Legal Aid While driving, if you are pulled over for a minor infraction (such as speeding), never attempt to pay the fine directly to a police officer; this could be construed as attempted bribery, a much more serious crime. Pay fines by mail, or directly into the hands of the clerk of the court. If accused of a more serious offense, say and do nothing before consulting a lawyer. In the U.S., the burden is on the state to prove a person's guilt beyond a reasonable doubt, and everyone has the right to remain silent, whether he or she is suspected of a crime or actually arrested. Once arrested, a person can make one telephone call to a party of his or her choice. The international visitor should call his or her embassy or consulate.

LGBT Travelers For such a licentious, permissive town, Las Vegas has its conservative side, and it is not the most gay-friendly city. This does not manifest itself in any signs of outrage toward open displays of gay affection, but it does mean that the local gay community is largely confined to the bar scene. See listings for gay bars in chapter 8.

Mail At press time, domestic postage rates were 34¢ for a postcard and 49¢ for a letter. For international mail, a first-class letter of up to 1 ounce or a postcard costs $1.15. For more information go to **www.usps.com**.

Always include a zip code when mailing items in the U.S. If you don't know a zip code, visit www.usps.com/zip4.

The most convenient post office to the Strip is immediately behind Circus Circus at 3100 S. Industrial Rd., between Sahara Avenue and Spring Mountain Road (ℭ **800/275-8777**). It's open Monday through Friday from 8:30am to 5pm. You can also mail letters and packages at your hotel.

Mobile Phones Just because your mobile phone works at home doesn't mean it'll work everywhere in the U.S. (thanks to our nation's fragmented mobile phone system). Whether or not you'll get a signal depends on your carrier and where you happen to be standing when you are trying to make a call. Hotel rooms and casinos are notoriously bad places to be if you want to chat with someone back home on your cellphone, but step outside and things usually improve

dramatically. Note that if you can get a signal in a casino, don't try to use your phone while sitting at a gaming table—that's a big no-no.

Once you leave Las Vegas proper, you are in the wilds of the Nevada desert, so unless you are near a major byway (like I-15), expect to get very few, if any, bars on your phone.

THE VALUE OF THE U.S. DOLLAR VS. OTHER POPULAR CURRENCIES

US$	Aus$	Can$	Euro (€)	NZ$	UK£
1	A$1.31	C$1.24	€.90	NZ$1.42	£.65

Money & Costs

Because Las Vegas is a town built on the concept of separating you from your money, it should come as no surprise that gaining access to money is very easy—sometimes too easy. There are ATMs (also known as "cash machines" or "cashpoints") conveniently located about every 4 feet (okay, an exaggeration, but not by a lot); and check cashing, and credit card–advance systems are omnipresent. Note that using any of these to access your money will cost you money; ATMs charge upward of $6 per transaction, and that's before whatever fees your bank will add.

And while Vegas visitors used to require a great deal of change in order to play the slots and other gaming machines, few, if any, still accept coins. Gone are the once-prevalent change carts. All machines now take bills in most denominations, and you get "change" in the form of a credit slip that appears when you cash out. You then take this slip to

the nearest cashier's cage to exchange for actual money.

So getting to your money isn't a problem. Keeping it may be.

Las Vegas has grown progressively more expensive, with the concept of a cheap Sin City vacation a distant memory. The average room rate on the Strip on weekends is over $200 a night, those formerly cheap buffets have been replaced by $40-a-person lavish spreads, and top-show tickets easily surpass $100 a head. And then, of course, there are the casinos, a money-losing proposition if there ever was one.

But there are Las Vegas vacations available for just about any budget, so pay (no pun intended) close attention to chapter 4, "Where to Stay," and chapter 5, "Where to Eat," which break down your choices by cost.

Beware of hidden credit card fees while traveling. International visitors should check with their credit or debit card issuer to see what fees, if any, will be

charged for transactions in the U.S.

Newspapers & Magazines The *Las Vegas Review-Journal* is the major daily periodical in the city, which is now partnered with the *Las Vegas Sun*, its former newspaper rival. Both offer the latest news, weather, and information and can be valuable resources for coupons and up-to-the-minute show listings.

LVM is a local magazine usually available in-room, listing shows, restaurants, and more, and it often features discount offers to attractions that could save you some dough.

Packing Most Las Vegas hotel rooms are fully stocked with basics—shampoo, conditioner, hand lotion, mouthwash, and in some cases things like sewing kits and cotton swabs. If you don't have allergy or skin sensitivity issues to contend with, you may want to consider leaving those types of sundry items at home to free up some room in your suitcase. The same goes for

WHAT THINGS COST IN LAS VEGAS	US$
Taxi from the airport to the Strip	15.00–25.00
Taxi from the airport to Downtown Las Vegas	18.00–27.00
One-way Las Vegas monorail ticket	5.00
All-day Deuce or SDX bus pass	8.00
Standard room at Bellagio, Fri–Sat	175.00–400.00
Standard room at MGM Grand, Fri–Sat	150.00–300.00
Standard room at Bally's, Fri–Sat	100.00–200.00
Dinner for two at Guy Savoy, prix fixe	580.00
Dinner for two at Pizza Rock	45.00
Wynn Las Vegas buffet, weekend champagne brunch	35.00
Main Street Station Garden Court buffet champagne brunch	12.00
Ticket to Cirque du Soleil's O	109.00–180.00
Ticket to Mac King (comedy magic show)	30.00
Domestic beer at Light	10.00
Domestic beer at the Double Down Saloon	5.00

your travel iron, as most rooms have a full-size iron and ironing board or they are available by request through housekeeping.

Comfortable walking shoes are a must for Las Vegas as you'll be doing a lot of it. Yes, your Jimmy Choo's will look fabulous for your night out at the party spots, but do you really want to navigate the crowds across a 100,000-square-foot casino in them?

Checking the weather forecast before your trip can provide you with guidance on what types of clothes to bring, but packing a light sweater or jacket even during the summer months is not a bad idea. It gets windy in Las Vegas and there can be a chill in the evenings, plus many of the casinos and showrooms set the air-conditioning on "Siberia," so light layers that you can peel off when you go back outside into the heat are recommended.

If you are bringing your computer or other mobile devices, don't forget to bring your power cords, and chargers.

Lastly, consider safety when packing by tossing in a small flashlight. During an emergency, this could become invaluable in helping you navigate your way out of a 4,000-room hotel.

Police For non-emergencies, call ℂ **702/795-3111.** For emergencies, call ℂ **911.**

Safety *CSI: Crime Scene Investigation*, a popular U.S. TV show, may turn up new corpses in Vegas each week, but the crime rate in real-life Vegas isn't higher than in any other major metropolis of its size.

With all that cash floating around town, pickpockets and thieves are predictably active. At gaming tables and slot machines, men should keep wallets well concealed and out of the reach of pickpockets, and women should keep handbags in plain sight (on laps). If you win a big jackpot, ask the slot attendant to cut you a check rather than give you cash—the cash may look nice, but flashing it can attract the wrong kind of attention. Outside the casinos, popular spots for pickpockets and thieves are restaurants and outdoor shows, such as the volcano at the Mirage or the fountains at Bellagio. Stay alert. Unless your hotel room has an in-room safe, check your valuables into a safe-deposit box at the front desk.

When in your room, be sure to lock and bolt the door at all times and only open it to hotel employees that you are expecting (such as room service).

A special safety concern for women (and even men occasionally) centers on behavior at nightclubs. Do not ever accept a drink from a stranger no matter how handsome he is, and keep your cocktail in your hand at all times, even while on the dance floor. Instances of people getting something slipped into their drink are rare but they have happened—singer John Popper of the band Blues Traveler was drugged and robbed in 2014—so it's best to take precautions.

Senior Travel One of the benefits of age is that travel to most destinations often costs less—but that's rarely true in Las Vegas. Discounts at hotels, shows, restaurants, recreation, and just about anything else you want to do are rare. About the only discounts offered to seniors are at some of the local attractions, which will give a few bucks off to those over 62 or 65 (see chapter 6).

Members of **AARP** (www. aarp.org; ✆ **888/687-2277**), get discounts on hotels, airfares, and car rentals. But be sure to check them against the discount websites we recommend earlier in the book, because

sometimes these "special discounts" aren't as good as the normal ones.

The U.S. National Park Service (NPS) offers an **America the Beautiful—National Park and Federal Recreational Lands Pass—Senior Pass.** You'll find it useful for some of the day trips covered in chapter 9. The pass gives U.S. residents 62 years or older lifetime entrance to all properties administered by the National Park Service—national parks, monuments, historic sites, recreation areas, and national wildlife refuges—for a one-time processing fee of $10. The pass must be purchased in person at any NPS facility that charges an entrance fee. Besides free entry, the America the Beautiful Senior Pass also offers a 50% discount on some federal-use fees charged for such facilities as camping, swimming, parking, and tours. For more go to **www.nps.gov/findapark/passes.htm**.

Smoking Vegas is decidedly no longer a smoker's haven. Increasingly strict smoking laws prohibit puffing virtually everywhere indoors except in designated hotel rooms, nightclubs, bars, and on the casino floor itself. Because it's frequently hard to tell where a casino ends and basic public area begins, don't fret too much about stepping across some invisible line. Hotels still have dedicated floors for smokers and nonsmokers. There

is a significant charge, approximately $300, for smoking anything in a non-smoking room.

Taxes The United States has no value-added tax (VAT) or other indirect tax at the national level. Every state, county, and city may levy its own local tax on all purchases, including hotel and restaurant checks and airline tickets. These taxes will not appear on price tags.

The sales tax in Las Vegas is 8.1% and is added to food and drink bills. Hotel rooms on the Strip come with a 12% tax, while those in the Downtown area carry 13%. Taxes are also added to show tickets.

Telephones Generally, Vegas hotel surcharges on long-distance and local calls are astronomical. You are often charged even for making a toll-free or phone-card call. You're better off using your **cellphone** since pay phones are almost nonexistent these days. Some hotels are adding on an additional "resort fee" to the cost of the room, which sometimes covers local calls (as well as using the pool and other elements that ought to be givens). The fee can range from $3 to $25 per day.

Most long-distance and international calls can be dialed directly from any phone. **To make calls within the United States and to Canada,** dial 1 followed by the area code and the seven-digit number. **For**

other international calls, dial 011 followed by the country code, city code, and the number you are calling.

Calls to area codes **800, 888, 877, 866,** and **855** are toll-free.

For **reversed-charge or collect calls,** and for person-to-person calls, dial the number 0 then the area code and number; an operator will come on the line, and you should specify whether you are calling collect, person-to-person, or both. If your operator-assisted call is international, ask for the overseas operator.

For **directory assistance** ("Information"), dial 411 for local numbers and national numbers in the U.S. and Canada. For dedicated long-distance information, dial 1, then the appropriate area code plus 555-1212.

Time The continental United States is divided into **four time zones:** Eastern Standard Time (EST), Central Standard Time (CST), Mountain Standard Time (MST), and Pacific Standard Time (PST). Alaska and Hawaii have their own zones. Las Vegas is in the Pacific Time zone, 8 hours behind Greenwich Mean Time (GMT), 3 hours behind the East Coast, and 2 behind the Midwest. For example, when it's 9am in Las Vegas (PST), it's 7am in Honolulu (Hawaii Standard Time), 10am in Denver (MST), 11am in Chicago (CST), noon in New York

City (EST), 5pm in London (GMT), and 2am the next day in Sydney.

Daylight saving time (summer time) is in effect from 1am on the second Sunday in March to 1am on the first Sunday in November, except in Arizona, Hawaii, the U.S. Virgin Islands, and Puerto Rico. Daylight saving time moves the clock 1 hour ahead of standard time.

Tipping Las Vegas is a hospitality-driven economy, meaning many of the people you encounter depend on tips for their livelihood. This doesn't necessarily mean you *need* to tip more than you would anywhere else, but average tips in other cities can be viewed as somewhat stingy here.

In the casinos, it's common to tip **cocktail waitresses** $1 to $2 per drink and to tip **dealers** 5% of any big wins.

In hotels, tip **bellhops** at least $1 per bag ($2–$3 if you have a lot of luggage) and tip the **chamber staff** $3 to $5 per day (more if you've left a big mess to clean up). Tip the **doorman** or **concierge** only if he or she has provided you with some specific service (for example, calling a cab for you or obtaining difficult-to-get theater tickets). Tip the **valet-parking attendant** $2 to $5 every time you get your car.

In restaurants, bars, and nightclubs, tip **service staff** and **bartenders** 15% to 20% of the check, and tip

checkroom attendants $1 per garment.

As for other service personnel, tip **cabdrivers** 15% of the fare; tip **skycaps** at airports at least $1 per bag ($2–$3 if you have a lot of luggage); and tip **hairdressers** and **barbers** 15% to 20%.

Toilets In Las Vegas, you are almost always near a bathroom as long as you are in one of the tourist areas, with the casinos being the most obvious example. All have multiple facilities and they are usually among the cleanest you'll find in any public location. One small annoyance is that many hotel restaurants do not have their own restrooms, meaning you may need to go into the casino to find the nearest one.

Large hotels and fast-food restaurants are often the best bet for clean facilities. Restaurants and bars in resorts or heavily visited areas may reserve their restrooms for patrons.

Visitor Information The Las Vegas Convention and Visitors Authority (www.lasvegas.com; © **877/847-4858** or 702/892-7575) provides information, hotel reservation assistance, show guides, convention calendars, and more.

Other popular Las Vegas travel websites include www.vegas.com, www.vegas4visitors.com, and www.cheapovegas.com.

Many hotels have their own mobile apps that you

can download for special information and offers.

Water Ongoing drought conditions mean water is a concern in terms of its long-term availability, but for now it is plentiful from faucets, drinking fountains, and endless bottles of the stuff. As in most of the United States, the drinking water is considered safe and there have been no reported instances of sickness from it. Still, bottles of water are often free in the casinos, so you might as well pick one up.

Women Travelers
Thanks to the crowds, Las Vegas is as safe as any other big city for a woman traveling alone. A woman on her own should, of course, take the usual precautions and should be wary of hustlers and drunken businessmen.

Many of the big hotels have security guards stationed at the elevators at night to prevent anyone other than guests from going up to the room floors. If you're anxious, ask a security guard to escort you to your room. *Always* double-lock your door *and* deadbolt it to prevent intruders from entering.

Index

See also Accommodations and Restaurant indexes, below.

General Index

A

Absinthe, 205
Accommodations, 41–91. *See also* Accommodations Index
best, 5–6
chains, 80
Downtown, 72–78
family-friendly, 55
getting the best deal, 42–44
Just Off the Strip, 79–85
locals', 86
Mid-Strip, 56–68
North Strip, 68–72
North & West of the Strip, 89–91
online savings, 43
pet-friendly hotels, 52
practical information, 41–45
resort fees, 50
South & East of the Strip, 85–89
South Strip, 45–56
Adapting to Las Vegas, 28
Adventuredome, 157
Air tours, 16
Air travel, 257–258
Alibi, 225
American Restoration, 200
Amtrak, 259
Angel, Criss, 209–210
Angel Park Golf Club, 187
Ante and Play, 176
Aquae Sulis Spa, 189
Area codes, 266
Aria Las Vegas
accommodations, 45
casino, 7–8, 178
entertainment and nightlife, 225, 237
pools, 64
restaurants, 99, 101, 140, 143
Arroyo Golf Club, 187
Artifice, 228
Art museums and galleries
The Arts Factory, 159
Bellagio Gallery of Fine Art, 154
City Center Fine Art Collection, 152
Emergency Arts, 160
The Neon Museum, 161–162
The Arts Factory, 159
Aston MonteLago Village, 248
ATMs, 270
Atomic Liquors, 219
Axis Theater, 66, 207

B

Baccarat, 172–173
Bachelorette party shows, 210
Backstage Bar & Billiards, 219, 221

Bali Hai Golf Club, 187
Bally's Las Vegas
accommodations, 61
tennis, 186
The Bar at Times Square, 227
Bare, 237
Bars, 219–227
Bear's Best Las Vegas, 188
Beauty Bar, 221
Beerhaus, 221
Beer Park, 221
Bellagio, 112, 140, 144, 145
accommodations, 57
entertainment and nightlife, 226, 229, 234
shopping, 197
spa, 191
weddings, 185
Bellagio Conservatory, 158
Bellagio Fountains, 158
Bellagio Gallery of Fine Art, 154
Bell Transportation, 259
Big Apple Coaster & Arcade, 151
Big Shot, 159
Biking, 184
Red Rock Canyon, 252
Binion's, casino, 7
Bitcoin, 73, 77
Blackjack, 173
Blue Man Group, 205–206
Boating, 184
Lake Mead area, 245
Bodies . . . The Exhibition, 152
Bonanza Gift and Souvenir Shop, 197–198
Bond, 225
Bonnie Springs Ranch, 252
The Boulevard, 200
Bound, 225
Bowling, 190
Brad Garrett's Comedy Club, 213, 236
Brooklyn Bowl, 190, 216
Buffets, 142–149
Business hours, 266
Bus travel, 258, 266

C

Caesars Palace
accommodations, 57
casino, 7, 178
entertainment and nightlife, 205, 207, 216, 223, 232, 240
The Forum Shops at restaurant, 115
shopping, 195
restaurants, 111–112, 115, 116, 119–121, 145
spa, 189, 191
Calendar of events, 38–40
Calico Basin, 252
Calico Hill, 251
California Hotel & Casino, 74
Callville Bay Resort & Marina, 245
Camping
Lake Mead area, 246
Mount Charleston, 253
Canoeing, Lake Mead area, 246
Canyon Ranch SpaClub, 189

Carnaval Court, 235
Carrot Top, 213
Car travel and rentals, 258, 260–261
Casino gambling, 171–180
baccarat, 172–173
blackjack, 173
free gambling lessons, 171–172
players' clubs, 172
poker, 174–176
roulette, 176–177
slots, 177–179
sports books, 179–180
video poker, 180
Casinos, best, 7–8. *See also* *specific resorts and casinos*
CAT (Citizens Area Transit), 259–260
Cellphones, 269–270
The Chandelier, 226
Chapel of the Bells, 181
Chapel of the Flowers, 181–182
Chateau, 228–229
Cheetah's, 239
Chippendales, 210
Circus Circus Hotel & Casino, accommodations, 71–72
for families with children, 55
Circus Circus Midway, 157
Cirque du Soleil, 34
KÀ, 206
LOVE, 206
Michael Jackson ONE, 206, 208
Mystère, 208
O, 208–209
Zumanity, 209
Citizens Area Transit (CAT), 259–260
City Center Fine Art Collection, 152
Civillico, Jeff, 212
Clark County Marriage License Bureau, 180
Clark County Museum, 166
Climate, 36
Club and music scene, 227–236
"Come" bet, 174
Comedy clubs, 236
The Commonwealth, 222
Convention dates for 2017, 38
Copperfield, David, 210–211
The Cosmopolitan of Las Vegas
accommodations, 58–59
casino, 8, 178
entertainment and nightlife, 216, 225, 226, 231, 232, 237
pools, 64
restaurants, 110, 113, 115, 118, 146
shopping, 194–195
skating rink, 186
Craps, 173
Crazy 4 Poker, 176
Criss Angel: *Mindfreak Live!*, 209–210
The Cromwell of Las Vegas
accommodations, 60
nightlife, 225, 229, 230
restaurant, 116

Map List

Photo Credits

Published by
FROMMER MEDIA LLC

ISBN 978-1-62887-270-5 (paper), 978-1-62887-271-5 (e-book)

Editorial Director: Pauline Frommer
Editor: Pauline Frommer
Production Editor: Donna Wright
Cartographer: Liz Puhl
Indexer: Maro Riofrancos
Photo Editor: Meghan Lamb
Cover Designer: Howard Grossman

For information on our other products or services, see www.frommers.com. Frommer Media LLC also publishes its books in a variety of electronic formats.

Manufactured in the United States of America

5 4 3 2 1

HOW TO CONTACT US

In researching this book, we discovered many wonderful places—hotels, restaurants, shops, and more. We're sure you'll find others. Please tell us about them, so we can share the information with your fellow travelers in upcoming editions. If you were disappointed with a recommendation, we'd love to know that, too. Please write to: Support@FrommerMedia.com

ABOUT THE AUTHOR

Grace Bascos—too short to be a showgirl, too bad at math to be a card dealer—has earned her survival in Las Vegas in the next best possible way: as a freelance food and travel writer dedicated to all things Sin City. Bascos keeps up with all the food that's fit to eat through her weekly *Dishing with Grace* column in *Vegas Seven* and as the dining editor for *Vegas/Rated*. She is also a regular contributor to *USA Today*'s Experience Las Vegas Blog, as well as several other local and regional publications. When she isn't eating, drinking, partying, and relaxing through town for her craft, she occasionally leaves her pampered bubble to tour musical festivals around the world.

ABOUT THE FROMMER'S TRAVEL GUIDES

For most of the past 50 years, Frommer's has been the leading series of travel guides in North America, accounting for as many as 24% of all guidebooks sold. I think I know why.

Although we hope our books are entertaining, we nevertheless deal with travel in a serious fashion. Our guidebooks have never looked on such journeys as a mere recreation, but as a far more important human function, a time of learning and introspection, an essential part of a civilized life. We stress the culture, lifestyle, history, and beliefs of the destinations we cover and urge our readers to seek out people and new ideas as the chief rewards of travel.

We have never shied from controversy. We have, from the beginning, encouraged our authors to be intensely judgmental, critical—both pro and con—in their comments, and wholly independent. Our only clients are our readers, and we have triggered the ire of countless prominent sorts, from a tourist newspaper we called "practically worthless" (it unsuccessfully sued us) to the many rip-offs we've condemned.

And because we believe that travel should be available to everyone regardless of their incomes, we have always been cost-conscious at every level of expenditure. Although we have broadened our recommendations beyond the budget category, we insist that every lodging we include be sensibly priced. We use every form of media to assist our readers and are particularly proud of our feisty daily website, the award-winning Frommers.com.

I have high hopes for the future of Frommer's. May these guidebooks, in all the years ahead, continue to reflect the joy of travel and the freedom that travel represents. May they always pursue a cost-conscious path, so that people of all incomes can enjoy the rewards of travel. And may they create, for both the traveler and the persons among whom we travel, a community of friends, where all human beings live in harmony and peace.

Arthur Frommer